MW00577909

European Social Policy and
the COVID-19 Pandemic

INTERNATIONAL POLICY EXCHANGE SERIES

Published in collaboration with the Center for International Policy Exchanges
University of Maryland

Series Editors
Douglas J. Besharov
Neil Gilbert

Recently published in the series:

*Decent Incomes for All:Improving Policies in Europe*Edited by Bea Cantillon, Tim
Goedemé, and John Hills

Social Exclusion in Cross National Perspective:
Actors, Actions, and Impacts from Above and Below
Edited by Robert J. Chaskin, Bong Joo Lee, and Surinder Jaswal

The "Population Problem" in Pacific Asia
Stuart Gietel-Basten

United States Income, Wealth, Consumption and Inequality
Edited by Diana Furchtgott-Roth

Europe's Income, Wealth, Consumption and Inequality
Edited by Georg Fischer and Robert Strauss

The World Politics of Social Investment: Volume 1
Edited by Julian Garritzman, Bruno Palier, and Silja Hausermann

The World Politics of Social Investment: Volume 2
Edited by Julan Garritzman, Bruno Palier, and Silja Hausermann

Work and the Social Safety Net: Labor Activation in Europe and the United States
Edited by Douglas J. Besharov and Douglas M. Call

The Public/Private Sector Mix in the Financing and Delivery of Healthcare
Services: Some Impacts on Health Equity and the Quality of Healthcare Services
Edited by Howard A. Palley

Revitalizing Residential Care for Children and Youth:
Cross-National Trends and Challenges
Edited by James K. Whittaker, Lisa Holmes, Jorge F. del Valle, Sigrid James

European Social Policy and the COVID-19 Pandemic
Edited by Stefanie Börner and Martin Seeleib-Kaiser

SCHOOL *of*
PUBLIC POLICY

European Social Policy and the COVID-19 Pandemic

Challenges to National Welfare and EU Policy

Edited by

STEFANIE BÖRNER AND
MARTIN SEELEIB-KAISER

OXFORD
UNIVERSITY PRESS

Oxford University Press is a department of the University of Oxford. It furthers
the University's objective of excellence in research, scholarship, and education
by publishing worldwide. Oxford is a registered trade mark of Oxford University
Press in the UK and certain other countries.

Published in the United States of America by Oxford University Press
198 Madison Avenue, New York, NY 10016, United States of America.

The open access publication of this book was supported by the Otto-von-Geuericke-University
Magdeburg and the Eberhard Karls Universität Tübingen.

Library of Congress Cataloging-in-Publication Data
Names: Börner, Stefanie, 1980- editor. | Seeleib-Kaiser, Martin, editor.
Title: European social policy and the COVID-19 pandemic : challenges to
national welfare and eu policy / Stefanie Börner, Martin Seeleib-Kaiser.
Description: New York, NY : Oxford University Press, [2023] |
Series: International policy exchange series |
Includes bibliographical references and index.
Identifiers: LCCN 2023003846 (print) | LCCN 2023003847 (ebook) |
ISBN 9780197676189 (hardback) | ISBN 9780197676202 (epub) |
ISBN 9780197676219
Subjects: LCSH: European Union countries—Social policy—21st century. |
Welfare economics—European Union countries. | Unemployment
insurance—European Union countries. | European Union
countries—Economic policy—21st century. | COVID-19 Pandemic, 2020—Influence.
Classification: LCC HN373.5 .E833 2023 (print) | LCC HN373.5 (ebook) |
DDC 306.0940905—dc23/eng/20230209
LC record available at https://lccn.loc.gov/2023003846
LC ebook record available at https://lccn.loc.gov/2023003847

DOI: 10.1093/oso/9780197676189.001.0001

Printed by Integrated Books International, United States of America

Contents

PART I: NATIONAL WELFARE REGIMES DURING THE COVID-19 PANDEMIC

PART II: CHALLENGES AND RESPONSES IN SPECIFIC POLICY DOMAINS

List of Figures

List of Tables

Contributors

Klaus Armingeon is Professor Emeritus of Comparative and European Politics, University of Bern; associated researcher at the University of Zurich; and guest professor at the universities of Milan and Trento. He works on topics of comparative political economy, comparative political sociology, and European integration. Recent publications include: Redistributive preferences: Why actual income is ultimately more important than perceived income (with David Weisstanner), *Journal of European Social Policy* (forthcoming); Objective Conditions Count, Political Beliefs Decide: The Conditional Effects of Self-Interest and Ideology on Redistribution Preferences (with David Weisstanner) *Political Studies* 2021; Trade-Offs between Redistribution and Environmental Protection: The Role of Information, Ideology, and Self-Interest (with Reto Bürgisser) *Journal of European Public Policy* 2021; Fiscal Solidarity: The Conditional Role of Political Knowledge." *European Union Politics* 2021.

Eduardo Barberis is Professor of Sociology at the University of Urbino Carlo Bo, Italy. His research interests include the territorial dimension of social welfare policy and immigrant incorporation, and the role of welfare professions—with an attention to non-metropolitan areas. Among his recent publications: (2022) Handbook on Urban Social Policies (coedited with Y. Kazepov, R. Cucca, E. Mocca); (2022) Inside the Emergency: Digital Teaching from the Point of View of Teachers (with N. Bazzoli, D. Carbone, Y. Dagnes), in Education and Emergency in Italy (edited by M. Colombo, M. Romito, M. Vaira, M. Visentin).

Daniel Béland is Director of the McGill Institute for the Study of Canada and James McGill Professor in the Department of Political Science at McGill University. He is also the Executive Editor of the *Journal of Comparative Policy Analysis*, editor (French) of the *Canadian Journal of Sociology*, and the president of the Research Committee 19 (on Poverty, Social Welfare and Social Policy) of the International Sociological Association. A student of social, fiscal, and health care policy, he has published more than 160 articles in peer-reviewed journals as well as more than 20 books and monographs, including *How Ideas and Institutions Shape the Politics of Public Policy* (Cambridge University Press, 2019) and *An Advanced Introduction to Social Policy* (Edward Elgar, 2016; with Rianne Mahon).

Stefanie Börner is Junior Professor of Sociology of European Societies at the Social Sciences Department of the Otto-von-Guericke University Magdeburg. Her main fields of research are EU integration, the sociology of social policy, social theory (especially autonomy and solidarity), and welfare state transformation. She is the author of *Belonging, Solidarity and Expansion in Social Policy* (Palgrave 2013) and the editor of several books and special issues (among others *European Integration, Processes of Change and the National Experience,* together with Monika Eigmüller, Palgrave 2015). She has published in journals such as *British Journal of Sociology, Journal of European Social Policy* or *European Union Politics.*

Rui Branco is Associate Professor at the Department of Political Studies, NOVA University (Lisbon) and Senior Researcher at IPRI-NOVA. His research interests focus on comparative state formation, democratization, and social protection. He has recently worked on civil society and democratization, fiscal welfare and inequality, and labor market reforms during the crisis.

Cecilia Bruzelius is Junior Professor of European Public Policy at the Institute of Political Sciences at the University of Tübingen. Her research focuses in particular on comparative social policy, citizenship, social rights, migration, and EU integration. She has published in the *Journal of European Public Policy, West European Policy* and the *Journal of European Social Policy* among others.

Bea Cantillon is Professor of Social Policy and Member of the Herman Deleeck Centre for Social Policy at the University of Antwerp. She has acted as a consultant to, among others, the OECD, the European Commission, and the Belgian government. Currently, she is member of the Belgian High Council for Employment and of the Belgian Commission on Pension Reform. Bea Cantillon is fellow of the Royal Belgian Academy of Sciences and corresponding fellow of the British Academy. She was awarded a Doctorate honoris causa by UC Louvain Saint-Louis Brussels and the Van Doorn Chair at the Erasmus School of Social and Behavioural Sciences in Rotterdam. Recent book publications include *Reconciling Work and Poverty Reduction* (with F. Vandenbroucke) and *Decent Incomes for All* (with Tim Goedemé and John Hills), both with Oxford University Press. She co-authored the book *Social Indicators, The EU and Social Inclusion* with Tony Atkinson, Erik Marlier, and Brian Nolan, also with Oxford University Press.

Caroline de la Porte is Professor at the Department of International Economics, Government and Business, Copenhagen Business School. She is currently CBS lead for the Nordforsk-financed collaborative project, "Reimaging Norden in an Evolving World" (ReNEW) (2018–2023), and an EU Horizon 2020– financed project "The Future of European Social Citizenship" (EUSocialcit) (coordinator Amsterdam University), where she leads a WP on Fair Labor Markets (2020–2023). Recent publications include "The Next Generation EU: An analysis of the Dimensions on Conflict behind the Deal" (with Mads Jensen), *Social Policy & Administration,* 55: 388–402 and "The politics of European Union social investment initiatives" (with Bruno Palier), in Garritzmann, Häusermann, and Palier, *World Politics of Social Investment* (Oxford University Press 2022).

Matthew Donoghue is Assistant Professor and Ad Astra Fellow in Social Policy at the School of Social Policy, Social Work and Social Justice, University College Dublin. His research interests include social citizenship and social rights, poverty and inequality, cohesion and resilience, and the politics and ideology of policy. He is co-editor of *Whither Social Rights in (Post-) Brexit Europe? Opportunities and Challenges* (Social Europe and Friedrich Ebert Stiftung London), and has recent articles published or forthcoming in *West European Politics, Journal of Social Policy, Social Policy and Society, Critical Social Policy, The Sociological Review* and *Political Studies*.

Natalie Glynn is a Research Officer and Lecturer in the Institute for Political Science at the University of Tübingen. Her main focus is on the translation of research into policy and practice for the common good, with specific interests in youth social policy, processes of social exclusion, and evidence-based policymaking. She has presented and published her research widely in both academic and professional settings, including the peer-reviewed journals *Children and Youth Services Review* and *Child Care in Practice*.

Bent Greve is Professor in Social Science at the University of Roskilde, Denmark. His research interest focuses on the welfare state, and social and labor market policy, often from a comparative perspective. He has published extensively on social and labor market policy, social security, tax expenditures, public sector expenditures, and financing of the welfare state. He is editor of *Social Policy & Administration*. Recent books include *Myths, Narratives and the Welfare State* (2021), Edward Elgar, *Austerity, Retrenchment and the Welfare State* (2020), Edward Elgar, *Poverty: The Basics* (2020), Routledge, *Routledge International Handbook of Poverty* (ed.) (2020), Routledge, *Welfare, Populism and Welfare Chauvinism* (2019), Policy Press, and the *Routledge Handbook of the Welfare State* (ed., 2nd Edition), (2019), Routledge.

Ana M. Guillén is Professor of Sociology at the University of Oviedo (Spain). She has published extensively on comparative social and labor policy, welfare state development, Europeanization, and European integration.

Mary Guy is Senior Lecturer in Public and EU Law at Liverpool John Moores University. Her main fields of research are health care reforms, law, and policy at national and EU levels. She is the author of *Competition Policy in Healthcare— Frontiers in Insurance-Based and Taxation-Funded Systems* (Intersentia 2019) and editor (with Eleanor Brooks) of the *Health Economics, Policy and Law* special issue, "The Future of EU Health Law and Policy" (2021). Her recent articles have been published in *Legal Studies, Health Economics, Policy and Law*, and the *European Journal of Risk Regulation*. Together with Eleanor Brooks (Edinburgh) and Charlotte Godziewski (Aston), Mary Guy coordinates the interdisciplinary (law/political science/sociology) EU Health Governance research network funded by the University Association of Contemporary European Studies between 2021 and 2024.

Rune Halvorsen is Professor of Social Policy, co-director of CEDIC (Center for the Study of Digitalization of Public Services and Citizenship), and coordinator of the Euroship Research Programme to provide an original and gender-sensitive assessment of the current gaps in social protection across Europe. https://www.oslomet.no/en/about/employee/runeh.

Elke Heins is Senior Lecturer at the University of Edinburgh, working on comparative welfare state policies, in particular labor market and unemployment policy as well as the politics of welfare and well-being. Recent publications include among others: "Voices from the Past: Economic and Political Vulnerabilities in the Making of NGEU" (with K. Armingeon, C. de la Porte, & S. Sacchi), in *Comparative European Politics* (2021), Unemployment benefit governance, trade unions and outsider protection in conservative welfare states (with D. Clegg and P. Rathgeb) in Transfer (2022), and "European Futures: Challenges and Crossroads for the European Union of 2050" (co-edited with C. Damro and D. Scott (Routledge, 2021).

Rod Hick is Reader in Social Policy at Cardiff University. His research interests include the conceptualization and measurement of poverty; the analysis of social security, housing, and labor market policies and their joint role in securing decent living standards; and the capability approach. He is a co-editor of the *Journal of Poverty and Social Justice* and was the 2015 recipient of the Foundation for International Studies on Social Security prize. His recent papers include "Austerity, localism, and the possibility of politics: explaining variation in three local social security schemes between elected councils in England," published in *Sociological Research Online*, and "Tax credits and in-work poverty in the UK: An analysis of income packages and anti-poverty performance" (with Alba Lanau), published in *Social Policy & Society*.

Zyab Ibáñez is a senior researcher at the Institute of Government and Public Policies (IGOP) of the Universitat Autònoma Barcelona. His research combines cross-national institutional analyses and organizational case studies to explore how different institutional regimes shape public policies in the areas of employment, working-time, and migration. His work has been published in journals such as *Journal of European Social Policy, Journal of Youth Studies, Time & Society*; as well as in books (Palgrave, Ashgate Macmillan).

Zhen Jie Im is Postdoc at the Copenhagen Business School who, among other issues, focuses on the relationship between labor market risks such as workplace automation and political behavior. He is currently postdoctoral researcher at the Department of International Economics, Business and Government at Copenhagen Business School. He is part of the EU Horizon 2020–funded project "EUSOCIALCIT." He is also affiliated with the Faculty of Social Sciences at the University of Helsinki. Recent publications include "Automation and public support for workfare." *Journal of European Social Policy*, with Komp-Leukkunen, K. (2021): https://doi.org/10.1177/09589287211002432 and "The 'losers of automation': A reservoir of votes for the radical right?". *Research & Politics* (with N. Mayer, Bl Palier, and J. Rovny, 2019:https://doi.org/10.1177/2053168018822395.

Yuri Kazepov is Professor of Sociology at the Faculty of Social Sciences (University of Vienna). His research interests address the territorial dimension of social policies in a comparative perspective, a theme on which he carried out extensive research at European level. His publications include: (2017) "The territorial dimension of social policies and the new role of cities" (with Barberis), in P. Kennett and N. Lendvai (eds.), *Handbook of European Social Policy* (2020), Local social innovation to combat poverty: a critical appraisal (edited with Oosterlynck and Novy for Policy Press: Bristol). He is also the editor of the *Handbook on Urban Social Policy. International Perspectives on Multilevel Governance and Local Welfare* to be published in 2021 by Edward Elgar together with E. Barberis, Cucca, R. and E. Mocca.

Klara Kuhn is a Research Assistant at the University of Mannheim and the Research Center SFB 884, "Political Economy of Reforms." Her research focuses on gender inequality and life course research.

Katja Möhring is Professor of Sociology especially Family and Work at the University of Bamberg and an external fellow and project leader at the Mannheim Centre for European Social Research. Her research focuses on life course sociology, gender inequality, comparative welfare state research, political attitudes, work and pensions, and quantitative methods. She has published in *European Sociological Review*, *European Societies*, the *Journal of European Social Policy*, and *Social Policy & Administration* among others.

Amílcar Moreira is Assistant Professor at the Lisbon School of Economics & Management (ISEG), University of Lisbon; and a Researcher at CSG/SOCIUS, Research Centre in Economic and Organizational Sociology. Previously, he worked at Trinity College Dublin (Ireland) and Oslo Metropolitan University (Norway). His research revolves around aging, pensions and income distribution, labor market policies and welfare reform. More recently, he has published on the social policy response to the COVID-19 pandemic (Moreira & Hick, 2021; Moreira et al, 2021). He is also the Principal Investigator of DYNAPOR—Dynamic Microsimulation Model for Portugal.

Jacqueline O'Reilly is Professor of Comparative Human Resource Management and Director of the ESRC-funded Digital Futures at Work Research Centre and the University of Sussex Business School. https://digit-research.org/researcher/prof-jacqueline-oreilly/.

Emmanuele Pavolini is Professor in Economic Sociology and Social Policy at the University of Macerata (Italy). He has focused his research interests on welfare state studies from a comparative perspective, with specific attention to the Italian and Southern European welfare states, inequalities in the access to welfare state provision, occupational welfare, and third-sector organizations.

Maria Petmesidou is Professor Emerita of Social Policy at the Democritus University of Thrace (Greece). She has published numerous articles on social policy and development issues in Greece, and comparative social protection systems in Southern Europe.

Andrea Prontera is Associate Professor of Political Science at Department of Political Science, Communication and International Relations of the University of Macerata (Italy). His research focuses in particular on international political economy, comparative public policy, EU integration, and energy policy. He has published in the *Journal of Common Market Studies*, *New Political Economy*, *Environmental Politics*, and the *Journal of Public Policy* and *Energy Policy* among others.

Maximiliane Reifenscheid is a researcher at the University of Bamberg. Her research focuses on welfare state reforms, family and gender policies, public opinion, and the positioning of interest organizations.

Triin Roosalu is Associate Professor of Sociology at the Institute of International and Social Studies in the School of Governance, Law and Society at Tallinn University. Most of her research focuses on comparative studies of inequalities in labor market participation, work, and lifelong learning, with approaches ranging from survey data and individual accounts to policy discourse analysis, tracing changes over time. Beyond authoring research reports commissioned nationally or within international projects, her work has been published in journals such as *Higher Education*, *Transfer—European Review of Labour and Research*, and *Human Arenas*, as well as in books published by Palgrave, Springer, and Peter Lang.

Stefano Sacchi is Professor of Political Science at the Polytechnic University of Turin. His current research focuses on the political economy of welfare and labor policy, the digitalization of public policies, and the socioeconomic and political impact of technological change. He has recently co-edited a World Bank volume on pensions systems (*Progress and Challenges of Nonfinancial Defined Contribution Pension Schemes*, Washington DC, World Bank, 2020) and published on industrial relations and corporatism ("A biased pendulum: Italy's oscillations between concertation and disintermediation," with A. Tassinari, in Ebbinghaus and Weishaupt, *The Role of Social Partners in Managing Europe's Great Recession*, Routledge, London, 2021) and on the relationship between exposure to technological risk and support for social policy ("Technology, risk, and support for social safety nets," with D. Guarascio, in Busemeyer et al., *Digitalisation and the Welfare State*, Oxford, Oxford University Press, 2022).

Tatiana Saruis is a Ph.D. in Sociology. She works as a sociologist within the Sector Innovation in health and social services of Emilia-Romagna Region (Italy). Her research topics are social innovation, education and welfare policies and services, governance, public organisations and street-level professionals. Among her recent publications: Oosterlynck S., Saruis T. (2022), Urban Social Innovation and the European City: Assessing the Changing Urban Welfare Mix and Its Scalar

Articulation, in: Kazepov Y., Barberis E., Cucca R., Mocca E., a cura di, *Handbook on Urban Social Policies. International Perspectives on Multilevel Governance and Local Welfare*, Cheltenham, Elgar, pp. 72–84; Raspanti D., Saruis T. (2021) Trapped into Reverse Asymmetry: Public Employment Services Dealing with Employers, *Journal of Social Policy*, 51(1), pp. 173–190.

Mi Ah Schoyen is Senior Researcher at NOVA Norwegian Social Research, Oslo Metropolitan University. She works in the field of comparative welfare state research. Her interests include the welfare mix, the politics and social consequences of welfare state reforms, intergenerational solidarity, and the interplay between climate and social policy.

Martin Seeleib-Kaiser is Professor of Comparative Public Policy at the Institute of Political Science of Eberhard Karls University Tübingen and editor of the *Journal of European Social Policy*. Prior to his appointment at Tübingen in 2017, he held appointments at the University of Oxford (2004–2017), Duke University (North Carolina, USA) (1999–2002), and Bremen University (1993–1999; 2002–2004). His research focuses on the politics of social policy and comparative social policy analysis, with a special focus on the social rights of EU citizens. He has published nine books and more than 70 articles in edited volumes and international journals, including the *American Sociological Review, British Journal of Industrial Relations, Journal of Common Market Studies, Journal of European Social Policy, Policy and Politics, Politics and Society, Politische Vierteljahresschrift, Social Politics, Social Policy and Administration, West European Politics*, and *Zeitschrift für Soziologie*.

Dorota Szelewa is Assistant Professor in Social Justice at University College Dublin, and Editor in Chief of the *Journal of Family Studies*. Recent publications include: "Populism, Religion and Catholic Civil Society in Poland: The Case of Primary Education," *Social Policy & Society* 2021 (2): 310–25, and "Social Policy in the Face of a Global Pandemic: Policy Responses to the COVID-19 Crisis in Central and Eastern Europe." *Social Policy & Administration* with Aidukaite, J., S. Saxonberg, and D. Szikra 2021 55(2): 358–73.

Marge Unt is Professor of Comparative Sociology and the Head of Institute of International Social Studies Education at Tallinn University and Principal Investigator (PI) of the H2020 project Social exclusion of Youth in Europe: Cumulative Disadvantage, Coping Strategies, Effective Policies and Transfer (EXCEPT-project. eu). https://www.tlu.ee/en/node/106116.

Rachel Verdin is a researcher on Euroship and Associate Researcher at the Digital Futures at Work Research Centre and the University of Sussex Business School https://digit-research.org/researcher/rachel-verdin/.

Georg Vobruba is Professor Emeritus of Sociology at the University of Leipzig. His main areas of research are Sociology of Social Security, Sociology of European Integration, and Sociological Theory of Society. His recent publications include: *Die*

Kritik der Leute. Einfachdenken gegen besseres Wissen. Weinheim, Basel 2019: *Beltz Juventa; Kritik zwischen Praxis und Theorie.* Weinheim, Basel 2020: *Beltz Juventa; Aktualität der Demokratie Weinheim*, Basel 2020: Beltz Juventa (together with Martin Endreß and Sylke Nissen).

Andreas Weiland is a researcher at the University of Bamberg. His work focuses in particular on life courses, gender inequality, and retirement. He has published in the *European Sociological Review, Work, Aging and Retirement* and *Quality & Quantity* among others.

Introduction

Stefanie Börner and Martin Seeleib-Kaiser

COVID-19, the Welfare State, and EU Social Policy

The COVID-19 pandemic constitutes "a distinct kind of crisis" (Béland et al. 2021, 249; Börner 2021; Moreira and Hick 2021) with respect to both the nature of the crisis and the subsequent social policy responses. It affects all domains of state action and all areas of public life. Although recent crises triggered a scholarly debate on welfare states' responses *to* crises (Starke et al. 2013), replacing the long dominant reading of the welfare state *in* crisis (Pierson 1994; Bonoli et al. 2000), the pandemic-induced crisis differs in several respects from previous big crises such as the European debt crisis and the refugee reception crisis. While all these crises were transnational in scope, only COVID-19 has made its effects felt on everyone, albeit to varying degrees. Moreover, the pandemic leaves less room to blame others than previous crises. From a time perspective, the pandemic triggered a long-term process with slowly unfolding enduring effects (Pierson 2000) which "challenge[s] the ways in which we live and the demands on social policy and public health and other areas of regulation" (Daly 2022, 115). Hence, this volume addresses the potential long-term effects for European welfare states and EU social policy. The chapters in this book analyze the different paths taken by policymakers as crisis managers in key domains of national welfare states and EU action. The common aim of the contributions to this volume is to identify areas of change and continuity and ask how welfare state futures and positive European integration might evolve in the medium and long term.

Not only the crises, but also the policy responses to the Great Recession and the COVID-19 pandemic differ significantly. While the *Great Recession* did not seem to contribute to social policy innovation, the pandemic triggered many path-deviating (temporary) measures, such as elements of the CARES Act in the United States and the furlough program in the United Kingdom. Among others, the US law provided unemployment benefits at a comparatively generous level of $600 per week

European Social Policy and the COVID-19 Pandemic. Stefanie Börner and Martin Seeleib-Kaiser, Oxford University Press. © Oxford University Press 2023. DOI: 10.1093/oso/9780197676189.001.0001

to individuals who previously had not been covered by unemployment insurance (Fischer and Schmid 2021), as well as child benefits (Parolin et al. 2021). Germany and other European countries facilitated access to minimum income schemes for self-employed workers. The Spanish government enacted a long-debated minimum-income scheme. In Belgium social assistance recipients received a monthly supplementary payment of €50 for six months. These approaches strengthened citizens' social rights by weakening deservingness considerations (Murphy and McGann 2020). Among the most popular crisis responses have been short-time work allowance or furlough schemes, indicating on the one hand a spillover effect of the policy instrument successfully used in several countries during the financial crisis (Konle-Seidl 2020, 5) and on the other hand that labor market insiders were a key focus of the crisis responses (Fischer and Schmid 2021). Konle-Seidl distinguishes three versions of short-time work in Europe: While most states modified existing schemes in order to ease access or extend time periods and the level of benefits, some states replaced the existing programs by more generous Corona short-time work schemes (e.g., Austria, Netherlands), and some states without a short-time work tradition such as Denmark, Ireland, and the UK introduced new programs. The most generous regulations with benefit duration periods of twelve or even 24 months are to be found among the first group (Belgium, Germany, France, Italy, Spain) (Konle-Seidl 2020, 9).

At the EU level, the Next Generation EU (NGEU) initiative represents a departure from the path firmly established in 2012 when the Member States of the EURO area adopted the European Stability Mechanism, which made support via bailout loans conditional upon Member States implementing austerity programs to promote their fiscal consolidation (de la Porte and Jensen 2021, 389). NGEU does not only show that EU Member States are able "to deal with large-scale crises" (ibid.), but NGEU's design also illustrates that the COVID-19 responses are not isolated from ongoing challenges (de la Porte and Heins 2022, 2). Furthermore, the steps taken by the European Commission in 2020 to extend the competencies of the European Medicines Agency and the European Centre for Disease Prevention and Control represent another successful policy initiative (Rhodes 2021), which culminated in two European Commission proposals to establish a new EU4Health program (May 2020) and to create a European Health Union (November 2020) that will allow the EU to expand its public health capacities in the future.

The health and social crisis caused by COVID-19 has not only pointed to the immense importance of the public sector in providing and allocating social benefits and services, but with new urgency has also drawn attention to the institutional weaknesses and deficits of public welfare systems. We are faced with the paradox that on the one hand, the welfare state has the means to distribute huge amounts of money and to provide large quantities of medical supplies and healthcare services, while on the other hand it is precisely the public welfare state structure that creates disturbing inequalities, at times neglecting the needs of the most vulnerable. According to the literature the main challenges are the following:

(1) Funding and modernization of health systems: COVID-19 shed light on the consequences of privatizations and cutbacks in public health systems; also, a lack of epidemiological knowledge, crisis-management plans, and a reliable supply of medical products and protective equipment became evident in many affluent countries. Even though Europe had faced previous epidemics such as SARS, swine flu, or bird flu, think tanks and international organizations like the WHO and the Bertelsmann Foundation characterized many European states as having been poorly prepared for the pandemic (WHO 2020; Schiller and Hellmann 2021).

(2) Job quality and income: The past two years have seen a worsening of existing social inequalities along familiar lines of social conflict in various affluent countries, as many of the short-term responses to the crisis have been aimed at preserving jobs and stimulating the economy (Cantillon et al. 2021). Numerous studies following the first wave of infection have shown that the pandemic hit the most vulnerable groups in the labor market the hardest. Low-wage workers have been particularly exposed to COVID-19–related health and social risks (Gustafsson and McCurdy 2020, 14–16) because they often work in essential economic sectors as well as frontline services and therefore were unable to work from home. COVID-19 has shed new light on the working conditions and workplace security in key economic sectors such as agriculture and food production, retail, inpatient and home care, and the service sector as a whole; whether in future European governments will deviate from their endorsement of "labour market flexibility towards a model that provides greater security for workers" (Bergsen et al. 2020, 8) remains an open question.

(3) Labor migration: In many essential economic sectors migrants are disproportionately employed, pointing to the transnational dimension of labor supply and job quality. Media attention of the horrendous conditions of pseudo self-employed and posted migrant workers in the German meat-processing industry during the beginning of the pandemic has contributed to a subsequent resolution by the European Parliament emphasizing the labor rights of cross-border and seasonal workers in the context of the COVID-19 crisis (EP 2020).

(4) Care sector: The care sector for the frail and elderly became a focal point for public health specialists and politicians given that infection and mortality rates in care homes have been high across countries and care regimes. According to Daly (2021, 114–116), COVID-19 experiences provide a set of insights on the future of elderly care with respect to agency, resources, and organization that do not only include staff working conditions but also the care relationship, the question of informal care, and the boundaries between paid and unpaid as well as public and private care. During the pandemic, social services were often not equipped to adequately deal with the challenges of COVID (Eurofound 2020), which raises questions about funding for a sector that has been widely under-resourced prior to the pandemic.

(5) Family and female workforce: Although family policies in Europe differ quite strongly in how they affect or support families' care arrangements, there is a broad consensus that "the old gender division of care labor manifested quite early in lockdown with women far more likely than men to undertake caring activities, especially those occasioned by the closure or cutback of services" (UN Women 2020). The shift toward working from home placed reconciliation of work and family once again on the top of the agenda and impacted the well-being and work–life balance of many female carers. Yet, different welfare regimes reacted differently to this situation. While Denmark was among the first to reopen schools and childcare facilities, and thereby facilitated parents' return to work, Germany stood for a prolonged closure of schools and kindergartens, which "has triggered a step backwards in gender equality" (Allmendinger 2022). Unsurprisingly, these strategies reflect the two countries' overall gender equality approaches in family policy (Bariola and Collins 2021).

Given this long and far from exhaustive list of challenges, as well as the situation of public finances with high rates of public debts—"a left-over from the *Great Recession*" (de la Porte and Heins 2022, 2)—what have been the responses by civil society and governments? Especially the first months of the pandemic were marked by an impressive degree of voluntary support at neighborhood and local levels (e.g., the sewing of masks or the staffing of helplines), and professional help from existing civil society organizations and charities (for an overview see Börner 2021). In addition to such flexible and grassroots-driven activities, public social policies became crucial. Although the welfare state has often been declared dysfunctional or even dead during past decades, the responses to the pandemic have demonstrated that the modern welfare state can deliver and might even emerge as *the* lasting winner of the crisis. Quite a few of the commentaries that have been written during the first year of the pandemic made cautious predictions in which solidarity and the public sector rank high. Sandher and Kleider (2020) see the welfare state as "back in" and "here to stay." At a European level, supranational initiatives such as the European Health Union and NGEU have raised hope that the EU will advance its social dimension (Guy 2020). Altogether, this might possibly result in a revival of the civic and "public sector after years of neoliberal folly" (Zielonka 2020, 3) in its local, national, and European dimensions. In particular, since policy responses "reflect at least in part existing national policy legacies" (Béland et al. 2021), the pandemic has thrown new light on the long-term effects of privatization and retrenchment policies (Giraud et al. 2021). It raises the question to which extent Europe-wide cooperation will gain importance, and whether the EU might even assume new competencies.

Overall, Dubet (2020, 4–5) sees a "return of society" as both the virus and the related, often highly improvised interventions have made us aware not only of the social division of labor but of the functioning of organizations and the way individual members of society depend on each other and the intersection with personal autonomy, as well as fundamental and social rights. Although the burden-sharing within families, municipalities, national societies, and beyond is nothing new for the welfare state, COVID-19 has rendered these social interdependencies particularly visible. Zielonka writes:

> "The shock of 2020 may leave us shattered and divided, but it may also mobilize us to rebuild and enlarge the public sphere, to offer citizens meaningful forms of participation in public affairs, to bring markets under

democratic scrutiny, and perhaps even to create a caring society able to respect labor (including migrant labor), the environment, and citizens' health." (Zielonka 2020, 1)

So, from a welfare-state theoretical point of view one of the most intriguing questions is whether the health and economic challenges caused by the COVID-19 pandemic will accelerate welfare state change and if so, in which direction.

Comprehensive Welfare State Change or Continuity?

During the past five decades, much of the comparative welfare state literature has focused on assessing and analyzing social policy continuity and change. The diagnoses differ significantly. For many social scientists the "golden welfare state era" or the *Trente Glorieuses* (Fourastié 1979)—a stylized and often idealized thirty years of post-WWII development—had come to an end by the 1970s. Ever since the mid-1970s the welfare state in affluent democracies was said to be in crisis according to some observers (cf. O'Connor 1973; OECD 1981; Offe 1984), while Flora (1986) hypothesized that we would be witnessing a "growth to limits" regarding the future development of welfare states, as major advances had been achieved. Moreover, the development of mature welfare states would tend to slow down or even stagnate without a severe economic or political crisis.

The subsequent comparative welfare research focused on the differentiation between distinct welfare systems or regimes (Esping-Andersen 1990). While Esping-Andersen's regime theory quickly became a modern classic (Emmenegger et al. 2015), many of his critics debated the applicability of the regime theory from the perspectives of certain policy or geographical areas. However, it is now widely acknowledged that welfare states can indeed be categorized into different welfare state regimes (Ferragina and Seeleib-Kaiser 2011) and that regimes are associated with specific social outcomes (Ferragina et al. 2015). Nevertheless, the literature focusing on welfare regimes was often limited to comparing the institutional designs or outcomes for average (production) workers in affluent welfare democracies at specific points in time. Longitudinal research with a regime perspective was relatively rare (but see Danforth 2014; Seeleib-Kaiser and Sowula 2021).

A further strand of research delved into the issue of whether the nature of the welfare state was changing. While Gilbert and Gilbert (1990) highlighted the concept of the *enabling state*, Jessop (1993) identified a transformation from a Keynesian welfare state to a Schumpeterian *workfare state*, Cerny (1997) diagnosed that the welfare state had mutated into a *competition state*, emphasizing the subordination of social policy to market logics and privatizations. By the late 1990s and early 2000s, observers identified new social risks and a shift toward a more active social policy (Bonoli 2013). Hemerijck (2017), and others (Morel et al. 2012) promoted a (normative) turn toward a welfare state more clearly focused on so-called social investments, emphasizing employability and human capital—a social investment turn, it was argued, would contribute to a virtuous cycle of social and economic development.[1] Although observers agreed that welfare states were undergoing significant changes, they disagreed about their directions.

Despite all the identified conceptual changes of welfare states, the overall social policy effort, as measured by spending data, *grosso modo* did not decline. Pierson (1994, 2001) in his influential work analyzed the politics of welfare state change and argued that we are witnessing a "new politics of the welfare state," whereby the welfare state clientele would oppose comprehensive cutbacks, making retrenchment difficult. Subsequently the literature on welfare state change differentiated between cost containment, retrenchment, recommodification, and recalibration. Pierson (2001) also argued that an era of permanent austerity had characterized social policy development since the 1990s. However, if we take social spending relative to Gross Domestic Product (GDP) as the indicator to assess welfare state development over the past decades, the highly aggregated data of public social spending suggests a picture of welfare state stability or a "growth to limits" for affluent countries of northwestern Europe and a rapid catch-up process and significant increases of public social spending in Southern European countries (see Figure. I.1), which in some countries, for instance in Spain, also was associated with a process of modernization for much of the 1990s and early 2000s (Guillén and Petmesidou 2008).

During the *Great Recession* (2007–2009), social policy *grosso modo* functioned as an automatic stabilizer, as is evidenced by the significant

---

[1] For analyses of the increased focus on social investment globally, see Garritzmann et al. (2022). The approach was criticized from conceptual (Nolan 2013) and empirical perspectives (Cantillon 2011; Parolin/Van Lancker 2021).

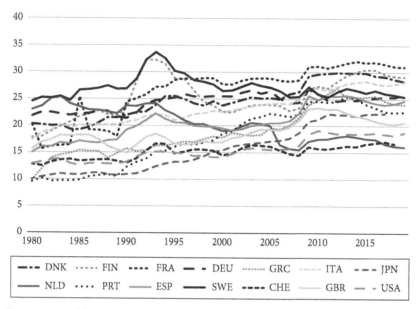

Figure I.1 Public Social Expenditure in % of GDP, 1980–2019. Source: OECD.

increase in spending in all OECD countries (see Figure I.1; OECD 2012). In several countries, particularly Germany, short-time work schemes were used to stabilize employment during the crisis, highlighting the economic benefits of social policy that were conceptually already identified in the 1930s (Briefs 1930). Empirical research demonstrates that government support through the tax and benefit system provided a cushion against the downturn during the Great Recession (Jenkins et al. 2013). However, this does not mean that we did not witness significant cutbacks in public social spending in relative and absolute terms in particular countries during the early 2010s, especially in the two Eurozone countries Greece and Portugal, but also in the United Kingdom (Figure I.1 and Figure I.2; cf. Taylor-Gooby et al. 2017).

Although the early 2010s were characterized by measures of budget con-solidation, social spending continued to be higher in the OECD world after the Great Recession than in the "golden welfare state era" (see Figure I.1; OECD 2020).[2] Holding prices constant and taking purchasing power into

---

[2] The Netherlands seems to be an exception; but the decline in public spending is largely related to reforms in health care and sick pay, as the compulsory basic health insurance is being financed through private funds since 2006 and sick pay provided through mandated employer-provided sick pay since the mid-1990s.

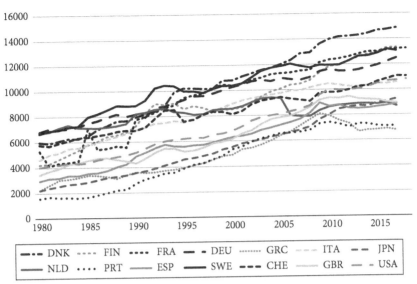

Figure I.2 Social Spending per Capita in Constant USD, 1980–2019.
Source: OECD.

account, OECD spending data per capita shows a clear increase in absolute terms in the *longue durée* (Figure I.2), reflecting overall economic growth and improvement in economic welfare during the past decades. From this perspective, the concept of *permanent austerity*, which has had significant traction in the social sciences and welfare state research (cf. Blyth 2013), seems to be misleading to characterize *overall* welfare state developments since the 1990s (Greve 2020; Reinprecht et al. 2018).

Irrespective of these macro spending data, analyses show that the protective capacity of social policies has declined, leading to increased inequality and poverty in many affluent democracies (Nolan 2018; Fischer and Strauss 2020; Cantillon 2022). At the policy level this development can be partially explained by welfare states that have undergone a "dual transformation" (Bleses and Seeleib-Kaiser 2004; Fleckenstein et al. 2011). The process of dual transformation can be characterized as retrenchment of earnings-related benefits for (long-term) unemployed and insufficient social protection coverage of atypically employed people on the one hand, and on the other an expansion of social policies addressing "new social risks," often disproportionately benefiting two-earner families in higher income groups (Cantillon 2011; Pavolini and Van Lancker 2018). Policies of social protection dualism, as part of overall dualization processes (Emmenegger et al. 2012), continue to largely protect labor market insiders and neglect or cut back social policies for labor market outsiders, leading to increasing social divides and dependence on social assistance programs among people in need (Seeleib-Kaiser et al. 2012). Yet, social assistance programs in the EU do not provide support above the risk-of-poverty threshold of 60% of median income (Konle-Seidl 2021); hence an increased dependence on social assistance programs, instead of reliance on universal or earnings-related social protection programs providing benefits above the poverty threshold in times of need, inevitably leads to increased poverty. In addition, the normative frames and concepts that have guided social policy for decades, namely continuous long-term employment in standard employment relationships and the dominance of stable two-parent families (with a female carer and a male worker) apply to ever fewer people, leading to increased risks. Homogamy (Blossfeld and Buchholz 2009) as well as migration (Eurostat 2021) have further contributed to inequality and poverty in Europe in the first couple of decades of the 21st century.

Social policy within the EU largely remained a matter of national welfare states, as European social policy was mainly limited to measures of social security coordination for mobile and migrant workers (Pennings 2015). Although the EU developed several social policy initiatives and strategies based on soft law in the 2000s, the results have been rather modest (Börner 2020). For instance, the Europe 2020 strategy, agreed upon in 2010, called for improved educational attainment of young people, high employment rates of the working-age population, and a reduction of people living in poverty and at the risk of social exclusion (Barcevičius et al. 2014). However, as a consequence of the economic and sovereign debt crisis as well as due to a lack of effective political effort (Offe 2016), poverty increased in a number of countries (Fischer and Strauss 2020). Especially in Greece, the conditionality of the bailout is said to have exacerbated the socioeconomic situation (De la Porte and Heins 2016; Petmesidou and Guilén 2014). In this context some observers and political actors have been calling for a so-called transfer union or the introduction of an unemployment reinsurance scheme to deal with asymmetric shocks and stabilize economies in crisis within the Eurozone (cf. Andor 2017). At that point in time, however, these proposals could not garner sufficient support, and the EU was left once again with the proclamation of a set of principles and soft law as part of the European Pillar of Social Rights established in 2017.

The social policy responses to the COVID-19 pandemic by the EU and affluent European nation states have demonstrated the economic and political benefits of social policies across the worlds of welfare, despite the fact that the policy responses by national welfare states were significantly influenced by the logics of existing welfare state regimes and national contexts. Moreover, the pandemic provided a window of opportunity to enact new or recalibrate existing social policy programs (Béland et al. 2021). The response by the EU to the pandemic was very different to its response to the Great Recession, as the EU provided large sums of money in form of loans *and* grants through its temporary "Support to mitigate Unemployment Risks in an Emergency" (SURE) and Next Generation EU (NGEU) programs to stabilize national economies and support social policy arrangements (Armingeon et al. 2022).

Structure of the Volume and Chapter Outlines

The edited volume provides an encompassing and longer-term analysis of social policy responses during the COVID-19 crisis. The book asks in which direction the European welfare states on the one hand, and EU social policy on the other hand, are developing as a result of the pandemic with respect to polity, politics, and policy instruments. What will be the medium- and long-term effects of the current social policy crisis responses on different welfare states? Will the partly improvised, partly only temporary but in every respect diverse and often unprecedented measures lead to novel reform trajectories, or even a new welfare state model? The questions raised do not only concern the future of welfare states in Europe but also EU-level social policymaking and European integration in general. The book focuses on the tension between continuity and change from different interdisciplinary and theoretical perspectives. Contributions range from single case studies to comparative policy analyses.

The chapters in Part I study welfare state change during the pandemic in order to contribute to welfare state and regime theory: How did different welfare state regimes in Europe react to the pandemic and its subsequent social problems? What were the greatest challenges across national borders? Will the crisis give birth to a new welfare state model and thus potentially alter the underlying normative beliefs on issues such as social spending, deservingness, and social justice? And with respect to future challenges, will the social policy crisis responses allow building a bridge between social and climate protection policies, and what new conflicts might arise from these policy processes?

In Chapter 1 Daniel Béland, Bea Cantillon, Bent Greve, Rod Hick, and Amílcar Moreira explore potential patterns of convergence and divergence in the social policy responses to the COVID-19 pandemic in four distinct welfare regimes: the Bismarckian regime, the Nordic regime, the liberal regime, and the Southern European regime. The analysis focuses on the policies introduced to protect workers against the risk of unemployment and the loss of income in two countries per regime (Ireland and the UK, Belgium and Germany, Denmark and Sweden, Greece and Portugal). The main conclusions are twofold: First, regardless of the regime type, countries have generally enacted emergency measures to expand and/or supplement existing policy instruments. Second, national policy legacies help explain key differences in the design of the policies adopted as a consequence of this pandemic.

Chapter 2, by Klaus Armingeon and Stefano Sacchi, place the public spending hike in the wake of the pandemic into a longer-term perspective, by studying the long-term spending patterns in the EU and the OECD world since 2010. The chapter examines the political strategies and options of governments, using a new dataset for 30 democratic nations. They analyze under which conditions democratic politics mattered for austerity policies from the Great Recession to the COVID-19 pandemic. The analysis shows that exiting a policy of austerity cannot be sufficiently explained by changed economic fundamentals. Rather, the longer governments pursue austerity, the more likely they are to exit it, even if the economic fundamentals would suggest otherwise. The quantitative findings are further corroborated by a case study on Italy showing the complex influences of economic constraints, political factors, and public discourse.

Chapter 3, by Tatiana Saruis, Yuri Kazepov, and Eduardo Barberis, studies the impact of COVID-19 on local social policies considering the subsidiarization process by focusing on the relevance of local and subnational levels of governance. Based on a classification of long-term welfare arrangements in five countries (France, Italy, Germany, Norway, Poland) the chapter addresses how the territorial dimension of social policies and its reconfiguration intersects with the COVID-19 pandemic, focusing primarily on the local dimension but embedding it in the complex multilevel governance arrangements that characterize social politics. The COVID-19 pandemic is a stress test and—as other crises such as the 2008 financial crisis—has territorial impacts and implications, redrawing the boundaries of inclusion and exclusion. This process is not free from inter-institutional conflict that may well hinder the implementation of potentially effective measures.

In Chapter 4 Matthew Donoghue uses a case study to examine how different crises connect with each other and affect a country's social policy strategy. The chapter considers how the framing of the UK social policy response reflects an active change in the United Kingdom's "imagined community," contextualized by its new position as an "independent" nation state outside of the EU. Drawing on an analysis of speeches, media reports, and policy literature focused on the pandemic response, particularly in health care and social protection, it argues that the COVID-19 pandemic presents the government with an opportunity to renew and bolster a sense of nation, not only in terms of the United Kingdom reasserting its position in the international order but also in terms of reasserting what it means to be a British citizen in the post-Brexit era. In doing so the chapter contributes to the literature on social policy and nation building, as well as literatures on the territorial politics of social policy.

Part II studies policy responses in specific social policy domains, their socio-structural effects for particular social groups, as well as their potential future effects on the social security systems in different countries. Following on from the finding that the coronavirus is exacerbating the existing social inequalities and divisive tendencies in the labor market, the authors ask which social groups are better or worse off as a result of the pandemic-induced reforms. For example, in many EU Member States, young labor market participants are more affected by the impact of the crisis on the labor market than are prime-age workers. Another focus is on the implementation of minimum labor and social standards in economic sectors in which EU migrant workers are overrepresented.

Chapter 5, by Emmanuele Pavolini, Rui Branco, Ana M. Guillén, and Maria Petmesidou, zooms in on health care systems in Southern Europe (Greece, Italy, Portugal, and Spain) that have been especially crises-ridden during the last two decades. The chapter analyzes whether the public health crisis in face of the pandemic and the recovery prospects—particularly under the Next Generation EU plan—represent a critical juncture for health care policy. The main findings indicate a variegated picture of piecemeal recalibration trends that, however, are short of addressing long-overdue challenges in a comprehensive manner and therefore show little evidence of this juncture turning into a window of opportunity for radical change. Chapter 6, by Jacqueline

O'Reilly, Rune Halvorsen, Marge Unt, Mi Ah Schoyen, Rachel Verdin, Triin Roosalu, and Zyab Ibáñez examines the impact of the pandemic on youth labor markets in Europe, focusing on four countries illustrating distinctive models of youth social citizenship: Estonia, Norway, Spain, and the United Kingdom. One of the key insights the analysis reveals is that government responses did not benefit (all) young people equally. The impact of the pandemic is likely to strengthen the significant challenges to previous underlying structural inequalities related to forms of education, training, and the quality of employment offered to young people.

Chapter 7, by Cecilia Bruzelius and Martin Seeleib-Kaiser, focuses on basic labor rights of mobile seasonal EU workers and the national enforcement thereof in the agricultural and forestry sector. It is demonstrated that although the EU has explicitly acknowledged the precarious working conditions of seasonal agricultural workers and the need to change policies in the wake of the COVID-19 pandemic at the discursive level, the EU continues to have very limited enforcement capacities and competencies and plays an ambivalent role. As enforcement continues to depend on Member States' policies and measures, the authors compare enforcement practices across four countries with different enforcement regimes: Austria, Germany, Sweden, and the United Kingdom. The analysis suggests that seasonal workers' rights are neglected across countries, irrespective of enforcement regime. They argue that the scant efforts made to enforce these seasonal workers' rights amounts to institutionalized exploitation.

In Chapter 8 Katja Möhring, Maximiliane Reifenscheid, Andreas Weiland, and Klara Kuhn study gender inequality in employment risks during the first and the second wave of the COVID-19 pandemic in Germany. Using individual-level panel data, the authors examine the risks of short-time work, job loss, and unpaid furlough, as well as having to work on-site. Although women, and in particular working mothers, are known to have suffered from a triple burden during the lockdowns, the results reveal no particularly high labor market risk exposure of women. Access to crisis measures, which serve as a buffer against risks of income loss and job loss, does not differ between genders. Furthermore, there is no increased likelihood of job loss and unpaid furlough among women, and women do not show a significantly higher probability of working on-site during the early phase of the pandemic than men. Regarding the risk of unemployment in the first and second wave of the pandemic, the results rather suggest that individual characteristics such as low income and education are important drivers. This also applies to the likelihood of short-time work during the second wave of the pandemic.

The chapters in Part III shift the main locus of the analysis from the national to the EU level and address social policymaking as a multilevel process by discussing the implications for European integration and EU social policy: What role do the different territorial levels play in the response to the crisis? Which (de)centralization processes can be observed? What new forms of international cooperation and conflict resolution mechanisms may arise in the EU context? What implications do the adopted and debated instruments have for the European integration process? Will the new conflicts cause another legitimation crisis in the EU? Is the "Corona crisis" leading EU social policy into a new era?

Chapter 9, by Zhen Jie Im, Caroline de la Porte, Elke Heins, Andrea Prontera, and Dorota Szelewa, deals with the EU's fiscal and policy response to the COVID-19 pandemic—Next Generation EU (NGEU), which represents an institutional and instrumental break to the previous policy trajectory. It examines the recovery and resilience programs of four different types of political economy (Denmark, Germany, Poland, and Spain), to discern whether and to what extent the NGEU is leading to green growth and a just transition. The authors argue that Member States differ both in their greening and just(ing) strategies; countries with robust social investment institutions may encounter less political resistance if they pursue more difficult decarbonization industrial reforms. If displaced workers can be offered better economic prospects, there may be less political resistance to such reforms. Member States that face less resistance are better able to adapt to the Green Economy and benefit from it more than Member States which face higher resistance and are less able to adapt.

Chapter 10, by Mary Guy, analyzes EU health policy since COVID-19 and how it raised the profile as well as led to an acceleration of EU-level activity in health. Notable developments since spring 2020 include calls for a European Health Union and the launch of the EU4Health program to underpin this. What emerged were two differing visions of a European Health Union: one primarily focused on the EU's ability to respond to health crises, and the other premised on the need to address wider health concerns, and the interaction between the EU and Member State competence.

In Chapter 11 Natalie Glynn utilizes the COVID-19 pandemic as a focusing event and seeks to integrate insights from comparative federalism and EU integration studies to further our understanding of how transnational problems are managed in multilevel systems, especially the role that non-centralization can play in this process. Using a small-n qualitative case study approach, including Australia, Canada, the European Union, and the United

States of America, the chapter examines how pandemic-induced internal border controls were managed between February 2020 and October 2020. The chapter then discusses insights about the role that non-centralization played in responding to these policy challenges. Glynn concludes that the intergovernmental–supranational dynamics can have implications for social policymaking in the EU.

Chapter 12, by Georg Vobruba, focuses on three specific areas of European social policy that dealt with particular pandemic-related problems under time pressure—health, mobility, and public finances. European policymaking, the chapter argues, follows a pattern of complementary insti-tutionalization. The pandemic revealed a particular state of insufficient in-stitutionalization of the EU, and as soon as this diagnosis was adopted by relevant actors, it contributed to triggering policies which resulted in com-plementary institution building. The application of the explanatory pattern to the three political areas reveals three different modes of pre-pandemic in-stitutionalization and hence also different institutional consequences for the policy domain. While the integration of health policies started from a low pre-pandemic level and allowed for an accelerated path-dependent institu-tionalization process, policies on freedom of movement had already reached a high level of institutionalization before the pandemic, and thus challenges could be dealt with within the framework of existing regulations. In the field of public finances, in which integration had been a highly contested matter in previous crises, Vobruba observes the most far-reaching and dynamic effects on complementary institution building.

Overall, the different social policy areas, European countries and so-cial groups studied in this volume do not only show that the welfare state is here to stay, but also that social policy may potentially develop and expand its competences at the European level. The epilogue discusses the volume's major insights and summarizes the results from a perspective of continuity and change in social policy.

References

Allmendinger, Jutta. 2022. "Auf dem Rücken der Frauen." *Die Zeit*, March 1, 2022.

Andor, László. 2017. "The Impact of Eurozone Governance on Welfare State Stability." In *A European Social Union after the Crisis*, edited by Frank Vandenbroucke, Catherine Barnard, Geert De Baere, 172–91. Cambridge: Cambridge University Press.

Armingeon, Klaus, Caroline de la Porte, Elke Heins, and Stefano Sacchi. 2022. "Voices from the past: economic and political vulnerabilities in the making of next generation EU." *Comparative Eurorpean Politics* 20: 144–65. https://doi.org/10.1057/s41295-022-00277-6.

Barcevičius, Egidijus, Timo Weishaupt, and Jonathan Zeitlin. 2014. *Assessing the Open Method of Coordination*. London: Palgrave Macmillan.

Bariola Nino, and Caitlyn Collins. 2021. "The gendered politics of pandemic relief: Labor and family policies in Denmark, Germany, and the United States during COVID-19." *American Behavioral Scientist*, 65 (12): 1671–1697.

Béland, Daniel, Bea Cantillon, Rod Hick, and Amílcar Moreira. 2021. "Social policy in the face of a global pandemic: Policy responses to the COVID-19 crisis." *Social Policy and Administration* 55 (2): 249–60.

Bergsen, Pepijn, Alice Billon-Galland, Hans Kundnani, Vassilis Ntousas, and Thomas Raines. 2020. *Europe After Coronavirus: The EU and a New Political Economy*. London: Chatham House.

Bleses, Peter, and Martin Seeleib-Kaiser. 2004. *The Dual Transformation of the German Welfare State*. Basingstoke: Palgrave.

Blossfeld, Hans-Peter, and Sandra Buchholz. 2009. "Increasing resource inequality among families in modern societies: The mechanisms of growing educational homogamy, changes in the division of work in the family and the decline of the male breadwinner model." *Journal of Comparative Family Studies* 40 (4): 603–15.

Blyth, Mark. 2013. *Austerity: The History of a Dangerous Idea*. New York/Oxford: Oxford University Press.

Bonoli, Giuliano, Victor George, und and Peter Taylor-Gooby. 2000. *European Welfare Futures: To-wards a Theory of Retrenchment*. Cambridge: Polity Press.

Bonoli, Guiliano. 2013. *The Origins of Active Social Policy*. Oxford: Oxford University Press.

Börner, Stefanie. 2020. "Marshall revisited. EU social policy from a social-rights perspective." *Journal of European Social Policy* 30 (4): 421–35.

Börner, Stefanie. 2021. "Practices of solidarity in the COVID-19 pandemic." *Culture, Practice and Europeanization* 6 (1): 1–14.

Briefs, Götz. 1930. "Der wirtschaftliche Wert der Sozialpolitik." In *Die Reform des Schlichtungswesens—Der wirtschaftliche Wert der Sozialpolitik*, edited by Vorstand der Gesellschaft für Soziale Reform. Bericht über die Verhandlungen der XI. Generalversammlung der Gesellschaft für Soziale Reform in Mannheim am 24. und 25. Oktober 1929, 144–170. Jena: G. Fischer.

Cantillon, Bea. 2011. "The paradox of the social investment state: Growth, employment and poverty in the Lisbon era." *Journal of European Social Policy* 21 (5): 432–49.

Cantillon, Bea. 2022. "The Tragic Decline of the Poverty Reducing Capacity of the Welfare State: Lessons from Two Decades of Social Policy Research." *Working Paper*, No 22/01. Herman Deleeck Centre for Social Policy, University of Antwerp.

Cantillon, Bea, Martin Seeleib-Kaiser, and Romke van der Veen. 2021. "The COVID-19 crisis and policy responses by continental European welfare states." *Social Policy Administration* 55: 326–38. https://doi.org/10. 1111/spol.12715.

Cerny, Paul. 1997. "Paradoxes of the competition state: The dynamics of political globalization." *Government and Opposition* 32 (2): 251–74. https://doi.org/10.1111/j.1477-7053.1997.tb00161.x.

Daly, Mary. 2021. "The concept of care: Insights, challenges and research opportunities in COVID-19 times." *Journal of European Social Policy* 31 (1): 108–18.

Danforth, Benjamin. 2014. "Worlds of welfare in time: A historical reassessment of the three-world typology." *Journal of European Social Policy* 24 (2): 164–82.

De la Porte, Caroline, and Elke Heins (eds.). 2016. *The Sovereign Debt Crisis, the EU and Welfare State Reform*. London: Palgrave Macmillan.

Emmenegger, Patrick, Silia Häusermann, Bruno Palier, and Martin Seeleib-Kaiser (eds.). 2012. *The Age of Dualization: The Changing Face of Inequality in Deindustrializing Societies*. New York/Oxford: Oxford University Press.

Emmenegger, Patrick, Jon Kvist, Paul Marx, and Klaus Petersen. 2015. "Three worlds of welfare capitalism: The making of a classic." *Journal of European Social Policy* 25 (1): 3–13. doi:10.1177/0958928714556966.

EP (European Parliament). 2020. "European Parliament resolution on European protection of cross-border and seasonal workers in the context of the COVID-19 crisis (2020/2664(RSP))." B9-0172/2020/REV. Available at https://www.europarl.europa.eu/doceo/document/B-9-2020-0172_EN.pdf.

Esping-Andersen, Gøsta. 1990. *Three Worlds of Welfare Capitalism*. Cambridge: Polity.

Eurofound. 2020. *COVID-19: Policy Responses Across Europe*. Luxembourg: Publications Office of the European Union.

Eurostat. 2021. "Migrants and the risk of poverty or social exclusion." Available at https://ec.europa.eu/eurostat/web/products-eurostat-news/-/ddn-20210202-2.

Ferragina, Emanuele, and Martin Seeleib-Kaiser. 2011. "Welfare regime debate: Past, present, futures?" *Policy and Politics*, 39 (4): 589–817.

Ferragina, Emanuele, Martin Seeleib-Kaiser, and Thees Spreckelsen. 2015. "The Four worlds of 'welfare reality': Social risks and outcomes in Europe." *Social Policy & Society* 14 (2): 287–307.

Fischer, Georg, and Günther Schmid. 2021. "Unemployment in Europe and the United States under Covid-19: Better constrained in the corset of an insurance logic or at the whim of a liberal presidential system?" *Discussion Paper* EME 2021–001. WZB Berlin Social Science Center.

Fischer, Georg and Robert Strauss (eds.). 2020. *Europe's Income, Wealth, Consumption, and Inequality*. New York/Oxford: Oxford University Press.

Fleckenstein, Tim, Adam Saunders, and Martin Seeleib-Kaiser. 2011. "The dual transformation of social protection and human capital: Comparing Britain and Germany." *Comparative Political Studies* 44 (12): 1622–50.

Flora, Peter (ed.). 1986. *Growth to Limits: The Western European Welfare States since World War II*. Vol. 1: Sweden, Norway, Finland, Denmark. Vol. 2: Germany, United Kingdom, Ireland, Italy. Berlin: Walter de Gruyter.

Fourastié, Joan. 1979. *Les Trente Glorieuses: Ou la révolution invisible de 1946 à 1975*. Paris: Fayard.

Garritzmann, Julian, Silja Häusermann, and Bruno Palier (eds.). 2022. *The World Politics of Social Investment: Welfare States in the Knowledge Economy*. Vol. I + II. New York/Oxford: Oxford University Press.

Gilbert, Neil, and Barbara Gilbert. 1990. *The Enabling State. Modern Welfare Capitalism in America*. Oxford: Oxford University Press.

Giraud, Oliver, Nikola Tietze, Tania Toffanin, and Camille Noûs. 2021. "The scalar arrangements of three European public health systems facing the COVID-19 pandemic: Comparing France, Germany, and Italy." *Culture, Practice & Europeanization* 6 (1): 89–111.

Greve, Bent. 2020. *Austerity, Retrenchment and the Welfare State:* Cheltenham: Edward Elgar.

Guillén, Ana M., and Maria Petmesidou. 2008. "The Public-Private Mix in Southern Europe: What Changed in the Last Decade?" In *Welfare State Transformations. Comparative Perspectives*, edited by Martin Seeleib-Kaiser, 56–78. Basingstoke: Palgrave.

Hemerijck, Anton (ed.). 2017. *The Uses of Social Investment*. Oxford: Oxford University Press.

Jenkins, Stephen P., Andrea Bandolini, John Micklewright, and Brian Nolan. 2013 *The Great Recession and the Distribution of Household Income*. Oxford: Oxford University Press.

Konle-Seidl, Regina. 2020. *Short-time Work in Europe: Rescue in the Current COVID-19 Crisis? IAB-Forschungsbericht*. Nuremberg: IAB.

Konle-Seidl, Regina. 2021. "Strengthening minimum income protection in the EU." Briefing: Policy Department for Economic, Scientific and Quality of Life Policies, Directorate-General for Internal Policies, European Parliament. PE 662.900— March 2021.

Morel, Natalie, Bruno Palier, and Joakim Palme. 2012. *Towards a Social Investment State? Ideas, Policies and Challenges*. Bristol: Policy Press.

Murphy, M., and M McGann. (2020): *Renewing welfare through universal entitlement: Lessons from Covid-19*. Social Europe, September 24, 2020.Available at https://www.socialeurope.eu/renewing-welfare-through-universal-entitlement-lessons-from-covid-19.

Nolan, Brian. 2013. "What use is 'social investment'?" *Journal of European Social Policy* 23 (5): 459–68. https://doi.org/10.1177/0958928713499177.

Nolan, Brian (ed.). 2018. *Generating Prosperity for Working Families in Affluent Countries*. Oxford: Oxford University Press.

OECD. 1981. *The Welfare State in Crisis*. Paris: OECD.

OECD. 2012. *Social spending during the crisis: Social expenditure (SOCX) data update 2012*. Paris: OECD.

OECD. 2020. *Social Expenditure (SOCX) Update 2020: Social spending makes up 20% of OECD GDP*. Paris: OECD.

Offe, Claus. 1984. *Contradictions of the Welfare State*. Cambridge, MA: MIT Press.

Offe, Claus. 2016. *Europa in der Falle*. Frankfurt am Main: Edition Suhrkamp.

Parolin, Zachary, Sophie Collyer, Megan Curran, and Christopher Wimer. 2021. "Monthly Poverty Rates among Children after the Expansion of the Child Tax Credit." Poverty and Social Policy Brief 20412, Center on Poverty and Social Policy, Columbia University.

Parolin, Zachary, Wim Van Lancker. 2021. "What a social investment 'litmus test' must address: A response to Plavgo and Hemerijck." *Journal of European Social Policy* 31 (3): 297–308. https://doi.org/10.1177/09589287211012974.

Pavolini, Emmanuele, Wim Van Lancker. 2018. "The Matthew effect in childcare use: a matter of policies or preferences?" *Journal of European Public Policy* 25 (6): 878–93. https://doi.org/10.1080/13501763.2017.1401108.

Pennings, Frans. 2015. *European Social Security Law*, 6th edition. Cambridge: Intersentia.

Petmesidou, Maria, Ana M. Guilén. 2014. "Can the welfare state as we know it survive? A view from the crisis-ridden South European periphery." *South European Society and Politics* 14 (3): 295–307.

Pierson, Paul. 1994. *Dismantling the Welfare State. Reagan, Thatcher, and the Politics of Retrenchment*. Cambridge: Cambridge University Press.

Pierson, Paul. 2000. "Increasing returns, path dependence, and the study of politics." *American Political Science Review* 94: 251–67.

Pierson, Paul (ed.). 2001. *The New Politics of the Welfare State.* Oxford: Oxford University Press.

de la Porte, Caroline, and MD Jensen. 2021. "The next generation EU: An analysis of the dimensions of conflict behind the deal." *Social Policy Administration* 55: 388–402. https://doi.org/10.1111/spol.12709.

de la Porte, Caroline, and Elke Heins. 2022. "Introduction: EU constraints and opportunities in the COVID-19 pandemic—the politics of NGEU." *Comparative European Politics* 20: 135–43. https://doi.org/10.1057/s41295-022-00276-7.

Reinprecht, Constantin, Martin Seeleib-Kaiser, and Jakub Sowula. 2018. "Mythen der vergleichenden Sozialpolitikforschung? Permanente Austerität und wohlfahrtstaatliches Retrenchment." *Sozialer Fortschritt* 67: 783–804.

Rhodes, Martin. 2021. "'Failing forward': a critique in light of Covid-19." *Journal of European Public Policy* 28 (10): 1537–54.

Seeleib-Kaiser, Martin, Adam Saunders, and Marek Naczyk. 2012. "Shifting the Public-Private Mix: A New Dualization of Welfare?" In *The Age of Dualization,* edited by Patrick Emmenegger, Silja Häusermann, Bruno Palier, and Matrin Seeleib-Kaiser, 151–75. Oxford: Oxford University Press.

Seeleib-Kaiser, Martin, and Jakub Sowula. 2021. "The Genesis of Welfare Regime Theory." In *Ideal Types in Comparative Social Policy,* edited by Christian Aspalter, 41–59. London: Routledge.

Starke, Peter, Alexandra Kaasch, and Franca van Hooren. 2013. *The Welfare State as Crisis Manager: Explaining the Diversity of Policy Responses to Economic Crisis.* Hampshire, England: Palgrave Macmillan.

Taylor-Gooby, Peter, Benjamin Leruth, and Heejung Chung (eds.). 2017. *After Austerity: Welfare State Transformation in Europe after the Great Recession.* Oxford: Oxford University Press.

UN Women. 2020. *Addressing the Economic Fallout of COVID-19: Pathways and Policy Options for a Gender-Responsive Recovery.* New York: United Nations.

PART I
NATIONAL WELFARE REGIMES DURING THE COVID-19 PANDEMIC

1

Policy Legacies, Welfare Regimes, and Social Policy Responses to COVID-19 in Europe

Daniel Béland, Bea Cantillon, Rod Hick, Bent Greve,
and Amílcar Moreira

Introduction

Much has been written since the publication in 1990 of Esping-Andersen's *The Three Worlds of Welfare Capitalism* on the concept of welfare regime as an analytical tool to study social policy stability and change in Europe and beyond. As a concept, welfare regime emphasizes both stability over change and divergence between country clusters over convergence. Studying concrete policy instruments rather than spending patterns and focusing on policies introduced to protect workers against the risk of unemployment and the loss of income, this chapter explores potential patterns of commonality and difference in the social policy responses to the COVID-19 pandemic in four distinct welfare regimes: the Bismarckian, the Nordic, the liberal, and the Southern European regimes. To add focus to our comparison, we focus on policies introduced to protect workers against the risk of unemployment or the loss of income as result of non-pharmaceutical interventions (lockdowns, school closures, etc.) to contain the spread of the virus. The emphasis of the analysis is on concrete policy instruments that have been expanded or even created to address the COVID-19 crisis with regard to employment and unemployment. Simultaneously, the analysis concentrates on national rather than subnational or supranational policies.

The main conclusions of our comparative analysis are twofold. First, we show that regardless of the regime in which they belong, countries have generally enacted emergency measures to expand and/or supplement existing

Daniel Béland, Bea Cantillon, Rod Hick, Bent Greve, and Amílcar Moreira, *Policy Legacies, Welfare Regimes, and Social Policy Responses to COVID-19 in Europe* In: *European Social Policy and the COVID-19 Pandemic*. Edited by: Stefanie Börner and Martin Seeleib-Kaiser, Oxford University Press. © Oxford University Press 2023. DOI: 10.1093/oso/9780197676189.003.0001 employment and unemployment-related policy instruments. This swift reaction in all the countries under consideration has been part of a broader effort to "save" the economy as part of both "emergency Keynesianism" (Bremer and McDaniel 2020, 439) and, at a deeper level, the economic imperative of preventing a collapse of capitalist markets (Béland et al. 2021). Second, we show that existing national policy legacies help explain differences in the design of the policies adopted as a consequence of this imperative. At the same time, we suggest that cross-national differences in policy legacies within the same regime cluster help account for intra-regime variation in social policy responses to COVID-19. This suggests that, ultimately, the weight of national policy legacies remains strong.

Three main sections comprise the remainder of this chapter. The first section provides a short theoretical discussion about convergence and divergence in social policy during the pandemic centered on the concepts of "emergency Keynesianism" and "welfare regimes." The second section, which comprises the bulk of the chapter, provides a discussion of the social policy responses to COVID-19 mainly addressing the risk of unemployment and the loss of income in the liberal, Bismarckian, Nordic, and Southern European welfare regimes, in that order. More specifically, a separate subsection is devoted to each regime, with a particular focus on two countries per regime: respectively (liberal) Ireland and the United Kingdom, (Bismarckian) Belgium and Germany, (Nordic) Denmark and Sweden, and (Southern European) Greece and Portugal. We selected two countries per regime to increase the number of cases and stress potential intra-regime variation from one country to the next. Although the discussion of these two cases per regime is not necessarily symmetrical, the empirical sections discuss eight cases in total (two per regime), which makes it easier to get a better sense of the social policy dynamics witnessed in each regime at hand during the pandemic. At the same time, perhaps with the exception of the liberal regime, we could not include all the main countries featured within each regime, which is a limitation of our analysis. The final section compares these cases directly before summarizing the findings and sketching an agenda for future research on welfare regimes and social policy stability and change during the COVID-19 pandemic and beyond.

Welfare Regimes in Times of Crisis

Much has been written about how many social policies tend to reproduce over time through self-reinforcing feedback effects, leading to what is known as path dependence (Pierson 1994, 1996, 2000; for a critical perspective see Jacobs and Weaver 2015). This perspective is consistent with punctuated equilibrium theory, an approach that claims that path-departing change typically occurs during rare episodes called "critical junctures," which can be triggered—among other factors—by global crises (Capoccia and Kelemen 2007).

The work of Gøsta Esping-Andersen (1990, 1999) and his many followers on welfare regimes stresses policy stability over time (Béland and Mahon 2016). A welfare regime is a cluster that gathers countries featuring a relatively similar articulation of the relationship between states, markets, and families (Esping-Andersen 1999). The original typology of welfare regimes as developed by Esping-Andersen (1990, 1999) only featured three regimes: (1) the liberal regime (e.g., Canada, Ireland, the United Kingdom, and the United States), which is dominated by market forces and relatively modest and targeted social programs; (2) the Bismarckian regime, which is centered on social insurance and traditional gender roles; and (3) the Nordic welfare regime, which features large universal social programs.

Although these regimes are understood as relatively stable over time, scholars have long pointed to path-departing pressures that may gradually transform them over time (Palier 2010). This type of scholarship is associated with a broader stream of research in comparative policy analysis that has challenged the previously dominant focus in institutional scholarship on path dependence and punctuated equilibrium (Streeck and Thelen 2005). Simultaneously, it is clear that policy legacies and trajectories can vary greatly from country to country within the same regime cluster, not to mention the heterogeneity of social programs across policy areas and instruments within the same country (Myles 1998; Béland 2010). Yet, even scholars like Bruno Palier (2010) and colleagues, who study both policy change and cross-country variation within specific welfare regimes, recognize the value of the concept, which allows us to systematically explore and compare the institutional dynamics of social policy beyond individual measures and policy instruments.

In the following analysis, we study how social policies designed and used to address employment and unemployment issues during the COVID-19 pandemic have fared in four welfare regimes present in Europe. Our analysis looks at key measures enacted during the initial phase of the pandemic in 2020 and assesses to what degree they are consistent with the specific policy legacies and dominant institutional logics associated with the four welfare regimes under consideration, as well as the variation from country to country within the same regime cluster. Simultaneously, we explore the possibility of convergence among these regimes triggered by the pandemic. The idea of a potential convergence among countries and welfare regimes is hardly a new question (Gilbert 2002), but it takes a new meaning during the COVID-19 pandemic, which has witnessed major economic disruptions that might have the potential to trigger path-departing pressures leading to a convergence among the four regimes to which we now turn.

Four Welfare Regimes during the COVID-19 Crisis

The Liberal Regime

The United Kingdom and Ireland are typically located within the liberal regime, emphasizing relatively unrestrained market forces in determining the living standards of the many, and with social protection modest in generosity and targeted largely at the poor. Ireland's position within the liberal grouping is sometimes contested—its scores in relation to degree of liberalism are low in Esping-Andersen's study (1990, 74; see Deeming et al. 2017 for a discussion). Irish authors have sometimes been dissatisfied with this classification, with The National Economic and Social Council (NESC) (2005, 140) suggesting that the welfare system contains elements of hybridity and therefore "resists easy classification." Central to this claim, and of importance here, is that Irish social protection rates were increased in the late 1990s and early 2000s and, despite significant restraint in the years following the Great Recession, remained considerably more generous than those paid in the United Kingdom at the onset of the pandemic. In concrete terms, the weekly rate of Universal Credit in the United Kingdom pre-pandemic was £73, with additional amounts possible on behalf of children or housing costs, while Ireland's primary social protection rate was €203 per week (approximately £180 at March 2020 exchange rates) with, similarly, additional amounts payable in cases of dependent adults and children.

In terms of employment-related support, the United Kingdom's response to the pandemic contained aspects of originality combined with a commitment to existing policy pathways. For those who could not work as a result of stay-at-home orders but who had jobs to go back to, the government announced the Coronavirus Jobs Retention Scheme (CJRS, or "furlough") on March 20. Under the furlough scheme, the UK government agreed to fund 80% of the gross salary of retained workers, up to £2,500 per month for an initial three months. A separate scheme was rolled out for self-employed people, providing equivalent levels of support, though the schemes operated quite differently in practice. By May 2020, there were almost nine million people relying on furlough (Tomlinson 2021).

While furloughed workers received generous provision that operated outside of the social security system, those who lost jobs were reliant on much less generous provision via the government's flagship means-tested social security payment, Universal Credit. Three changes were made to Universal Credit, each of which had the effect of increasing the generosity of awards (Hick and Murphy 2021). First, the standard allowance for Universal Credit (and for Working Tax Credits as part of the "legacy" system of payments that were in the process of being amalgamated into Universal Credit) was increased by £20 to £94 per week for 2020/21, representing a significant rise—the most generous of unemployment supports relative to earnings since 1998/9 (Brewer and Gardiner 2020). Second, Local Housing Allowance, which determines the level of support for housing costs within Universal Credit, was increased, reversing cuts that had been made to the scheme since 2012. Third, the Minimum Income Floor, which served to limit awards for self-employed people, was scrapped. While there were proposals to waive the capital limits on Universal Credit during the crisis (e.g., Brewer and Handscomb 2020), which would result in a reduced award for any household with more than £6,000 savings (and a nil award for a household with £16,000 or more in savings), these were ignored.

These changes all increased the generosity of support provided via the social security system, but they still implied a level of support that was much less generous for newly unemployed than for furloughed workers. In terms of levels of support, workers could receive up to £500 per week from furlough but just £94 from the basic rate of Universal Credit. There was added complexity in that the schemes were not mutually exclusive: furloughed workers who were in receipt of low earnings could, if they met the relevant conditions, top up their furlough payments with Universal Credit and, unlike in some other countries, the enhancements in relation to generosity were applicable to *all* claimants, not only those newly unemployed as a result of the pandemic (Hick and Murphy 2021).

Yet, there were also significant gaps in the support package announced. Geiger et al. (2021a) estimate that about 500,000 people were entitled to

Universal Credit but did not claim it. Lack of knowledge about entitlements played a part here; they also find that nearly a quarter of a million people (220,000) believed they were eligible but did not want to claim Universal Credit. Moreover, Geiger et al. (2021b) estimate that 290,000 people applied for Universal Credit but had their claims rejected, the key reason being for partner's earnings and having savings that denied entitlement. Throughout the pandemic, there has also been an absence of attention to the contributory social security system, which some newly unemployed workers would likely have been entitled to (Hick 2020). In general, gaps in provision, where identified, did not gain political traction.

Overall, in the United Kingdom, the initial response consisted of a high degree of support provided to furloughed workers, with much lower levels of support to those who lost work (or were denied furlough by their employers), and no support for some. It consisted of the introduction of a novel short-time work scheme (furlough) as well as embedding the existing policy pathway (in terms of the rollout of Universal Credit), with most of those who lost work reliant on the more generous provision via the furlough scheme.

The response package in Ireland took a different shape, though it was motivated by a similar view that income support during the pandemic would need to be more generous than was provided for by the pre-pandemic social protection system. There was a superficial similarity in terms of reliance on both job retention (the Temporary Wage Subsidy Scheme, or TWSS) and social protection (Pandemic Unemployment Payment) instruments. On its introduction the TWSS was paid at a rate of 70% of net earnings up to a ceiling of €410 per week; the Pandemic Unemployment Payment was paid at a flat rate of €350 per week. This implied an important commonality between the responses in Ireland and the United Kingdom—namely, that payments in both countries were for most people significantly higher than regular social security rates (Hick and Murphy 2021). However while there was, as in the United Kingdom, a reliance on both job retention and job loss payments, in practice these schemes looked quite different. The Irish instruments in most cases provided more equal payments than those from furlough and Universal Credit. Increased payments in cases of job loss (via the Pandemic Unemployment Payment) were made only for those who lost work due to COVID and paid at rates far exceeding those already unemployed (€350 vs €203 per week). This was contrary to the experience in the United Kingdom, where the (initial) 12-month £20 weekly uplift to Universal Credit was paid to all claimants whether impacted by the pandemic or not. Moreover, the

Pandemic Unemployment Payment was paid to those who lost their jobs as a result of the pandemic without any reference made to either social insurance contribution records or to means tests, and thus stood outside of the pre-pandemic social security system. Unlike in the United Kingdom, where most people whose work was affected by the initial lockdowns claimed the short-time work payment (the Coronavirus Job Retention Scheme), in Ireland more of these affected claimed the out-of-work Pandemic Unemployment Payment (Garcia-Rodriguez et al. 2021, 6). There are thus commonalities and differences between Ireland's and the United Kingdom's responses (Hick and Murphy 2021).

In terms of the social impacts of the crisis, both job loss and furlough were significantly correlated with low pay in the United Kingdom, but a combination of the policy responses discussed above, and families acting as buffers to individual labor market change, has meant that there was only a moderate relationship between households reporting a significant fall in income during the pandemic and economic position (Bell and Brewer 2021, 13; see also Sánchez et al. 2021). While data from Ireland is less extensive, Beirne et al. (2020) finds, similarly, that the Irish government's primary pandemic responses served to cushion losses for the lowest four income deciles. In this sense, the fortunes of those less well-off have been shielded significantly by the policy responses in both countries, but we will need better quality micro-data to understand the true effects on household living standards, including whether the different policy choices adopted in the United Kingdom and Ireland have identifiable consequences in terms of well-being outcomes.

The Bismarckian Regime

Germany and Belgium are typical social insurance states characterized by the predominance of institutionally segmented social insurance systems stemming from the Bismarckian legacy (Hinrichs 2010). Employees, the self-employed, and civil servants each have their own social security system; protection is, in principle, earnings-related and contribution-based. In these settings, means-tested social assistance remains rather marginal. In recent decades, however, in both countries social protection systems were subjected to sequential reform processes that weakened social insurance and, as a consequence, increased the share of social assistance in overall social protection: wage replacement schemes were partly reoriented toward minimum income protection, protection shifted toward activation, and social insurance contributions were replaced by an increasing share of tax-funding (Hinrichs 2012; Hemerijck and Marx 2012). These developments occurred in both countries but with different strength and at different paces.

In Belgium, social insurance for the unemployed became less generous and less accessible, but the duration of benefits remained unlimited, while social protection for the self-employed was strengthened significantly, *inter alia* by introducing a system that provides income support in the event of bankruptcy (OECD 2017). In Germany the role of social insurance in protecting the unemployed is more limited: long-term unemployed must rely on means-tested benefits, and so do the self-employed with no economic activity. As a consequence, the share of social assistance in total social protection expenditure is more than double in Germany than in Belgium (12.4% and 5.4% respectively, see OECD 2020). The traditional strength of social insurance in both countries on the one hand, and the stronger reliance of the unemployed on social assistance in Germany compared to Belgium on the other hand, explain the similarities and differences in the responses to the COVID-related labor market crisis in these two countries.

In Belgium[1] the negative impact of the crisis on household incomes was largely cushioned by the operation and the reinforcement of existing social insurance schemes, most notably by the lay-off scheme for employees, the bridging right for the self-employed, and the parental leave scheme. As a result, the number of people relying on social insurance increased dramatically while dependence on means-tested social assistance remained at a comparatively low level. The social partners played a crucial role in implementing very quickly the measures needed to adapt the existing social insurance systems to such unprecedented conditions.

Unlike in the United Kingdom, where a new short-term unemployment scheme had to be created, and unlike in Ireland, where a new wage subsidy system was installed (see above), in Belgium and Germany the existing short-term unemployment schemes were made more accessible while benefits became more generous. In Belgium, the replacement rate was increased from 65% to 70% of the monthly wage (capped at €2,754.76), while additional

---

[1] We focus on federal measures in social security and social assistance. In addition, the regions took measures such as child benefit supplement for temporary unemployed in Flanders, child benefit supplement for low-income families in Brussels, energy and water subsidies in Flanders, and measures related to housing support.

supplements were introduced for workers who had been laid off for a long period. The lay-off scheme provided Belgium with a strong instrument to protect workers and employers against the negative consequences of the public health measures implemented rapidly to stop the spread of the coronavirus. During the first lockdown, more than 29% of the workforce benefited from temporary unemployment benefits. Social protection for the regular unemployed remained at the same level, but activation measures were de facto relaxed while the "degressivity" of the social benefits for the regular long-term unemployed was temporarily frozen.[2]

In Belgium, social insurance has also been used to support the self-employed. The existing "bridging right" for self-employed—which in the event of bankruptcy assures for a maximum of 12 months the retention of the rights to child benefits and medical care (for a maximum of four quarters) and provides a monthly flat rate payment equal to the minimum pension—was extended to support the self-employed who had to cease their activities as a consequence of COVID-related health measures.[3] In April 2020, more than 400,000 self-employed received a bridging right.

Estimates of the total cost of COVID-19-related social protection measures in Belgium amounts to 10% of the social protection budget, or 2.3% of GDP. Only a tiny fraction of these efforts stem from social assistance. Although there has been some increase in the number of people who had to rely on means-tested benefits, welfare recipiency remained surprisingly stable (Marchal et al. 2020). As a result, in Belgium the existing social insurance schemes for employees and the self-employed mitigated the income shock substantially, especially for lower- and middle-income households. Simulations have shown that temporary unemployment and bridging right schemes effectively absorbed the massive economic impact of COVID-19. Yet, there are also indications that even among workers being entitled to compensatory measures, a non-negligible share experienced a substantial fall in household incomes and in their living standard (Marchal et al. 2020; Sanchèz et al. 2021).

Germany responded to COVID-19 in ways that were very similar to the responses in Belgium, but reliance on social assistance was more important.

---

[2] The Belgian mandatory unemployment insurance is quite unique in Europe in that benefits last in principle for the full duration of unemployment; yet the allowances decrease with the duration of unemployment.
[3] In addition, in Belgium, self-employed can fall back upon the unemployment insurance for employees if they had a prior insurance record built up as a wage earner.

As in Belgium, the negative impact of the restrictions on employees were cushioned by the existing short-time work scheme (Kurzarbeit), access to which was made easier. In May 2020, approximately 19% of the labor force were in receipt of short-time work benefits.[4] Long-term unemployed and the self-employed could rely on the existing social assistance scheme in which, however, the wealth test was temporarily suspended.[5] Unemployment benefits for long-term unemployed workers whose regular earnings-related benefits were extended by three months. However, benefits for the long-term unemployed or those without entitlement to earnings-related benefits, such as the self-employed or certain atypical workers, were not increased. As a result, as in Belgium, the gap between social protection for the long-term unemployed and the temporarily unemployed was significantly increased.

Overall, responses to COVID-19 in these two countries have a number of key characteristics. First, both countries did not revert to wage subsidy systems but responded by using existing social insurance and social assistance systems. Second, the extent to which these welfare states made use of either social insurance or social assistance schemes seems to be related to the extent to which these welfare states have moved in a liberal direction. Belgium, arguably still the most Bismarckian of the two countries, has relied almost entirely on social insurance. Germany also made use of existing systems, but self-employed persons were covered by unemployment assistance. Third, in both countries the policy responses reinforced the dual transformation of social protection that took place in recent decades, with retrenched earnings-related benefits for long-term unemployed and atypically employed people on the one hand and expanded social security to so-called new social risks on the other. Fourth, the reinforcements should, however, also be seen as major departures from the policy route that in recent decades has focused heavily on activating the unemployed by tightening eligibility criteria and decreasing social protection benefits.

---

[4] https://www.ifo.de/node/55800
[5] https://www.bmas.de/DE/Schwerpunkte/Informationen-Corona/Sozialschutz-Paket/sozialsch utz-paket.html. According to figures from the Federal Employment Agency, approximately 81.000 unemployed self-employed received unemployment assistance payments for at least part of the time in the months from April to September.

The Nordic Regime

The Nordic welfare states, historically known for their relatively high levels of social benefits and an active labor market policy since the 1950s (Greve 2016; Kangas and Kvist 2019), could be expected to have active responses to support employment and living standards during the pandemic. Overall, this is exactly what happened in all the Nordic countries (Greve et al. 2021).

The Nordic countries had different strategies with regard to how to cope with the crisis. Although the following discussion keeps an eye on the developments taking place in the other Nordic countries, the focus is mainly on Denmark and Sweden, especially due to the fact that the strategy to cope with the virus varied greatly between these two countries, which had a strong impact on the need to intervene in the economy. While Sweden became the country with the most limited lockdown policies, other countries, including Denmark, faced stronger negative pressures on economic activity due to more and larger restriction of their economic activities. Yet, when Sweden kept more economic activities running, albeit at the same time facing stronger pressures on its health care system than the other Nordic countries, there was a lesser need than in Denmark to compensate workers and companies negatively affected by the COVID crisis.

Overall, there has been an active fiscal policy in all the Nordic countries with high levels of government support to reduce the level of economic contraction and ensure that there was purchasing power among citizens in what can be characterized as an active Keynesian demand management policy—albeit, as indicated above, this was less the case in Sweden, given its different approach to lockdowns. This Keynesian reality combined with the fact that in Nordic countries during the pandemic, there was an extension of, and a number of different initiatives related to, active labor market policy. In Denmark, for example, unemployment benefits and cash benefit periods were extended, and the requirements for activation were relaxed.[6]

In the Nordic countries during the pandemic, fewer people on average than in other OECD countries have faced job disruptions and/or losses, with only Belgium and the Netherlands doing better than Denmark, who has performed best among the Nordic countries in this regard. It is also the case that in Nordic countries, job losses affected only about 6% of the workforce

---

[6] For more information on specific measures in each of the Nordic countries see Coronavirus country measures see the data provided by the International Social Security Association (ISSA).

and between a quarter and a third of households faced job-related disruption because of the pandemic (OECD 2021a). This also meant that fewer people in the Nordic countries than in other welfare regimes coped with financial difficulties as a consequence of the pandemic. This reality confirms the Nordic tradition of focusing on keeping people in jobs, employment creation, and income security. Yet unemployment levels remain higher in Sweden than in Denmark, and the Swedish ministry of finance expected the unemployment rate to continue to be at 7.9% in 2022.[7] Furthermore in Denmark, as in the other Nordic countries but higher than in Sweden, there was significant public support for the private businesses facing closures through direct state subsidies to companies. Simultaneously, companies that retained employees could receive state support because of this.

At the peak of the use of retention schemes, around 10% of all employees in Nordic countries were using such schemes (Drahokoupil and Müller 2021). Rates of unemployment are now almost back to pre-crisis level in Denmark and Norway, and there, unemployment is also lower than in Sweden and Finland (OECD 2021c). Denmark and Sweden had a solid economic foundation that enabled the adoption of comprehensive support packages, which included several public works and construction activities and thus stimulated both employment and economic demand. Furthermore, the period has seen a comprehensive set of tripartite agreements between the state, employers, and employees, all of which in various ways have directly helped Denmark get through the COVID crisis.

Overall, Denmark maintained a universal approach to social benefits while keeping the labor market partners involved in decision-making as part of a consensus-seeking approach. At the same time, during the pandemic, Denmark supported companies much more directly than is traditionally the case in that country. Denmark has a decentralized welfare state and, during the pandemic the state has, in the context of annual bargaining with municipalities and regions, compensated these subnational units for additional health care and social spending incurred to avoid reductions in other welfare services amid higher than usual health and social spending (see www.fm.dk).

Unemployment rates in all four Nordic countries in 2022 were expected to be lower than in 2020 (OECD 2021b). Overall, compared to other OECD countries the Nordic countries, despite massive investment in supporting

---

[7] Upswing for resilient Swedish economy in 2021—Government.se, accessed on August 30, 2021.

businesses and the unemployed, retained low levels of gross public debt in 2022 while being expected to move close to balancing public budgets. Yet, this discussion about debt and fiscal policy does not say anything about the distributional effects of social policies. As in most countries, some industries in Denmark were hit harder than others (especially tourism and the experience industry), where employees faced a higher risk of unemployment, whereas investments in the construction sector led to full employment in that sector. Thus, the overall macroeconomic balance does not mean that there was any redistribution taking place. There were indeed winners and losers of economic development in the wake of the COVID crisis. The scope of its redistribution effects remains unclear for the time being, but these effects might average out so that at the macro-level, the degree of inequality remains the same as before that crisis.

To conclude, in general the Nordic countries were able to cope with COVID-19 presumably much better than expected, and also with a relatively quick rebound in economic activity, implying that the use of Keynesian demand management in combination with the automatic stabilizers at play meant that loss of jobs has been more limited and for a shorter time and less widespread than initially expected. Thus, despite the negative impact of the pandemic on specific groups, during the pandemic Nordic welfare states proved able to support companies and those at risk of losing their jobs with extensive interventions. Thereby we witnessed a continuation of traditional Nordic social policies, which is a sign of institutional continuity in the context of entrenched policy legacies.

The Southern European Welfare Regime

Together with Italy and Spain, Portugal and Greece belong to a group of countries which, in the literature on comparative welfare states, is known as the "Latin" rim (Leibfried 1993), the Southern model (Ferrera 1996) or, more recently, the "familistic" model (Papadopoulos and Roumpakis 2013). These terms have been used to classify a particular model of social protection that combines a Bismarckian pension system with a universal health care system; where families, namely women, are called to play the protective role that the state plays in other models of social protection (namely in northern Europe); and where labor market institutions are designed to favor those in dependent employment.

As they were faced with the emergence of the COVID-19 pandemic, the Portuguese and the Greek welfare states were still recovering from the impact of the Eurocrisis that began in late 2009. During this crisis, having asked for financial assistance from the International Monetary Fund (IMF) and the European Union (EU), both countries had to pursue severe fiscal austerity measures, which translated into tax increases and cuts in social transfers—both in pensions and in social assistance (Guillén et al. 2016). Health expenditure was also significantly reduced (see Petmesidou et al. 2014). Finally, as part of the pursuit of an (externally imposed) internal devaluation strategy, measures were introduced to reduce the protection given to those in employment and to the unemployed as well (see Moreira et al. 2015). Still, after 2015, at least in Portugal, significant steps were taken to revert some of the harshest measures introduced in the initial aftermath of the Eurocrisis—even if most of labor market changes remained (see Moreira and Glatzer, 2022).

As Moreira et al. (2021) make clear, there were important differences in how the COVID-19 pandemic hit Portugal and Greece. At the health level, up until December 2020, Portugal had already been significantly hit by the pandemic. Greece, on the other hand, had been one of the least hit countries in the OECD. Economically, however, Portugal and Greece were both among the most affected countries in the OECD.

In Portugal the backbone of the response to the economic toll of COVID-19 involved the introduction of a derivative of the "lay-off scheme" that had been a feature of the social security edifice since 2003—even if a marginal one. The "Extraordinary Support to the Maintenance of Employment Contracts"—or "Simplified Lay-off" scheme—was introduced in March 2020 and allowed companies that suffered a significant drop in turnover (at least 40%)—or that were forced to close/reduce activities as part of the measures to reduce the spread of the pandemic—to reduce the number of hours worked or to suspend work contracts. During this period, employees would be entitled to a payment worth two-thirds of their gross salary, subject to a minimum equivalent to the national minimum wage—adjusted to the number of hours effectively worked. This payment was to be 70% subsidized by social security.

In July 2020, the "Simplified Lay-off" scheme was replaced by (yet) another derivative of the original lay-off scheme: the "Support for Progressive Recovery."[8] This new scheme reduced the threshold of losses that would

[8] Decree n.º 46-A/2020.

qualify employers for this type of benefit; allowed more flexibility in terms of the hours reductions that employers could apply for; increased the generosity of workers' payments from 2/3 to over 4/5 of their gross salary; and increased the state's contributions.

It is fair to say that social assistance played a minor role in dealing with economic toll of the crisis. Despite measures to automatically renew the entitlement to the Social Integration Income (RSI) and the Assistance-Based Unemployment Benefit,[9] the number of beneficiaries did not increase significantly. In fact, the number of RSI beneficiaries actually fell (by 3.5%) compared to 2019.

Although these were not excluded from the range of measures introduced during this period, the support given to self-employed and atypical workers was clearly less generous than that given to employees. The initial scheme targeting self-employed workers—the "Extraordinary Support for the Reduction of Economic Activity"[10]—was subject to a (social insurance) contribution requirement (of up to 3 months of contributions in the last 12 months) and subject to a ceiling equal to the Social Support Indexer (SSI), whose value is below the official poverty line. Subsequent revisions sought to expand its coverage (to company managers), to allow for the possibility of reducing work hours, and to increase the generosity of the payments.[11]

The response to the COVID-19 crisis in Greece was strikingly different both in size and in the type of measures adopted. Data from the IMF Fiscal Monitor (2021, June) show that (non-health-related) additional spending in Greece (in 2020) amounted 13.2% of GDP, which contrasts with 4.5% in Portugal.

Despite a much stronger fiscal response, the employment-related measures adopted in Greece are significantly less robust than those adopted in Portugal (see Moreira et al. 2021). The Greek government's initial reaction involved the introduction of a number of special allowances worth €800 for a 45-day period and targeting employees, self-employed workers, and people affiliated with individual businesses of up to 20 workers (Ministry of Finance 2020). The government also decided to provide a one-time payment to cover the Easter bonuses that employers were expected to pay in April. Unemployment benefits were extended by two months, and a special

[9] Order n.º 94-A/2020.
[10] Order n.º 94-A/2020.
[11] Decree n.º 14-F/2020 and Law n.º 31/2020.

allowance (worth €400) was introduced for individuals who became long-term unemployed beginning April 2020 (Leventi et al. 2020). Guaranteed minimum beneficiaries were also allocated a one-off sum, with a maximum ceiling of €300 (Leventi et al. 2020).

In June 2020, Greek authorities introduced a short-time work scheme— "SYN-ERGASIA"[12]—which allowed employers with significant turnover losses to reduce work hours and pay by 50%. The government would pay the 30% of the gross wage, though workers on minimum wages would receive their salaries in full. However, the take-up of the scheme remained consistently low—covering 52,000 workers up to June 2020 and 17,000 in February 2021 (Moreira et al. 2021; European Commission (2021). Finally, a special leave scheme—partially funded (25%) by the Greek state—was also introduced to support parents who needed to provide care to their children during school closures (Leventi et al. 2020).

Discussion

Considering the sheer scope of the COVID-19 crisis, macroeconomic imperatives that transcend the boundaries among the four welfare regimes under investigation seem largely responsible for the fact that all the countries studied here, regardless of the welfare regime and of country-specific policy legacies, enacted prompt policy responses to the pandemic with regard to unemployment and income loss. This reality is consistent with "emergency Keynesianism" (Bremer and McDaniel 2020; on this issue see also Hall 2013), which is largely about saving capitalism from itself through emergency measures aimed at preventing a recession from becoming an outright depression (Béland et al. 2021). The European Union played an important role in this regard by supporting unemployment protection systems, particularly in the Southern European countries but also, for the first time, by deploying more general recovery packages financed out of common EU resources (on the role of the EU during the COVID crisis, see de la Porte and Jensen 2021).

As far as the country-specific use of policy instruments is concerned, the existence of similar cross-national emergency response patterns during the COVID-19 crisis suggests that economic developments can shape social policy change over time, a claim associated with the work of scholars such as

[12] SYN-ERGASIA was funded by SURE (see https://primeminister.gr/en/2020/05/20/24004).

Harold Wilensky (1975) and, more recently, Branko Milanović (2016), who claims public policy is rooted in economic preconditions. From this perspective, welfare regimes are not only the product of "politics against markets" (Esping-Andersen 1985) but also of "politics for markets" (on this topic see Iversen and Soskice 2015). In the context of this chapter, it means that to mitigate the negative economic and social impacts of the COVID-19 pandemic, countries with specific policy legacies belonging to different welfare regimes all adopted emergency social policy measures to support the people and businesses while avoiding a deep and durable economic downfall (Béland et al. 2021).

While our analysis suggests that many countries witnessed similar developments—for example, expanded access to existing schemes and extended entitlement duration—the way these developments played out bears the hallmarks of specific welfare regimes and, especially, country-specific differences in national policy legacies. In this context, we do observe variation within each regime cluster stemming at least in part from *national* policy legacies specific to each country. This subtle understanding of both regime-based and country-based continuity in the social policy responses to COVID-19 complements our above claim that all the countries under investigation embraced "emergency Keynesianism" and adopted swift counter-cyclical policies to mitigate the negative impact of the pandemic on the economy as well as on workers and families.

In the liberal welfare regimes of the United Kingdom and Ireland, the policy response was more discontinuous than in some of the other regimes under consideration in this chapter, but these discontinuities can also be explained by regime characteristics. The modest rate of payment of pre-existing social protection schemes required a novel response once the pandemic hit, given that lockdown resulted in a substantial minority of society, including many middle-income earners, losing employment income. This required COVID response schemes that were much more generous than existing social security provision. Novel short-time work (UK) and wage subsidy schemes (Ireland) were introduced for those whose jobs were retained. For those who became unemployed as a result of the pandemic, the United Kingdom continued to rely on means-tested provision via Universal Credit, while Ireland, by contrast, introduced a new payment that made no reference to means tests or social insurance contributions.

In Belgium and Germany (albeit to a lesser extent in the latter case), two Bismarckian welfare regimes, the main policy responses to the COVID-19

Table 1.1 Emergency Unemployment Benefits

	2019	2020 (COVID-19 related)	2019	2020 (COVID-19 related)
LIBERAL REGIME		UK		IRELAND
	New Style Jobseeker's Allowance (UB)	New Style Jobseeker's Allowance (UB) / Universal Credit (SA)	Jobseeker's Benefit (UB)	Pandemic Unemployment Payment
		Higher benefits (if Universal Credit only)		*Higher Benefits*
BISMARKIAN REGIME		GERMANY		BELGIUM
	Unemployment Benefit[a] *(UB)*	Unemployment Benefit[a] (UB)	Unemployment Benefit[b] (UB)	Unemployment Benefit[b] (UB)
		Extended Duration		*Benefits long-term unemployed frozen*
NORDIC REGIME[1]		DENMARK		SWEDEN
	Unemployment Insurance[c] (UB)	Unemployment Insurance[c] (UB)	Income-related Unemployment Insurance[d] (UB)	Income-related Unemployment Insurance[d] (UB)
		Extended Duration		*Expanded Access by relaxation of eligibility conditions; Increased Benefits*
SOUTHERN EUROPEAN REGIME		PORTUGAL		GREECE
	Unemployment Insurance[e] (UB)	Unemployment Insurance[e] (UB)	Unemployment Insurance[f] (UB)	Unemployment Insurance[f] (UB)
		Expanded Access		*Extended Duration*

[1]Important to note that job-retention schemes have been more important during the crisis than earlier.

Notes: [a]Arbeitslosengeld I; [b]Assurance Chômage; [c]Arbejdsløshedsdagpenge og andre Akasseydelse; [d]Arbetslöshetsförsäkring inkomstrelaterad; [e]Subsídio de Desemprego; [f]Τακτική Επιδότηση Ανεργίας.

Legend:

UB—Unemployment Benefit, Insurance-Based;

UA—Unemployment Benefit, Assistance-Based;

SA—Social Assistance; SE—Subsidy to Employer;

STUB—Short-Time Unemployment Benefit;

STWS—Short-Time Work Scheme.

Table 1.2 Emergency Employment Benefits

	2019	2020 (COVID-19 related)	2019	2020 (COVID-19 related)
LIBERAL REGIME	**UK**		**IRELAND**	
	Universal Credit (SA)	Coronavirus Jobs Retention Scheme (STWS)	Short-Time Work Support (STUB)	Temporary Wage Subsidy Scheme (Wage Subsidy)
BISMARKIAN REGIME	**GERMANY**		**BELGIUM**	
	Short-Time Work Scheme[a] (STWS)	Short-Time Work Scheme[a] (STWS)	Short-Term Unemployment Benefits[b] (STUB)	Short-Term Unemployment Benefits[b] (STUB)
		Expanded Access; Increased Benefits; Extended Duration; Reduced Employers' Costs		*Expanded Access; Increased Benefits*
NORDIC REGIME	**DENMARK**		**SWEDEN**	
	Work Sharing[c] (STUB)	Work Sharing[c] (STUB)	Short-Time Work Allowance[d] (STWS)	Short-Time Work Allowance[d] (STWS)
		Expanded Access; Reduced Employers' Costs; Extended Duration		*Reduced Employers' Costs*
SOUTHERN EUROPEAN REGIME	**PORTUGAL**		**GREECE**	
	Lay-Off Scheme[e] (STWS)	Simplified Lay-Off Scheme[f] (STWS)	Temporary Lay-off Allowance[g] (STWS)	Special Purpose Allowance[h] *(STUB)*
		Expanded Access		*One-Off, Flat Rate Allowance*
				Syn-Ergasia (STUB)

Notes: [a]Kurzarbeit; [b]Tijdelijke Werkloosheid; [c]Arbejdsfordeling; [d]Korttidsarbete; [e]Lay-Off; [f]Lay-Off Simplificado; [g]Επίδομα διαθεσιμότητας; [h]Ειδικού Σκοπού σε εργαζόμενους των οποίων η σύμβαση εργασίας έχει λυθεί από.

Legend:

UB—Unemployment Benefit, Insurance-Based;

UA—Unemployment Benefit, Assistance-Based;

SA—Social Assistance;

SE—Subsidy to Employer;

STUB—Short-Time Unemployment Benefit;

STWS—Short-Time Work Scheme

crisis proved consistent with the Bismarckian model. In both countries, existing social insurance systems were expanded temporarily, and the social partners played an important role. Social assistance was deployed only residually (that was certainly the case in Belgium).

In the Nordic welfare states, institutional continuity proved especially strong, as existing job-retention schemes were temporarily expanded to support keeping persons in their existing jobs. The social policy response proved stronger in Denmark than in Sweden, although this was mainly due to a stronger lockdown approach in Denmark. Changes seemed to be temporary, so that from 2022 on, the Nordic welfare states are likely to look like they did before, which points to both institutional continuity within that regime and a strong ability to cope with external shocks to protect Nordic societies and economies.

Finally, the differences in policy responses in Greece and Portugal reflect a long-term process of policy divergence within the Southern European cluster (Petmesidou and Guillén 2021), where the Portuguese welfare state has evolved over time to become more inclusive and, despite some expansionary attempts such as the introduction of a minimum income scheme or the simplification of the pension system, the Greek model of welfare provision has remained largely fragmented and inadequate. In that sense, there are key country-specific path dependencies in how these two countries responded to the crisis. Portugal opted for a more comprehensive response, involving a fairly encompassing short-time work scheme; Greece introduced a very limited wage subsidy, complemented by a plethora of partial and paltry schemes. Still, in both countries, reflecting the dualized nature of labor market institutions in Southern European countries, the level of protection awarded to self-employed and atypical workers was significantly below that of employees.

The above discussion illustrates the diversity of policy responses to COVID-19, which reflect in part institutional logics embedded in existing national legacies, which often mirror welfare regime type. Our analysis suggests that both similarities and cross-national differences within each welfare regime cluster under consideration have shaped social policy responses to COVID-19 in Europe. Simultaneously, while our above empirical analysis does point to inter-welfare regime differences in policy legacies and in social policy responses to the pandemic, the fact that all the countries under consideration reacted swiftly to the crisis suggests that economic shocks can trigger some level of social policy convergence, although only time will tell whether, in the case of COVID-19, this relative convergence is only temporary or more durable in nature. Regardless, by stressing both the enduring weight of national policy legacies and the powerful impact of economic crises on social policy development, our chapter should help social policy scholars craft more sophisticated and generalizable frameworks to study both national convergence and divergence in social policy responses to global crises, in Europe and beyond.

Keeping people in jobs instead of supporting them with economic transfers has the further positive side effect that well-being is higher for those keeping their job than those who are unemployed, even if they get unemployment benefits (Cotofan et al. 2021). Hence for well-being purposes, a strategy of keeping people in jobs can be an important factor in choosing policy instruments.

Our chapter has also three main limitations worth spelling out at this stage. First regarding case selection, while the sections on the liberal and the Nordic welfare regimes cover the main country cases within each regime, this is not the case for the sections on the Bismarckian and Southern European regime cluster, which each highlight major cases not featured in our comparative analysis due to space limitation. More research about these welfare regimes is needed to provide a more systematic "big picture" about the social policy impact of the pandemic in employment-related policies and beyond.

Second, the events discussed in this chapter are very recent, so the compressed time frame used is a clear limitation of our comparative analysis. While the section on Nordic countries makes it clear that the situation might return to the pre-pandemic "normal" soon, the truth of the matter is that it is too early to assess the long-term consequences of the pandemic on most of the countries under consideration in this chapter. This is why more research will be needed in the future to explore continuity and change in social policy response to COVID-19 in Europe. Finally, a third limitation of the chapter is that it focuses almost exclusively on national policies. In Europe, the EU has played a direct role during the pandemic, first with SURE (Support to mitigate Unemployment Risks in an Emergency) and, later, with Next Generation (de la Porte and Dagnis Jensen 2021). Future research could explore the interaction between this involvement of the EU and national policy legacies and decisions across different European welfare regimes during the COVID-19 pandemic.

References

Beirne, Keelan, Karina Doorley, Mark Regan, Barra Roantree, and Dora Tuda. 2020. "The potential costs and distributional effect of COVID-19 related unemployment in Ireland." *ESRI Budget Perspectives* 2021. Dublin: ESRI. https://www.esri.ie/system/files/publications/BP202101%20%281%29.pdf.

Béland, Daniel. 2010. *What is Social Policy? Understanding the Welfare State.* Cambridge: Polity.

Béland, Daniel, and Rianne Mahon. 2016. *Advanced Introduction to Social Policy.* Cheltenham: Edward Elgar.

Béland, Daniel, Bea Cantillon, Rod Hick, and Amílcar Moreira. 2021. "Social policy in the face of a global pandemic: Policy responses to the COVID-19 crisis." *Social Policy & Administration* 55: 249–60.

Bell, Torsten, and Mike Brewer. 2021. *The 12-month Stretch: Where the Government Has Delivered—And Where It Has Failed—During the COVID-19 Crisis.* London: Resolution Foundation.

Bremer, Björn, and Sean McDaniel. 2020. "The ideational foundations of social democratic austerity in the context of the great recession." *Socio-Economic Review* 18 (2): 439–63.

Brewer, Mike, and Karl Handscomb. 2020. *This Time Is Different—Universal Credit's First Recession: Assessing the Welfare System and Its Effect on Living Standards during the Coronavirus Epidemic.* London: Resolution Foundation. https://www.resolutionfoundation.org/publications/this-time-is-different-universal-credits-first-recession/

Brewer, Mike, and Laura Gardiner. 2020. "The initial impact of COVID-19 and policy responses on household incomes." *Oxford Review of Economic Policy* 36 (S1): S187–S199.

Capoccia, Giovanni, and R. Daniel Kelemen. 2007. "The study of critical junctures: Theory, narrative, and counterfactuals in historical institutionalism." *World Politics* 59 (3): 341–69.

Cotofan, Maria, Jan-Emmanuel De Neve, Marta Golin, Micah Kaats, and George Ward. 2021. "Work and Well-Being during COVID-19: Impact, Inequalities, Resilience, and the Future of Work." In *World Happiness Report*, edited by Helliwell, John F., Richard Layard, Jeffrey Sachs, and Jan-Emmanuel De Neve, 153–90, Chapter 7. Published online at https://worldhappiness.report/ed/2021/.

Deeming, Christopher. 2017. "The lost and the new 'liberal world' of welfare capitalism: A critical assessment of Gøsta Esping-Andersen's the three worlds of welfare capitalism a quarter century later." *Social Policy and Society* 16 (3): 405–22.

de la Porte, Caroline, and Mads Dagnis Jensen. 2021. "The next generation EU: An analysis of the dimensions of conflict behind the deal." *Social Policy & Administration* 55 (2): 388–402.

Drahokoupil, Jan, and Torsten Müller. 2021. "Job retention schemes in Europe: A lifeline during the Covid-19 pandemic." 2021.07. Brussels, ETUI Research Paper–Working Paper.

Esping-Andersen, Gøsta. 1985. *Politics against Markets: The Social Democratic Road to Power.* Princeton: Princeton University Press.

Esping-Andersen, Gøsta. 1990. *The Three Worlds of Welfare Capitalism.* Princeton: Princeton University Press.

Esping-Andersen, Gøsta. 1999. *Social Foundations of Postindustrial Economies*. New York: Oxford University Press.

European Commission. 2021. "Enhanced Surveillance Report—Greece, June 2021." https://economy-finance.ec.europa.eu/system/files/2021-06/ip150_en.pdf.

Ferrera, Maurizio. 1996. "The 'Southern Model' of welfare in southern Europe." *Journal of European Social Policy* 6: 17–37.

Garcia-Rodriguez, Abian, Adele Bergin, Luke Rehill, and Éamonn Sweeney, E. 2021. "Exploring the impact of COVID-19 and recovery paths for the economy." ESRI Working Paper No. 706. Dublin: Economic and Social Research Council.

Geiger, Ben Baumberg, Lisa Scullion, Kate Summers, Phil Martin, Cormac Lawler, Daniel Edmiston, Andrea Gibbons, Jo Ingold, David Robertshaw, and Robert de Vries. 2021a. "Non-take-up of benefits at the start of the COVID-19 pandemic." *Welfare at a (Social) Distance Project Report*. The Welfare at a (Social) Distance Project. http://www.distant welfare.co.uk/take-up

Geiger, Ben Baumberg, Lisa Scullion, Kate Summers, Phil Martin, Cormac Lawler, Daniel Edmiston, Andrea Gibbons, Jo Ingold, Eleni Karagiannaki, David Robertshaw, and Robert de Vries. 2021b. "Should social security reach further? A study of those not claiming benefits at the start of the COVID-19 pandemic." *Welfare at a (Social) Distance Project Report*. The Welfare at a (Social) Distance Project. http://www.distant welfare.co.uk/ineligibility-report

Gilbert, Neil. 2002. *Transformation of the Welfare State: The Silent Surrender of Public Responsibility*. Oxford: Oxford University Press.

Glatzer, Miguel, and Amílcar Moreira. 2022. "The Portuguese Welfare State." In *The Oxford Handbook of Portuguese Politics*, edited by Jorge M. Fernandes, Pedro C. Magalhães, and António Costa Pinto, 507–27. New York: Oxford University Press.

Greve, Bent. 2016. "Denmark: Still a Nordic welfare state after the changes of recent years?" In *Challenges to European Welfare Systems*, edited by Klaus Schubert, Paloma Villota, and Johanna Kuhlman, 159–76. Cham: Springer International. Chapter available online at https://doi.org/10.1007/978-3-319-07680-5_8.

Greve, Bent, Paula Blomqvist, Bjørn Hvinden, and Minna van Gerven. 2021. "Nordic Welfare states—still standing or changed by the COVID-19 crisis?" *Social Policy & Administration* 55 (2): 295–311. https://doi.org/10.1111/spol.12675

Guillén, Ana Marta, Sergio González-Begega, and David Luque Balbona. 2016. "Austeridad y ajustes sociales en el Sur de Europa. La fragmentación del modelo de bienestar Mediterráneo." *Revista Española de Sociología* 25 (2): 261–72.

Hall, Peter. 2013. "The Political Origins of our Economic Discontents: Contemporary Adjustment Problems in Historical Perspective." In *Politics in New Hard Times*, edited by Miles Kahler, and David A. Lake, 129–49. Ithaca: Cornell University Press.

Hemerijck, Anton, and Ive Marx. 2012. "Continental Welfare at a Crossroads: The Choice between Activation and Minimum Income Protection in Belgium and the Netherlands." In *A Long Goodbye to Bismarck? The Politics of Welfare Reforms in Continental Europe*, edited by Bruno Palier, 129–56. Amsterdam: Amsterdam University Press.

Hick, Rod. 2020. "COVID-19 and the bypassing of contributory social security benefits." https://blogs.bath.ac.uk/iprblog/2020/05/22/covid-19-and-the-bypassing-of-contr ibutory-social-security-benefits/.

Hick, Rod, and Mary P. Murphy. 2021. "Common shock, different paths? Comparing social policy responses to COVID-19 in the UK and Ireland." *Social Policy & Administration* 55 (2): 312–25.

Hinrichs, Karl. 2012. "A Social Insurance State Withers Away. Welfare State Reforms in Germany—Or: Attempts to Turn Around in a Cul-de-Sac." In *A Long Goodbye to Bismarck? The Politics of Welfare Reforms in Continental Europe*, edited by Bruno Palier, 45–72. Amsterdam: Amsterdam University Press.

IMF. 2021, June. "Fiscal monitor database of country fiscal measures in response to the COVID-19 pandemic." https://www.imf.org/en/Topics/imf-and-covid19/Fiscal-Polic ies-Database-in-Response-to-COVID-19

Iversen, Torben, and David Soskice. 2015. "Politics for markets." *Journal of European Social Policy* 25 (1): 76–93.

Jacobs, Alan M., and R. Kent Weaver. 2015. "When policies undo themselves: Self-undermining feedback as a source of policy change." *Governance* 28 (4): 441–57.

Kangas, Olli, and Jon Kvist. 2019. "Nordic Welfare States." In *Routledge Handbook of the Welfare State*, edited by Bent Greve, 2nd edition, 124–36. Oxon: Routledge.

Leibfried, Stephan. 1993. "Towards a European Welfare State? On Integrating Poverty Regimes into the European Community." In *New Perspectives on the Welfare State in Europe*, edited by C. Jones, 120–43. London: Routledge.

Leventi, Chrysa, Maria Flevotomou, and Manos Matsaganis. 2020. "EUROMOD—Greece Country Report." https://euromod-web.jrc.ec.europa.eu/resources/country-reports/latest

Marchal, Sarah, Jonas Vanderkelen, Bea Cantillon, Koen Decancq, André Decoster, Sarah Kuypers, et al. 2021. "The distributional impact of the COVID-19 shock on household incomes in Belgium." *COVIVAT Working Paper* 2, (January 7). Leuven/Antwerpen.

Milanovic, Branko. 2016. *Global inequality: A new approach for the age of globalization.* Cambridge, MA: Harvard University Press.

Ministry of Finance. 2020. "Stability Programme 2020." Athens: Helenic Republic. https:// ec.europa.eu/info/business-economy-euro/economic-and-fiscal-policy-coordinat ion/eu-economic-governance-monitoring-prevention-correction/european-semes ter/european-semester-timeline/national-reform-programmes-and-stability-or-conv ergence-programmes/2020-european_en

Moreira, Amílcar, Margarita León, Flavia Coda Moscarola, and Antonios Roumpakis. 2015. "In the eye of the storm . . . again! Social policy responses to COVID-19 in Southern Europe." *Social Policy & Administration* 55 (2): 339–57. https://doi.org/ 10.1111/spol.12681

Moreira, Amílcar, Angel Alonso Domínguez, Cátia Antunes, Maria Karamessini, Michele Raitano, and Miguel Glatzer. 2021. "Austerity-driven labour market reforms in Southern Europe: Eroding the security of labour market insiders." *Journal European Journal of Social Security* 17(2): 202–26.

Myles, John. 1998. "How to design a 'liberal' welfare state: A comparison of Canada and the United States." *Social Policy & Administration* 32 (4): 341–64.

OECD. 2017. https://www.oecd.org/els/soc/3_Vanderstappen_Providing_Social_Protect ion_to_the_Self-Employed.pdf.

OECD. 2020. "OECD Social Expenditure database." Paris: Organisation for Economic Co-operation and Development (OECD).

OECD. 2021a. "Main findings from the 2020 Risks That Matter Survey." Paris: Organisation for Economic Co-operation and Development (OECD). https://doi.org/10.1787/b9e85 cf5-en.

OECD. 2021b. "OECD Economic Outlook, Volume 2021, Issue 1." Paris: Organisation for Economic Co-operation and Development (OECD). https://doi.org//10.1787/edfbca02-en.

OECD. 2021c. "OECD Employment Outlook 2021." Paris: Organisation for Economic Co-operation and Development (OECD). https://doi.org/10.1787/5a700c4b-en.

Palier, Bruno. 2010. *A Long Goodbye to Bismarck? The Politics of Welfare Reforms in Continental Europe.* Amsterdam: Amsterdam University Press.

Papadopoulos, Theodoros, and Antonios Roumpakis. 2013. "Familistic welfare capitalism in crisis: Social reproduction and anti-social policy in Greece." *Journal of International and Comparative Social Policy* 29 (3): 204–24.

Petmesidou, Maria, Emmanuele Pavolini, and Ana M. Guillén. 2014. "South European healthcare systems under harsh austerity: A progress–regression mix?" *South European Society and Politics* 19 (3): 331–52.

Petmesidou, Maria, and Ana M. Guillén. 2021. "South Europe: Reclaiming Welfare post-Crisis?" In *Handbook on Austerity, Populism and the Welfare State*, edited by Bent Greve, 186–206. Cheltenham: Edward Elgar.

Pierson, Paul. 1994. *Dismantling the Welfare State? Reagan, Thatcher, and the Politics of Retrenchment.* New York: Cambridge University Press.

Pierson, Paul. 1996. "The new politics of the welfare state." *World Politics* 48: 143–79.

Pierson, Paul. 2000. "Increasing returns, path dependence, and the study of politics." *American Political Science Review* 94: 251–67.

Sánchez, Olga Canto, Francesco Figari, Carlo Fiorio, Sarah Kuypers, Sarah Marchal, Marina Romaguera de la Cruz, et al. 2021. "Welfare resilience at the onset of the COVID-19 pandemic in four European countries: Impact on public finance and household incomes." COVIVAT Working Paper Number 3, https://sites.google.com/view/covivat/publicaties#h.9gbn1086rydt.

Streeck, Wolfgang, and Kathleen Thelen (eds). 2005. *Beyond Continuity: Institutional Change in Advanced Political Economies.* Oxford: Oxford University Press.

Tomlinson, Daniel. 2021. *The Beginning of the End.* London: Resolution Foundation.

Wilensky, Harold L. 1975. *The Welfare State and Equality: Structural and Ideological Roots of Public Expenditures.* Berkeley: University of California Press.

2

Austerity and Adjustment from the Great Recession to the Pandemic—and Beyond

Klaus Armingeon and Stefano Sacchi

Introduction

In the period between 2010 and 2015, almost all democratic countries pursued austerity in an attempt to reduce public deficits. Then countries exited austerity, although following different paths. The onset of the COVID-19 pandemic brought about a hike in public spending to cope with its social and economic consequences that did, however, plant the seeds of future economic adjustments. On September 10, 2021, finance ministers of eight European Union (EU) Member States—among them the Netherlands—signed a letter calling for a renewed effort to "reduce excessive debt" among EU member states (EUObserver 2021). In particular in the Eurozone, the constraints of a monetary union without a fiscal union may force political leaders to think about another round of austerity after the pandemic, at the same time monetary policy will have become less accommodating. The basic rationale for such austerity may be to avoid the possibility that high levels of public debt in some Member States will pave the road to increasing spreads, thereby increasing the likelihood of a need for bailouts.

Fiscal policy in the Great Recession and its aftermath may offer some lessons for fiscal policy in the aftermath of the pandemic. Since fiscal policy sets the framework for social policy spending, insights from the period between 2010 and 2019 may be helpful to understand policymakers' options once governments exit from expansion and are once again forced to embark on the reduction of excessive debt.

In this chapter we study the political strategies and options of governments during austerity periods using a new dataset on austerity during the 2010s for 30 democratic nations. We complement that quantitative analysis with a case study of Italy, showing the processes and causal relationships leading to the

Klaus Armingeon and Stefano Sacchi, *Austerity and Adjustment from the Great Recession to the Pandemic—and Beyond*
In: *European Social Policy and the COVID-19 Pandemic*. Edited by: Stefanie Börner and Martin Seeleib-Kaiser,
Oxford University Press. © Oxford University Press 2023. DOI: 10.1093/oso/9780197676189.003.0002

decisions to enter and to exit austerity. We ask where and when democratic politics mattered in designing and implementing austerity, from the Great Recession to the COVID-19 pandemic. Our main finding is that austerity policy—defined as cutting the deficit—was mostly driven by economic forces and institutions. Then we focus on the process of exiting austerity. Contrary to our findings regarding entry into austerity, we show that exit from austerity cannot be sufficiently explained by changed economic fundamentals. Rather, the longer governments pursue austerity, the more likely they are to exit it, even if the economic fundamentals do not support it.

Theory and Hypotheses

Austerity can be understood as an economic requirement under specific economic conditions that cannot be disregarded by political actors. This widely shared belief can be traced back to John Locke and others (see Blyth 2013, chs. 4–6). If a national government continuously spends more than it receives, this will result in economic problems such as inflation and rising public debt that must be serviced with ever-increasing interest payments. In addition, expansive policies reduce the credibility of national governments in international financial markets, thereby increasing the risk premiums on interest rates of government bonds. Therefore, in order to sustain the system, the function of government is to ensure that fiscal policy is not crisis-prone. The greater the economic problems, the greater the necessity of fiscal consolidation. This is a standard argument that underlies the debates that took place in the world of politics during the "Great Recession," such as in the European Council, by policy advisors such as the International Monetary Fund (IMF 2010a), or in scientific debates (Wagschal and Wenzelburger 2008; Schäfer and Streeck 2013, 1).

This is a biased perspective, however. It ignores the possibility that public spending may boost economic growth and thereby lead to increased tax revenues, which may cover even more than the previous spending. It also ignores the fact that austerity may shrink the economy and increase unemployment because of decreased demand. As a consequence, tax revenues decrease and result in increasing public debts and deficits. All this makes clear that austerity is just a policy idea—and, some hold, it is a very bad idea (Blyth 2013). Hence there is no such thing as an "Iron Fist" that necessarily forces governments onto a path of austerity once spending exceeds revenues. Rather, the pressure to pursue austerity is the outcome of the perceptions and evaluations of economic and political actors. If, for example, an international rating agency concludes that a given level of debts and deficits is unsustainable for a country, this country may run into problems with borrowing on international financial markets (Barta and Johnston 2018, 2021). The reason is that banks receive the signals of the rating agencies and start to lose trust that the government will be able to pay back its debts. By implication, interest rates may then spiral upward, making debt service by that government increasingly difficult.

The economic ideas of powerful actors have far-reaching consequences for democratic politics on the level of the nation state. For example, between 2010 and 2015 the Greek government had to pursue tough austerity policies. However, Greek citizens were not convinced of the appropriateness of this strategy and did not mandate their government to accept austerity requests by international and supranational organizations such as the IMF and the EU backed by German or Dutch governments. At the same time, the German citizens—based on their views on fiscal policy—did not mandate their government to be generous to Greece. Greek austerity was not compatible with Greek democracy, while an expansive policy was not compatible with German democracy. But in the end, the most powerful actors acted on their ideas and realized their goals.

At the beginning of the Great Recession, governments initially reacted with a short-term Keynesian policy by expanding domestic demand. However, by 2010 they started to exit this strategy and increasingly opted for austerity. They were pressured to do this by international financial markets following the advice by rating agencies and by international and supranational actors such as the IMF and the EU. The perspective of the IMF, EU, and international markets was based on the notion that austerity was the only game in town (Armingeon and Baccaro 2012). The worse the fiscal situation of countries was, the more this notion applied. Hence under strong market and political pressure, such as in the Great Recession, governments had little choice in designing fiscal policies: they were forced onto a path of austerity, otherwise international financial markets or international institutions would have sanctioned them. One of the major factors that preempt political decisions in fiscal policy are the rules of the Economic and Monetary Union (EMU) to impose prudent fiscal policy on all EU members, and on the Eurozone members in particular (Heins and de la Porte 2015. Even if governments doubt the beneficial effects of austerity on economic growth under severe external constraints, during the Great Recession they felt forced to implement austerity. For these reasons, we assume that in a severe fiscal crisis the size of austerity is initially determined by the levels of economic and fiscal problems.

H1: At the beginning of a severe crisis, austerity is determined by economic and fiscal fundamentals.

In theory, in the medium to long run austerity may lead to more growth, less unemployment, and reduced debts and deficits (Alesina, Favero, and Giavazzi 2019). In the short run however, it may be contractionary and lead to less growth and more unemployment. Already in 2010, the IMF argued that austerity typically leads to reduced economic growth for about two years after the policy has been implemented (IMF 2010b, 93–124). In 2016 IMF economists argued that "(f)aced with a choice between living with the higher debt—allowing the debt ratio to decline organically through growth—or deliberately running budgetary surpluses to reduce the debt, governments with ample fiscal space will do better by living with the debt. . . . Austerity policies not only generate substantial welfare costs due to supply-side channels, they also hurt demand—and thus worsen employment and unemployment" (Ostry, Loungani, and Furceri 2016, 40).

Austerity inflicts pain on the citizenry: welfare expenditures writ large are reduced, while unemployment increases. Hence the economic benefits of austerity are at best uncertain. The longer a government sticks to tough austerity while the policy does not quickly ameliorate the economic and fiscal situation, the higher the likelihood that the administration will find that it is riding a dead horse; then this learning should motivate political elites to dismount the beast. At least over time, and lacking economic success, it will get harder and harder for the governing coalitions to craft consensus for further reducing the deficit, and it will be increasingly difficult to defend arguments against such policy.

In addition to learning effects and policy disappointment, politicians must fear that they will be punished by citizens. While there is some (limited) empirical support for the notion that citizens recognize and support austerity policies (Alesina, Favero, and Giavazzi 2019; Arias and Stasavage 2019, Bechtel, Hainmueller, and Margalit 2017, 2014; Bansak, Bechtel, and Margalit 2021), evidence is accumulating that long-term austerity measures are risky from an electoral perspective (see, e.g., Bojar et al. 2022; Bremer and Bürgisser 2023a, 2023b). According to the literature on economic voting and welfare state retrenchment, we would expect that austerity damages the reelection prospects of governments, particularly if austerity is at the center stage of the electoral campaign (Hübscher and Sattler 2017; Giger and Nelson 2011). This applies in particular to the post-2010 crisis period (Talving 2017). During periods of fiscal consolidation, the tensions between the assumed long-term benefits of the policy and the short-term electoral risks increase (Fernandez-Albertos and Kuo 2020; Hübscher, Sattler, and Wagner 2021; Jacques and Haffert 2021). Therefore, rational governmental parties should shy away from fiscal consolidation the longer it lasts, unless the beneficial effects for growth and employment have kicked in.

Relatedly, the less citizens support austerity, the less governments may feel legitimized to cut deficits and therewith public spending. If citizens are strongly convinced of the beneficial effects or the unavoidability of austerity, this creates quite different room for maneuver by the national governments as compared to a situation when a large share of the citizenry is convinced that austerity is a bad thing. Hence decisions to enter or quit austerity may also reflect the opinions of the citizens on spending and saving policies. Arguably, at the beginning of a phase of austerity policy, many citizens may agree on fiscal reforms. However, the longer the policy lasts and the less the beneficial effects of the policy are visible, the more citizens may lose trust in the policy.

Finally, and closely related to potential electoral punishment and receding public support for austerity, governing parties may fear the rise of challenger parties, which are in almost all cases at the extreme left or right of the political spectrum. These challenger parties may even gain sufficient votes to enter government. They criticize the precedence of international decision-making and fiscal criteria over the national welfare state and its underlying democratic politics (on the left), or they point to the loss of national sovereignty (on the right). Famous examples are the "Lega" in Italy or "SYRIZA" in Greece. Under these conditions, and depending on national configurations of political power outside and within parliament, mainstream governing parties come under considerable pressure when pursuing austerity.

To summarize, political disappointment combined with policy learning, potential electoral punishment, and the growing weight of challenger parties in national politics provide strong incentives for governments to relax their austerity policies, even as external pressures from international markets and organizations continue.

H2: The longer governments pursue austerity, the less ambitious their plans for fiscal consolidation become.

While we argue that learning, potential punishment, low or declining public support for austerity, and the rise of challenger parties are the causes of waning government willingness to give in to external pressures for austerity, it is of course difficult to model statistically these interrelated causes and their outcomes. In the statistical analysis we will present some direct effects, but this is insufficient for a systematic quantitative test. For these reasons, in a qualitative case study on Italy, we will illustrate the size and interaction of these causes of declining governmental willingness to pursue austerity policies—something that can be called "austerity fatigue."

There may be additional competing or complementary hypotheses about entering and exiting austerity based on such variables as the ideology of political parties, an electoral calendar that puts competing elites under pressure, or the options in decision-making of minimal winning versus broad coalitions in government. We will enter these variables into our statistical models.

Cases, Data, and Methods

Data and Dependent Variable

When the Great Recession started in 2007 in the United States, initially most governments in democratic capitalist nations embarked on temporary counter-cyclical policies. By around 2010, these strategies were replaced by tough austerity. We focus on this period of comprehensive austerity and its aftermath until the start of the pandemic in 2020. In the spring of 2020, governments and international institutions concluded that only expansionary policies would be able to combat the economic consequences of the COVID-19 pandemic crisis. Therefore, they buried the idea of austerity—at least for the time being.

Austerity is defined as cutting public deficits. Synonymously, we speak of fiscal consolidation. In our statistical analysis we focus on planned consolidations, namely what governments intend to do compared to the status quo. These data are provided by the IMF. They are based on information given by governments about budget decisions and their fiscal implications. Based on adopted public policies with fiscal implications, the IMF calculates the future public deficits of a member country. The IMF starts from information of national administrations on budgetary and macroeconomic data. It adjusts for its own macroeconomic and fiscal assumptions.[1] It goes without saying that there may be deviations from these projected deficits if economic growth, revenues, or expenditures do not correspond to projections due to unforeseeable economic changes such as an international crisis, or unforeseeable changes in expenditures due to events like a natural catastrophe or unexpected migration influx. However, these data on planned deficits are not mere window dressing for the general public and international markets. They reflect adopted policy measures and credible commitments of tax and spending policies.

We use 19 editions of the IMF *Fiscal Monitor* and their underlying electronic databases. The first *Fiscal Monitor* was published in the fall of 2010; the latest *Monitor* we use is from October 2019. There are two editions of the *Fiscal Monitor* in every year, one in spring and one in fall. Each of these publications lists the historical data on deficits and the planned deficit, calculated according to the methodology described above. We calculate the intended change of structural primary deficits ("cyclically adjusted primary balance"), or primary deficits that are already adjusted for cyclical influences. Primary balances are balances net of interest payments. Structural balances are adjusted for the business cycle. Hence, our measure indicates discretionary governmental decisions on budgets net of interest payments. Arguably, this is exactly what governments can and do decide about.

For each *Fiscal Monitor*, our measure of austerity is the difference between planned cyclically adjusted primary balances in the year after the publication of the *Fiscal Monitor* and the actual cyclically adjusted primary balance in the year before the publication of the *Monitor*. A positive value means that the government strives for a smaller deficit in the coming year as compared to the previous year, hence it is engaging in austerity. A negative value indicates expansionary policy, that is, the government plans a deficit in the coming year that is larger than the deficit in the previous year. This operationalization is superior to outcome measures such as actual changes in deficits, which reflect many more economic and societal changes rather than just political decisions on revenues and spending. Likewise, it is more precise than vague statements about fiscal planning that are not transposed into policy decisions. Finally, some austerity plans cover various years. By using

---

[1] See for example https://www.imf.org/en/Publications/FM/Issues/2019/09/12/fiscal-monitor-october-2019 and the respective section on methodology.

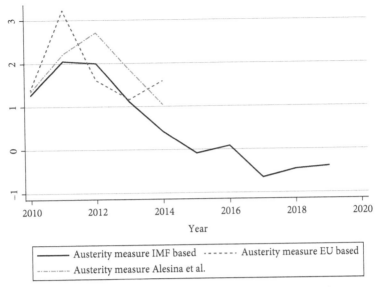

Figure 2.1 Austerity measures. Sources: IMF (various years) *Fiscal Monitor*; Alesina/Favero/Giavazzi 2019; Guthmann 2021.

annual data, we cover all austerity programs that are in effect for a given year. We have data for 30 countries of the democratic OECD and EU countries (excluding Bulgaria, Cyprus, Croatia, Estonia, Luxembourg, and Malta, for which long-term series of cyclically adjusted primary balances are not available).[2] Since we use the information from 19 editions of the *Fiscal Monitor*, we have 19 observations of fiscal policy for each country.

We checked our data against other datasets that are based on "narratives" of spending plans. These are the time series produced by Alesina and colleagues (Alesina, Favero, and Giavazzi 2019) and by Guthmann (2021, 40). Figure 2.1 depicts the average austerity in 30 countries based on our measure as compared to the figures by Alesina et al. and Guthmann for their respective samples. The obvious advantage of our dataset is that it ranges to the fall of 2019, while the time series by Alesina et al. and Guthmann stop in 2014. We believe that the similarities among the three time series are substantial, giving us confidence in our measurement.

---

[2] For Latvia, data are available only for *Fiscal Monitor* April 2013 and later.

Independent and Control Variables

Economic Variables

We measure *fiscal pressures* by the interest rates (10-year interest rates on government bonds), the level of sovereign debt, and the current account, with the expectation that countries that have a negative current account are under much greater pressure to adjust. Likewise, we used economic openness (imports and exports as % of GDP) as an indicator of the extent to which a country is integrated in (and vulnerable to) world markets.

Another set of variables indicates the *economic costs of internal devaluation*. Following Stefanie Walter (2016; Walter et al. 2020) we assume that these costs correspond to the pains of implemented austerity. Prominent among them is depressed economic growth and rising unemployment.[3] If the previous level of growth is high, and the increase of unemployment is low, governments should be less hesitant to pursue fiscal consolidation. In contrast, if a country was already suffering from low growth and rising unemployment, austerity policies would intensify these problems. Therefore, governments may shy away from introducing further fiscal consolidation.

Also, austerity can be avoided—at least in the short run—if a country pursues *external devaluation*.[4] Countries can only externally devaluate if they are not in a currency union; that is (as in our sample), if they are not members of the Eurozone. Being in the Eurozone shifts all efforts onto internal devaluation, since external devaluation is not feasible—unless governments accept the costs and risks of leaving the EMU. Hence, other things being equal, we expect a generally higher level of austerity within the group of Eurozone members.

Political Variables

Moving to political variables, we test whether, once in government, *left parties* are most hesitant to translate external pressure for internal devaluation into austerity programs, or whether these are instead the parties that are most likely to implement far-reaching fiscal consolidation, following a

---

[3] Since change in real GDP and change in level of unemployment are strongly correlated, we only enter GDP growth in our models.

[4] There are of course also risks and costs of external devaluation, for example, if the public and private debt of a country is denominated to a large extent in a foreign currency (see Walter 2016).

"Nixon goes to China" logic. We also consider the strength of center parties in government (mostly Christian-Democratic). Thus, we consider the strength of left and center parties with respect to that of right (conservative, liberal) parties. We measure the strength of parties as reflected in their share in cabinet posts.

In planning fiscal consolidation, all political parties may be influenced by the timing and the competitive landscape of the *next election*. The closer the next election is, the less they may be willing to take the risk of fiscal consolidation that could lead to an electoral backlash. Therefore, we counted the time since the last election (with '1' being the year of the last national election).

Both left-socialist or communist and right-populist parties tend to fight against austerity imposed by external actors such as the IMF or the EU. In addition, at least in Italy, even a center party such as the Five Star Movement acted as a *challenger* party. We used the vote share of these parties as an indicator of the strength of challenger parties. For definition of left-socialist, communist, and right-populist parties, see Armingeon et al. (2021).

Broad coalitions may be less vulnerable to major political conflict. Therefore, they may be in a better position to pursue austerity. In operationalizing the type of government studied, we followed Armingeon et al. (2016, 629), classifying surplus coalitions and minority governments (both depending on broad parliamentary support) as *broad coalitions*. For definitions of types of government see Armingeon et al. (2021).

The Eurobarometer surveys of the European Commission asked for the *public support of austerity measures*. We used the share of respondents that agreed (totally, and tended to agree) with the statement, "Measures to reduce the public deficits and debt in our country are not a priority for now" as an indicator of skepticism about austerity—calculated from the semi-annual Eurobarometer Survey between May 2010 and November 2019 (https://www.gesis.org/en/eurobarometer-data-service/home).

Finally, we operationalize our main independent variable in our second hypothesis, *austerity duration*, as follows: We identified the *Fiscal Monitor* which reported the highest level of austerity in the period 2010–2019. If this was a Spring issue of the *Fiscal Monitor*, we coded this year as a duration of 0.5 years; the next year was coded as 1.5 years, and so on. In cases where a maximum of austerity was reported in a Fall issue, duration in this year was coded as 0, in the next year as 1, and so on.

Further Variables

For a separate analysis of the consequences of austerity, we calculated the average number of *changes of governments* in the years 2010–2019 minus the average number of changes of governments in the years 2000–2009.

For a separate analysis we also needed information on the economic *vulnerability to austerity* of a country. We started from the work of Walter et al. (2020) and combined the level of debts, the size of deficits, the level of unemployment, and the private savings of citizens (as % of GDP) into an additive index to measure economic vulnerabilities. For deficits, debts, and unemployment with considerable volatility over time, we calculated three-year averages (2010–2012 and 2016–2018) to smooth out short-term fluctuations, while for private savings we used data for 2010 and 2018. We calculated the z-scores for all variables and added up these scores. High scores indicate high vulnerability.

Econometric Model

We estimated autoregressive distributed lag (ADL) models. In the ADL models, the dependent variable is entered in levels, and it is also entered as a lagged variable on the right-hand side of the equation. Standard errors are robust standard errors. (See De Boef and Keele 2008; Beck and Katz 2011). Data for political and economic variables come from Armingeon et al. (2021) if not otherwise indicated.

Analyses and Findings

Quantitative Analysis

Figure 2.2 depicts the average size of austerity between 2010 and 2019 in 30 countries (for a country-by-country graph, see Figure 2.6 at the end of this chapter). It shows the average austerity for all 30 countries under study (blue line) as well as the average austerity in all European countries of the sample (red line) and in all non-European countries (grey-green line). There are two basic findings: (1) Although non-European countries embarked on a slightly more austere path between 2013 and 2016, the general pattern of policy development is very similar in Europe and outside Europe. (2) On average, austerity peaked in 2010–2013, then receded until 2015 and vanished thereafter.

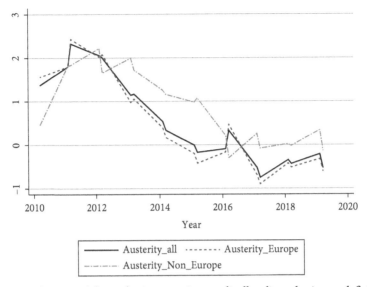

Figure 2.2 Austerity (planned minus previous cyclically adjusted primary deficits). Source: IMF *Fiscal Monitor* (various years). Note: averages for all countries (30 countries), for all European countries and for all non-European countries. For each year there are two entries (Spring and Fall issue of the *Fiscal Monitor*).

Therefore, we adopted a two-step strategy. We first estimated a model using only economic variables (and EMU membership) for the initial period of the Great Recession, namely 2010–2014 (see Table 2.1). We estimated these models for all countries, and separately for the European countries (All: Models 1 and 3; Europe: Models 2 and 4), as well as with and without interest on government bonds, since there could be a concern about endogeneity: international financial markets could define interest rates on the basis of the perceived future austerity plans of governments. However, substantively, these models—with and without interest rates— produce similar results. If we know the previous size of austerity, the current accounts, the long-term interest rate, and the previous economic growth rates, we can explain a large part of variance in austerity. At the same time, political factors—such as the partisan composition of government, public opinion, or the strength of challenger parties—turn out not to be significantly correlated with austerity policies in the beginning of the period under study (data not reported here). In other words, in the beginning of the major wave of austerity policies, the significant explanatory variables were only economic.

Table 2.1 Baseline Models (2010–2014)

	(1)	(2)	(3)	(4)
	Austerity All	Austerity Europe	Austerity All	Austerity Europe
Austerity, lag1	0.30***	0.32***	0.30***	0.32***
	(3.73)	(3.86)	(3.73)	(3.86)
Current accounts, lag1	−0.10**	−0.11***	−0.10**	−0.11***
	(−3.19)	(−3.33)	(−3.19)	(−3.33)
Long-term interest, lag1	0.09*		0.09*	
	(2.32)		(2.32)	
Debt, lag1	0.00	0.00	0.00	0.00
	(0.32)	(0.29)	(0.32)	(0.29)
Openness, lag1	−0.00	−0.00	−0.00	−0.00
	(−0.65)	(−0.01)	(−0.65)	(−0.01)
Real growth, lag1	0.16**	0.11*	0.16**	0.11*
	(3.09)	(2.06)	(3.09)	(2.06)
Economic and Monetary Union (EMU) member state	0.49*	0.48	0.49*	0.48
	(2.01)	(1.88)	(2.01)	(1.88)
Constant	0.30	0.46	0.30	0.46
	(0.56)	(0.67)	(0.56)	(0.67)
Observations	115	95	115	95
R^2	.49	.49	.49	.49

t statistics in parentheses

* $p < 0.05$, ** $p < 0.01$, *** $p < 0.001$

Thus, in a next step we predicted the size of austerity for the period 2010–2019 based on the coefficients of this economic model. If the economic variables were equally important for size and development of austerity in the latter period (2015–2019) as in the initial period (2010–2014), predicted and actual austerity should, on average, develop in sync. Figure 2.3, however, shows that this is not the case.

Based on the economic fundamentals and their impact on austerity decisions in the initial years of the Great Recession, austerity should have receded much less since 2013, and therefore should have stayed on a much higher level than it actually has. In the theoretical section we have argued that governments have a hard time sustaining austerity in the long run, either

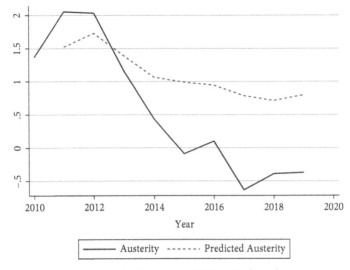

Figure 2.3 Actual and predicted austerity 2010–2019 based on estimations for 2010–2014. (Model 1; ADL, all, including interest.)

because they learn that it does not work as well as expected in the short run, and/or because they fear that it might become electorally risky. By implication the validity of our argument on duration of austerity rests critically on the absence of a correlation between austerity and economic success and/or electoral success. This indeed seems to be the case, as Figures 2.4 and 2.5 indicate.

If austerity were economically successful, the more governments cut back deficits, the more economic vulnerability should have been reduced by the year 2018 as compared to 2010. This is true for Ireland, but for all the other countries there is a zero correlation between austerity and improvement of their economic position.

Similarly, based on Alesina et al. (2019), we would expect austerity to be beneficial not only for the economy but also for the current government's reelection prospects. However, those governments that were particularly diligent in austerity were not systematically more likely to remain in office, as shown in Figure 2.5

The vertical axis of the graph in Figure 2.5 is the difference in number of changes of governments in two different periods: 2010–2019 and 2000–2009. This indicates whether governmental volatility was higher or lower in 2010–2019 as compared to 2000–2009. If austerity were to increase the chances of reelections, this indicator should be lower for high-austerity countries. This however is not the case.

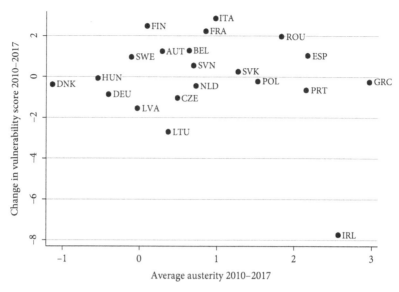

Figure 2.4 Austerity and the reduction of economic vulnerability.

This evidence leads us to consider alternative explanations. Is the pure economic model simply mis-specified, since political variables—such as governments' ideological composition, type of government, or closeness of next general election—are not included, which may have been consequential

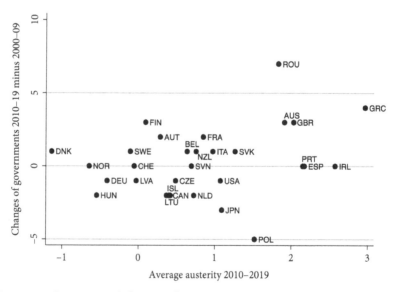

Figure 2.5 Austerity and changes of governments.

in a second phase of austerity? Table 2.2 summarizes the estimation results of five models. Model 1 is the baseline economic model. Over the whole period of 2010–2019, only the "current accounts" variable has a significant coefficient.

This does not change if additional political variables are entered pertaining to the size of the coalition, the share of left and center parties in government (base category: right parties), the time elapsed since the last election, the vote share of challenger parties, or the annual growth rate of challenger parties (measured as the average change in their vote share over the last four years, which usually includes at least one election). This conclusion is not altered if we interact interest rates with left governments, as suggested by Raess (2021).[5]

However, substantial improvements in the model can be observed if variables on public opinion and duration of austerity policies (Models 3 and 4) are included. If the share of citizens with a skeptical stance on austerity ("reducing debt and deficits is not a priority") is integrated, this variable is significantly and negatively correlated with austerity. At the same time, economic variables and Eurozone membership gain significance, indicating that previous models may have been mis-specified. By the same token, inclusion of duration of austerity clearly supports our main "political" hypothesis of austerity fatigue: the longer governments pursue austerity, the less pronounced their efforts in cutting deficits become. Interestingly there is no significant interaction effect of duration with challenger parties or critical stances on austerity.

The main problem with Models 3 and 4 is their focus on EU member states, as Eurobarometer data on austerity skeptics are only available for these countries. Therefore, we re-run the models excluding public opinion variables (Model 5). These estimations corroborate our previous central finding: Over the course of austerity policy, governments increasingly deviate from the goal of reducing the public deficit. Comparing Models 2 and 5—which differ only with regard to the duration variable—it is clear that the duration of austerity increases the explained variance considerably.

The highly significant result of our variable "duration" is also surprising given that we estimate it in a very conservative way. We expect the variable

---

[5] Data not reported here. Raess (2021) argues that in the Great Recession financial markets were suspicious about the willingness of Social Democratic parties to pursue austerity, which in turn led such parties to implement austerity policy in order to build reputation.

Table 2.2 Austerity 2010–2019

	Model 1	Model 2	Model 3	Model 4	Model 5
Austerity[a]	0.27	0.22	0.32***	0.30***	0.14
	(1.45)	(1.23)	(4.63)	(4.72)	(0.81)
Current accounts[a]	−0.10*	−0.10	−0.10***	−0.11***	−0.13*
	(−2.09)	(−1.90)	(−3.49)	(−3.84)	(−2.57)
Long-term interest[a]	0.06	0.10*	0.13**	0.05	−0.02
	(1.11)	(1.99)	(2.75)	(1.25)	(−0.48)
Debt[a]	−0.00	−0.00	−0.01**	−0.01	−0.00
	(−0.50)	(−0.33)	(−2.64)	(−1.93)	(−0.51)
Openness[a]	−0.00	0.00	−0.00	−0.00	0.00
	(−0.28)	(0.14)	(−0.49)	(−0.40)	(0.22)
Real growth[a]	−0.03	−0.05	0.04	0.04	−0.04
	(−0.46)	(−0.72)	(1.21)	(1.13)	(−0.63)
Member Eurozone	0.21	0.32	0.64**	0.75**	0.66**
	(0.82)	(1.43)	(3.02)	(3.28)	(2.76)
Broad coalition[a]		0.30	0.18	0.22	0.33
		(1.65)	(1.31)	(1.63)	(1.80)
Left govt.[a]		−0.00	−0.00	−0.00	0.00
		(−0.10)	(−1.25)	(−0.78)	(0.36)
Center govt.[a]		0.00	−0.00	−0.00	−0.00
		(0.57)	(−0.74)	(−1.07)	(−0.03)
Time since last election, yrs.		−0.03	−0.03	−0.03	−0.02
		(−0.53)	(−0.67)	(−0.75)	(−0.45)
Challenger parties[a]		−0.02	−0.02*	−0.02**	−0.03*
		(−1.58)	(−2.01)	(−2.66)	(−2.35)
Growth of challenger parties, past 4 yrs.[a]		0.03	0.06	0.08	0.06
		(0.49)	(1.55)	(1.92)	(1.16)
No Priority[a]			−3.17**	−2.38*	
			(−3.29)	(−2.39)	
Duration austerity, yrs.				−0.13***	−0.24***
				(−4.07)	(−4.23)
Constant	0.45	0.42	2.55**	2.58***	1.43**
	(0.94)	(1.01)	(3.18)	(3.39)	(3.10)
Observations	259	259	192	192	259
R^2	.33	.35	.59	.61	.43

t statistics in parentheses
* $p < 0.05$, ** $p < 0.01$, *** $p < 0.001$
(a): Variable lagged for one year

to have a monotonic and linear effect. With each additional time unit of "duration" the extent of austerity is expected to decrease by the same amount. If for example in one country, austerity were to vanish already one year after its peak while in another country it remains at a high level and is reduced only after some years, the chances for significant results to emerge would be very low. In fact, scatterplots of estimated austerity (based on our general model) for periods immediately after austerity's peak and after about three years (the median category of austerity) do not signal any extreme distributions.

At this point, however, the explanatory power of statistical models built on linearity and, at best, two interactions becomes problematic. How do economic constraints and political factors such as the rise of challenger parties, the change in public opinion, the discourse in the political systems between all major actors, and the duration of austerity policies interact? Such complex causal networks require qualitative case studies capable of tracing processes of political conflict and compromise as well as policy processes. It is to such a study of a critical case—Italy—that we now turn.

Italy: The Interaction of Economic Constraints and Politics

Although it was never subject to explicit conditionality by the EU or the IMF, Italy went through austerity in the early 2010s. In the following years, governments tended to scale back their austerity efforts. Forceful budgetary consolidation was pursued through welfare (in particular pension) cuts, foregone social investments (in health care, education, and social safety nets), and rising taxes. Later governments increasingly shed further consolidation as support for austerity decreased over time. Populist parties capitalized on such sentiment, putting forward a platform aimed at reversing welfare cuts and actually promoting new welfare programs, which was partly realized by the populist government in 2018–2019. Our case study makes it plausible—in addition to the model estimations that reduce societal complexity to simple models (see Hall 2003)—that at least in Italy, the causal factors behind the duration effect of austerity are learning and policy disappointment among the political elite, the fear of increasing electoral punishment, and the frustration of citizens with lack of policy success. These developments supported the rise of populist parties: the Five Star Movement being neither left nor right, and the right-populist Lega. In addition, also on the right end of the spectrum of the party system, "Brothers of Italy" substantially gained votes in recent elections, becoming the most voted party in 2022 general elections.

While Italy recorded an almost continuous increase of public debts, from 50% of GDP in the 1960s to about 150% at the beginning of the pandemic, it has nonetheless managed to keep a primary budget surplus for most of the time since the early 1990s. This used to be acknowledged by international rating agencies and their very positive scores (Lenzi 2018). It was with the Eurozone crisis of 2011 that fears mounted about the sustainability of Italian public debt, due to its high level. In addition, the then-conservative government under Berlusconi failed to introduce unpopular reforms, first and foremost pension reform (Sacchi 2015). Italy was on the verge of default in late fall 2011 when, under the aegis of the European Union, the Berlusconi government was replaced by a technocratic government led by the economist and former EU Commissioner Mario Monti. Under the pressure of economic fundamentals (and implicit conditionality by European institutions), this liberal and technocratic government introduced fiscal consolidation worth 3% of GDP (1.3% of GDP in expenditure cuts, 1.7% of GDP in new taxes). Austerity in Italy peaked in 2011 and 2012 and greatly overshot values predicted by our economic model based on all 30 countries. After 2012, however, austerity efforts abated almost continuously, and since 2015 Italy has exited austerity, although the economic fundamentals (and in particular the level of debt) should have caused much stronger and longer austerity policies.

Arguably the policy did not work as expected, and this may be linked also to credit rating agencies not buying into the hope that austerity would in the short run lead to economic expansion. Rather, notwithstanding tough austerity, between summer 2011 and spring 2013, the Italian public debt was downgraded by Moody's, Fitch, and Standard and Poor's (Lenzi 2018). Likewise, citizens became frustrated and, while still worrying over debt, they were increasingly disillusioned by the real economy's dismal performance. Support for the Monti government plunged from 78.6% in November 2011 to 43.9% in December 2012 (Atlante Politico 2012).

This fits into findings from opinion polls showing a declining trend in support for austerity in Italy. The share of respondents in Eurobarometer data who believe that reducing deficit and debt is *not* a priority shows an upward yet modest trend over the years; the share of those who believe that reducing debt and deficit cannot be delayed has gone down more emphatically over the years, from 90% to 75% (calculated from Eurobarometer surveys, see above). At the same time, at the end of the austerity period in 2016, half of respondents believed that EU austerity policies were a hindrance to Member

States' growth, while a third supported them as the only way public finances can be kept under control (IPSOS 2017). In summer 2017, austerity was believed to have brought more disadvantages than advantages by 65% of respondents, and more advantages by only 10% (SWG 2017a); by the same token, 72% of respondents believed the EU should ease up on rigorous fiscal policies and favor growth-oriented investments, while 12% supported fiscal rigor (SWG 2017b). Arguably, the increasing austerity skepticism of the governments with Social Democratic orientations (under Enrico Letta, Matteo Renzi, and Paolo Gentiloni between 2013 and 2018), the fear of electoral punishment and public opinion turning against austerity made fiscal consolidation increasingly difficult in political terms, although economic fundamentals would have justified a tougher policy of welfare retrenchment and tax increases. By 2018 the Social Democrats, who had pursued a very mild austerity, were ousted by the populist Five Star Movement and Lega, for which austerity was a clear no-go—at least in their rhetoric.

The rise of these populist challenger parties help qualify our argument and reconcile it with findings by Bansak et al. (2021), who find that austerity was supported as a general policy response to the financial crisis (as shown by Eurobarometer data above). The same authors highlight the importance of the austerity package actually put in place, finding that support for austerity is greatly reduced if it involves social and education policy cuts, and pension cuts in particular, which is exactly what was done in the Italian case.

Some policy examples may illustrate this process of austerity fatigue. The 2012 pension reform of the liberal technocratic Monti government created a rift in the political community. People about to retire discovered that they had to wait up to six more years. Elderly workers who had accepted farewell packages from their companies on the assumption that this would be a walkway to retirement were left on their own, becoming unemployed at over 55 or even 60 years of age in a depressed labor market. While the Social Democratic Renzi and Gentiloni governments from 2014 to 2018 adopted a piecemeal approach and tackled some of the outstanding issues, the basic structure of the reform—which had attracted praise from the EU and international organizations such as the OECD—was maintained. By the same token, a wide-ranging labor market reform was introduced in 2015, which was meant to increase employment opportunities for the outsiders by de-segmenting the labor market and substantially expanding unemployment benefits (Sacchi 2018). However, its policy narrative made it a highly contentious reform, and it was generally perceived as reducing rather than increasing workers' rights (Galanti and Sacchi 2019). At the same time, a

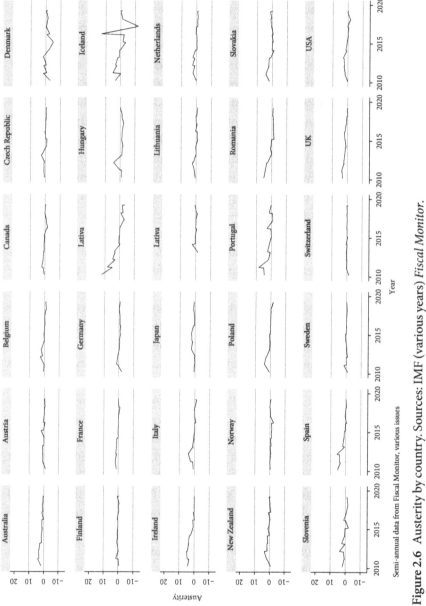

Semi-annual data from Fiscal Monitor, various issues

Figure 2.6 Austerity by country. Sources: IMF (various years) *Fiscal Monitor*.

minimum income scheme was introduced for the first time in Italian history in 2018, but it was criticized as being too little and too late. This all paved the way to the center-right-populist coalition government of Lega and the Five Star Movement. This coalition, led by Giuseppe Conte, immediately took a confrontational stance with the EU, blatantly questioning the validity of the deficit rule and introducing two costly expansionary social policy measures in early 2019. First was a temporary reversal of the 2012 pension reform, allowing early retirement with no adverse impact on the amount of the pension benefit (a measure that had featured prominently in Lega's electoral campaign). Second, the minimum income scheme introduced in 2018 was replaced by a much larger one (pompously called citizenship income), still means-tested and subject to an activation requirement, which had been the electoral flagship issue of the Five Star Movement. These two measures marked the end of austerity in citizens' perceptions and was the ultimate vindication of austerity fatigue—even before expansionary budgetary responses to the COVID-19 pandemic introduced by a different coalition government (still led by Mr. Conte and including the Five Star Movement) with the Social Democrats replacing Lega as a junior partner.

Conclusion

What explains austerity since the beginning of the Great Recession? In examining its evolution during the Great Recession and beyond, we have shown that austerity was initially strongly correlated with economic and fiscal fundamentals. However, the explanatory power of the economic model diminishes as austerity policies continue over time. Controlling for economic variables, we have argued that governments became increasingly unwilling to pursue an austerity strategy. The main reasons for this could be learning effects, that the policy is not as successful as planned in terms of economic or fiscal variables, or that governments become concerned about the electoral costs of austerity the longer it is in place—and, by implication, the rise of challenger parties. While we have strong evidence of the explanatory power of an economic model at the outset of austerity policies and of increasing austerity fatigue with the duration of spending cuts, the causal pathways—which arguably differ across countries—could not be clearly identified in the quantitative study. However, our case study of Italy illustrates how, in that country, challenger parties, electoral concerns, and both public and elite dissatisfaction with austerity policies dovetailed to bring about increasing austerity fatigue.

What are the lessons for post-pandemic fiscal policy and related welfare state policies in Europe? We expect that after the health shock and the temporary fiscal and monetary expansionary policy, international financial markets will factor in the level of sovereign debt when setting the interest rates of sovereign bonds. This is all the more likely as the consequences of the Ukrainian war may offset the expected economic growth stemming from recovery from the pandemic. Since some countries, in particular in Southern Europe, may be in a bad position in this regard after the pandemic—something that was already the main rationale of the Next Generation EU initiative (Armingeon et al. 2022)—their governments may be forced to cut back deficits. True, it is likely that EU institutions will not prescribe that those countries come off their expansionary policies cold turkey this time, particularly if the consequences of the Ukraine war should be serious. The Growth and Stability Pact was temporarily suspended by the European Commission in March 2020. This suspension is set to expire by the end of 2023 but might be further extended. Speaking to the European Parliament in March 2022, EU Commission executive vice president Dombrovskis recognized that "debt reduction strategies should be sustainable, credible and growth-friendly. This implies *gradual* fiscal adjustment" (Dombrovskis 2022, our italics). Yet, debt reduction should eventually be, while high-debt countries may also be forced to cut their deficits more abruptly if growth turns sluggish and international markets start questioning debt sustainability. That may trigger another round of support from the EU institutions, which would likely be made conditional on "structural reforms." Since welfare state expenditures are the bulk of public expenditures, high-debt governments in the Eurozone may have little option but to again shrink the welfare state, as they do not have the option of external devaluation of their own currency. It seems therefore not unlikely that in a few years we will come full circle again: introducing austerity first and exiting austerity afterward because it is unsuccessful or electorally unsustainable.

References

Alesina, Alberto,Carlo Favero and Franceso Giavazzi. 2019. *Austerity. When It Works and When It Doesn't*. Princeton and Oxford: Princeton University Press.

Arias, Eric, and David Stasavage. 2019. "How large are the political costs of fiscal austerity?" *The Journal of Politics* 81 (4): 1517–22.

Armingeon, Klaus, and Lucio Baccaro. 2012. "The Sorrows of Young Euro: The Sovereign Debt Crisis of Ireland and Southern Europe." In *Coping with Crisis: Government*

Responses to the Great Recession, edited by Nancy Bermeo and Jonas Pontusson, 162-97. New York: Russel Sage.

Armingeon, Klaus, Caroline De La Porte, Elke Heins, and Stefano Sacchi. 2022. "Voices from the past: Economic and political vulnerabilities in the making of Next Generation EU." *Comparative European Politics* 20 (2): 144–65.

Armingeon, Klaus, Sarah Engler, and Lucas Leemann. 2021. Comparative Political Data Set 1960-2019 Zürich: Institute of Political Science, University of Zurich. https://www.cpds-data.org

Armingeon, Klaus, Kai Guthmann, and David Weisstanner. 2016. "Choosing the path of austerity: how parties and policy coalitions influence welfare state retrenchment in periods of fiscal consolidation." *West European Politics* 39 (4): 628–47.

Atlante Politico. 2012. "35° Atlante politico—primarie, tecnici, prossime elezioni." https://www.demos.it/a00785.php

Bansak, Kirk, Michael M. Bechtel, and Yotam Margalit. 2021. "Why austerity? The mass politics of a contested policy." *American Political Science Review* 115 (2): 486–505.

Barta, Zsófia, and Alison Johnston. 2018. "Rating politics? Partisan discrimination in credit ratings in developed economies." *Comparative Political Studies* 51 (5): 587–620.

Barta, Zsófia, and Alison Johnston. 2021. "Entitlements in the crosshairs: How sovereign credit ratings judge the welfare state in advanced market economies." *Review of International Political Economy* 28 (5): 1169–95.

Bechtel, Michael M., Jens Hainmueller, and Yotam Margalit. 2014. "Preferences for international redistribution: The divide over the Eurozone bailouts." *American Journal of Political Science* 58 (4): 835–56.

Bechtel, Michael M., Jens Hainmueller, and Yotam Margalit. 2017. "Policy design and domestic support for international bailouts." *European Journal of Political Research* 56 (4): 864–86.

Beck, Nathaniel, and Jonathan Katz. 2011. "Modeling dynamics in time-series–Cross-section political economy data." *Annual Review of Political Science* 14: 331–52.

Blyth, Mark. 2013. *Austerity. The history of a dangerous idea*. Oxford: Oxford University Press.

Bojar, Abel, Björn Bremer, Hanspeter Kriesi, and Chendi Wang. 2022. "The effect of austerity packages on government popularity during the great recession." *British Journal of Political Science* 52 (1): 181–99.

Bremer, Björn, and Reto Bürgisser. 2023a. "Do citizens care about government debt? Evidence from survey experiments on budgetary priorities." *European Journal of Political Research* 62: 239–63.

Bremer, Björn, and Reto Bürgisser. 2023b. "Public opinion on welfare state recalibration in times of austerity: evidence from survey experiments." *Political Science Research and Methods* 11(1): 34–52.

De Boef, Suzanna, and Luke Keele. 2008. "Taking time seriously." *American Journal of Political Science* 52 (1): 184–200.

Dombrovskis, Valdis. 2022. "Opening statement at European Parliamentary Week 2002 on stability and growth pact." March 15, 2022. https://ec.europa.eu/commission/commissioners/2019-2024/dombrovskis/announcements/speech-executive-vice-president-dombrovskis-european-parliamentary-week-economic-and-social_en

EUObserver. 2021. "'Frugals' renew effort to reduce excessive debt." https://euobserver.com/green-economy/152882

Fernandez-Albertos, Jose, and Alexander Kuo. 2020. "Selling austerity: Preferences for fiscal adjustment during the Eurozone crisis." *Comparative Politics* 52 (1): 197–227.

Galanti, Maria Tullia, and Stefano Sacchi. 2019. "When words matter: Narratives and strategies in the Italian Jobs Act (2014–2016)." *Policy and Society* 38 (3): 485–50.

Giger, Nathalie, and Moira Nelson. 2011. "The electoral consequences of welfare state retrenchment: Blame avoidance or credit claiming in the era of permanent austerity?" *European Journal of Political Research* 50 (1): 1–23.

Guthmann, Kai. 2021. *Fiscal Consolidation in the Euro Crisis. Politico-economic and Institutional Causes.* Cham: Springer.

Hall, Peter A. 2003. "Aligning Ontology and Methodology in Comparative Research." In *Comparative Historical Research in the Social Sciences,* edited by James Mahoney and Dietrich Rueschemeyer, 373–404. Cambridge: Cambridge University Press.

Hübscher, Evelyne, and Thomas Sattler. 2017. "Fiscal consolidation under electoral risk." *European Journal of Political Research* 56 (1): 151–68.

Hübscher, Evelyne, Thomas Sattler, and Markus Wagner. 2021. "Voter responses to fiscal austerity." *British Journal of Political Science* 51 (4): 1751–60.

IMF. 2010a. *Fiscal Monitor. Fiscal Exit. From Strategy to Implementation. November 2010.* Washington, DC: IMF.

IMF. 2010b. *World Economic Outlook. October 2010. Recovery, Risk and Rebalancing.* Washington, DC: IMF.

IPSOS. 2017. *Italia 2017: la realtà su misura.* Milan: Ipsos edizioni.

Jacques, Olivier, and Lukas Haffert. 2021. "Are governments paying a price for austerity? Fiscal consolidations reduce government approval." *European Political Science Review* 13 (2): 189–207.

Lenzi, Francesco. 2018. "Lo spread, l'austerity e il vero problema della manovra, al di là degli zero virgola." *il Sole 24ore,* October 29, 2018.

Ostry, Jonathan D., Prakash Loungani, and Davide Furceri. 2016. "Neoliberalism: Oversold?" *Finance and Development* 53 (2): 38–41.

Raess, Damian 2021. "Globalization and austerity: Flipping partisan effects on fiscal policy during (recent) international crises." *Political Studies,* https://journals.sagepub.com/doi/10.1177/00323217211015811

Sacchi, Stefano. 2018. "The Italian welfare state in the crisis: Learning to adjust?" *South European Society and Politics* 23 (1): 29–46.

Schäfer, Armin, and Wolfgang Streeck. 2013. "Introduction: Politics in the Age of Austerity." In *Politics in the Age of Austerity,* edited by Armin Schäfer and Wolfgang Streeck, 1–25. Cambridge: Polity.

SWG. 2017a. "La metamorfosi del Paese." *POLITICAPP.* 7 luglio 2017. https://www.swg.it/politicapp?id=rnce

SWG. 2017b. "Fiscal compact." *POLITICAPP.* 21 luglio 2017. https://www.swg.it/politicapp?id=afri

Talving, Liisa. 2017. "The electoral consequences of austerity: Economic policy voting in Europe in times of crisis." *West European Politics* 40 (3): 560–83.

Wagschal, Uwe, and Georg Wenzelburger. 2008. "Roads to success: Budget consolidations in OECD countries." *Journal of Public Policy* 28 (3): 309–39.

Walter, Stefanie, Ari Ray, and Nils Redeker. 2020. *The Politics of Bad Options: Why the Eurozone's Problems Have Been So Hard to Resolve.* Oxford: Oxford University Press.

3

The Territorial Dynamic of Social Policies during COVID-19 Lockdowns

Tatiana Saruis, Eduardo Barberis, and Yuri Kazepov

Introduction: The Pre-COVID-19 Pandemic Context and Dynamics

Analyzing social policy changes from a territorial perspective is not a common exercise—particularly when adopting a comparative perspective—but it is increasingly gaining relevance (Kazepov et al. 2022). The issue's complexity pertains to not only the scarcity of data at the urban local level but also to the fragmentation of social policies into many specialized sub-fields, as well as their varying levels of territorial outreach. Consequently, scholars often pursue a single-case-study approach or—at best—consider a few case studies on specific policy fields in different cities comparatively. However, to understand policies' role in shaping citizens' lives during COVID-19 through a territorial lens, we must consider different analytical dimensions and the changes they are undergoing. In particular, we must understand the interaction among changing contexts, the regulatory principles behind specific policies, their jurisdictions, and the political dynamic accompanying the relation among all of them.

Contextual changes are well known. The structural socioeconomic transformation that started in the industrialized countries in the 1970s has deeply affected European welfare states' territorial dimension (Kazepov 2010), bringing about a reconfiguration of labor markets and production systems (Amin 1994; Crouch 2008). Moreover, relevant changes in the population's socio-demographic structure and new migration flows have challenged welfare structures that were institutionalized during the *Trente Glorieuses*. Both these processes contributed to the spread of new social risks that received limited response within consolidated social policies (Bonoli 2006; Ranci 2010) and were distributed unequally across social groups and territories.

Tatiana Saruis, Eduardo Barberis, and Yuri Kazepov, *The Territorial Dynamic of Social Policies during COVID-19 Lockdowns*
In: *European Social Policy and the COVID-19 Pandemic*. Edited by: Stefanie Börner and Martin Seeleib-Kaiser,
Oxford University Press. © Oxford University Press 2023. DOI: 10.1093/oso/9780197676189.003.0003

From a political perspective, these contextual changes fueled public and policy debates on the welfare state and the need to change it. The spread of neoliberal ideologies and the fall of the Eastern Bloc contributed to framing the debate on public expenditure and on policy's capacity to address the new risks. In doing so, these events inspired various reforms mainly aimed at containing costs and increasing welfare's efficiency and effectiveness (Gilbert 2004; Jenson 2004). A long period of reforms took place in most European countries (Esping-Andersen et al. 2002), varying in relation to timing, national models, and local specificities (Barbier 2008; Kazepov 2010). Two coexisting trends can be depicted: attempts to pursue budgetary cuts within a neoliberal retrenchment agenda on the one hand, and recalibration of social expenditure (including the promotion of citizens' participation and of new services) on the other (Ferrera and Hemerijck 2003). Such trends also had an often underestimated territorial dimension. In this chapter we frame our territorial lens within a scalar approach—in which the local is defined not as a bounded territory but rather according to its vertical positioning within changing, multi-tier spatial configurations (Brenner 2019). The emerging rescaling process and dynamic implies that economic, social, and institutional changes might affect spatial relations—including the re-articulation of welfare policies within multilevel governance systems.

Analytically, such a process can be divided into two connected dimensions: vertical and horizontal. Vertically, a strong tendency toward decentralization characterized many welfare reforms after the *Trente Glorieuses*. These reforms were aimed to de-bureaucratize social policies and get closer to citizens. The result was that up to the mid-2000s, the institutional level at which policies were designed, managed, funded, and implemented moved for some policy fields from national states to regions and local authorities. According to the principle of subsidiarity, which legitimized this shift, more innovative, adequate, and timely solutions arise from organizations closest to citizens (Fung and Wright 2003; Moulaert et al. 2010). Therefore, the local dimension has been considered a privileged entry point not only for satisfying needs but also for mobilizing resources to do so. In practice, however, these reforms often had to account for budgetary constraints and tended not to be particularly favorable to either social or territorial redistribution. The consequence—particularly debated in recent crises such as the 2008 economic crisis and more recently the 2020 pandemic—is that subnational bodies often lack adequate capacity to manage systemic shocks—or, rather, that their capacity is highly fragmented, hence adding new dimensions of territorial inequalities. These effects, as we will see, have been legitimizing—at different paces and in different forms—recentralization pressures in some European contexts (for an overview, see CEMR 2013).

Moreover, the vertical rescaling process can take place in different forms and within different configurations of power. A basic distinction can be drawn between implicit and explicit rescaling (Kazepov 2008). In the first case of implicit rescaling, there is no policy reform, but institutions operating at different levels change in relevance. An example is the impact of growing long-term unemployment in the 1980s on the relationship between unemployment benefits and social assistance. The social protection schemes put in place during the *Trente Glorieuses* and the postwar economic growth foresaw that the unemployed would be covered for a relatively limited period of time by national contributory social insurance schemes. The longer the duration of unemployment spells, the more claimants ran out of their unemployment benefits and fell into social assistance—commonly managed at the local level. In the second case of explicit rescaling, the reconfigurations of tasks, duties, responsibilities, and funding occurs through changes in regulations at different levels—from constitutional changes to procedures defined by middle managers (Kazepov and Barberis 2013).

Horizontally, welfare policies increasingly opened to a diversified number of profit and nonprofit organizations, variously involved in policy design, funding, management, and implementation (Ascoli and Ranci 2002; Kazepov 2010). Horizontal and vertical subsidiarity are supposed to be interconnected: the assumption is that plural and complementary (Amable 2016) organizations and networks can respond more effectively than other entities to complex needs (Ascoli and Ranci 2002; Ferrera and Hemerijck 2003). Furthermore, civil society's involvement was aimed to renew democracy and ensure transparency and accountability (Fung and Wright 2003; Goodin 2003). However, these purposes require specific conditions, such as a coherent system to manage vertical subsidiarity, the renewal of the public institutions to carry out coordination tasks, and the synchronization of different dimensions (tasks, competences, and resources). Decentralization and externalization did not necessarily imply de-bureaucratization, nor did they guarantee the improvement of social interventions or accountability (Christensen and Lægreid 2007; Somerville and Haines 2008). The re-articulation of institutional levels, the redistribution of policy tasks, and the creation of the welfare mix can produce complex organizational frameworks that are difficult to coordinate and connect in pursuit of consistent policy goals.

Overall, this process of institutional reorganization and externalization has had context-related effects, often leading to negative consequences related to social rights (Andreotti, Mingione, and Polizzi 2012). Forms of institutional de-responsibilization (Swyngedouw 2009) and the transfer of functions to local administrations without adequate resources (the decentralization of scarcity was highlighted by Keating 1998) increased territorial inequalities in Europe. Vested interests and reactions of stronger lobbies tended to not only challenge retrenchment trends but also influence the allocation of available resources, excluding new and vulnerable target groups or specific territories. The austerity policies fielded after 2008, aimed at reducing government budget deficits by combining spending cuts and tax increases, brought about a partial recentralization of institutional power, with a reinforcement of the European authority and central state control on expenditure (van Berkel et al. 2011; Canavire-Bacarreza et al. 2021). Such retrenchment also had a territorial dimension, with urban-based forms of austerity (Peck 2012) and institutional conflicts among central and subnational authorities (Bonoli and Trein 2022). As a general outcome, the boundaries of social citizenship were redesigned, also contributing to an increasing territorial inequality in Europe (Rodríguez-Pose 2018).

Within this frame, considering differences in how rescaling takes place in varied national welfare models, this chapter is aimed at analyzing the territorial dimension of welfare policies and measures enacted in Europe to face the socioeconomic consequences of the COVID-19 outbreak. The policy area considered here includes interventions and provisions—cash support, care, and in-kind benefits—aimed at compensating for the increase in social risks due to the pandemic outbreak and its syndemic effects. Analyzing both new social dynamics and the institutional responses to the pandemic, we aim to inscribe emergency-based changes within ongoing rescaling processes of welfare policy in Europe. We derive illustrative evidence of such trends from five European countries with different welfare and territorial organization models (Kazepov 2010): France and Germany as continental corporatist welfare states—the former centrally framed, and the latter regionally framed with a coordinated system; Italy as a Mediterranean familistic welfare state, regionally framed with a weakly coordinated system; Norway as a Nordic welfare system with a local autonomy/centrally framed spatial configuration; and Poland as a Central Eastern European (CEE) welfare state, characterized by one of the most articulated transformations of spatial configuration among post-Socialist countries.

We maintain that it remains unclear whether or not the pandemic will be a critical juncture—a point in time that may steer long-term institutional processes with new durable outcomes (Capoccia and Kelemen 2007)—in the spatial organization of welfare. On the one hand, preexisting spatial configurations affect preparedness and fragmentation in early institutional responses, and rescaling trends are likely to follow paths established before the pandemic. On the other hand, there remain open questions related to new needs for coordination and multilevel governance brought about in the pandemic management, which might lead to path adaptations. Will the pandemic produce structural changes? This chapter will lay down some analytical insights that could help frame this question, enabling us to parse how different welfare systems might be able to be reconfigured. Accordingly, the first section introduces the social dynamics generated by the pandemic outbreak and the spatial dimension of vulnerability. The second section—the core of our argument—analyzes institutional responses to the pandemic in reference to their territorial governance. The concluding section summarizes the main insights and proposes questions for further reflection and research.

Socio-spatial Dynamics

Aside from COVID-19's general socioeconomic consequences, discussed both in this volume and in a growing body of literature (Buheji et al. 2020; Grasso et al. 2021), the COVID-19 outbreak's socio-spatial dimensions are gaining relevance. To frame our understanding of it, we should consider the lines along which its impact spatially differs.

First, the pandemic hit hardest in specific hotspots. Different vulnerability indicators show intranational variations (OECD 2020). High shares of old-age residents and/or those with health conditions, people's high density and mobility (particularly if associated with socioeconomic vulnerabilities), and weak territorial health infrastructure were crucial factors of differentiation (see, for example, Ehlert 2021 on Germany; Consolazio et al. 2021 on Italy). In particular, peri-urban/suburban areas of the Global North seem to have been hit the hardest (Biglieri, De Vidovich and Keil 2020)—often due to their marginal position in the territorial governance.

In this respect, intranational variations in the institutional structure and a related uneven capacity to curb inequalities are issues (Rodriguez-Pose and Burlina 2021; McCann, Ortega-Argilés, and Yuan 2022). Institutional infrastructures and preparedness are key to understanding the differences between areas recovering quickly and areas suffering from long-term consequences—institutions have a role to play in the construction of disasters (Bifulco, Centemeri, and Mozzana 2021). Not by chance, there is consistent evidence that important economic hubs were hit first (due to their global connectedness) but reacted more effectively, whereas further waves and long-term effects affected more vulnerable groups and areas (OECD 2020; Woolford 2021). Furthermore, politics matter because political polarization and political leanings of regional elites do play roles in mortality differentials—in promoting, supporting, implementing, and following restrictions (Charron, Lapuente, and Rodriguez-Pose 2020).

Second, COVID-19's syndemic effects—that is, "the social and environmental factors that promote and enhance the negative effects of disease interaction" (Singer et al. 2017, 941)—and the consequences of early policy responses (particularly lockdowns) were highly selective. Areas with economies based on tourism and leisure were likely to be particularly affected, as well as areas that had already accumulated vulnerabilities (Bohme and Besana 2020; Belaid, Flambart, and Mongo 2021 for France). The share of jobs that can be performed remotely is variable in most countries—usually along an urban–rural divide (OECD 2020), but also in reference to the spatial concentration of vulnerabilities at the neighborhood level (Fu and Zhai 2021).

Furthermore, recovery measures' impact may suffer from territorial biases. National-level emergency cash measures that were implemented in most European countries may imply a selective redistribution of resources by design. In some cases, resources flow toward the most affected areas. In others, however, they flow toward specific recipients who meet eligibility criteria while others who might be in greater need are excluded. A couple of examples might clarify this point: areas characterized by higher levels of non-standard and/or undeclared work may be less endowed with contributory labor-based measures. Moreover, areas and social groups with weaker abilities to voice their needs may not find adequate resources to fill them. This might not be the case in contexts where local measures address these needs explicitly, adding yet another source of differential impact.

Ideally, local measures should complement national ones to address place-specific vulnerabilities. Nevertheless, they may have the unintended consequence of magnifying inequalities. On the one hand, more resourceful locales may be better able to implement their own measures, thus widening the gap between strong and weak areas—especially considering uneven losses of fiscal revenues at the subnational level (OECD 2020). On the other hand, localized measures necessarily provide place-specific responses to common problems, thus fragmenting the effectiveness of safety nets.

Institutional Dynamics and Responses

Preparedness to Respond to the Crisis

Preparedness to cope with the crisis may be influenced by many factors. As disaster sociology underlines, such crises usually sprout from existing societal configurations and do not create radical path breaks, but rather selectively speed up existing processes, mirroring and amplifying previous vulnerabilities (Plümer and Neumayer 2020).

Not by chance, social welfare policies have been fundamental to the management of the COVID-19 crisis (Greer et al. 2020; Cantillon et al. 2021). In the early phases they were mainly aimed at integrating and supporting health interventions and at mitigating the immediate effects of the lockdown and isolation measures on households and their economic and social conditions.

The duration of the pandemic and its foreseen medium-term consequences on the labor market, along with the resulting social stratification, challenge policy capacity to re-adapt to new conditions and to learn lessons from the crisis. Béland and colleagues (2021) highlighted the fact that responses to the crisis first relied on existing welfare programs and were congruent with the related welfare regimes. However, they also underlined the trend toward a new "emergency Keynesianism" that considers welfare policies not in contrast with markets but as a support to them (Bremer and McDaniel 2020, 439; Iversen and Soskice 2015). This trend was particularly evident in European institutions' response to the pandemic, which was opposite to austerity measures adopted after the financial crisis in 2008.

The territorial organization, as part of the welfare policy production, was one of the key factors shaping decisions and their implications for both immediately coping with the emergency and developing potential future practices. The coordination capacity during the first wave appeared particularly challenging in federal and devolved states, which had to cope with multiscale institutional systems to approve prompt and relevant decisions and guarantee their implementation. However, centralized states also had difficulties considering the fact that the pandemic's effects were not territorially homogeneous but rather were influenced by the variable distribution of weaker social groups and territorial resources. The balance between universalistic and context-specific interventions was already a challenge for many welfare policies. However, the pandemic pressure called into question the organization of institutional responsibilities in relation to their effectiveness and promptness in facing systemic challenges (Dodds et al. 2020). Some subnational authorities asked for more coordination and support from the central state, whereas others requested more decisional autonomy to respond to the pandemic's different territorial impacts.

As we mentioned above, the vertical dimension must be analyzed together with the horizontal one. The multi-scalar governance systems, which include regional, local, and national public institutions, involve private actors as well. In modern welfare states, the responsibility for health, social, educational, and labor programs is—at least partially and to varying degrees—shared across levels of government, integrated with markets of services and provisions and/or with civil society organizations. This setting is supposed to be based on institutional complementarities (Amable 2016). However, while addressing policy problems in emergency situations requires cooperation and coordination across levels of government and variable mixes of private interests, it does not exclude opportunistic and competitive dynamics. The outcome is a mix of opportunities, constraints, and incentives—and of conflicts, with policy games characterized by textbook collective action problems: cooperation would be the best options, but conflicting interest discourage collaborative actions. Different public interests in the political arena (e.g., economic or fiscal advantages) intermingle (Rodden 2006; Bonoli and Trein 2022). Responsibilities and blame for unpopular decisions, such as those limiting freedoms and those having unfavorable economic consequences, can be shifted spatially. Subnational institutions' autonomy is variably designed and differently combined with market and civil society. Their games could produce clashes and disagreements over the imposition and severity of public health measures as well as the redistribution of compensatory social measures. Consolidated incompatibilities and conflicts could be temporarily overcome or set aside and left unsolved, but what may be sustainable during the emergency could be unsustainable over a longer period.

Responses to the Emergency—Between Path Dependency and Path Break

The COVID-19 outbreak and its consequences put the consolidated governance arrangements under pressure. The need for rapid action did not leave much time for the usual democratic debates, shared decision-making processes, or planning processes. Central states' roles were crucial because of the importance of coordination and systemic interventions. Their budgets were put under severe stress, requiring extraordinary expenditures for managing the health emergency and financing the mass vaccination; compensating the economic damages caused by the lockdowns and safety limitations; and providing ordinary and extraordinary welfare measures for sick people, quarantined people, and newly unemployed people (OECD 2020). The recentralization trends that could be traced to the time before the pandemic were accelerated by these events—whether temporarily or durably remains an open question.

Among the different types of territorial organization of social policies, those characterized by high degrees of coordination were probably under the least stress: *centrally framed* countries with clear command lines, *locally framed* ones with effective equalization arenas, and *local autonomy/centrally framed* ones providing a solid framework to subnational administrations. However, the new and temporary governance resources activated within the emergency could call into question previous power balances and allow new discussions to emerge regarding consolidated practices.

According to the OECD (2020), the crisis's consequences on public revenues and expenditures will be a key issue for central and subnational governments. In many countries, subnational institutions are (jointly) responsible for health care and welfare provision, including social assistance and social benefits. Furthermore, they are often involved in key areas impacted by the pandemic such as education, active labor market policies, public administration, economic development, transport, public order and safety, and various utilities. In the context of early lockdowns, these institutions had to contribute to and collaborate with the central state to enhance health interventions and to manage the full or partial closure of some services while ensuring the continuity of essential public services. Then they had to manage the reopening, with dual efforts to guarantee physical services (e.g., public transport or cleaning public spaces) while reinforcing or enacting digital services (e.g., remote health consultation or education).

In *locally framed* countries, where subnational revenues mainly come from direct sources such as taxes, user charges, fees, and income from assets, the crisis's impact may be more relevant because horizontal redistribution and compensation mechanisms tend to be weaker in these contexts. In the medium term, local claims for rebalancing institutional competences could arise as blame-avoiding strategies related to the financial effects of the crisis.

In *local autonomy/centrally framed* countries, in which the coordination is more important in the production process of national policies, the pandemic's management may have been smoother because of preexisting bargaining arenas. However, it is also possible that institutional mechanisms of negotiation were put under stress, bypassed, or reframed. Local institutions may have asked for stronger intervention from the central state to manage the emergency, or may have resisted the state's attempts to acquire greater control.

In *centrally framed* countries, the shrinking of top-down redistribution may have enhanced bottom-up vocal conflict.

The emergency may both provide constraints and generate opportunities for policy change (Campbell 2004) and may produce formal or informal change, or even a mix of them. Informal changes mean that institutional structures remain unchanged, but governance balances or policy practices take on new forms.

It usually takes considerable time to introduce formal institutional changes because they are based on democratic discussions and decisions, formalization, and implementation measures. Emergency regulations are foreseen by the legislation, but their implementation may follow its own (even unexpected) logic and produce lasting effects. The literature has highlighted a slow and often underestimated incremental change in public institutions' practices (Streeck and Thelen 2005). In particular, in street-level organizations (Brodkin 2013)—whose task is to respond to specific citizens' requests and conditions, resolve new problems, piece together resources, and manage relationships—continuous adaptation is likely. During the pandemic, street-level organizations such as hospitals or social services that were managing the emergency's front line had their routines disrupted. They had to provide responses to unexpected and increased demands for intervention; at the same time, they had to enable and organize at least part of their work remotely and/or implement new safety procedures and practices to work onsite (Brodkin 2021). Aspects of these changes will probably produce durable consequences, such as reinforcement of the digitalization process of public administrations and modification of practices and procedures, and even of contact with applicants and beneficiaries. Considering the territorial dimension, the institutional capacity to coordinate the policy implementation process—observing the front line, developing new practices, systematizing innovation, or contrasting unequal effects—might vary. This means the pandemic's effect could widen territorial differences through informal shifts.

To sum up, the emergency may not only provide constraints but also generate opportunities for policy change (Campbell 2004). Adaptation to the new conditions could consolidate or reverse, returning to previous arrangements. Alternatively, it might trigger incremental changes. The crisis might also become an opportunity to retreat from less-established reforms or innovations. A post-pandemic territorial rescaling could imply path-discontinuity processes, both upward and downward, as well as path-dependent reactions which reinforce the policies' already-consolidated territorial organization.

Consolidation Dynamics

Norway's case is an example of territorial consolidation. The Norwegian welfare state belongs to the Nordic group of European countries, characterized by generous and mainly universalistic policies. The central agency in the social policy administration is the Norwegian Labor and Welfare Administration (NAV), which is subordinate to the Ministry of Labor and Social Affairs. The 2005 reform of the welfare system merged the pensions and employment administrations and moved them to the local level. Local authorities and central government cooperate through offices in municipalities and city boroughs. This system of organization defines Norwegian social welfare, from the territorial point of view, as *local autonomy/centrally framed* (Kazepov 2010). According to Christensen (2021), the central institutions in the pandemic's management were the Ministry of Health and Care Services (MH) and its subordinate expert agencies (the Norwegian Directorate of Health and the Norwegian Institute of Public Health), together with the prime minister and the cabinet in collaboration with the parliament, because the government is supported by a minority coalition. The agenda has been dominated by the central political and administrative leadership and experts, in a typical top-down process based on health concerns and the precautionary principle, and supported by a large consensus of public opinion and a consolidated trust in the state that characterizes the Norwegian context (Christensen and Lægreid 2020; Christensen 2021). The measures addressing COVID-19's social consequences were mostly economic and aimed at compensating businesses, helping employees, and increasing risk coverage for self-employed individuals and freelancers. The role of the Ministry of Labor and Social Affairs has been marginal during most of the pandemic, and social policy measures overall received much less attention from central leadership than economic issues. These measures were rather loosely coupled to vulnerable groups such as children, youth, and elderly people that were not strong enough to push their problems into the political agenda (Martin-Howard and Farmbry 2020; Ursin et al. 2020; Christensen 2021). However, the government did not encounter much opposition to its failure to focus on vulnerable groups. A universalistic approach remained at the basis of Norwegian social policy, whereas targeted measures regarding vulnerable groups were usually marginal (Greve et al. 2021; Béland et al. 2021). The logic was that ordinary programs should receive additional funds or be extended to more people; thus, the eligibility criteria were relaxed during the pandemic, and the program of economic social assistance was also made more generous. The institutional reaction to the pandemic followed a path-dependent logic in both welfare intervention and the territorial distribution of power. Therefore, the central state's relevance was confirmed and reinforced during the pandemic (Christensen 2021).

One can see another example of path-dependent management of the crisis in France's case. No relevant power shifts took place, and central control was maintained to cope with territorial variations as well. The centrally framed leaning of most public institutions, including welfare institutions, was reaffirmed. Even in cases where territorially differentiated measures were enacted, as in the case of clustering to provide spatially differentiated measures according to the circulation patterns of COVID-19, they were determined and implemented in a centrally framed way (Vampa 2021). Indeed, most of the shock-absorbing measures (e.g., to limit and counteract unemployment) were national in scope and organization, with the risk of leaving particularly affected areas behind. Although the overall territorial inequalities did not grow, some scholars (Belaid, Flambard, and Mongo 2021) noticed that a few departments were hit remarkably hard, accumulating health and social disadvantages, and general emergency measures were not sufficient to address their problems. In emergency management itself, top-down public action may have prevented the use of resources by civil society and local players and hindered the identification of institutions not accustomed to coordinating horizontally and vertically (Giraud et al. 2021; Bergeron et al. 2020). Although the clear line of command (guaranteed at the regional level by the role of the prefects) and the shared legitimation of centrally framed decision-making was conducive to a smoother implementation of decisions (Kuhlmann et al. 2021), some scholars noted that newly established emergency bodies complicated coordination efforts (Bergeron et al. 2020).

Institutional Centralization

Recentralization trends may have been based on a redistribution of institutional competences toward national-level institutions because central players assumed a specific relevance during the pandemic emergency. Recentralization can also be shaped as a coordination effort, often based on soft policy instruments: new coordination arenas are created, and previous mechanisms of coordination are reinforced. That is, new practices of inter-institutional cooperation experiment with instituting new arenas without formally modifying previous assets.

In Italy, the central state's intervention in social policies was strongly re-inforced during the pandemic, partially bypassing the regions, which have exclusive constitutional competence in this field. Since the constitutional reform in 2001, the central state has had the function of defining the norma-tive framework and funding and establishing homogeneous levels of basic provisions. The latter were defined only in 2020–2021 through a long and complicated process of negotiation with the regions. The state's weak role in social welfare defines a weakly coordinated regionally framed welfare that is often residual and fragmented (Kazepov 2008). However, the process of the central level's enhancement started in 2016 with the institution of the first national minimum income measure, which was further expanded in the fol-lowing years. During the pandemic, state-mandated relief measures were ex-panded, providing both cash relief and some in-kind benefits that previously had been provided by regional and local institutions. The central govern-ment introduced extraordinary cash support for self-employed individuals and freelancers who had to interrupt or reduce their activities because of the lockdown, along with an emergency income measure (*reddito di emergenza*) for those excluded from existing national minimum income schemes. At the same time, the central state distributed funds for food stamps (*buoni spesa*) directly through the municipalities, thus bypassing the regions. Other in-kind benefits usually provided by the regions (e.g., active labor market policies) were largely suspended during the lockdown, producing an informal refocus on state-based measures. The regional role in the management of social measures during the pandemic was marginal overall, but this kind of management did not cause any uproar (whereas the regions were highly vocal in the field of health and prevention). Emergency intervention was discussed within the so-called state–regions conference—that is, the coordination arena usually dedicated to institutional negotiations. Furthermore, the high costs of emergency measures were fully covered by the state. It remains an open question whether and how the pace of recentralization will consolidate or slow down in the near future.

Poland's case may be quite similar, although from a different starting point. Since the 1990s, Poland has been one of the few CEE countries to establish and strengthen a multilevel organization with different layers. This resulted in almost two decades of growing regional and local roles in welfare policy planning, funding, and provision (Kazepov 2010) —under the aegis of the state—in ways that we may even classify as a peculiar kind of local autonomy/centrally framed model, albeit within the framework of quite residual welfare provisions. However, the first response to COVID-19's syndemic effects in Poland was centralized, based on the so-called anti-crisis shield (*tarcza antykryzysowa*), a set of norms issued in March 2020 that included mostly wage subsidies and job protection measures (Aidukaite et al. 2021). Subnational government bodies were only involved in the implementation of measures adopted at the national level, in policy areas usually managed at the subnational level (e.g., active labor market policy and mental health care; Marzec 2020). Although early national provisions were aimed at ensuring local authorities' functioning under pandemic conditions (e.g., by means of dedicated transfer and by introducing more flexibility to some tasks, including through the use of budgets and employees), bottom-up initiatives from subnational units were limited—at least during the first wave, which hit Poland less severely compared to other European countries (Glinka 2021). Some scholars do interpret this centralized management as an intensification of an early path change. A recent recentralization process has been starting to reverse the local autonomy that began in the 1990s. In particular, the revenue structure's transformation since 2016 has become a challenge for Polish multilevel governance (Rajca 2020; Turala 2020). This is especially true for new populist-authoritarian welfare reforms, which include an expansion of (state-based) cash measures (e.g., in family policy), as well as recentralization in areas such as health (Mikula and Kaczmarek 2019; Stubbs and Lendvai-Bainton 2020). Although this is not enough to reverse 30 years of decentralization, a creeping recentralization seems to be ongoing (Sześciło 2019; Gawlowski 2022).

Institutional Decentralization

Decentralization processes could be triggered by local protagonism prompted by the pandemic, evaluated as positive experiences in adapting policies to local specificities, or mobilizing local resources. An example is targeting vulnerable groups not yet covered by consolidated safety nets who find relief through specific local welfare measures or charities and civil society organizations. These trends could also reinforce the visibility and legitimization of new organizations that work on these issues.

According to Kuhlmann et al. (2021), Germany's response to the pandemic emergency was characterized by a complex dynamic: an initial bottom-up local and regional protagonism that gave way to a federal strategy in the next period, followed by a return to regional autonomy and local variation. Local governments were the first to enact mitigation measures. Land-level—and even municipal-level—responses differed, with a variety of measures, also according to the pandemic's differing impact. The German constitution provides both the *Länder* governors and city mayors considerable power. The federal government cannot impose rules, but only give recommendations and push for coordinated measures. However, federal government strategy and coordination were considered important for coping with the challenges posed by the pandemic. Some research (Bariola and Collins 2021; Dodds et al. 2020) underlines the importance of Chancellor Merkel's solid leadership as a factor in the success of this temporary scale-up process. The arenas of horizontal negotiation between the 16 Länder, and the vertical involvement of the federal level, became crucial to the achievement of nationwide solutions. Local solutions developed by lower-tier governments were scaled up and harmonized to finally be enacted by the 16 states in agreement with the federation (Kuhlmann et al. 2021). The coordination of federal and local strategies touched upon the regulation of lockdowns, health intervention, and social and economic compensation measures, and lasted throughout the pandemic's most severe phase in 2020. Then, a new re-appropriation of power by the *Länder* and municipalities occurred in the phase of dismissal policies (Kuhlmann et al. 2021). Regarding social policies, Germany substantially expanded existing programs and provided generous subsidies (Bariola and Collins 2021). As a conservative–corporatist welfare regime, most entitlements are employment-based (Esping-Andersen 1999). Beyond massive intervention to support firms and freelancers, the most relevant measure for coping with the pandemic's consequences was the expansion of the short-time work scheme, already used in response to the 2008 recession with the aim of guaranteeing workers' job stability. The measure is based on social insurance and support to employers and is aimed at reducing employees' working hours instead of laying them off. The government pays workers at least 60% (67% for working parents) of their usual pay for the hours not worked. The expansion of this benefit, among other measures, allowed Germany to keep its unemployment rate low, but reduced attention to most socially disadvantaged groups and efforts to maintain gender equality (Bariola and Collins 2021).

New Public–Private (Re-)Balances?

The decentralization processes triggered by the pandemic may concern both public and private organizations and should always be considered together with horizontal subsidiarization processes (Kazepov 2010). The pandemic may have weakened some organizations by, for example, interrupting externalized measures financed by public funds and exposing them to financial crisis. Other organizations may have been strengthened, depending on their capacity to address the emergency. The crisis may also have encouraged new civic activism on emerging problems.

Although cash measures have favored recentralization processes due to the redistributive role of central institutions, the outcome may be different in relation to care and in-kind benefits, which need direct contact and relational proximity. Cash measures, even when substantial and based on broad access criteria, can resolve only a portion of beneficiaries' needs. According to the principle of subsidiarity, local welfare systems are usually responsible for planning, organizing, and providing care measures and in-kind benefits, aiming for flexible and tailored interventions. The support of civil society and for-profit actors is often key in this area of welfare provision.

COVID-19 challenged standard arrangements in care, absorbing resources for their reorganization and reducing their room to maneuver. Care measures and in-kind benefits—health, social, relational and psychological support; food aid and other practical assistance; accommodation, activation policies—are based on direct interaction. The organizations providing them had to be reorganized to operate remotely, and even had to reduce or suspend their services during the pandemic. Restrictions on the use of public spaces and physical distancing have been key policy measures in pandemic times (Honey-Roses et al. 2020), which has affected service providers and their facilities. The complementarity of cash care, cash activation, and cash conditionalities in welfare measures tended to be misaligned and loosened as well. Care and in-kind provisions may have followed different dynamics compared to cash provisions. Central management was probably reinforced due to the need for coordinated interventions on pandemic effects, but these interventions still had to pass through local public and/or private organizations, mainly nongovernmental organizations.

Furthermore, many countries had to cope with a significant increase in demand for support due to both the increased vulnerability of some groups and the reinforcement of already-existing disadvantaged situations. The pandemic made structural inequalities embedded in many welfare systems more visible for fragile groups and territories. However, in general, measures aimed at broadening welfare coverage during the crisis tended to leave behind many vulnerable groups, including children, disabled people, homeless people, migrants, and victims of violence (Orru et al. 2021; Bergman et al. 2021; Leonardi 2020).

State-level authorities demonstrated varied responsiveness to NGOs' advocacy work, which seemed to be more successful in countries where stronger alliances between the state and nongovernmental care services existed before the crisis (e.g., Germany). By contrast, in some countries (e.g., Italy), many welfare facilities' closures could have been prevented if public authorities had been able to coordinate with social services to restructure their operations in a safe way instead of halting all face-to-face interactions; day care centers represent a good case in point (Orru et al. 2021).

Orru and colleagues (2021) claimed that in Germany and Norway, coordinated governance networks were stronger, and the public authorities were more open to the requests of NGOs and to the needs of vulnerable groups: "These positive exchanges and the clarity of information received were vital for staff morale and led to personnel not only feeling equipped to disseminate accurate information to clients, but also knowledgeable about ways to rearrange services to align with regulations" (p. 560). In other contexts, such as Italy, some organizations suspended their services whereas others resisted and were forced to make their own arrangements without much support or guidance from state institutions (Barberis and Martelli 2021). The challenges introduced by the COVID-19 pandemic for care organizations changed their routines, which reduced their capacity for direct intervention and possibly caused them to redistribute or even rethink their roles and tasks. One example is reported in Leonardi's (2020) case study in Turin (Italy). There, congregate homeless shelters managed by NGOs were closed during the pandemic without any resources or strategies aimed at finding alternative and safe solutions. Instead of disbanding, they readdressed their efforts from provision of housing to protest and advocacy actions, demanding public intervention for housing solutions. Despite their flexibility and capacity for innovation and activism, they could not directly and autonomously provide accommodation for homeless people, highlighting their financial fragility and potential vulnerability to the crisis. This case clearly represents an effect of governance relationships based on passive subsidiarity (Kazepov 2010), which occurs in contexts in which the delegation of social tasks to NGOs occurs without public institutions' attention and support (including funding).

To sum up, cash measures and care were provided differently than were in-kind measures. The former were mainly centrally managed, and the latter were decentralized to local public and private organizations that could guarantee direct contact and relational proximity. This double strategy seeks to reconcile the redistribution of resources and adaptation to territorial variations and groups. However, it also risks misaligning economic support and measures to encourage the empowerment and activation of welfare beneficiaries.

Conclusions

From a territorial point of view, social policy responses to the pandemic are mainly characterized by processes of centralization variously intertwined with health and safety strategies. These processes can be path-dependent or can present path breaks with previous forms of territorial organization. In the cases of Norway (local autonomy/centrally framed) and France (centrally framed), we observe a reinforcement of centralization in the management of the crisis in continuity with the already-consolidated models, and mainly based on informal power shifts toward the respective national governments. Germany, based on a consolidated regionally framed organization with institutional coordination across scales, shows a complex dynamic substantially reinforcing the arenas of institutional negotiation. Italy (uncoordinated, regionally framed) and Poland (local autonomy/centrally framed) reinforced recent trends, strengthening their centralization during the crisis.

However, this is an incomplete picture. The common trend of centralization of social welfare policies follows different strategies. On the one hand, it is based on the reduction of local authority through formal and informal shifts of power toward national institutions; on the other hand, it reinforces coordination and negotiation arenas with meaningful involvement of local authorities in the crisis's management. Poland accelerated recent centralization trends mainly through formal rules, moving power and competences toward the national level, whereas Italy increased centralization through a mix of formal and informal decisions—both indirectly by reinforcing the state–regions coordination arena, and directly by introducing new central social policy measures. France further reinforced a consolidated centralized policy system through an informal rebalance of power at the expense of local institutions, possibly challenging consolidated mechanisms of coordination between the different institutional levels. Norway increased the role of the national level through an informal strategy as well, but it started with a consolidated local autonomy/centrally framed system. Germany followed a similar strategy, informally strengthening the coordination between central and federal levels. Table 3.1 summarizes these trends.

In emergency management, coordination—realized through both centralization of authority and/or reinforcement of arenas of negotiation—is a key factor. According to a report describing the territorial impact of COVID-19 (OECD 2020), more than centralized or decentralized crisis responses, "a coordinated response by all levels of government, in both federal and unitary systems, can minimize crisis-management failures" (p. 55). This means that, rather than considering only the distribution of institutional competences at different territorial levels, what is relevant for analysis is how the levels interact and support one another (Vampa 2021). However, it is difficult to

Table 3.1 Summary overview of Strategies for Management of Social Policies during the Pandemic

Management of the pandemic	Territorial organization of social policies		
	Centrally framed	Local autonomy/ centrally framed	Regionally framed
Path dependency	France (informal shift toward stronger centralization)	Norway (informal shift toward centralization)	Germany (informal reinforcement of central–federal state coordination)
Path break, but accelerating previous trends		Poland (formal centralization)	Italy (formal centralization of policies and informal reinforcement of coordination arenas)

Source: author's elaboration based on Kazepov (2010).

formulate hypotheses about whether and how social policy management during the pandemic will produce durable effects on their territorial organization. Countries' emergency strategies have been mainly consistent with their central or regional frameworks and/or with already-ongoing trends toward centralization or decentralization—which they helped accelerate and further consolidate. The informal shifts introduced through soft law strategies are more likely to be temporary than new formal rules that rebalance institutional competences. In these countries, it does not seem like there is room for strong discontinuity or radical innovation.

References

Aidukaite, Jolanta, Steven Saxonberg, Dorota Szelewa, and, Dorottya Szikra. 2021. "Social policy in the face of a global pandemic: Policy responses to the COVID-19 crisis in Central and Eastern Europe." *Social Policy Administration* 55: 358–73. https://doi.org/10.1111/spol.12704.

Amable, Bruno. 2016. "Institutional complementarities in the dynamic comparative analysis of capitalism." *Journal of Institutional Economics* 12(1): 79–103. https://doi.org/10.1017/S1744137415000211.

Amin, Ash, ed. 1994. *Post-fordism: A Reader*. Oxford: Oxford University Press.

Andreotti, Alberta, Enzo Mingione, and Emanuele Polizzi. 2012. "Local welfare systems: A challenge for social cohesion." *Urban Studies* 49(9): 1925–40. https://doi.org/10.1177/0042098012444884.

Ascoli, Ugo, and Costanzo Ranci. 2002. "The Context of New Social Policies in Europe." In *Dilemmas of the Welfare Mix*, edited by Ugo Ascoli and Costanzo Ranci, 1–24. Nonprofit and Civil Society Studies. Boston: Springer US. https://doi.org/10.1007/978-1-4757-4992-2_1.

Barberis, Eduardo, and Alessandro Martelli. 2021. "Covid-19 e welfare dei servizi in Italia." *Politiche Sociali* no. 2 (May–August): 349–68. https://doi.org/10.7389/101684.

Barbier, Jean-Claude. 2008. "The Puzzling Resilience of Nations in the Context of Europeanized Welfare States" (Communication to the RC19 Meeting. "The future of social citizenship: politics, institutions and outcomes," Stockholm, September 2008).

Bariola, Nino, and Caitlyn Collins. 2021. "The gendered politics of pandemic relief: Labor and family policies in Denmark, Germany, and the United States during COVID-19." *American Behavioral Scientist* 65 (12): 1671–97. https://doi.org/10.1177/0002764221 1003140.

Belaid, Fateh, Véronique Flambard, and Michelle Mongo. 2022. "How large is the extent of COVID-19 on territorial inequality? France's current situation and prospects." *Applied Economics* 54 (12): 1432–48. https://doi.org/10.1080/00036846.2021.1976389.

Béland, Daniel, Bea Cantillon, Rod Hick, and Amílcar Moreira. 2021. "Social policy in the face of a global pandemic." *Social Policy and Administration* 55 (2): 249–60. https://doi.org/10.1111/spol.12718.

Bergeron, Henri, Olivier Borraz, Patrick Castel, and François Dedieu. 2020. *COVID-19. Une crise organisationelle*. Paris: Les Presses de Sciences Po.

Bergman, Solveig, Margunn Bjørnholt, and Hannah Helseth. 2022. "Norwegian shelters for victims of domestic violence in the COVID-19 pandemic. Navigating the new normal." *Journal of Family Violence* 37: 927–37. https://doi.org/10.1007/s10 896-021-00273-6.

Bifulco, Lavinia, Laura Centemeri, and Carlotta Mozzana. 2021. "For preparedness as transformation." *Sociologica* 15 (3): 5–24. https://doi.org/10.6092/ISSN.1971-8853/ 13939.

Biglieri, Samantha, Lorenzo De Vidovich, and Roger Keil. 2020. "City as the core of contagion?" *Cities and Health* 5 (s1): S63–5. https://doi.org/10.1080/23748 834.2020.1788320.

Böhme, Kai, and Flavio Besana. 2020. "Understanding the territorially diverse implications of covid-19 policy responses." *Spatial Foresight Brief* 13: 1–16.

Bonoli, Giuliano. 2006. "New Social Risks and the Politics of Postindustrial Social Policies." In *The Politics of Postindustrial Welfare States*, edited by Klaus Armingeon and Giuliano Bonoli, 3–26. London: Routledge.

Bonoli Giuliano, and Philipp Trein. 2022. "National-Regional-Local Shifting Games in Multi-tiered Welfare States." In *Handbook on Urban Social Policy. International Perspectives on Multilevel Governance and Local Welfare*, edited by Yuri Kazepov, Eduardo Barberis, Roberta Cucca and Elisabetta Mocca, 250–65. Cheltenham: Edward Elgar.

Bremer, Björn, and Sean McDaniel. 2020. "The ideational foundations of social democratic austerity in the context of the great recession." *Socio-Economic Review* 18 (2): 439–63. https://doi.org/10.1093/ser/mwz001.

Brenner, Neil. 2019. *New Urban Spaces*. New York: Oxford University Press.

Brodkin, Evelyn Z. 2013. "Street-level Organization and the Welfare State." In *Work and the Welfare State*, edited by Evelyn Z. Brodkin and Greg Marston, 17–34. Washington, DC: Georgetown University Press.

Brodkin, Evelyn Z. 2021. "Street-level organizations at the front lines of crises." *Journal of Comparative Policy Analysis: Research and Practice* 23 (1): 16–29. https://doi.org/10.1080/13876988.2020.1848352.

Buheji, Mohamed, Katiane da Costa Cunha, Godfred Beka, Bartola Mavrić, Yuri Leandro do Carmo de Souza, Simone Souza da Costa Silva, Mohammed Hanafi, and Tulika Chetia Yein. 2020. "The extent of COVID-19 pandemic socio-economic impact on global poverty." *American Journal of Economics* 10 (4): 213–24. https://doi.org/10.5923/j.economics.20201004.02.

Campbell, John L. 2004. *Institutional Change and Globalization.* Princeton University Press. https://doi.org/10.1515/9780691216348.

Canavire-Bacarreza, Gustavo, Pablo Evia Salas, and Jorge Martinez-Vazquez. 2021. "The Effect of Crises on Fiscal and Political Recentralization." Working Paper 21-11, Georgia State University, Georgia, GA, June 2021. https://bit.ly/3cj7A4m.

Cantillon, Bea, Martin Seeleib-Kaiser, and Romke Veen. 2021. "The COVID-19 crisis and policy responses by continental European welfare states." *Social Policy and Administration* 55 (2): 326–38. https://doi.org/10.1111/spol.12715.

Capoccia, Giovanni, and R. Daniel Kelemen. 2007. "The study of critical junctures." *World Politics* 59 (3): 341–69. https://doi.org/10.1017/S0043887100020852.

CEMR (Council of European Municipalities and Regions). 2013. https://www.ccre.org/

Charron, Nicholas, Victor Lapuente, and Andrés Ridriguez-Pose. 2020. "Uncooperative Society, Uncooperative Politics or Both? How Trust, Polarization and Populism Explain Excess Mortality for COVID-19 across European regions." QoG Working Paper Series 12, University of Gothenburg, Västra Götalands län, Hallands län, December 2021.

Christensen, Tom. 2021. "The social policy response to COVID-19." *Public Organization Review* 21 (4): 707–22. https://doi.org/10.1007/s11115-021-00560-2.

Christensen, Tom, and Per Lægreid. 2007. "The whole-of-government approach to public sector reform." *Public Administration Review* 67 (6): 1059–66. https://doi.org/10.1111/j.1540-6210.2007.00797.x.

Christensen, Tom, and Per Lægreid. 2020. "Balancing governance capacity and legitimacy: How the Norwegian government handled the COVID -19 crisis as a high performer." *Public Administration Review* 80 (5): 774–79. https://doi.org/10.1111/puar.13241.

Consolazio, David, Rossella Murtas, Sara Tunesi, Federico Gervasi, David Benassi, and Antonio Giampiero Russo. 2021. "Assessing the impact of individual characteristics and neighborhood socioeconomic status during the COVID-19 pandemic in the provinces of Milan and Lodi." *International Journal of Health Services* 51 (3): 311–24. https://doi.org/10.1177/0020731421994842.

Crouch, Colin. 2008. "Change in European societies since the 1970s." *West European Politics* 31 (1–2): 14–39. https://doi.org/10.1080/01402380701833699.

Dodds, Klaus, Vanesa Castan Broto, Klaus Detterbeck, Martin Jones, Virginie Mamadouh, Maano Ramutsindela, Monica Varsanyi, David Wachsmuth, and Chih Yuan Woon. 2020. "The COVID-19 pandemic: Territorial, political and governance dimensions of the crisis." *Territory, Politics, Governance* 8 (3): 289–98. https://doi.org/10.1080/21622671.2020.1771022.

Ehlert, Andree. 2021. "The socio-economic determinants of COVID-19: A spatial analysis of German county level data." *Socio-Economic Planning Sciences* 78 (December): 101083–92. https://doi.org/10.1016/j.seps.2021.101083.

Esping-Andersen, Gøsta. 1990. *The Three Worlds of Welfare Capitalism.* Cambridge, UK: Polity Press.

Esping-Andersen, Gøsta. 1999. *Social Foundations of Postindustrial Economies.* Oxford: Oxford University Press. https://doi.org/10.1093/0198742002.001.0001.

Esping-Andersen, Gøsta, Duncan Gallie, Anton Hemerijck and John Myles, eds. 2002. *Why We Need a New Welfare State.* Oxford: Oxford University Press.

Ferrera, Maurizio, and Anton Hemerijck. 2003. "Recalibrating Europe's Welfare Regimes." In *Governing Work and Welfare in a New Economy*, edited by Jonathan Zeitlin and David M. Trubek, 88–128. Oxford: Oxford University Press.

Fu, Xinyu, and Wei Zhai. 2021. "Examining the spatial and temporal relationship between social vulnerability and stay-at-home behaviors in New York City during the COVID-19 pandemic." *Sustainable Cities and Society* 67 (April): 102757–66. https://doi.org/10.1016/j.scs.2021.102757.

Fung, Archon, and Erik Olin Wright. 2003. *Deepening Democracy.* The Real Utopias Project, volume 4. London: Verso.

Gawlowksi, Robert. 2022. "Intergovernmental relations during the COVID-19 crisis in Poland." *Institutiones Administrationis* 2 (2): 88–98. https://doi.org/10.54201/iajas.v2i2.32.

Gilbert, Neil. 2004. *Transformation of the Welfare State.* Oxford: Oxford Scholarship Online. https://doi.org/10.1093/0195140745.001.0001.

Giraud, Olivier, Nikola Tietze, Tania Toffanin, and Camille Noûs. 2021. "The scalar arrangements of three European public health systems facing the COVID-19 pandemic." *Culture, Practice and Europeanization* 6 (1): 89–111.

Goodin, Robert E. 2003. "Democratic accountability: The distinctiveness of the third sector." *European Journal of Sociology* 44 (3): 359–96. https://doi.org/10.1017/S0003975603001322.

Grasso, Maria, Martina Klicperová-Baker, Sebastian Koos, Yuliya Kosyakova, Antonello Petrillo, and Ionela Vlase. 2021. "The impact of the coronavirus crisis on European societies." *European Societies* 23 (suppl): 2–32. https://doi.org/10.1080/14616696.2020.1869283.

Greer, Scott L., Elizabeth J. King, Elize Massard da Fonseca, and Andre Peralta-Santos. 2020. "The comparative politics of COVID-19." *Global Public Health* 15 (9): 1413–16. https://doi.org/10.1080/17441692.2020.1783340.

Greve, Bent, Paula Blomquist, Bjørn Hvinden, and Minna van Gerven. 2021. "Nordic welfare states—still standing or changed by the COVID-19 crisis?" *Social Policy and Administration* 55 (2): 295–311. https://doi.org/10.1111/spol.12675.

Glinka, Kamil. 2021. "The biggest Polish cities in response to the first wave of the COVID-19 pandemic." *Przegląd Politologiczny* 2: 47–69. https://doi.org/10.14746/pp.2021.26.2.4.

Honey-Roses, Jordi, Isabelle Anguelovski, Josep Bohigas, Vincent Chireh, Carolyn Daher, Cecil Konijnendijk, Jill Litt, et al. 2020. "The impact of COVID-19 on public space." *Cities & Health* 5 (S1): S263–79. https://doi.org/10.1080/23748834.2020.1780074.

Iversen, Torben, and David Soskice. 2015. "Politics for markets." *Journal of European Social Policy* 25 (1): 76–93. https://doi.org/10.1177/0958928714556971.

Jenson, Jane. 2004. "Canada's new social risks: Directions for a new social architecture." CPRN Social Architecture Papers Research Report F.43, Family Network. September 2004, Canadian Policy Research Networks.

Kazepov, Yuri. 2008. "The subsidiarization of social policies: Actors, processes and impacts." *European Societies* 10 (2): 247–73.

Kazepov, Yuri. ed. 2010. *Rescaling Social Policies towards Multilevel Governance in Europe.* Farnham: Ashgate.

Kazepov, Yuri, and Eduardo Barberis. 2013. "Social Assistance Governance in Europe: Towards a Multilevel Perspective." In Minimum Income Protection in Flux, edited by Ive Marx and Kenneth Nelson, 217–48. Houndmills Basingstocke: Palgrave McMillan.

Kazepov, Yuri, Barberis, Eduardo, Roberta Cucca, and Elisabetta Mocca, eds. 2022. *Handbook on Urban Social Policy.* Cheltenham: Edward Elgar.

Keating, Michael. 1998. *The New Regionalism in Western Europe.* Cheltenham, UK; Northampton, MA: E. Elgar.

Kuhlmann, Sabine, Mikael Hellström, Ulf Ramberg, and Renate Reiter. 2021. "Tracing divergence in crisis governance: Responses to the COVID-19 pandemic in France, Germany and Sweden compared." *International Review of Administrative Sciences* 87 (3) (September): 556–75. https://doi.org/10.1177/0020852320979359.

Leonardi, Daniela. 2020. "La pandemia raccontata dalla bassa soglia." *Welforum.it*, April 17, 2020. https://www.welforum.it/il-punto/emergenza-coronavirus-tempi-di-precari eta/la-pandemia-raccontata-dalla-bassa-soglia/

Martin-Howard, Simone, and Kyle Farmbry. 2020. "Framing a needed discourse on health disparities and social inequities." *Public Administration Review* 80 (5): 839–44. https://doi.org/10.1111/puar.13265.

McCann, Philip, Raquel Ortega-Argilés, and Pei-Yu Yuan. 2022. "The Covid-19 shock in European regions." *Regional Studies* 56 (7): 1142–60. https://doi.org/10.1080/00343 404.2021.1983164

Mikuła, Łukasz, and Urszula Kaczmarek. 2019. "From marketization to recentralization: the health-care system reforms in Poland and the post-New Public Management concept." *International Review of Administrative Sciences* 85(1): 28–44. https://doi.org/10.1177/0020852318773429.

Moulaert, Frank, Erik Swyngedouw, Flavia Martinelli, and Sara Gonzalez, eds. 2010. *Can Neighbourhoods Save the City?* London: Routledge.

OECD. 2020. "The territorial impact of COVID-19: Managing the crisis across levels of government." OECD Policy Responses to Coronavirus (COVID-19), *oecd.org*, November 10, 2021. https://www.oecd.org/coronavirus/policy-responses/the-territor ial-impact-of-covid-19-managing-the-crisis-across-levels-of-government-d3e314e1/

Orru, Kati, Kristi Nero, Tor-Olav Nævestad, Abriel Schieffelers, Alexandra Olson, Merja Airola, Austeja Kazemekaityte, et al. 2021. "Resilience in care organisations: Challenges in maintaining support for vulnerable people in Europe during the Covid-19 pandemic." *Disasters* 45 (S1): 48–75. https://doi.org/10.1111/disa.12526.

Marzec, Małgorzata. 2020. "Evaluation of the effectiveness of social economy entities during the coronavirus pandemic in Poland." *Hyperion International Journal of Econophysics and New Economy* 13 (1): 99–112.

Plümper, Thomas, and Eric Neumayer. 2020. "The pandemic predominantly hits poor neighbourhoods? SARS-CoV-2 infections and COVID-19 fatalities in German districts." *European Journal of Public Health* 30 (6): 1176–80. https://doi.org/10.1093/eurpub/ckaa168.

Rajca, Lucyna. 2020. "Reforms and centralization trends in Hungary and in Poland in a comparative perspective." *Przegląd Sejmowy* 5: 133–51. https://doi.org/10.31268/PS.2020.69.

Ranci, Costanzo, ed. 2010. *Social Vulnerability in Europe*. Basingstoke: Palgrave Macmillan.

Rodden, Jonathan. 2006. *Hamilton's Paradox: The Promise and Peril of Fiscal Federalism.* Cambridge; New York: Cambridge University Press.

Rodríguez-Pose, Andrés. 2018. "The revenge of the places that don't matter (and what to do about it)." *Cambridge Journal of Regions, Economy and Society* 11 (1): 189–209. https://doi.org/10.1093/cjres/rsx024.

Rodríguez-Pose, Andrés, and Chiara Burlina. 2021. "Institutions and the uneven geography of the first wave of the COVID-19 pandemic." *Journal of Regional Science* 61 (4): 728–52. https://doi.org/10.1111/jors.12541.

Singer, Merrill, Nicola Bulled, Bayla Ostrach, and Emily Mendenhall. 2017. "Syndemics and the biosocial conception of health." *Lancet* 389 (10072): 941–50.

Sześciło, Dawid. 2019. "Is there a room for local and regional self-government in the illiberal democracy?" *Studia Iuridica* 79: 176–79

Somerville, Peter, and Nathan Haines. 2008. "Prospects for local co-governance." *Local Government Studies* 34 (1): 61–79. https://doi.org/10.1080/03003930701770488.

Streeck, Wolfgang, and Kathleen Thelen, eds. 2005. *Beyond Continuity: Institutional Change in Advanced Political Economies*. Oxford: Oxford University Press.

Stubbs, Paul, and Noémi Lendvai-Bainton. 2020. "Authoritarian neoliberalism, radical conservatism and social policy within the European Union." *Croatia, Hungary and Poland, Development and Change* 51(2): 540–60.

Swyngedouw, Erik. 2009. "Civil Society, Governmentality and the Contradictions of Governance-Beyond-The-State: The Janus-face of Social Innovation." In *Social Innovation and Territorial Development*, edited by Diana MacCallum, Frank Moulaert, Jean Hillier, and Serena Vicari Haddock, 63–78. Ashgate: Farnham.

Turala, Maciej. 2020. "Subsidiarity, fiscal decentralisation and financial autonomy of local and regional governments in Poland." *Studia Prawno-ekonomiczne*, CXVII: 335–55. https://doi.org/10.26485/SPE/2020/117/18

Ursin, Gøril, Ingunn Skjesol, and Jonathan Tritter. 2020. "The COVID-19 pandemic in Norway." *Health Policy and Technology* 9 (4): 663–72. https://doi.org/10.1016/j.hlpt.2020.08.004.

Vampa, Davide. 2021. "COVID-19 and territorial policy dynamics in Western Europe: comparing France, Spain, Italy, Germany, and the United Kingdom." *Publius: The Journal of Federalism* 51 (4): 601–26. https://doi.org/10.1093/publius/pjab017.

van Berkel, Rik, Willibrord de Graaf, and Tomáš Sirovátka. 2011. *The Governance of Active Welfare States in Europe*. Basingstoke: Palgrave Macmillan.

Woolford, Jayne L. 2021. *Territorial impact and responses to COVID-19 in lagging regions. The Coronavirus Response Investment Initiative (CRII) and Cohesion Policy related responses*. JRC Science for Policy Report, European Commission, https://doi.org/10.2760/000780.

4

The United Kingdom in Search of a New "Imagined Community"?

Social Cohesion, Boundary Building, and Social Policy in Crisis Periods

Matthew Donoghue

Introduction

The welfare state originated as a project of nation states, with roots in the 19th and early 20th centuries. Advances in social policy were often related to processes of nation building, like the introduction of social insurance by Bismarck (1883–1889) that followed German unification (1871). Critical periods in a country's history that went along with a renewal of the national spirit also propelled social reform, like the New Deal during the Great Depression in the 1930s and the creation of the British "welfare state" in the immediate aftermath of the Second World War (Leisering 2003, 175).

The United Kingdom is facing a critical period in its history, in which its territorial integrity and nationhood is under significant pressure. Since the financial crisis of 2008, it can be argued, the country has been engaged in a prolonged period of crisis response—first dealing with the financial crisis and its fallout; second, instigating a debate on, and subsequently withdrawing from, European Union (EU) membership, thus creating a range of economic, social, and political crises that vary in size and scope; and third, managing the COVID-19 pandemic and the associated significant social and economic problems it brought to the fore.

Addressing these crises is dependent on developing and implementing appropriate social and public policies that not only deal with the immediate crisis (be it Brexit or COVID in the current period) but crucially, any knock-on effects. This is made more difficult by the evident fractures in

Matthew Donoghue, *The United Kingdom in Search of a New "Imagined Community"?* In: *European Social Policy and the COVID-19 Pandemic.* Edited by: Stefanie Börner and Martin Seeleib-Kaiser, Oxford University Press.
© Oxford University Press 2023. DOI: 10.1093/oso/9780197676189.003.0004

society driven, as Scambler (2020) argues, by the inequalities and power imbalances inherent in contemporary financial capitalism. Ironically, events such as Brexit can be argued to have been driven by such fracturing and now necessitate—or legitimize—a shift in focus away from addressing these long-term imbalances to focus instead on shorter-term political problems. The UK, entering a new historical era, must work to address—or suppress—these divisions.

This chapter considers how the framing of the United Kingdom's social policy response to the COVID pandemic has been used to rejuvenate the British "imagined community," contextualized by its new position as an "independent" nation state outside of the European Union. It argues that the COVID pandemic presents the government with an opportunity to renew and bolster a sense of nation, not only in terms of the United Kingdom reasserting its position in the international order but also in terms of reasserting what it means to be a British citizen in the post-Brexit era, and in a "union state" in which multiple nations within the state have varying levels of autonomy, and integration is "less than perfect" (Mitchell 1996, 608). It also considers how elements of public health, labor, and economic policy, developed in the context of both Brexit and COVID, are framed, legitimized, and facilitated by the rejuvenation of the imagined community. It draws upon in-depth qualitative analysis of policy literature and speeches focused on (public) health policy and social security policy during the pandemic—analyzed through a theoretical framework that highlights the role of social cohesion and, to a lesser extent, nation-building strategies—to understand how the UK policy response to COVID contributes to social cohesion within and across the nations of the United Kingdom.

There are many ways a government can bring people together and strengthen a nation. However, social policy responses provide an ideal prism through which to consider social cohesion and nation in the context of crisis. First, social policy and the welfare state in general are underpinned by practices of solidarity. Generally, these are structured and upheld by norms of citizenship and membership of a polity. All welfare states, regardless of those with a strong or weak sense of social citizenship, must, at some level, have public buy-in; and even in liberal states such as the United Kingdom, this includes a sense of duty to the less fortunate. Second, there is a well-established literature that demonstrates the role of social policy and welfare politics in developing and maintaining territorial solidarity and cohesion (Rokkan and Urwin 1982; McEwen and Moreno 2005; Ferrera 2005), as well as growing literature on the role of social policy as a nation-building tool, especially for subnational units (e.g., Béland and Lecours 2008).

The chapter begins by considering the context of the imagined community, alongside the idea of "imagined solidarities," that fuses welfare politics with Anderson's landmark work. This outlines the importance of understanding the relationship between the pandemic response, social policy, and the rhetoric of cohesion and the nation. Next, the methodological approach taken in the chapter is outlined. The following sections provide the empirical evidence and analysis of the UK pandemic response and the role of social policy in promoting a specific form of social cohesion focused on territorial integrity and promoting the United Kingdom over the constituent nations. Finally, the chapter concludes.

Imagined Communities and Imagined Solidarities

The boundaries of the British state and nation are being challenged by Scottish agitations for independence, growing instability in Northern Ireland, the "north–south divide" within England, and spatial inequality in general, exacerbated significantly by the Brexit process and by the COVID pandemic. In a multinational state such as the United Kingdom, the idea of the "imagined community" is particularly stark: "Britishness" is contingent and unstable as a cultural and political identifier, the connotations of which have become increasingly more polarized over recent years. Anderson's (1991) concept of imagined communities asserts that nations, by necessity, must be social constructions: "the members of even the smallest nation will never know most of their fellow-members, meet them, or hear of them yet in the mind of each lives the image of their communion" (Anderson 1991, 6). Central to this is the construction of a "we"—a shared identity united by membership and articulated by the products of that membership. This "we" has become significantly fragmented due to deep inequalities and events such as Brexit, becoming further entrenched by the COVID pandemic and the UK state's response to it.

Yet somewhat ironically, the state's response to the pandemic, via its social policy response and the communication of this response, provides an opportunity (however slim) for the UK to re-imagine the community. Alongside generating and entrenching division, crises can galvanize populations especially when crises represent an existential threat to a way of life. COVID is exemplary of this and, either through a sense of fear or a sense of solidarity, encourages people and communities to come together. This is something that clearly has been identified and utilized by the UK government, not only in its messaging throughout the pandemic but also in its social policy responses.

There are important differences in terms of policy possibilities with the COVID crisis and the crises associated with Brexit and the Great Recession. The most prominent of these is that the nature of the COVID crisis means that the usual constructed rules and norms on acceptable state spending and state intervention, embedded during the latest phase of neoliberalism post-2010, do not hold—even if this turns out to be temporary. Vast public spending projects are not questioned, while emergency state intervention in multiple facets of public and private life is readily accepted in the name of the greater good. Yet, hanging over this is a tacit commitment to return to pre-pandemic fiscal politics. As stated in Budget 2021, "it will be necessary to take steps to get the public finances back on track once the economic recovery is durably underway" (HM Treasury 2021a, 3). This does not diminish the power of crisis as a path-breaking moment. It is open to discussion what "back on track" signifies: a new economic orthodoxy with more balance between borrowing, spending, and saving, or a return to austerity. In a crisis, opposing positions and outcomes can be entertained simultaneously because there is unlikely to be a clear consensus on what action is needed, or the depth and longevity required.

Daniel Wincott (2020) develops Anderson's work on imagined communities to consider the concept of imagined solidarities in the United Kingdom. Focusing on the privileged position of the National Health Service (NHS), he argues that it is "a shared national symbol: by 2012 it was firmly established as the vessel, *par excellence,* of imagined community in and across the United Kingdom. As a symbol and an imagined embodiment of values, the NHS became available to a diverse range of political projects" (Wincott 2020, 8–9). Wincott et al. (2021, 2) argue that Brexit was influenced by a "distinctly English version of the UK," "rooted in an *Anglo-British imaginary.*" Brexit has also thrown into serious question the future territorial integrity of the United Kingdom.

After Brexit, across Great Britain and Northern Ireland, the ambiguities, structures, and practices of the territorial constitution have become the stuff of intense contestation and conflict. Its future remains unsettled: the United Kingdom might break up, recentralize, or be reconstructed as a devolved or multilevel state. It is, though, hard to see how it could retain its current form (Wincott et al. 2021, 2).

It is this context in which the UK government (and indeed the devolved governments) develops its political and policy response to COVID. Crises present challenges and opportunities, especially to political actors. Policymaking itself has increasingly been characterized by "crisis" (Peck and Theodore 2015, 14–26). While it is certainly true that the government has had to respond quickly to the COVID crisis, often with unreliable information (either due to insufficient or volatile data), its social and economic response has also been characterized by preceding crises such as the 2008 financial crisis and Great Recession and the harsh austerity measures that followed, and now the multifaceted crises generated by the (post-) Brexit process, which are economic, social, political, and constitutional in nature.

Some crises quickly lock in actions, such as the lock-in effects of the financial crisis on economic and social austerity policy. Yet these lock-in effects do not appear out of nowhere; the ostensible choices on offer to policymakers are restricted by previous actions and context. Austerity measures in those European countries that faced sovereign debt crises was mandated, and support was made conditional on implementing such measures. States in the Global South have in many cases only been able to avail of economic support and investment after economic restructuring and trade liberalization. In the UK case, austerity was only one potential response among many to the economic shock felt in the City of London. Yet the government chose to shift much economic burden onto ordinary citizens in order to stabilize financial markets (e.g., Glynos et al. 2012; Stanley 2014; Ferragina and Zola 2021). The decision to pursue austerity has profoundly affected the United Kingdom, especially in the context of the COVID pandemic, including social policy (Lupton et al. 2016; Farnsworth and Irving 2015) and inequality, especially health (Bambra et al. 2020; Keys et al. 2021) and regional (Tubadji et al. 2020; Bhattacharjee et al. 2020) inequalities.

The response of "personalizing" the financial crisis was successful because it could be framed as an endogenous crisis, one of our own making (Stanley 2014; Glynos et al. 2012). By contrast, the COVID pandemic is quintessentially *exogeneous* from a policy and health response perspective.[1] This creates many opportunities, as it is the type of crisis during which

---

[1] I remark that it is exogenous from a policy and health perspective, and not necessarily exogeneous in itself, because of the impact that developments such as climate change and the birth of the Anthropocene have on the ability of pandemics to spread (Hulme et al. 2020).

rules and conventions can be put on hold. The exemplar of this is the speed at which states worldwide abandoned principles of "cost containment" and surplus operation to fund "emergency" rescue packages for businesses and individuals (Ferragina and Zola 2021). Notwithstanding many finance ministers' indications that once the pandemic is over there will be a return to a more or less austere economic and social policy regime, it is still notable that the nature of the crisis enabled governments to ignore their own (largely socially constructed) rules around economic and social governance.

The implication is that the UK government has an opportunity to use the COVID pandemic and the state's response to it to build cohesion around a renewed or reinvigorated (yet still *imagined*) sense of Britishness. A central question however is does this imagined community remain "Anglo-British," or does it work to incorporate the other nations of the United Kingdom in a bid to stabilize and reinforce the territorial integrity of the United Kingdom? The Brexit process was as much about presenting a new Britain/United Kingdom to the population as it was the technical act of leaving the EU. Given the clear divide on EU membership in the United Kingdom, especially from the nations (England and Wales voted to leave, while Northern Ireland and Scotland and voted to remain), it was in the UK government's interest to emphasize crisis management. Wincott et al. (2021, 12) demonstrate that during the negotiations, the government downplayed the level of autonomy the devolved nations received thanks to the EU, instead emphasizing the binding effect of EU law, restricting autonomy for all nations in the United Kingdom. Furthermore, the complexities of devolution make the repatriation of powers to the United Kingdom difficult. There is a question about whether powers would need to be centralized first, then devolved, which increases the power of Westminster. At the same time, emphasizing the binding nature of EU law provides an opportunity for Westminster to argue that Brexit is ultimately in the interests of all nations in the United Kingdom.

The United Kingdom, despite its arguably "core" position in the EU, has tended to be peripheral to Europe not just geographically but politically. Once a "great power," the United Kingdom has retained a commitment to unilateralism, or at least a "first among equals" approach to politics and policy, as this chapter will demonstrate. This British exceptionalism has had a significant influence on policymaking, in which domestic policymaking is either perceived as insulated from international pressures or is developed with a sense that what is good for the United Kingdom will also benefit its neighbors. This is not necessarily vastly different from some of the larger European nations, except its biggest comparators remain in the EU and have indeed been politically committed to the European project since its beginnings. This has an effect on the construction of discourse in these countries and the implications for domestic as well as international policymaking. Seeing itself as a voluntary outsider, the United Kingdom has not felt encumbered by other nations. This is another reason that UK policymaking in crisis periods is such an important case study, and demonstrates the importance of understanding how the response to crises is framed and promoted in terms of the general population and the nations of the United Kingdom—especially Scotland, given its current position in the union.

Methodology

Data was collected from public announcements—the regular televised government COVID briefings,[2] statements in the House of Commons, press releases, and newspaper articles—from Prime Minister Boris Johnson, the then–Secretary of Health Matt Hancock, and Chancellor of the Exchequer Rishi Sunak. Data was also collected from key policy documents from the Department of Health and the Treasury. These actors and departments were chosen because of their centrality to the state's response to the pandemic. Johnson, Hancock, and Sunak have been the primary public face of the *political and policy* response to the pandemic.[3] It has been their job to communicate policy decisions and to "sell" them to the public. In some cases this has been purely to the English public, given the level of social policy devolution to Scotland and Northern Ireland, and to a lesser extent Wales, but in many cases it has been to the United Kingdom as a whole. Even in those cases where the devolved nations had autonomy, it was (and remains) important for Westminster to appear "in control" of the situation or to sell an ethos to a *United* Kingdom, even if concrete policy decisions ultimately differ.

---

[2] At the beginning of the pandemic, these briefings were daily. As the pandemic developed, the regularity of the televised briefings changed in line with the severity of different waves, the status of national and local lockdowns, and the prominence of particular developments of interest to the public, such as vaccines.

[3] This is in contrast to the *public health* response, led by Prof. Chris Whitty, Prof. Patrick Vallance, Prof. Jonathan Van Tam, etc. This is a largely arbitrary division between political and non-political, considering the burgeoning work on the politics of expertise, and the politics of the public health response itself (e.g., Hulme et al. 2020). However, given the focus of this chapter on the relationship between policy and imagined communities, it is an appropriate distinction to define the boundaries of the study.

The data collected spans from the beginning of the pandemic in February 2020 to January–February 2021, when the United Kingdom was emerging from its second wave. This period was chosen as it represents the period in which the UK state was on its most reactive footing. The period from January 2021 onward was epitomized by the roll-out of the various COVID-19 vaccines, which enabled the state (and the devolved administrations) to develop new policy and public health strategies to address the pandemic. The initial phase of the pandemic and the UK response came at a time when the United Kingdom was deeply embroiled in fairly hostile negotiations with the EU (in rhetoric, if not in practice) over the Northern Ireland Protocol. This was also the "crisis response" phase, in which policy had to be made quickly, without precedent, and while attempting to not compromise on other policy priorities and to maintain a strong position in negotiations with the EU. At the time of writing, the United Kingdom is entering a different phase of the COVID response in which policy could be designed with the longer term in mind. This is a limitation of the current study, given that longer-term policy planning will likely include a more considered and calculated approach to nation building and the building of imagined community. Nevertheless, it is important to understand how the United Kingdom's sense of itself and its projected political and social future was represented in, and perhaps influenced, policy. Further research will capture developments in the later phases of the pandemic response and compare them to the initial crisis-response phase.

Data was organized and coded using NVivo 12. This ensured that data was treated systematically, following a consistent coding process, and allowed for a large amount of qualitative data to be produced, handled, and analyzed. Nevertheless, coding was conducted manually via the software, and abductively; initial coding involved a set of codes generated deductively from scholarly literature, news sources, and general context. This code list was then refined inductively, allowing a select number of codes to emerge from a close reading of the raw data.

The data was subjected to a combination of content analysis and thematic analysis. Vaismoradi and Turunen (2013) argue that notwithstanding the many similarities—identification of patterns and themes, providing cross-sections of data—the main difference is that content analysis allows for "quantification" of qualitative data. This chapter does not embark on a quantification of data; it does not engage in "keyword counting" or similar. Rather, a combination of the two methods allows the analysis to not only highlight core themes and relationships in the data pertaining to building cohesion and the imagined community of the British nation, but also to highlight salient ideas worthy of deeper consideration by virtue of their prominence in the data.

Table 4.1 shows the most prevalent codes in the data. However, this cannot speak to the prominence of the codes. It is possible that not-very-prevalent codes carry significant importance.

Table 4.1 Major Codes with Description and Number of References

Code	Description	References
"National effort"	Explicit or implicit references to making a national effort (e.g., use of a phrase or phrases that invoke a sense of nation and (common) endeavor.	95
British(ness)	Words, phrases, or passages that talk about the British, British traits, or carry connotations of "Britishness."	75
Solidarity and cooperation	References to working together, particularly when invoking sense of solidarity (national or otherwise) or community level.	65
NHS plus institutions	References to the NHS primarily, but also to public institutions, especially when relevant to COVID or Brexit.	64
"War" language	Linguistic references that make use of tropes related to war (e.g., fighting a common enemy, vanquishing the virus, "frontlines"), military operations, or wartime civilian conduct.	58
Responsibility	References to the need to take responsibility, identifying loci of responsibility, particularly regarding public health.	54
National pride	Reference to being proud of the nation. Britain/ UK, etc., or implicit references that have connotations of pride.	37
Devolved nations	Direct references to the devolved nations.	27
Hero(es)	Invocation of heroism or labeling heroic.	26
Border(ing)	Invocation or discussion of physical or metaphorical borders; using rhetoric to draw borders, especially between "British" and non-British.	24
We and us	Invocation of a collective "we" that is otherwise not defined (e.g., as British, etc.).	20
Community	References to "community"—be that local neighborhoods or international.	16

These codes share similarities. For example, an intuitive link can be made between *collective memory, we/us, national pride,* and *Britishness.* Yet the codes are also discrete and contain unique elements. So although they present differently, they interact and combine to strengthen particular tropes, emphasize some rhetoric over others, and frame issues in particular ways. This all contributes to the presentation of a specific imagined community. Also, given the focus of the subject matter, it is not surprising that codes focused on the nation and on cooperation, national or otherwise important institutions are most prominent. It is what is said within these codes that is significant.

Codes were then organized into overarching themes. Each theme connected a group of codes, providing an opportunity to analyze their interrelation and the implications of these connections. Given the overlaps between codes in terms of their content and their potential for alternative interpretation, Figure 4.1 represents an organization of themes that makes sense in the context of the overarching question of the chapter.

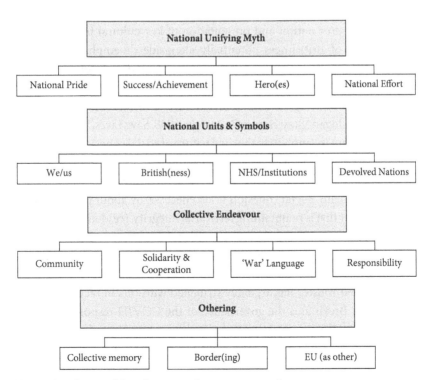

Figure 4.1 Overarching themes and component codes.

It is feasible, therefore, that organizing these codes differently may give rise to different themes. The organization was driven by central questions and the theoretical framework employed in the analysis, which privileges and makes sense of social cohesion building and to a lesser extent nation building.

The "thematic content" analysis was structured through a theoretical framework that draws upon Scheifer and Van der Noll's (2017) review of the state of the art of social cohesion. Scheifer and Van der Noll's starting point is to address the prominent issue of a lack of consensus in the social cohesion literature. Through an in-depth engagement with the literature, they identify three "constitutive elements" of social cohesion: social relations, identification with the social entity, and orientation toward the common good (Scheifer and Van der Noll 2017, 595). During the coding process and the re-reading of the data, components of these elements were highlighted. For example, under the umbrella of *social relations* one could expect to find allusions to or explicit discussion of social networks, trust, acceptance (or otherwise) of diversity, participation, and relations between nations. For *identification with the social entity* in the context of this study one would expect to see mentions of the state and/or nation and presentation of key cultural institutions, an enhancement of Britishness potentially alongside de-emphasizing or selectively contextualizing the constituent nations. Under *orientation toward the common good* one may expect invocations of a common enemy against which "all" can rally against, or exhortations to protect sacred institutions, such as in the slogan "Stay Home, *Protect the NHS*, Save Lives."

It is important to emphasize the dual nature of social cohesion. On the one hand it is about creating a common bond across a social and political unit, in which there is cooperation, solidarity, and (some) acceptance of difference. On the other hand, social cohesion is also necessarily about power maintenance, whether that is maintaining territorial integrity, (re)defining who may and may not become a member of the national "club." A crucial task for social cohesion in the United Kingdom is maintaining "the ties that bind." Yet, as argued earlier, "Britishness" has always largely been Anglo-Britishness. Although Westminster has arguably struggled with this in recent years, especially with Brexit and the governance of the COVID response, England remains core to Britain, while Scotland, Wales, and Northern Ireland remain in the periphery (e.g., Findlay et al. 2002; Steed 1986; Smout 1980). The following sections explore these elements in the context of the UK government's framing of its policy response to COVID.

(Re)Building the National Myth

In terms of social cohesion, a national myth provides a rallying point that is unaffected by circumstance. It facilitates identification with a/the social entity, which in itself could help define the "common good" toward which communities (imagined or otherwise) may orientate. All nations have their creation myths and stories, either from ancient times or from the birth of the modern nation.

The United Kingdom is not in the process of creating a "new" nation. In this sense the government is not embarking on a process of nation building in the traditional sense. Rather, it draws upon well-embedded tropes and imagery in order to (re)construct particular narratives of what it means to be British and a part of the United Kingdom.

Throughout the briefings a clear message was adhered to, involving the need to act as a nation. Equally important was the reason for the nation to come together. In the briefings this was partly to protect vulnerable citizens, but especially to protect health care workers. These actors were afforded a kind of "hero" status at the same time as being labeled as needing protection; this is somewhat of a paradox, given that traditionally heroes protect the vulnerable and are not usually vulnerable themselves.

> Central to this work is the retention of those staff who have returned to help the NHS in our hour of need. I would like to take this opportunity to pay tribute and say thank you to the thousands of healthcare students, and former NHS staff who have played their part in helping the NHS tackle COVID-19. For some this has meant learning new skills or working in a different speciality—each individual will have had different experiences—but each has a place in the NHS if they want to remain and HEE will have an important job in equipping them to do so. (DHSC 2020)

The above extract places returning and trainee health care workers as exemplars of a national effort. Their actions are painted as a sacrifice. Here, health care workers are not vulnerable, but are instead helping *protect* the NHS, itself framed as vulnerable. On the other hand, this is less about a heroic national effort, given that the document itself is essentially focused on labor policy and employee retention. Historic staff shortages in the NHS require innovative solutions, such as accelerating training programs, recruiting retirees, and so on. The COVID-19 pandemic provided the context to legitimize action that would have not been possible in normal times.

The role of health care workers as prominent and upstanding members of the nation was also deployed to emphasize the perceived importance of maintaining the United Kingdom. Again, a practical consideration was framed in such a way as to highlight potential (if implied) deficiencies that needed neighborly support to address:

> I want to extend thanks also to our ambulance service workers and in particular I want to thank ambulance service staff who stepped up over the weekend when an appeal went out from the Scottish ambulance service for extra help and ambulance services from the other nations stepped forward. (Health Secretary Statement on Coronavirus, January 25, 2021)

The implicit message here, quite clearly, is that the nations of the United Kingdom must work together in times of crisis. However, it may imply something potentially more damaging. Scotland in recent years has edged closer toward independence from the United Kingdom, itself using social policy as a technique of nation building, articulating differences between Scotland and England (Mooney and Williams, 2006). The focus on Scotland needing to appeal to the other UK nations carries the implication that it cannot resource its own health care system without help from the rest of the United Kingdom. Although this is in the context of a crisis, and as such may not happen in normal times, it nevertheless paints the Scottish NHS as in a precarious position and in need of support if there are surges in need.

The careful framing of the originally daily coronavirus briefings was designed on the one hand to inform the public about developments with the virus and how the government was responding. However, as this chapter will make clear, the briefings were also used to "showcase" the United Kingdom, primarily to those within the country but also further afield. The United Kingdom is known for its "theatrical" political style (e.g. Te Velde 2019), which facilitates promotion. In the post-Brexit context, in which the United Kingdom must forge new relationships and find its place in the international order, the state must first promote the United Kingdom, but must also reassure the populace of the geopolitical importance of the UK:

> And of course, while this is a national effort to find these treatments, it's also an international effort. In the same way that we have donated more money

to the global search for a vaccine than any other country, so too we will lead the world in this science of treatments and whatever we learn, we will share, because we are all on the same side in this war. (Health Secretary Statement on Coronavirus, April 3, 2020)

The thrust of this extract is to place in parity the national and international effort; one is of little use without the other. This signals that the United Kingdom is outward looking, encapsulating the slogan of "global Britain." Yet this imagery of international player or collaborator soon morphs into international leader. The United Kingdom has donated more money, leads the world in treatments, and the like. Finally, the international leader is pitched as benevolent, returning to the imagery of collaboration, in sharing "whatever we learn."

It is clear that this national effort is led by talismanic figures in health, but also from the corporate world:

Many businesses have generously come forward with offers to turn over their production lines as part of this national effort. In particular, I want to thank Burberry, with their offers of gowns; Rolls-Royce and McLaren, who are creating visors; Ineos and Diageo, who are producing hand sanitizer. We're talking to many others and we want more to step up to the plate. (Health Secretary Statement on Coronavirus, April 10, 2020)

The businesses the health secretary chose to mention here are important, as they are quintessentially British. It implicitly highlights a supposed innovation but also an independence from reliance on other states. These are not companies who manufacture the required products. Indeed, as was well publicized at the time, the equipment and PPE procurement process was significantly flawed (e.g., McKee 2021). Again, this is an advertisement for "Global Britain" dressed up as a response to a health crisis. The social policy implications of this bolster the *nation* but weaken the role of the *state*. It is a social policy framework that prioritizes private actors and interests, while government agencies scramble to fill vacancies in the NHS, as highlighted earlier.

Part of this response, then, is to demonstrate a strong and dynamic social entity that a population can rally round, especially in a crisis. It attempts to demonstrate an "all in the same boat" mentality that is important to building social cohesion. Another core element of this is emphasizing national symbols.

National Symbols for All?

National symbols can be built through the construction of national myths, or they can support those myths. They can also act as a shorthand for particular values that the nation upholds, which tend to be required for membership of the polity. These national symbols also provide visual representations for the social entity, shared values and common goals toward which a polity and society should orient themselves.

Unsurprisingly, the most prominent national symbol deployed was the NHS. As Wincott (2020) has demonstrated, the NHS occupies a privileged position in the UK national imaginary, often referred to by politicians as "our NHS." It is deployed variously, to encourage personal responsibility, to ask for sacrifices, as well as to highlight perceived unique strengths of the United Kingdom:

> The single most important economic policy in the short term is rolling out the vaccine as quickly as possible, where thanks to *our extraordinary NHS*, we have already vaccinated over 20 million people across the UK. But as restrictions ease we need to look ahead to the future sources of jobs and growth. Now that we have left the EU we have the opportunity to forge a new path as a fully sovereign trading nation, doing things differently, more nimbly and better. (HM Treasury 2021b, 8; emphasis added)

This passage from HM Treasury's *Build Back Better: Our Plan for Growth* highlights the government's thinking in terms of the timeline on which it has placed itself: moving from the Brexit process, through the pandemic, and into the post-Brexit, post-COVID era. Although not a revelation, passages such as this highlight that the vaccination program can just as much be seen as an economic and/or labor policy as a public health policy. The public is understandably worried about jobs and growth, thanks to the immediate impact of the pandemic, but this has also been a well-publicized impact of the Brexit process. The COVID pandemic allows the partial sanitization of the negative political and economic effects of the UK withdrawal from the EU, leaving only the positive story of a sovereign trading nation, doing things "differently, more nimbly and better."

It is important to consider the presentation of the NHS as a national symbol to "all" against the policy realities. Tensions between the impacts of Brexit and the pandemic are evident, especially with regard to ensuring adequate labor supply. The message from public statements was one of collective sacrifice, solidarity, and diversity, acknowledging the contribution of economic migrants to the United Kingdom:

> I am awed by the dedication of my colleagues on the frontline—every single person who contributes to the running of this *diverse and caring institution* that our nation holds so dear. These were people who *came to this country to make a difference*. And they did. And they have given their lives in service, in sacrifice. We salute you. (Health Secretary Statement on Coronavirus, 2nd April 2020—emphasis added)

The contribution of migrants is the clear focus, although implicitly it is a focus on the "right kind" of migrant: one who, in the public eye, contributes positively to the economy and society.[4] This invokes a subtle process of bordering and othering, in which migrants are required to demonstrate a much higher level of deserving or virtuousness to integrate into British society. It follows Wingard's (2012) use of the "other" and "other-other" in a process of neoliberal nation building: the other is an outsider who is nevertheless redeemable, while the other-other has no hope of integrating and is thus kept outside the borders for the good of both the migrant and the nation. This idea of good and bad "others" can also be seen in NHS recruiting strategy in the post-Brexit and post-COVID context:

> We remain committed to delivering 50,000 more nurses in the NHS, but clearly the context for the delivery of that commitment has changed. While we will continue to welcome overseas staff as an invaluable part of the NHS team, the pandemic poses extra challenges for the recruitment of staff from overseas and justifies an even greater focus on enlarging our home grown workforce. (DHSC 2020, np)

The Department of Health and Social Care's mandate to Health Education England provides an interesting case study of how policy may react to public discourse, or vice versa. The mandate focuses on the challenges posed by COVID on recruitment of international staff, thus justifying a more

---

[4] This is a common trope, especially in UK social policy discourse, concerned with whether migrants are net contributors or beneficiaries of various supports available in the UK. There is not time to discuss this in this chapter.

intensive domestic labor recruitment and training strategy. Yet, it is well known that prior to the pandemic, and still today, Brexit has had a huge effect on NHS recruitment (BMJ 2017; McHale et al. 2020). Furthermore, the legacy of Theresa May's "hostile environment" and the aggressive anti-migrant rhetoric of Home Secretaries Priti Patel and now Suella Braverman should not be underestimated. This was compounded by the comments of the (until July 2021) heir apparent chief of the NHS, Dido Harding, who caused controversy after remarks that the NHS should become "less reliant on foreigners"—a challenge, given that at least 14% of the NHS workforce have a nationality other than British (McKay 2021; see also Faragher 2021; Hinsliff 2021; Pogrund 2021).

The COVID pandemic has been used to launch a rallying call in defense of the most emotive and evocative national symbol in the modern United Kingdom. Yet, despite the prominent framing in public statements of commitment to diversity and solidarity, the policy underpinning the NHS tends toward more nativist labor strategies, in line with domestic policy developments in the wake of Brexit. Furthermore, the overriding message from the "Build Back Better" strategy and Budget is the imperative to maintain UK territorial integrity. Given the difficulty of rolling back existing devolution, this is likely to involve consolidation of economic and political competences where possible post-Brexit, alongside the warnings that the constituent nations cannot "go it alone" when it comes to developing and financing their own social and economic programs. The COVID pandemic has proved useful in this respect, facilitating these developments as a response to the pandemic and the need to remain united.

Collective Endeavor

This chapter so far has emphasized the importance of forms of solidarity and collective action, whether this is in service to a core social entity, to uphold particular values, or to strive toward a common good. These activities are core to social cohesion building. Imagery around collective endeavor can be deployed in terms of carrot *and* stick: a positive sense of groups and individuals coming together to work for the common good on one hand, or admonishment of those slow to answer the call or who may refuse.

Another key element of building social cohesion is the premise of breaking down barriers. Although a clear (social) division of labor—which can be based upon various social groupings and divisions—is central to a socially cohesive unit such as a country so that every member knows their role, it can also help to break these barriers down. A crisis such as the COVID pandemic is the ideal opportunity in which to remove such barriers, at least figuratively:

> And it really inspires me, how people are helping in adversity. Like a grandson, helping their grandma to book an appointment online, or neighbours dropping off essentials on the doorstep, or the community groups that are getting together to help drive people to a vaccination centre so that people can get that all important jab. (Health Secretary Statement on Coronavirus, January 18, 2021)

The image here is of resourceful local communities, helping one another within and beyond the family unit. It is clearly evocative of the rhetoric of David Cameron's "Big Society" and of Conservative approaches to social welfare in general. It also plays into embedded tropes of the resourcefulness of the British people, something which Prime Minister Boris Johnson referred to often throughout the pandemic. The salient point is that just as "the virus does not discriminate," nor should the nation. All groups have their part to play, regardless of the scale.

However, there are clear, if implicit, divisions that are constructed through the government's messaging, especially on the relationship between employment and public health policy. Compare the two extracts below and the loci of responsibility in each:

> *It is your civic duty*, so you avoid unknowingly spreading the virus and you help to break the chain of transmission. This will be voluntary at first, because we trust everyone to do the right thing. But we can quickly make it mandatory if that's what it takes. (Health Secretary Statement on Coronavirus, May 27, 2020—emphasis added)
>
> And my message to employers is crystal clear. Please work with us to ease the transition back to a more normal way of life for shielding employees. *We expect you to do the right thing.* (Health Secretary Statement on Coronavirus, June 22, 2020—emphasis added)

For individuals, following public health guidance is *civic duty*, which can be enforced if compliance is not satisfactory. For businesses, compliance is *expected*. The former is essentially a legal threat, while the latter is a moral exhortation. There is little to no coercion implied in the latter extract. This encapsulates the Conservative government's self-imposed dilemma regarding trade-offs between public health and economic growth. Following the argument that social policy is subordinated to economic policy (e.g., Walker and Wong 2009), this is perhaps no surprise. However, alongside the first extract in this section, the message is that social support is something that should be decentralized to individuals where possible, either through concrete policy mechanisms or through "soft power" and "nudge" style initiatives. Again, the pandemic provides an opportunity to solidify such approaches through a (legitimate) need for all members of society (individuals, businesses, or other institutions) to "do their part."

This is reinforced through a link to national heroes or prominent national institutions, which can be imbued with desirable values and normative:

I want to start by thanking everyone who is staying at home, even in this sunshine. Together, we are slowing the spread of this virus. And I want to pay a special tribute today to Captain Tom Moore who, at the age of 99, has raised over £7 million so far for NHS charities by completing 100 laps of his garden. Captain Tom, you're an inspiration to us all and we thank you. (Health Secretary Statement on Coronavirus, April 12, 2020)

The elevation of a 99-year-old ex-military officer to the status of national institution plays a multifaceted role. Firstly, the military connection connotes service to the nation. In this case it is to raise money for the NHS. This reinforces the tropes of protection discussed earlier, but also reinforces a subtext of individual responsibility; if a 99-year-old man with mobility issues can raise so much money, what are others doing to help? The framing is one of "inspiration," that simultaneously responsibilizes others. Furthermore, it reinforces implicit assumptions around the financing and development of social policy from a Conservative standpoint, that is, largely hands-off and left to individuals and communities where possible (beyond the obvious need for the state to legislate for and regulate key institutions and actors associated with social policy). Again, this is wrapped in the context of a crisis necessitating everyone to work beyond usual expectations of citizens. The COVID pandemic facilitates a sense of necessity for individuals to struggle together to fund and support basic services, the impetus for which may not exist as prominently in "normal" times.

Additionally, one person's perceived sacrifice in service of the "greater good" serves to emphasize the detrimental effects of division, whether that is between classes, ethnicities, or nations. "Captain Tom" serves as an artefact for a sense of not just collective but *national* endeavor, while also lauding individual entrepreneurship and industriousness.

Just as membership means little without those denied membership, a social cohesion that includes all groups, all people, at all times would mean little in practice. Social cohesion in the context of the nation tends to require something to be cohesive against, as well as something to be cohesive for. For the United Kingdom in the current period the nation requires cohesion against COVID but also against the European "other" (see Donoghue and Kuisma 2021). It attempts to build cohesion for the "British" nation, through (among other things) policy that is expansive in terms of who it claims to include or represent, while remaining restrictive in terms of funding but also eligibility and deservingness.

Defining Members and Others

As Joppke (2008, 533; see also Nassehi and Schroer 1999, 83) highlights, modern citizenship has been marked by a tension between "universal inclusion and particularistic exclusion." One the one hand, the rise of modern citizenship thrives on the idea of shared humanity and of universal human rights, as developed by the European Enlightenment. On the other hand, such universalism had to be reconciled with the particularism of states, without which the promise of "liberty, equality, solidarity" could never be a reality.

Social cohesion is, in essence, a representation of the universalistic element of citizenship. Every member is to be included and has a role to play, and these roles contribute to the health of the polity, nation, and state. In order to have a cohesive entity, it needs boundaries that distinguish it from the "other" (different nations and values are two examples; even where programs of social cohesion laud diversity of values, they are set within certain tolerances).

The promotional nature of the coronavirus briefings especially enabled ministers to respond to a range of issues under the guise of the COVID crisis. These were framed by the implicit and explicit calls for unity and cooperation to fight the virus. It thus facilitated ministers to appear to address pressing issues, while using the crisis to suppress discussion. For example, around the time of the Black Lives Matter Protests, the then–health secretary used the briefings as an opportunity to address division and diversity, both society-wide and within the NHS:

> Black lives matter and I want to say this to everyone who works in the NHS and in social care. I value the contribution that you make, everybody equally. And I want to say it right across society too. I want to thank you and I want you to know that our whole country cares about your wellbeing. And I value too those who come to our country to work in the NHS and in social care. And I love that this country is one of the most welcoming and tolerant and diverse. That goes for the whole country and it goes especially for the health and social care system. (Health Secretary Statement on Coronavirus, June 2, 2020)

While the ostensible purpose of the COVID briefings was to share information about the response to the pandemic, they were also used to shore up social institutions against criticism, or to help rebuff criticisms of the government's stewardship of these institutions. This extract can be read in the light of previous discussions in this chapter on the tension between promoting diversity and the realities of employment policy in the NHS, and indeed labor policy in the UK post-Brexit. COVID has acted as a useful smokescreen for such reforms, given that a state of crisis allows for more executive-style decision-making, especially compared to a political decision upon which the country remains almost equally split.

Given that division of labor is core to social cohesion, one would expect to find tensions between or acknowledgments of multiple loci of responsibility within the entity. Regarding the public health response, the UK government employed such a strategy:

> Although we are tackling this virus as one United Kingdom, it remains the case that the devolved administrations are responsible for lockdown in Scotland, Wales and Northern Ireland. And it is right that they move at the right pace for them, according to their circumstances. (Prime Minister's Statement on Coronavirus, June 10, 2020)

This can be read in two ways. On the one hand it is a simple acknowledgment that the United Kingdom is a multinational state that is operating a multispeed public health response. On the other, it subtly highlights loci of responsibility for public health, helping Westminster shift some responsibility. It highlights the fractured nature of policymaking in the United Kingdom. Here, it is important to understand the other messages circulating from central government, especially the Treasury. As has been shown, a strong focus of the Treasury has been emphasizing the importance of the Union, especially for the devolved nations:

> Today's figures speak for themselves [...] As we continue to see throughout this pandemic, the strength of the Union and support offered by the UK Treasury has never been more important. (GOV.UK 2021)

The image presented by the briefings and by government policy is the necessity of unity. This is unity of the public to fight the virus, unity of the nations of the United Kingdom to work together, and a reminder of the "ties that bind." Contrasting this extract with the previous extract, the composite image is a union in which membership is technically voluntary, but presented as a practical necessity. Again, the pandemic has been used to bolster the message that everyone (nation or otherwise) needs to stick together.

Allowing the COVID crisis to be the prism for the negative, recent budgets have been able to present post-Brexit developments in a positive light, while also emphasizing the role of a united UK in a post-EU world:

> In repatriating the EU structural funds, the government has an historic opportunity to design a UK Shared Prosperity Fund to match domestic priorities. The UK Shared Prosperity Fund will replace the overly bureaucratic EU structural funds, levelling up opportunity in each of the four nations of the country. Funding will be realigned to match domestic priorities, not the EU's, with a focus on investing in people. (HM Treasury 2020, 49)

The extract is designed to promote an innovative, efficient United Kingdom in contrast to an overly burdensome and bureaucratic EU. This is significant given that the Shared Prosperity Fund would be a key economic support for many social policies. It promises "levelling up opportunity in each of the four nations," yet the Institute for Government asserts that it "risks further damaging trust between the UK and devolved administrations and undermining the UK government's objective of binding the four nations of the UK closer together" (Nice et al. 2021, 30). This supports the argument that a core aim of the UK government is to centralize power (economic, social, and political) where possible, while appearing committed to a more open and conciliatory method of securing the union. As Wincott demonstrates:

> In July 2020, the UK Government's Internal Market White Paper heralded the end of the Brexit transition/implementation period as bringing with it the 'single biggest transfer of powers to the devolved administrations in history', but one which is predicated on the UK being 'a unitary state' which would also see an expanded role for Whitehall in overseeing these new arrangements. (Wincott et al. 2021, 12; see also BEIS 2020, para 12; para 16)

This strategy can only be achieved if the United Kingdom can sell itself as an open, global actor that is committed to diversity and integration at home. As this chapter has demonstrated, references to this reimagined United Kingdom are peppered throughout the coronavirus statements and grey literature. The core takeaway is that the new United Kingdom remains at the forefront of the global order and in control of both its internal and external borders. It is at once global and national:

> We reject narrow nationalism. We support a global effort, because this virus respects no borders. And we are all on the same side. This morning I held a global conference call with other health leaders, including from Germany, Australia, Canada, Switzerland and the United States and others, to discuss the need for global licensing access for any successful vaccine. (Health Secretary Statement to Parliament, July 20, 2020—HC Deb. July 20, 2020)

Conclusions

This chapter has focused on Westminster's (presentation of its) response to the COVID pandemic and the implications for public and social policy in service of rebuilding the (Anglo-)British imagined community. The research was constrained in scope, but has provided a compelling foundation for further exploring the phenomena in this chapter. In particular, future research should focus on the policy pronouncements of the other nations of the United Kingdom, especially Scotland (e.g., Law and Mooney 2012), which can be compared to the UK-wide framing, drawing out tensions around the reconstruction of the imagined community.

As the saying goes, don't let a good crisis go to waste. The UK government has utilized the COVID crisis as a means of reasserting the territorial integrity of the United Kingdom and attempted to reinvigorate the imagined community. The COVID briefings in particular, but also important policy documents in the areas of health and finance, have been used as a platform to promote Britain to both its own citizens and to the wider world. They have also been used to reassert the "ties that bind" the United Kingdom, using a blend of the carrot and the stick: an acknowledgment and even embrace of devolution on the one hand, with sometimes subtle and sometimes not so subtle assertions of the constituent nations of the UK's need for one another.

This could be achieved partly because of the nature of the crisis, which elevated the importance of the social policy response (especially in health) and emphasized the social aspects of other policy areas. The importance of solidarity, whether implicit or explicit, lent itself to calls for unity and cooperation. This in turn provided an ideal platform to promote social policy. However, what can be seen is a tension between the solidaristic and cooperative rhetoric seen in much of the briefings and policy literature against a typical Conservative approach to welfare and social policy that continues to prioritize individual endeavor and a largely hands-off role for the state. This means that, notwithstanding the crucial role of the state during the pandemic, in the reimagined community of the United Kingdom a reimagined approach to social policy seems unlikely. The ultimate conclusion, then, is that the COVID briefings in particular can be seen largely as a coordinated PR exercise for the Conservative government in the United Kingdom, attempting to rebrand "Global Britain" and reinforce the territorial integrity of the Union, legitimized via prominent elements of the social policy response to the pandemic.

Bibliography

Anderson, Benedict. 1991. *Imagined Communities: Reflections on the Origin and Spread of Nationalism*. London: Verso.

Bambra, Clare, Ryan Riordan, John Ford, and Fiona Matthews. 2020. "The COVID-19 pandemic and health inequalities." *Journal of Epidemiology and Community Health* 74 (11): 964–68. https://doi.org/10.1136/jech-2020-214401

BEIS (Department for Business, Energy and Industrial Strategy). 2020. UK Internal Market (CP 278). Available at: https://assets.publishing.service.gov.uk/government/uploads/system/uploads/attachment_data/file/901225/uk-internal-market-white-paper.pdf (accessed 28/02/2023)

Béland, Daniel, and André Lecours. 2008. *Nationalism and Social Policy: The Politics of Territorial Solidarity*. Oxford: Oxford University Press.

Bhattacharjee, Arnab, David Nguyen, and Tony Venables. 2020. "The prospects for regional disparities in the UK in times of Brexit and Covid-19." *National Institute Economic Review* 253: R1–R3.

DHSC (Department of Health and Social Care). 2020. *The Department of Health and Social Care mandate to Health Education England: April 2020 to March 2021*. https://www.gov.uk/government/publications/health-education-england-mandate-2020-to-2021/the-department-of-health-and-social-care-mandate-to-health-education-england-april-2020-to-march-2021

Farnsworth, Kevin, and Zoe Irving. 2015. *Social Policy in Times of Austerity: Global Economic Crisis and the New Politics of Welfare*. Bristol: Policy Press.

Ferragina, Emanuele, and Andrew Zola. 2021. "The end of austerity as common sense? An experimental analysis of public opinion shifts and class dynamics during the Covid-19 crisis." *New Political Economy* 27 (2): 239–346.

Ferrera, Maurizio. 2005. *The Boundaries of Welfare: European Integration and the New Spatial Politics of Social Protection*. Oxford: Oxford University Press.

Findlay, A.M., Aileen Stockdale, and Emma Stewart. 2002. "Professional and managerial migration from core to periphery: The case of English migration to Scottish cities." *Population, Space and Place* 8 (3): 217–32.

Glynos, Jason, Robin Klimecki, and Hugh Willmott. 2012. "Cooling out the Marks: The ideology and politics of the financial crisis." *Journal of Cultural Economy* 5 (3): 297–320.

GOV.UK. 2020. *Health and Social Care Secretary's statement on coronavirus (COVID-19): 3 April 2020*. https://www.gov.uk/government/speeches/health-and-social-care-secretarys-statement-on-coronavirus-covid-19-3-april-2020.

GOV.UK. 2020. *Health and Social Care Secretary's statement on coronavirus (COVID-19): 10 April 2020*. https://www.gov.uk/government/speeches/health-and-social-care-secretarys-statement-on-coronavirus-covid-19-10-april-2020.

GOV.UK. 2021. *Health and Social Care Secretary's statement on coronavirus (COVID-19): 25 January 2021*. https://www.gov.uk/government/speeches/health-and-social-care-secretarys-statement-on-coronavirus-covid-19-25-january-2021.

HC Deb. July 20, 2020. vol. 678, col. 1850. https://hansard.parliament.uk/commons/2020-07-20/debates/CEB1C545-2E55-4CD7-84D4-5CDC09C5F357/CoronavirusResponse.

HM Treasury. 2020. *Budget 2020*. London: Stationery Office.

HM Treasury. 2021a. *Budget 2021*. London: Stationery Office.

HM Treasury. 2021b. *Build Back Better: Our Plan for Growth*. London: Stationery Office.

Hulme, Mike, Rolf Lidskog, James M. White, and Adam Standring. 2020. "Social scientific knowledge in times of crisis: What climate change can learn from coronavirus (and vice versa)." *WIREs Climate Change* 11 (4): e656.

Joppke, Christian. 2008. "Immigration and the identity of citizenship: the paradox of universalism." *Citizenship Studies* 12 (6): 533–46.

Keys, Clare, Gowri Nanayakkara, Chisa Onyejekwe, Rajeeb Kumar Sah, and Toni Wright. 2021. "Health inequalities and ethnic vulnerabilities during COVID-19 in the UK: A reflection on PHE Reports." *Feminist Legal Studies* 29: 107–18.

Law, Alex, and Gerry Mooney. 2012. "Devolution in a 'stateless nation': Nation-building and social policy in Scotland." *Social Policy and Administration* 46 (2): 161–77.

Leisering, Lutz. 2003. "Nation state and welfare state: An intellectual and political history." *Journal of European Social Policy* 13 (2): 175–85.

Lupton, Ruth, Tania Burchardt, John Hills, Kitty Stewart, and Polly Vizard. 2016. *Social Policy in a Cold Climate: Policies and Their Consequences since the Crisis.* Bristol: Policy Press.

McEwen, Nicola, and Luis Moreno. 2005. *The Territorial Politics of Welfare.* Basingstoke: Routledge.

McKee, Martin. 2021. "The UK's PPE procurement scandal reminds us why we need ways to hold ministers to account." *BMJ* 372: n639.

Mitchell, James. 1996. "From unitary state to union state: Labour's changing view of the United Kingdom and its implications." *Regional Studies* 30 (6): 607–11.

Mooney, Gerry and Charlotte Williams. 2006. "Forging new 'ways of life'? Social policy and nation building in devolved Scotland and Wales." *Critical Social Policy* 26 (3): 608–629.

Nassehi, Armin, and Markus Schroer. 1999. "Integration durch Staatsbürgerschaft? Einige gesellschaftstheoretische Zweifel." *Leviathan* 27 (1): 95–112.

Peck, Jamie, and Nik Theodore. 2015. *Fast Policy: Experimental Statecraft at the Thresholds of Neoliberalism.* Minneapolis: Duke University Press.

Rokkan, Stein, and Urwin, Derek W. 1982. *The Politics of Territorial Identity: Studies in European Regionalism.* London: Sage.

Scambler, Graham. 2020. "Covid-19 as a 'breaching experiment': Exposing the fractured society." *Health Sociology Review* 29 (2): 140–48.

Schiefer, David, and Jolanda van der Noll. 2017. "The essentials of social cohesion: A literature review." *Social Indicators Research* 132: 579–603.

Smout, T.C. 1980. "Scotland and England: Is dependency a symptom or a cause of underdevelopment?" *Review* 3 (4): 601–30.

Stanley, Liam. 2014. "'We're reaping what we sowed': Everyday crisis narratives and acquiescence to the age of austerity." *New Political Economy* 19 (6): 895–917.

Steed, Michael. 1986. "The core-periphery dimension of British politics." *Political Geography Quarterly* 5 (4): S91–S103.

Te Velde, Henk. 2019. "Parliamentary 'theatre', dignity and the public side of parliaments." *Redescriptions* 22 (1): 35–50.

Tubadji, Annie, Don J. Webber, and Fred Boy. 2020. "Cultural and economic discrimination by the great leveller: The COVID-19 pandemic in the UK." *Covid Economics* 13: 48–67.

Vaismoradi, Mojtaba, Hannele Turunen, and Terese Bondas. 2013. "Content analysis and thematic analysis: Implications for conducting a qualitative descriptive study." *Nursing and Health Sciences* 15 (3): 398–405.

Wincott, Daniel. 2020. "Imagined Solidarities: Brexit, Welfare, States, Nations and the EU." In *Whither Social Rights in (Post-) Brexit Europe? Opportunities and Challenges,* edited by Matthew Donoghue and Mikko Kuisma, 7–15. London: Social Europe Publishing.

Wincott, Daniel, C.R.G. Murray, and Gregory Davies. 2021. "The Anglo-British imaginary and the rebuilding of the UK's territorial constitution after Brexit: Unitary state or union state?" *Territory, Politics, Governance* 10 (5): 1–18. https://doi.org/10.1080/21622671.2021.1921613.

Wingard, Jennifer. 2012. *Branded Bodies, Rhetoric, and the Neoliberal Nation State.* Lanham, MD: Lexington Books.

PART II
CHALLENGES AND RESPONSES IN SPECIFIC POLICY DOMAINS

5

From Crisis to Opportunity?

Recalibrating Health Care in Southern Europe in the Wake of the Pandemic

Emmanuele Pavolini, Maria Petmesidou, Rui Branco,
and Ana M. Guillén

Introduction

Southern European welfare states have been going through turbulent times since the mid-2000s. The financial crisis that started in 2007–2008 was followed by austerity policies. It soon turned into a "Great Recession" that accompanied these countries for a good part of the 2010s. Once Greece, Italy, Portugal, and Spain seemed to have partially recovered from this socioeconomic crisis, the COVID-19 pandemic set in. This chapter focuses on the health care sector of the social protection system for two reasons. First, Southern European welfare states display a hybrid institutional design (Ferrera 1996): sectors such as pensions and unemployment protection are regulated according to a social insurance principle, while others follow a universalistic principle. Health care is the most important social protection sector, where the shift from social insurance to universalism took place in recent decades with the creation of National Healthcare Systems (NHSs). In other terms, it is one of the few strongholds of a universalist approach to social needs. Second, the pandemic hit health facilities hardest, and the capacity of NHSs to react played a pivotal role in the countries' strategies to cope with COVID-19. The NHSs of these four countries are financed mostly through taxation (Greece being the main and partial exception). The Spanish and the Italian NHS are highly decentralized at the regional level. However, when the pandemic broke out, their public per capita expenditure was lower in comparison to Nordic and Anglo-Saxon NHSs, and especially Italy and Greece faced greater access problems (Petmesidou et al. 2020). In light of the medium-term trends emerging over the last 15 years, the chapter addresses

Emmanuele Pavolini, Maria Petmesidou, Rui Branco, and Ana M. Guillén, *From Crisis to Opportunity?* In: *European Social Policy and the COVID-19 Pandemic*. Edited by: Stefanie Börner and Martin Seeleib-Kaiser, Oxford University Press. © Oxford University Press 2023. DOI: 10.1093/oso/9780197676189.003.0005 the question of whether the pandemic public health crisis and the recovery prospects—particularly under the Next Generation EU (NGEU) plan, which seemingly breaks with austerity—represent a "critical juncture" for health care policy change. Our main findings indicate a variegated picture of piecemeal recalibration trends that, however, fall short of addressing some long-standing challenges in a comprehensive way.

The first section of the chapter briefly introduces our analytical framework, followed by an overview of the situation before the onset of the COVID-19 pandemic. Then follows a detailed analysis of how the four health care systems have fared during the pandemic, and of the forward-looking policy options as laid out in the countries' recovery plans. The conclusion provides an overall assessment of the combined effect of the crisis-induced policy changes during the Great Recession, the responses to the pandemic since its outbreak, and any ensuing game-changing triggers.

Analytical Framework

The assessment of change over time in this policy field will draw from two well established analytical tools. The first frames social policy change in terms of retrenchment versus expansion (e.g., Levy 2010), while the second looks at social policy change in relation to what extent recalibration has taken place (e.g., Ferrera, Hemerijck, and Rhodes 2000). Regarding the latter, we look mainly at three dimensions: functional, distributive, and institutional recalibration. Functional recalibration refers to the type of social risks against which the welfare state protects. Distributive recalibration concerns the rebalancing of social protection provision across different social groups. Institutional recalibration deals with the design of institutions, levels of decision-making, and the roles given to states, markets, families, and individuals within the policy regime. Applying the concept of recalibration specifically to health care means looking at the following issues:

- Functional recalibration concerns the type of care provided. In particular, health care systems currently have to deal with how to allocate resources among prevention, primary care, hospital care, and various forms of outpatient care (including long-term care—LTC—for a growing elderly population). Functional recalibration is expected to occur after decades in which hospital care has become the main pillar of health care systems, especially across Southern Europe.

- Distributive recalibration points to substantive and not only formal inclusion of specific social groups within health care systems' protection, depending also on the extent of the use of co-payments required for accessing public health care.
- Institutional recalibration refers, on one hand, to the role different government levels (central, regional, and local) play in the planning and organization of health care services, and, on the other hand, the role of private provision within (and outside) the NHS.

In the years prior to the 2008 global financial crisis, the trajectories and profiles of Southern European NHSs diverged considerably, as consolidation of universal coverage at all levels of care (including long-term care) and system integration proceeded faster in Spain and Italy compared to Greece and Portugal. At the beginning of the 2010s, austerity policies brought about a convergence trend, as all four NHSs underwent severe spending cuts. Though to varying degrees, this impacted access in care and the quantity and quality of provisions, indicating a "subtractive recalibration" (Guillén and Pavolini 2015). Retrenchment in expenditure disproportionally hit welfare services (childcare, long-term care, education, and health care) relative to social transfers (pensions and unemployment benefits). Austerity in the last decade also meant less investment in infrastructure, worsening labor conditions in this sector (freezes in salary increases, career progression and new hires), and significant functional and organizational problems. The pandemic put huge pressure on these (already weakened) health care systems, exacerbating their recalibration needs.

The Situation on the Eve of the Pandemic

At the outbreak of the pandemic the four Southern European health care systems were still recovering from a decade of economic crisis and austerity measures. Spending apparently picked up, though at varying pace among the four countries, but human resources deficiencies and health infrastructure inequalities persisted. In addition, Greece and Portugal were still confronting long-standing challenges of unequal distribution of primary care coverage.

Public Expenditure Trends

Public health expenditure grew in all countries in the noughties and then fell afterwards (Figure 5.1). Not only had they far less health care resources than Western European countries (EU-15) on average, but they also stopped converging toward the EU-15 average expenditure after 2007 (Table 5.1).

However, the trajectory of health care spending in Spain and Portugal partly differs from that of Italy and Greece. The two Iberian countries were able to recover from the austerity years' cuts quite rapidly: from 2012 to 2019, their per capita expenditure increased by 10.7% and 17.9% respectively, and overall, from 2007 to 2019 expenditure grew by 10%–11%. On the other hand, Italy adopted severe cuts between 2007 and 2012 and recorded a very slow growth afterwards, which was unable to get expenditure back to the 2007 levels (-3% between 2007 and 2019). Finally, Greece registered a collapse, with continuous cuts over time: expenditure decreased in real terms by almost a third between 2007 and 2019. The overall result was that in 2019, the Greek per capita public health expenditure (in PPPs) was around half of what was spent on average in the EU-15 (Table 5.1).

The availability of human resources was hit hard by the onset of austerity (Table 5.2). However, as with expenditure, Southern European trajectories varied over the decade (except for the shared decline in hospital beds). In Greece and Italy, the policy measures greatly accentuated staff shortages, as the hiring

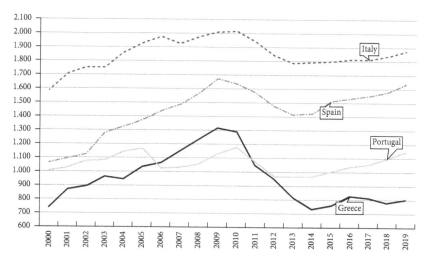

Figure 5.1 Public per capita current expenditure on health over time (2000–2019) in Southern Europe (constant prices; OECD base year; euros).

Table 5.1 Public per capita current expenditure on health over time in Southern Europe in comparative perspective (PPP constant prices; EU-15 unweighted average public expenditure = 100)

	2000	2007	2012	2019
EU 15 average	100.0	100.0	100.0	100.0
Greece	63.4	74.7	56.5	48.3
Italy	93.1	83.0	77.1	73.6
Portugal	78.3	69.8	64.0	69.6
Spain	70.7	76.6	72.4	75.0

Source: Authors' elaboration from OECD (2022)

Table 5.2 Variation in the availability of different types of health care resources between 2010 and 2019 in Southern Europe (percentages)

	Greece	Italy	Portugal	Spain
NHS employed personnel	n.a.	−6.6	+5.0	+5.0
Nurses employed by the NHS	n.a.*	−2.8	+11.2	+11.1
Doctors employed by the NHS	approx. −15**	−4.8	+12.9	+10.9
General Practitioners (contracted by the NHS)	approx. −25***	−7.5	n.a.	+3.1
Hospital beds	−10.1	−12.5	−2.4	−4.2

* According to data provided by the Panhellenic Federation of Public Hospital Employees, nursing and associated staff decreased by over 30% between 2010 and 2017. ** 2010–2017. *** 2013–early 2019. The data for 2013 include private physicians (GPs, pathologists, and pediatricians) contracted by EOPYY, while for 2019 they also include family doctors under contract in Local Health Units established in 2017. Pay cuts and unfavorable working conditions for contracted-out physicians, introduced in early 2018, partly account for the significant decrease of their number.

Sources: Istat Health for All (2021) for Italy; for Portugal, *Balanço Social Global do Ministério da Saúde 2010* and *Relatório Social do Ministério da Saúde e do SNS* (December 2018); for Greece, EOPYY data base (March 2013; January 2019) and Petmesidou (2020: 516); for Spain, *Recursos Humanos, ordenación profesional y formación continuada en el Sistema Nacional de Salud, 2019 (2021), SIS.*

freeze in combination with retirements contributed to a considerable decrease in the number of medical personnel, while at the same time many doctors left the two countries. Somewhat differently, in Spain and Portugal health care personnel grew in the public system between 2009 and 2019. However, salaries in Spain only grew by 0.2%, while working conditions worsened and job insecurity increased. In Portugal, despite significant cuts during the Great Recession, NHS human resources and wage salary expenditure rebounded after 2015, ending the decade respectively up 5% and 12% from 2010.

Functional Recalibration

Variations in expenditure were not evenly distributed across health care functions. Spain and Portugal were better able to recalibrate their health care systems than Italy and Greece (Table 5.3). In the former countries, outpatient care and LTC expenditure grew. Only preventive care did not recover from the cuts of the austerity years. Instead, Italy followed a path of "light" retrenchment, continuing to cut further all main functions apart from prevention, and only trying to functionally recalibrate its system to a limited extent. Finally, Greece acted through plain retrenchment, practically cutting down strongly on every function.

Nevertheless, Greece and Portugal attempted reforms with medium- to long-term functional recalibration goals, also due to their bailout programs. These attempts are not easily captured by the data reported in Table 5.3. In Greece, reforms implemented in the last decade aimed at solving long-standing problems of system fragmentation: the various health social insurance funds were amalgamated into a single entity (the National Organization for the Provision of Health Services, EOPYY); regulative mechanisms for prescriptions and referrals were introduced, and hospital reforms were implemented aimed at improving pricing of services and management (Petmesidou 2020). In Portugal, reforms rationalized the hospital network, expanded LTC, and set up a palliative care network. From 2015, some measures pursued long-standing orientations, for example, cost containment, systemic integration of care levels, and LTC. The service basket expanded in primary care, mental health, and LTC (Nunes and Ferreira 2019).

Distributive Recalibration

Distributive recalibration can be assessed on two grounds: the share of individuals with unmet health care needs by socioeconomic characteristics, and reforms and policy changes that might have affected social inequalities. Tables 5.4 and 5.5 provide data of self-reported unmet needs for medical examination by income quintile (Table 5.4 focuses on the lowest and highest quintiles) and by migratory background (defined in terms of country of birth). Four main findings emerge. First, social inequality in the access to health care was a much more pronounced problem in Greece and Italy than in Spain and Portugal, with the latter countries performing similarly

Table 5.3 Variation in per capita public expenditure on health by function over time in Southern Europe (percentages, constant prices)

	Greece			Italy			Portugal			Spain		
	2007–2012	2012–2019	2007–2019	2007–2012	2012–2019	2007–2019	2007–2012	2012–2019	2007–2019	2007–2012	2012–2019	2007–2019
Total	−17.1	−15.7	−30.1	−4.4	1.6	−2.9	−5.8	17.9	11.1	−0.8	10.7	9.8
Inpatient curative and rehab. care	−13.4	−19.1	−29.9	n.a.	−5.3	n.a.	−13.8	10.8	−4.5	6.1	14.2	21.2
Outpatient curative and rehab. care	−16.8	5.8	−12.0	−49.2	8.2	−45.1	1.7	17.4	19.3	−0.1	11.2	11.1
Long-term care (health)	407.0*	62.0	721.2	n.a.	5.2	n.a.	36.6	35.6	85.3	12.8	16.8	31.7
Ancillary services	−33.7	48.1	−1.8	n.a.	−0.1	n.a.	−18.8	15.4	−6.4	4.9	8.8	14.2
Medical goods	−21.9	−33.4	−48.0	−1.5	15.4	13.7	−25.8	15.1	−14.6	−18.3	2.4	−16.4
Preventive care	−18.6	6.5	−13.3	30.9	17.3	53.5	−23.7	4.8	−20.1	−13.6	11.3	−3.9
Governance and administration	−11.5	−2.0	−13.3	1.2	−16.1	−15.1	−4.6	−4.1	−8.5	−8.1	−3.4	−11.3

Source: Authors' elaboration from OECD (2022)
* Due to a very low figure at the base year, the high increase rates do not reflect any substantial expansion of this function.

Table 5.4 Self-reported unmet needs for medical examination due to costs, availability, or waiting lists by income quintile

	2008			2015			2019		
	Total	First quintile	Fifth quintile	Total	First quintile	Fifth quintile	Total	First quintile	Fifth quintile
European Union-27	3.0	5.7	1.4	3.3	5.6	1.5	1.7	3.2	0.7
Greece	5.4	8.8	1.8	12.3	18.3	4.0	8.1	17.6	1.0
Spain	0.4	0.7	0.4	0.6	0.7	0.4	0.2	0.1	0.2
Italy	5.2	10.4	2.0	7.2	15.5	1.5	1.8	4.1	0.4
Portugal	1.1	2.6	0.3	3.0	6.4	0.6	1.7	3.5	0.2

Source: Eurostat online database (2022) (indicator: HLTH_SILC_08)

Table 5.5 Self-reported unmet needs for medical examination due to costs, availability, or waiting lists by country of birth

	2008		2015		2019	
	Foreign country	Reporting country	Foreign country	Reporting country	Foreign country	Reporting country
EU-27	2.9	3.2	3.6	3.2	1.5	1.7
Greece	6.6	5.3	18.4	11.8	12.8	7.8
Spain	0.8	0.3	0.6	0.6	0.3	0.2
Italy	6.1	5.1	12.2	6.6	1.7	1.8
Portugal	0.5	1.2	3.9	2.9	1.6	1.7

Source: Eurostat online database (2022) (indicator: HLTH_SILC_29)

(Portugal) or better (Spain) relative to the EU average. Second, inequalities peaked in Greece, Portugal, and Italy around the mid-2010s, and then abated. Third, on the eve of the pandemic, social inequalities were still very strong in Greece and partially so in Italy. In these two countries (and mostly in Greece) access inequalities were related both to income level and migratory background. Last, in Spain all types of inequalities were persistently low, while in Portugal they were not very strong and mainly related to income level.

In Greece, reforms tried to tackle social inequalities but with limited success. For instance, the health benefits basket was standardized across occupational groups, but it became leaner, and co-payments for pharmaceuticals and laboratory tests (outside hospitals) increased (Petmesidou 2020). Drastic public expenditure contraction shifted the cost to patients, and barriers to system permeability and navigation rose, especially for the more disadvantaged groups (Petmesidou et al. 2020).

In Portugal, access inequalities worsened during the early 2010s. The reforms instigated by the 2011 bailout program doubled user charges. Excepting LTC, austerity across all functions undermined universal access, shifting costs to patients when private spending was frozen by the economic crisis without relevant efficiency gains. Overall, state responsibility narrowed while the NHS service basket shrank (Petmesidou et al. 2014). User charges were ended in 2019 for primary care and all primary care referrals within the NHS. Despite reversals from 2015, policies still adversely impacted access, for example through less scope and depth of provision (particularly of pharmaceuticals), personnel shortages, and system integration and rationalization issues (Petmesidou et al. 2020). Inequalities persisted due to fragmented ambulatory and hospital care and geographical imbalances (Perista 2018).

Similarly, the Italian NHS on the eve of the pandemic clearly showed severe inequalities in access to care, also related to the increase of fees to access provision. These inequalities were not just based on income level but also were territorial in nature, with a big gap between northern and southern Italy (Vicarelli and Neri 2021). Spain suffered from territorial imbalances too, albeit much less marked than the north–south divide in Italy, and in general Spain was the country that had fewer distributional recalibration problems.

Institutional Recalibration

As for institutional recalibration, all countries shifted decision-making from local/regional to central government level (Guillén and Pavolini 2013, 2015). This development was particularly important in Spain and Italy, where decentralization had been implemented in the previous decades. In both countries, the strong regional autonomy was limited by central governments during the 2010s, not through a legislative reform but simply by introducing more limits on public health care spending (Petmesidou et al. 2020). In Portugal and Greece, the weak regional autonomy was further undermined by a centralist turn, displacing decision-making to the top of the ministries of health and finance. Also, in Spain and Italy an incremental rise of supplemental private coverage (of an "occupational-mutualist" type; Petmesidou et al. 2020) indicated a "hidden privatization," though this has not led to substantial enhancement of the role of private provision. Portugal and Greece followed a different path. They never developed a fully-fledged NHS, given the large private sector (in both countries) and generous health insurance schemes for public servants and private subsystems, particularly in Portugal. During the past decade occupational subsystems and private insurance covered 16% and 26% of the population, respectively, in Portugal. Austerity stimulated the transfer of services to nonprofit institutions and an increase of out-of-pocket spending. As for Greece, where the shift to an NHS model remained deeply incomplete for about three decades, the financial crisis and bailout conditions enforced reform toward a more unified structure. But greatly strained budgetary conditions placed a brake on effective implementation, and private (mostly out-of-pocket) spending remained high.

Finally, no significant shifts in normative patterns were observed. By using citizens' satisfaction with health care services during the Great Recession (Petmesidou et al. 2014, 334–5) in combination with the size of private health spending as a proxy for normative orientation, we find two highly contrasting cases: sustained predominance of universalism in Spain (comparatively high satisfaction with public provisions and limited private spending) versus a highly negative appraisal of public provision and high private health spending in Greece. Within this range of proxy normative attitudes, Italy fell closer to Spain, and Portugal to Greece (though with some distance). Overall, Janus-faced trends were varyingly manifest in the four countries at the turn of the 2020s. Health care spending was on the rise, but upward convergence to the EU-15 average per capita rate was slower compared to the pre-crisis years. Rules regulating access were reviewed (e.g., some fees were reduced or abolished) but significant inequalities in access persisted (except for Spain). Strong public budget pressures during austerity largely ran counter to primary-care reform and system integration in Greece (and partly in Portugal), limiting universal coverage. Also, increasing surveillance capacity on spending by central governments in the first half of 2010s sparked off worrisome central/regional tensions, particularly in Italy and Spain, which continue to significantly impact upon service provision.

The Main Measures Adopted During the Pandemic

To analyze how the countries recalibrated (or intended to) during the first year and half of the pandemic, we shall focus on three issues: funding, emergency measures adopted to cope with the health threat, and measures seeking to tackle health issues in the medium to long term.

Funding

Figure 5.2 and Table 5.6 display long-term trends in per capita public health expenditure, the rapid spending increase during the pandemic after a decade of austerity, and future investment in the health care sector under the countries' recovery plans. Between 2019 and 2020, per capita public expenditure on health care rose significantly in real terms in Spain and Portugal (by 7.6% and 7.4% respectively; Table 5.6). The corresponding rates for Italy and Greece were 4.8% and 6.1%. Portugal registered a strong upward trend in 2021 too (10.5%). These are substantial increases, which (with the exception of Greece) brought per capita expenditure slightly above the 2007 level (in Italy), and well above that level in Portugal and Spain. Looking at medium- to long-term investment choices between 2021 and 2026, the Italian National Recovery and Resilience

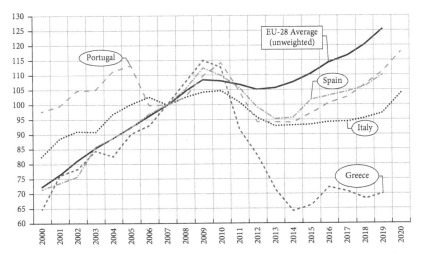

Figure 5.2 Public current expenditure on health care over time (2000–2020) in Southern Europe (per capita, constant prices; base 2007 = 100). Source: Author elaboration from OECD (2022).

Table 5.6 Expenditure and investment during the pandemic and in the road to recovery

	Per capita public health care spending*			Health spending as percentage of the total resources of the NRRPs (2021–2026)	Main health care sectors in NRRPs investment programs (2021–2026) in billion euros				
	Percentage change (in 2020 constant prices; euros)		In million constant 2020 prices; euros 2020 / 2021		Primary/ outpatient care and e-health	R&D, innovation and digitalization	Mental health	Infrastructure**	Public health and/ or other
	2019–2020	2020–2021							
Greece	6.1	n.a.	907 / n.a.	5.0	0.29	0.58	0.06	0.36	0.26
Spain	7.6	n.a.	1861 / n.a.	1.5***	0.10	0.09	0.003	0.79	0.08
Italy	4.8	4.7	2036 / 2131	9.0	7.00	9.60	-	-	-
Portugal	7.4	10.5	1273 / 1410	8.4	0.67****	0.3	0.09	0.31	0.01

* Government schemes and compulsory contributory health care financing schemes; ** Including investments for tackling territorial inequality in service provision; *** up to 2023; **** including LTC

Source: Authors' elaboration from WHO Global Health Expenditure Database (2022); NRRPs of the four countries

Plan (NRRP 2021) aims to devote €16.63 billion to health care, equal to around 9% of the total resources of the NRRP (QuotidianoSanità 2021). In Spain, a small increase (of 0.6%) was budgeted for 2021, 11% of which came from the Recovery and Resilience Fund (RRF) (MHyFP 2021; NRRP Spain 2021).

Portugal has witnessed a continuous and steep rise in public health spending since the end of the Memorandum of Understanding[1] in 2014 (by 28% up to 2020). Thus, in 2020 the NHS total expenditure rose by about €650 million (+5.8% compared to 2019) and in 2021 by another €1.4 billion (+11.9%). The government vowed to keep funding levels, and the NRRP included additional expenditure of €1.38 billion (12% of total NHS outlays) (NRRP Portugal 2021).

In contrast to the other three countries, where the government budget almost entirely covers public health spending, in Greece state budget sources fund only about 45% of public health expenditure. Between 2020 and 2022, government health spending ranged between 4 to 4.5 billion euros, 6%–7% deriving from EU resources (state budgets[2]; NRRP Greece 2021). Dedicated COVID-19 extra-budgetary funds were added to these, raising government spending by about 20% each year. These extra resources covered the increase of health care personnel (mainly on a temporary contract basis), the procurement of personal protective equipment, the expansion of intensive care beds and of diagnostic testing capacity, as well as subsidies to EOPYY to counterbalance its declining revenue due to falling social insurance contributions. However, this trajectory of government spending is insufficient for redressing decade-long, huge austerity-driven cuts.

Emergency Measures

As soon as the pandemic set in, Southern European countries introduced emergency measures (varyingly combining temporary and permanent elements), which addressed, to one extent or another, the demands for swift increases in the number of health care personnel, scaling-up of hospital capacity, improvement/reorganization of primary care response (including

[1] The MOU was a program of financial assistance signed in 2010 by the European Commission, the European Central Bank (ECB), and the International Monetary Fund (IMF), and separately by Greece and Portugal. Financial aid packages were provided in exchange for structural reforms and public debt reduction.
[2] https://www.minfin.gr/web/guest/oikonomika-stoicheia

home care), and acceleration of digital technologies. Logistics challenges linked to COVID-related procurement, mass testing, and vaccination had to be met, too. Italy had the most dramatic start of the four countries in terms of infections and deaths. The government passed two major bills (the "Care Bill" of March 2020 and the "Relaunch Bill" of May 2020) laying out the policy framework (Vicarelli and Neri 2021). Greece stands out for its early adoption of strict containment measures (March 2020), which contributed to managing at least the first wave comparatively better than the other countries. Yet, her performance deteriorated during the second and third wave of the pandemic due to public health capacity constraints and feeble random-sampling epidemiological surveillance (Kondylis et al. 2021, 65–70).

Health Care Personnel

Between March 2020 and April 2021, around 83,000 professionals (26% of which were doctors) were recruited ad hoc to cope with the pandemic emergency in Italy (Corte dei Conti 2021). This figure amounts to 12% of the total NHS employees and therefore represents a major effort to reverse the cuts in the personnel that were made in the previous decade (see Table 5.2). By the end of 2021, it was not clear if these new personnel would remain on a more permanent basis and/or if future retirements would not be replaced due to the ad hoc hiring during the pandemic. In Spain, retired doctors and medical students were encouraged to collaborate on a voluntary basis. New regulations (particularly those introduced in late March and September 2020) allowed the regional health care systems to recruit doctors, nurses, and other health care personnel. However, this was set up as an extraordinary measure: contracts were fixed-term for 12 months and could then be renewed every three months based on need. Approximately 92,000 contracts were signed from the onset of the pandemic up to June 2021. But only 8%–10% of all new contracts remained by the end of 2021. Several regions declared that all or part of the new take-ups were going to be kept due to personnel shortages related to retirement within the same year (Antena 3 Noticias June 6, 2021; Redacción Médica September 20, 2021). In Greece, more than 7,500 new medical, nursing, paramedical, and other staff have been recruited since March 2020, predominantly on short-term contracts. In addition, some permanent position openings were announced in 2020 and 2021 (for about 1,400 doctors and 4,000 nursing staff). As in Spain, doctors about to retire were asked to remain in the NHS for as long as the system was strained. Equally, special legislation simplified and facilitated the hiring of new professional staff in Portugal, as well as created banks of health students and retired professionals. There was a surge in hiring through fixed-term contracts, of which only a limited number had been converted into open-ended contracts by mid-2021 (NRRP Portugal 2021).

Hospital Capacity

In all four countries, the pressure on hospitals led to an expansion of acute care beds (partly through the transformation of hospital wards into Intensive Care Units [ICUs]), the designation of several public hospitals as dedicated CORONA hospitals for COVID-19 patients, the creation of field hospitals (including by the military), and partnerships with private for-profit and nonprofit hospitals (mainly in Portugal). In Italy, the above-mentioned bills fostered an expansion of acute care beds, especially those for intensive care. But, as with new recruitments, the two bills did not clarify if the measures would be just temporary or more long-standing after the pandemic. The goal of 3,500 ICU beds appears to be a medium to long-term choice. In Spain, under the steep increase in demand, 6,000 new ICU beds were added to the approximately 4,400 existing ones. In many cases, these were created in hospital wards previously used for other purposes and staffed with personnel that was quickly up-skilled (El País February 12, 2021). Many of such improvised ICUs were subsequently dismantled, except for those hospitals in which there was already a shortage before the pandemic (Redacción Médica June 1, 2020). Similarly, Greece increased the number of ICU beds in public hospitals from 565 to 840 at the height of the first wave, and added 32 ICU beds in military hospitals and about 145 in private hospitals. Total ICU capacity for NHS patients further increased during the second and third wave (close to 1,400 ICU beds in total). However, flexibility in the temporary deployment of acute care capacity has not been adequately matched with more lasting measures. Many of the new ICU units were makeshift arrangements within surgeries and/or "high dependency" wards; the ICU staffing shortage was largely met with the relocation of health care personnel (often lacking highly specialist intensive care skills) from other clinical areas, as well as from primary care units. Pressure to convert special ICUs for other diseases into acute care places exclusively for COVID-19 patients created serious treatment disruptions for patients with other critical diseases (like cancer, cardiac diseases, etc.). Therefore, about 45% of excess mortality was not COVID-19 related in 2020 (Kondylis et al. 2021, 73–75). Greece, also, stood out for the favorable treatment of the private sector, as private hospitals were shielded from COVID-19 incidences because the "requisitioning" of acute and non-acute care private hospital beds was mainly focused on the transfer of non-COVID-19 NHS patients, and at a very hefty compensation by the Ministry of Health (e.g., set at more than twice the cost in public hospitals). In Portugal, the further allocation of human and other technical resources resulted in a 35% increase in ICU bed capacity. Health services were reorganized to concentrate the response to COVID-19 cases in dedicated areas; military hospitals and hotels were deployed in the response to outbreaks, particularly those in nursing homes (Simões et al 2021). Yet, despite the surge of resources, a huge backlog of lack or delayed care emerged, especially worrying for acute and chronic care patients (e.g., hospital appointments fell by 1.2 million, and programmed surgical interventions by 100,000; NRRP Portugal 2021). A snapshot of the impact of disruption in service provision due to the pandemic is provided by a recent Eurofound e-survey of self-reported unmet need for health care. In all four countries, the rates of persons who declared that although they needed a medical examination or treatment, they had not received it, was well above the EU-27 average (20.7%), ranging from 23.2% in Italy to 34.2% in Portugal in February/ March 2021.[3]

Primary and Community Care

Investment in and reorganization of outpatient and domiciliary care have been prominent in Italy. An important intervention (with potentially long-lasting effects) was the creation of special care community units (USCAs), which are special treatment units providing care at home for COVID-19 patients. For the first time since the NHS's creation in 1978, young primary care doctors were directly hired, instead of being contracted out, to make the USCAs work. Furthermore, nursing home care was strengthened, with the attempt to involve also voluntary and community organizations. The USCAs and the strengthening of home care are considered as innovations that should last beyond the pandemic.

In contrast to Italy, the reorganization of outpatient and domiciliary care was not high on the agenda in Spain, though minor policy adjustments have been going on, particularly with the aim to reinforce home care. Portugal and Greece—which, as mentioned above, had embarked on a path toward achieving universal primary health care coverage in the last

---

[3] https://www.eurofound.europa.eu/data/covid-19.

decade—exhibited divergent trends during the pandemic. In Portugal the coronavirus crisis offered an opportunity to improve outpatient and domiciliary care, a long-standing goal to be addressed also through the NRRP. National coverage of the population unserved by a general practitioner (GP) is improving, though still short of the universal goal, all while broadening the basket of care and diagnostic services. In Greece, however, the pandemic has greatly slowed (or partly thrown into reverse) the realization of primary care reform. And even before the coronavirus health crisis, the implementation of reform has not been straightforward. Instead of strengthening primary care to reduce vulnerability in the community and mitigate pressure on hospitals, staff relocation from primary care units to other parts of the NHS greatly weakened its service delivery capacity. Nevertheless, an accelerated adoption of digital technologies in health care through emergency measures could potentially have a beneficial impact upon primary care integration and public health promotion. Digital technologies have been progressively introduced in the Greek NHS since the early 2010s, such as the Electronic Patient Record and the National Network of Telemedicine, servicing mainly NHS health care centers and hospitals on the Aegean islands. The pandemic has given an impetus to the expansion of these measures that can facilitate interoperability in health care.

Forward-Looking Policies in the NRRPs

In Italy and Spain, no drastic reform was envisaged under the NRRPs. The Italian NRRP proposed investment in and expansion of two health care sectors (Table 5.6), partly linked with the emergency measures discussed previously, namely outpatient care and e-health (about €7 billion), research and development, and digitization (about €9.6 billion). The first line of investment focused on strengthening prevention, home care, and several forms of outpatient care. It introduced 1,288 "community centers" where interdisciplinary teams of GPs, pediatricians, medical specialists, nurses, and social workers will work together in primary care and in coordinating home and outpatient care. The goal is for home care to cover 10% of the elderly population (practically doubling the current coverage). Also, 380 "community hospitals" are planned, to be run mostly by nurses and intended for short hospital stays of patients with a medium to low care complexity, often after an acute hospital discharge. The second line of investment aimed to modernize the NHS technological infrastructure, promote biomedical research (setting up "excellence research centers"), and support lifelong learning for health care personnel (in particular GPs). As part of these goals, e-health is framed as an important element of the future NHS in order to make it more sustainable and effective.

Investment in health care did not figure prominently in the Spanish NRRP (just over €1 billion for 2021–2023, Table 5.6). About 90% of the funds will be allocated to the renewal of high-tech equipment, the rationalization of consumption of health products and drugs, and surveillance of the pandemic by the newly established Public Health Center. A meager amount (€62 million) will be devoted to disease prevention and health promotion actions, and an even smaller amount (€13 million) to up-skilling of health professionals. Investment in primary care improvement is not included in the NRRP but will be supported by national/regional funding and other EU financial tools.

In Greece, the NRRP milestones and goals to be achieved with funding allocated to health care (about €1.5 billion between 2021 and 2026; 5% of the total funding to be received by the country, see Table 5.6) strongly embraced the digital transformation of health through integrated information systems and advancement of health promotion and disease prevention. A previous five-year plan for health promotion and disease prevention approved by Parliament in March 2020 partly informed the NRRP: its strategic goals embraced primary prevention of diseases, early detection interventions, and rehabilitation/palliative measures. Other projects in the NRRP included the upgrade of NHS infrastructure and medical equipment through energy-efficient renovations, the expansion of mental health units and of academic curricula in family medicine, as well as the establishment of eight staffed home care units across the country (a care sector least developed).

In Portugal, the NRRP embodied the core reforms for the NHS in the medium term (up to 2026). Three major reforms and €1.38 billion in investments (8.4% of total funding, Table 5.6) seek to balance fiscal sustainability and expansion to underserved types of care and social groups, while at the same time addressing traditional issues of vertical integration, hospital governance, and rationalization, via mainly functional and distributive recalibration. More than a third of these investments will be in primary care. The key aim is to broaden the diagnostic capacity and basket of services of the primary community care network and its physical infrastructure, while expanding community and domiciliary outreach. There is also a sizeable investment in LTC and palliative networks (€205 million) for enhancing capacity (e.g., 5,500 new long-term beds will be added, as well as 500 community beds, 50 domiciliary teams, and 20 palliative care units). Mental health is a major priority, too. A €88 million investment will focus on de-institutionalization, better integration with ambulatory and specialized hospital care, and expansion of community care and the National Network of Continuing Integrated Care (RNCCI) in the entire territory. Most of the planned measures indicate a shift toward attending an increasingly large elderly population with more chronic and degenerative diseases and rising multi-morbidity. Changes in the governance of public hospitals set specific financial goals, enact internal markets, and better integrate different care levels under the oversight of the Ministry of Finance, curbing "wasteful expenditure" for efficiency gains. Lastly, the forecasted hiring of 8,400 health professionals seeks to replenish and rebalance NHS personnel toward more nurses and technicians and away from doctors (excepting GPs still needed to universalize primary care).

Conclusion: An Overall Assessment of Potential Changes in Southern European NHSs

The coronavirus crisis brought significant challenges to Southern European NHSs. Before the COVID-19 crisis, health spending was on a growth path in Spain and Portugal, but less so in Italy and Greece. The health crisis has accelerated this trend in all four countries, representing a boost in the short term and, potentially, in the medium term too. Contrary to the 2010s, the pandemic seemed to be no time for "subtractive recalibration." Rather, it foregrounded the need for a stronger and more resilient public health care system. At least this is what public opinion conveyed by the unprecedented public displays of appreciation for and gratitude to health care workers across Southern Europe at the peak of the health crisis. Indeed, it seemed as though the pandemic presented a "terrible occasion" for those actors who believed in the strengthening and fine-tuning of the public health care systems after a decade of austerity. But, until early 2022, there was no evidence of this juncture turning into a "window of opportunity" that policy and political actors could exploit for a radical rethink of public health care. Instead, our analysis has shown piecemeal recalibration trends to be present in policy proposals (and emergency measures). Overall, these trends indicate two different paths among Southern European NHSs.

In Italy and Spain, the relaunch of the NHS was not a priority in the political agenda, nor in public opinion terms, before 2020. An incremental but potentially transformative change was taking place in these two health care systems toward a kind of partial hidden privatization (Petmesidou et al. 2020; Guillén and Luque 2019). During the pandemic the ad hoc measures adopted in Italy, as well as the investment plans included in its NRRP, go in the direction of a notable functional recalibration of the entire system toward outpatient and home care, with a better focus also on LTC combined with technological innovation. Although this policy orientation does not seem to be radically innovative, it might partially suffice to avoid the hidden privatization of the NHS. Functional recalibration among levels of care, together with prevention and health promotion, is less pronounced in Spain, and private complementary insurance due to growing waiting lists may well continue to expand. Institutional recalibration, be it the interplay among levels of government or the role of private provision within the NHSs, has not been contemplated so far, and distributional recalibration (in terms of access) has not been on the agenda, either. Evidently, in both highly decentralized countries, the most worrisome problem that is not seriously confronted either by the pandemic-induced measures or any planned policies, is that of territorial social inequalities. The whole issue has practically been forgotten in the first two years of the pandemic in Italy. The fact that COVID-19 hit particularly hard the central to northern Italian regions, which was where the NHS already worked better before 2020, largely contributed to this. The issue remains uncontemplated in Spain as well.

While radical recalibration has not been the case in Greece and Portugal either, policy trajectories have borne a different character compared to Italy and Spain. The Great Recession brought into sharp relief the fault lines of the Greek and Portuguese NHSs (weak integration, fragmentation, high private spending), which since then have been the focus of varyingly effective reforms. In Portugal, as soon as the austerity and downward drift of the Troika years was reversed, NHS reform acquired a renewed political impetus. With a left-wing coalition in office (*Geringonça*) since 2015,[4] health care recorded a significant rebound in the pre-pandemic years: more equitable access, rising NHS expenditure with personnel rebalance, and a larger

---

[4] The coalition (under the ruling of the center-left Socialist Party) collapsed in late 2021. Early elections in January 2022 gave an absolute majority to the Socialist Party. This indicates policy continuity.

service basket in primary care. In 2019, the new Health Basic Law passed by the left-wing majority enhanced NHS's centrality vis-à-vis the private and nonprofit sectors and ended NHS user charges. In Greece, a deeper and more protracted economic crisis followed by a weak rebound in public health spending prior to the pandemic constrained any recalibration moves toward an integrated universal health care system. Still, the public health care budget (partly relying on the Next Generation EU fund for major investments) over the coming years falls short of undoing the drastic cuts of the 2010s.

Seemingly, the political conjuncture creates a more amenable time for reform in Portugal. Pandemic policy measures garnered broad political support, including from the center-right opposition and social partners. Government and opposition cooperation was the Portuguese pattern during the pandemic, unlike in the other Southern European countries (De Giorgi and Santana-Pereira, 2020). Pandemic politics created a "rally around the NHS" effect; hence support for a strong public system seems to be set. This is corroborated by the significant steps in recalibration planned under the Portuguese NRRP. Nevertheless, enduring features of the austerity era raise questions as to the breadth of reform. Such features are the recentralization of an already weakly regionalized NHS, and the lasting importance of the private for-profit sector (both in primary and hospital care) and private nonprofit sector (especially in long-term, palliative, and elderly care), even though the 2019 reform stopped any further privatization trend. However, the persistence of generous public (but also private) occupational subsystems for civil servants and the military needs to be mentioned, which directs a considerable amount of spending toward private providers.

In Greece, the pandemic has blatantly exposed the need for universal primary care built around community-based multidisciplinary team practices (embracing domiciliary care) and able to coordinate actions and ensure continuity across primary, secondary, acute, and aged care services. But reform that tackles this problem head on is still very slow. A window of opportunity is provided, though indirectly, by the intended digital transformation that figures prominently in the Greek NRRP. This has the potential to recalibrate system governance and to bypass some of the NHS's traditional constraints. It can promote interoperability across the system, uphold better and faster coordination of care, and underpin optimal spatial arrangements of networked health care entities (e.g., along the lines of a hub-and-spoke network). In a highly centralized system like the Greek NHS, it can also make possible some de-concentration of functions to semi-autonomous agencies (e.g., the newly established quality assurance agency). Yet, in contrast to Portugal, sustained political (preferably cross-partisan) commitment to leverage such reforms does not seem to be on the horizon. Rather, it is likely that once the pandemic is over, under the pressure of Greece's exorbitantly high public debt, recalibration will again prioritize cost-cutting and hence increasingly co-opt universal public health care into private operators.

To conclude, during the health crisis and on the path to recovery, Southern European countries have undertaken interventions in public health, varyingly triggering NHS recalibration. No wholesale reform has taken place, but some decisive changes in terms of functional (and partly distributive) recalibration can be ascertained (e.g., in Italy and Portugal). Digitization potentially can be an indirect trigger of recalibration (e.g., in Greece). However, system governance and the public–private mix are not at the foreground in all four countries, and a meager opportunity for enhancement of universalism (in terms of equity and service quality) that opened up during the pandemic does not seem to be sustained. Finally, a cautionary remark is needed given two uncertain parameters that may weigh heavily on policy options and funding. The first parameter refers to the shape in which the Stability and Growth Pact will be reapplied. The second parameter concerns the unfolding global energy crunch, likely to intensify due to the geopolitical conflicts that erupted in Europe during the time of writing. These can overstretch public finances in Southern European countries and take their welfare states—and the NHSs as a main component of them—into uncharted territory.

References

Antena 3 Noticias. June 6, 2021. *Casi un tercio de los sanitarios contratados como refuerzo por la pandemia en España ya han sido despedidos.*

Corte dei Conti. 2021. *Rapporto 2021 sul coordinamento della finanza pubblica.* Corte dei Conti: Roma.

Council of Ministers/Consejo de Ministros. October 7, 2021. Referencia. Secretaría de Estado de Comunicación. www.lamoncloa.gob.es

De Giorgi, Elisabetta, and J. Santana-Pereira. 2020. "The exceptional case of post-bailout Portugal: A comparative outlook." *South European Society and Politics* 25 (2): 127–50.

El País. February 12, 2021. "El sobreesfuerzo de las UCI: el doble de camas desde el inicio de la crisis." Sociedad. EL PAÍS. (elpais.com): Madrid.

Ferrera, Maurizio. 1996. "The 'Southern Model' of welfare in Social Europe." *Journal of European Social Policy* 6 (1): 17–37.

Ferrera, Maurizio, Anton Hemerijck, and Martin Rhodes. 2000. *The Future of Social Europe: Recasting Work and Welfare in the New Economy.* Oeiras: Celta Editora.

Eurostat. 2022. *Eurostat online database.* Luxemburg: https://ec.europa.eu/eurostat/data/database.

Guillén, Ana M. and Emmanuele Pavolini (eds). 2013. *Health Care Systems in Europe under Austerity.* London: Palgrave.

Guillén, Ana M. and Emmanuele Pavolini. 2015. "Welfare states under strain in Southern Europe: Overview of the special issue." *European Journal of Social Security* 17(2): 147–57.

Guillén, Ana M. and David Luque. 2019. "La opinión pública sobre el sistema sanitario español." *Panorama Social* 30: 125–43.

Kondylis, Elias, Filippos Tarantilis, Stergios Seretis, and Alexis Benos. 2021. "The Covid-19 Pandemic in Greece: A Critical Assessment of the Policies to Deal with It." In *The Pandemic and Current Threats to Public Health,* edited by Elias Kondylis and Alexis Benos, 55–83. Athens: Topos (in Greek).

Legido-Quigley, Helena, Marina Karanikolos, Sonia Hernandez-Plaza, Cláudia de Freitas, Luís Bernardo, Beatriz Padilla, and Martin McKee. 2016. "Effects of the financial crisis and Troika austerity measures on health and health care access in Portugal." *Health Policy* 120 (7): 833–39.

Levy, Jonah D. 2010. "Welfare Retrenchment." In *The Oxford Handbook of the Welfare State* edited by Francis G. Castles, Stephan Leibfried, Jane Lewis, Herbert Obinger, and Christopher Pierson, 552–69. Oxford: Oxford University Press.

MH y FP, Ministerio de Hacienda y Función Pública. 2021. Presupuestos Generales del Estado para 2021 SEPG:Presupuestos Generales del Estado del año en curso. (hacienda.gob.es)

Ministério das Finanças (MF). *Orçamento do Estado para . . ., years 2020 and 2021.*

Nunes, Alexandre Morais, and Diogo Cunha Ferreira. 2019. "Reforms in the Portuguese health care sector: Challenges and proposals." *The International Journal of Health Planning and Management* 34 (1): e21–e33.

OECD. 2022. *OECD. Stat.* https://stats.oecd.org/, Paris: OECD.

Perista, Pedro 2018. *Portugal. ESPN Thematic Report on Inequalities in Access to Healthcare,* Brussels: ESPN.

Petmesidou, Maria, Emmanuele Pavolini, and Ana M. Guillén. 2014. "South European healthcare systems under harsh austerity: A progress–regression mix?" *South European Society and Politics* 19 (3): 331–52.

Petmesidou, Maria. 2020. "Health Policy and Politics." In *The Oxford Handbook on Modern Greek Politics,* edited by Kevin Featherstone and Dimitri A. Sotiropoulos, 505–20. Oxford: Oxford University Press.

Petmesidou, Maria, Ana M. Guillén, and Emmanuele Pavolini. 2020. "Health care in post-crisis South Europe: Inequalities in access and reform trajectories." *Social Policy and Administration* 54 (5): 666–83.

QuotidianoSanità. 2021. "A colloquio con Speranza." September 11, 2021. www.quotidianosanità.it.

Recovery and Resilience Plan Greece (NRRP). 2021. *Greece 2.0.* Athens: Greek Government. (https://greece20.gov.gr/en/the-complete-plan/)

Recovery and Resilience Plan Italy (NRRP). 2021. *Piano Nazionale de Ripresa e Resilienza. Italia Domani.* Rome: Italian Government. (https://www.italiadomani.gov.it/content/sogei-ng/it/it/home.html)

Recovery and Resilience Plan Portugal (NRRP). 2021. *Plano de Recuperação e Resiliência.* Lisbon: Portuguese Government. (https://recuperarportugal.gov.pt/documentacao/)

Recovery and Resilience Plan Spain (NRRP). 2021. Plan de recuperación, transformación y resiliencia. Madrid: Spanish Government (mineco.gob.es)

Redacción Médica. June 1, 2020. "Coronavirus España: menos camas UCI que Alemania." (redaccionmedica.com).

Redacción Médica. September 20, 2021. "Las CCAA quieren mantener a sanitarios de refuerzo Covid." (redaccionmedica.com)

Simões, Jorge, João Paulo Magalhães, André Biscaia, António da Luz Pereira, Gonçalo Figueiredo Gonçalo Figueiredo Augusto, and Inês Fronteira. 2021. "Organisation of the State, model of health system and COVID-19 health outcomes in six European countries, during the first months of the COVID-19 epidemic in 2020." *The International Journal of Health Planning and Management*, 36 (5): 1874–86.

Vicarelli, Giovanna, and Stefano Neri. 2021. "Una catastrofe vitale? Le scelte di politica sanitaria per far fronte al Covid-19." *Politiche Sociali* 2: 233–54.

6

Locked in Transition

Youth Labor Markets during COVID-19 in the United Kingdom, Norway, Estonia, and Spain

Jacqueline O'Reilly, Marge Unt, Rune Halvorsen, Mi Ah Schoyen, Rachel Verdin, Triin Roosalu, and Zyab Ibáñez

Introduction

Young people in education, working, or looking for work were locked in their transitions during the pandemic; these transitions were frequently mediated by digital technologies. School and university closures moved education online. Existing inequalities and digital divisions became more apparent as reflected in the ability of education systems to adapt, young people's own digital skills, and their access to high-speed internet at home. The younger and more socially deprived they were, the bigger the gaps. In-person businesses that employ many young people, such as hospitality and retail (O'Reilly et al. 2019) were shut. New job opportunities appeared in the gig and consumer economy, but often with inferior employment conditions (Rolf et al. 2022).

Those with the lowest levels of access to skills training and welfare provisions were among the most vulnerable to economic and job insecurity, as they had been during the economic crisis after 2008 (Unt et al. 2021; ILO 2020; O'Reilly et al. 2019; Halvorsen and Hvinden 2018). In addition, this time around the toll of restricted social interaction has had particularly detrimental effects on young peoples' mental health (Efuribe et al. 2020; Eurofound 2020; Orben et al. 2020). To address these challenges, exceptional government policies appeared to break with established path-dependent welfare practices. The combined short-term shock of the pandemic, alongside longer-run developments in digitalization, raises a question central to this volume: To what extent have policy regimes continued to be embedded in a pattern of path dependency? Or, have these developments catalyzed new processes of change?

Jacqueline O'Reilly, Marge Unt, Rune Halvorsen, Mi Ah Schoyen, Rachel Verdin, Triin Roosalu, and Zyab Ibáñez, *Locked in Transition* In: *European Social Policy and the COVID-19 Pandemic*. Edited by: Stefanie Börner and Martin Seeleib-Kaiser, Oxford University Press. © Oxford University Press 2023. DOI: 10.1093/oso/9780197676189.003.0006

Examining these questions, we draw on a comparative case study of four countries illustrative of distinctive policy regime types affecting youth in the United Kingdom, Norway, Estonia, and Spain (Pohl and Walther 2007).[1] We compare regime characteristics and performance, differences in skill attainment, and policies to address youth at risk. We conclude by examining how pandemic-related social policies have affected young people, what this can tell us about how social policy regimes are adapting to these challenges, and the consequences for intersectional inequalities. In conclusion, we discuss how these experiences illustrate a reinforcement of path dependencies or new patterns of hybridization in social policy delivery.

Comparing Youth Policy Regimes and their Effects

Comparative youth transition regimes of Pohl and Walther (2007, 545–46) distinguish between five main types of youth transition regimes: liberal, universalistic, post-socialist, subprotective, and employment-centered. Our four countries illustrate the liberal (United Kingdom), the universalistic (Norway), post-socialist (Estonia), and subprotective (Spain) types, whose characteristics are summarized in Table 6.1.

Country Case Studies

Liberal Regimes

Key policy trends in the United Kingdom's liberal model of the welfare state over the last 20–30 years include privatization of the public sector, moves to target benefits to the most in need, and "work first" activation measures (Gilbert and Van Voorhis 2017). There has been a wholesale reform of benefits and their delivery through the introduction of Universal Credit in 2013 and a strategy of access based on "Digital by Default," requiring all recipients to be online to access their benefits.

---

[1] This methodology includes extensive review of policy documents and academic literature, secondary data analysis of key comparative indicators of youth labor market performance, and primary data collection of expert interviews with policymakers, employer organizations, trade unions, and academic experts in each country as part of the EU H2020 EUROSHIP project (https://euroship-research.eu/).

Table 6.1 Comparing Youth Policy Regimes

Regime Type	Liberal (UK)	Universalistic (Norway)	Post-socialist (Estonia)	Subprotective (Spain)
Education and Skills	Comprehensive public education system, with private schools; predominance of general education Moderate levels of early school leaving Fragmented post-compulsory training Low status and standardization of VET Limited employer involvement Digital skills high	Comprehensive, free education system, few private schools High levels of early school leaving (compared to the other Nordic countries) High transitions to tertiary education Secondary role of VET Digital skills high	Comprehensive, free education system Secondary role of VET, high transitions to tertiary education Digital skills high	Comprehensive public education (65%), publicly funded private schools (30%), and 100% private schools (5%) Low status and take-up of VET High levels of early school leaving Weak linkages between education system and labour market Digital skills moderate
ALMP for youth at risk	Supply side, workfare activation model Focus on acquisition of employability skills and rapid labor market entry ("work–first" approach) Targeted remedial interventions for NEETs and vulnerable young people	Stronger measures on supply side than on demand side High ALMP investments in activation (Youth Guarantee since 1970s) High human capital investment	Youth Guarantee since 2015, focus on acquisition of employability skills (supply side) and stimulus of labor demand through wage subsidies	Underdeveloped ALMP and low PES capacity Focus on acquisition of first work experience Wage subsidies
Labor market regulation	Low levels of EPL Universalistic minimal social protection Statutory minimum wages age differentiation	Moderate EPL Universalistic social protection, differentiated according to contribution Collectively agreed minimum wages vary by sector and age differentiation	Low levels of EPL Employment and education status–based social protection Collectively agreed minimum wages No age differentiation	High EPL dualism between temporary and permanent employment Segmented social protection with high protection gaps No age-specific minimum wage

(continued)

Table 6.1 Continued

Regime Type	Liberal (UK)	Universalistic (Norway)	Post-socialist (Estonia)	Subprotective (Spain)
Family dependency	Low/Medium; High youth poverty	Low; High youth poverty	Low/Medium; Medium youth poverty	High; High youth poverty
COVID policies	Furlough—general not just youth-specific Kickstart T-level qualifications	Universal policies for employed and self-employed; Additional student loans	Youth Guarantee continued, universal not youth-specific policies, no/limited support for gig-workers	2021—new policies for youth—economic challenges to expenditure—biggest plan on youth in 40 years—EU funded
Performance	Low Unemployment	Low Unemployment	Medium unemployment	High NEETS
Quality of labor market transitions	Fast but unstable; high incidence of low-quality employment Skills mismatch	Fast and stable	Double status of student and full-time worker. High incidence of low-quality employment Skills mismatch	Lengthy and uncertain High levels of temporary employment Skills mismatch Low labor demand

VET, Vocational Education and Training; EPL, Employment Protection Legislation

Source: Adapted from Hadjivassiliou et al. (2019) and Pohl and Walther (2007)

Since the December 2019 reelection of the Conservative Party, the policies introduced during the COVID-19 pandemic have moved away from the austerity agenda, while the rolling out of Universal Credit (UC) has continued. The aim of this policy has been to simplify the array of benefits within one system and address the United Kingdom's "welfare dependency culture" (Hood and Keiller 2016). But the gradual introduction of UC regionally has been systematically linked to a growth in voluntary food banks, indicating the inadequacies of the welfare system to sustain survivable lives for those with precarious incomes (Trussell Trust 2021).

There has been an increased polarization in the youth labor market because of the pandemic, with fewer "steppingstones" to mid-skilled jobs for young people and an increase in insecure and part-time work. Unemployment rate for young Black people has been four times greater than for young white people, and three times greater for young Asian people (Williams et al. 2021).

Universalistic Regimes

The Norwegian welfare state, in contrast, is characterized by a high level of welfare generosity and comprehensive social services available across the entire country (Andersen et al. 2017; Halvorsen et al. 2015). Young people are less dependent on their families, with heavily subsidized services in health and education, public care services for the sick and elderly, and kindergartens for children.

To fund these systems, the state has promoted as high a labor market participation as possible. This goal has been pursued by a strategy of educational and active labor market policies, extensive public sector employment, and the provision of services that encourage female participation in the labor force (Kjeldstad 2001). Public authorities have taken an active role *vis-à-vis* other social institutions, stimulating tripartite collaboration and encouraging renewal and innovation in the economy in general (Moene, Barth, and Willumsen 2014). Full employment has further been supported by Keynesian fiscal and monetary policies fueled by abundant oil revenues (Dølvik and Oldervoll 2019). Job quality for young adults has remained largely unchanged since the mid-1990s (Schoyen and Vedeler 2016, 4). Overall, Norway has to a greater extent than most other European countries succeeded in safeguarding good-quality transitions from education to employment for young adults (Halvorsen and Hvinden 2018).

Post-socialist Regimes

The social, political, and economic transformations of the early 1990s resulted in Estonia opting for a very "thin" state, oriented to attracting foreign investment. Social rights have been gradually expanding since the late 1990s as the country adjusts to European integration, but a workfare ideology and activation dominate. Levels of social welfare expenditure were relatively low between 2005 and 2018, with labor market policy accounting for approximately half of the EU28 average, and social protection at 67% of the EU28 average (Taru et al. 2021).

Estonia is often considered a "deviant" case combining features from several welfare regime types. Liberal characteristics include low levels of employment protection, strict criteria for unemployment benefits, a means-tested minimum income far below the poverty threshold and of short duration, with few opportunities for early retirement (Unt and Saar 2016). "Conservative" characteristics include a generous contribution-based unemployment insurance benefit, and lengthy maternal leave dependent on 18 months' previous contribution; this creates a strong incentive for parents, predominantly mothers, to stay out of the labor market for extended periods. Nordic characteristics include public child care (from age 3) and free education at all levels; this is widely accessible, affordable, and of good quality.

Young Estonians leave home early but are considered as part of family by the state in cases of need up to the age 21 (or up to age 24 for students). While young people have the highest rates of unemployment, they are more likely to find a job quicker than older workers, but this tends to be for shorter periods of time. There has been an increased polarization in the youth labor market as a result of an increase in insecure and gig work.

Subprotective Regimes

In contrast to Estonia, the Spanish welfare state is biased toward the elderly, especially through contributory old age pensions (Ibáñez et al. 2021). By EU standards, the redistributive capacity of social transfers, other than pensions, is very limited, with the lowest impact in reducing poverty (European Commission 2020b). The social protection system suffers traditional gaps in adequacy and coverage, with weak capacities to support struggling people, especially the most vulnerable households and children. High levels of decentralization have aggravated territorial inequalities, with a heterogeneous range of programs and a diversity of bureaucratic requirements witnessing a decreasing take-up of these initiatives.

Most welfare benefits in Spain are dependent on contributions; social assistance benefits occupy a very residual place in the social protection scheme overall. Employment is the main strategy to tackle poverty, but this has seen a long-term growth in precarious and temporary contracts, in particular for young people, resulting in a progressively embedded dualization of the labor market.

During the boom years of the economic cycle (1994–2007), a low-paid temporary contract was the main step out of poverty for many women, migrants, and young people. While the economy was growing, most of these jobs led to situations of relative poverty. As soon as the economy started to falter, transitions were to unemployment with few if any benefits, often resulting in poverty.

Comparing Regime Performance Before and During the Pandemic

The differential effects of these regimes are particularly evident in the rates of those not in employment, education, and training (NEET) (Figure 6.1)—although this measure needs to be treated with caution (Mascherini 2019; O'Reilly et al. 2015)—and those at risk of poverty (Table 6.2).

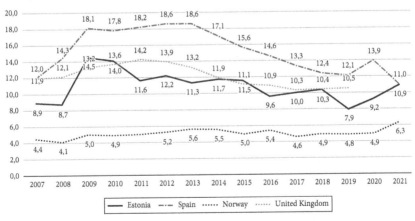

Figure 6.1 NEET Rates: Young people neither in employment nor in education and training, from 15 to 24 years of age (2007–2021). Source: Eurostat, EDAT_ LFSE_23. Note: no comparable data is available for United Kingdom in 2020–2021.

Table 6.2 At Risk of Poverty or Social Exclusion (AROPE), Severe Material Deprivation, In-Work-Poverty (IWP) and Income Inequality 2008–2018/20

		AROPE		Severe material deprivation		In-work-poverty		Income inequality (S80/S20)
		All	16–24	All	16–24	18 and over	16–24	All
European Union	2008	23.7%	28.3%	8.5%	10.8%	8.5%	10.9%	5.01
	2019	21.2%	27.4%	5.3%	6.3%	9.2%	11.7%	5.07
Norway	2008	15%	36.7%	2.0%	3.0%	5.4%	27.5%	3.73
	2020	15.9%	37.3%	2.0%	2.0%	6.0%	23.5%	3.78
United Kingdom	2008	23.2%	26.0%	4.5%	8.4%	8.0%	8.2%	5.63
	2018	23.1%	30.5%	4.6%	7.6%	10.4%	12.7%	5.63
Estonia	2008	21.8%	17.9%	4.9%	3.9%	7.4%	3.3%	4.99
	2020	23,3%	24.9%	2.8%	3.9%	10.5%	18.7%	5.03
Spain	2008	23.8%	26.0%	3.6%	4.8%	11.3%	13.3%	5.59
	2020	26,4%	33,0%	7.0%	10.0%	11.8%	15.7%	5.77

Sources: ilc_di11, ilc_peps01, ilc_mddd11, ilc_iw01

NEET rates have been quite variable across these four countries since the financial crisis and up until the pandemic (Figure 6.1). Since their peak in 2013, these were falling up until the pandemic. They increased most in Spain and Estonia, and even in Norway. The traditionally overall low NEET rate in Norway reflects the priority given to investments in education and active labor market policy measures for young adults. Lockdowns reduced job opportunities, and online teaching increased student dropout risks. NEET rates across Europe have been higher for young women than for young men (Eurostat 2021a).

After the 2008–2013 crisis, employment growth in several European countries (with few exceptions such as Norway) has been based, to a large extent, on downward pressure on wages for workers. For example, between 2008 and 2018, Spanish real average wages decreased and did not return to their pre-recession levels. And for those under 35, even nominal wages decreased, with those under 30, and especially under 24, bearing the higher decreases (CES 2020; INE 2021). Across all countries except for Norway, in-work poverty (IWP) increased between 2008 and 2019 for all age groups and especially for young people aged 16–24. These two measures indicate the increased vulnerability of young people in all four countries, albeit to a different extent.

Education and Skills Gaps Before and During the Pandemic

The long-term policy concern in education and skills gaps for young people were exacerbated during the pandemic, alongside the rapidly evolving digitalization of work and the need for new digital skills (Verdin and O'Reilly 2021). Concerns are not only about the overall level of education and skills but also with the polarized outcomes within countries of those attaining these skills. Here we focus on some key indicators on differences in rates of early school leavers, educational enrollment, and the graduate population in each country (Table 6.3), along with evidence of digital skills gaps (Table 6.4). We then examine policies to address these gaps in each country before and during the pandemic.

Early School Leavers, Enrollment in Education, and Education Performance Gaps

Early school leavers account for around 10% of all 18- to 24-year-olds in the United Kingdom, Norway, and Estonia. Despite regional differences in Spain, overall it has the highest proportion of early school leavers among the four countries compared here (Table 6.3);[2] this is especially high for students with disabilities and a non-EU-born background (Ibáñez et al. 2021).

Table 6.3 Skill Distribution and Levels

Country	% 18–24 Early School Leavers 2019	% 20–29 Education enrolment rates 2018	% 25–29 with tertiary education 2019
United Kingdom	10.9	20.1	44
Norway	9.9	32.2	37
Estonia	9.8	24.4	43
Spain	17.3	31.5	33

Source: Eurostat (2019a), OECD.Stat (2018), OECD (2018; 2020), Schleicher (2019)

[2] EUROSTAT defines an early leaver from education and training as a person aged 18 to 24 who has completed at most lower secondary education and is not involved in further education or training; the indicator "early leavers from education and training" is expressed as a percentage of the people aged 18 to 24 with such criteria, out of the total population aged 18 to 24.

Table 6.4 Digital Skill Level and Access to the Internet

Country	Individuals' level of digital skills, % of 16–24 years old who have above average overall digital skills[a] 2019	Daily use of internet, % of 16–24 years old 2021
Norway	67%	98%
Estonia	76%	99%
Spain	68%	97%
UK	75%	100%
EU average	59%	95%

Source: Eurostat (2019b) ISOC_SK_DSKL_I, ISOC_CI_IFP_FU

[a]It is assumed that individuals having performed certain activities have the corresponding skills. Therefore, the indicators can be considered as proxy of the digital competences and skills of individuals. According to the variety or complexity of activities performed, two levels of skills ("basic" and "above basic") are computed for each of the four dimensions. Finally, based on the component indicators, an overall digital skills indicator is calculated as a proxy of the digital competences and skills of individuals ("no skills." "low," "basic," or "above basic") (Eurostat 2021b).

Spain and Norway have the highest proportion of those aged 20–29 enrolled in education. In Spain, this in part can be attributed to the consistently high levels of youth unemployment over recent decades, with education providing an alternative to the lack of employment. In Norway there is greater support for young people: the educational system is universal, access to higher education is free, and participation is highly supported by the state. Enrollment rates are comparably lower in the United Kingdom and Estonia, but in both countries there is a very high share of tertiary graduates (44%) in the age group 25–34, as most university students complete their degrees by their mid-20s.

The OECD PISA 2018 results (Schleicher 2019; OECD 2020a; OECD 2020b) indicate that the level and distribution of reading and numeracy performance in the United Kingdom, Norway, and especially in Estonia was higher than the OECD average. The mean numeracy score is the lowest in Spain. In Estonia and Norway, there was very little relationship between socioeconomic status and poor reading performance, signaling an more inclusive school system, while the United Kingdom has a remarkable heterogeneity among schools, and around average OECD performance rates for those aged 15.

Digital Skills

Supporting digital skills is a key policy area of both national and EU governments (Hauben et al. 2020). The digital skills indicator from Eurostat

(Table 6.4) is a composite based on selected activities related to internet or software use performed by individuals in four specific areas (information, communication, problem solving, software skills). All four countries perform highly on this measure compared to the EU average, with the United Kingdom and Estonia doing particularly well. Daily use of internet among youth is high in all four countries.

Findings from the Eurobarometer by McDonnell et al. (2022) illustrate intersectional differences in individuals' subjective perceptions of their digital skills, and produce some expected differences in the gaps between different communities across all countries. For example, women, older people, the less well-educated, and those living in households without children have a lower evaluation of their digital skills compared to men, younger people, the better educated, and those living in households with children. However, while this is similar across all countries, the extent of these differences varies between countries. Italians and Hungarians have lower levels of confidence in their digital skills than those in countries like Estonia, Spain, and the United Kingdom, where confidence levels are higher.

These findings resonate with some of the evidence of cross-national differences in the roll out of e-government (O'Reilly and Verdin 2021) and the take-up of jobs on digital platforms (Verdin and O'Reilly 2021). Estonia, Spain, and Norway have the most extensive development of digital e-government in Europe. While the United Kingdom has a much poorer performance, it does better on human capital and business integration of digital technology (O'Reilly and Verdin 2021, 7–9). The United Kingdom has the highest incidence of platform work, accompanied by Germany, Spain, and Italy (Joint Research Centre 2018, 3), whereas this is relatively low in Norway (Dølvik and Jesnes 2018, 13).

Digital forms of employment, especially those on platforms, have increased during the pandemic, but they are often associated with poorer employment conditions and risks in relation to pay and job security (Verdin and O'Reilly 2021, 17–19; Rolf et al. 2022). In this context we turn to examine how governments have sought to support digital training and skills in each of these four countries prior to and during the pandemic.

Active Labor Market Policies to Support Training and Skills

The United Kingdom adopted several measures to enhance youth skills since 1990s. Following the Richard Review in 2012, the focus has been on expanding apprenticeships and creating standards-based programs

(HMGovernment 2015). The apprenticeship levy was introduced in April 2017 to support training. This employer-funded tax pays for the development and delivery of new apprenticeships and gives employers an allowance to encourage them to utilize the fund. It was hoped that the measure would enable an additional 3 million apprenticeships by 2020. However, apprenticeship starts have fallen since the measure was introduced. Attempts to revive the take-up of apprenticeships during the pandemic with the Kickstart Scheme have not been judged very successful, and it is viewed as a case of repeating characteristic errors from the past in not dealing with regional inequalities or providing sufficient incentives to meet employers' needs (Radiven and Prideaux 2022).

The importance of vocational training for those with lower academic attainment has led to the current overhaul of technical education and the introduction of T-levels, as an alternative to apprenticeships and A-levels (Newton et al. 2020). There has been limited development of lifelong learning. Despite the critical role of career guidance schemes for young people in periods of transition, and policy efforts to offset early job insecurity and resultant trajectories, support is limited, especially in comparison with that on offer in Norway (Lewis and Tolgensbakk 2019).

In Norway, a long tradition of supporting youth labor market was evident as early as 1979, with a youth guarantee for 16- to 19-year-olds. A new youth guarantee for the age group 20–24 was established in 2005, and a "follow-up guarantee" in 2007. The latter implied that young people (20–24) who had been unemployed for three months or more were guaranteed personal counseling (job search, activation) from the Norwegian Work and Welfare Administration (NAV). In 2009, the target group was further guaranteed participation in an active labor market measure. In 2013 the Youth Guarantee was extended to include those with reduced work capacity, and in 2014 also those with reduced work capacity in the 25–29 age group (Hardoy et al. 2016).

In 2017, the conservative Solberg government replaced the Norwegian Youth Guarantee with the "New Youth Effort" (*ny ungdomsinnsats*), arguing that this would enable the local offices of the Work and Welfare Administration to provide better and targeted follow-up of NEETS. The aim was to motivate more active job search and faster transitions to employment or education (The National Budget 2017, Meld. St. 1 [2016–2017], p. 71). The New Youth Effort entitled all registered employable jobseekers below the age of 30 to personalized employment support within eight weeks of registration (*Investing in Youth: Norway*, OECD 2018, 12, 18, 20). However, compared to other Northern European countries (Denmark, Finland, the Netherlands, and Sweden) Norway has had a lower share of job seekers of any age participating in active labor market programs between 2006 and 2015 (OECD 2018a, 135).

Although Estonian investment in active labor market policies (ALMPs) is below the EU average, the Public Employment Services system has been developing its services rapidly. In 2015, a "youth guarantee" program was launched to guarantee a training or workplace for all NEET youth, and in 2018 a digital system based on registry data was launched to proactively detect NEET youth to be contacted. During the COVID-19 pandemic in 2020, the provision of services at the local level changed in form as they moved online but were not interrupted, and cooperation with other stakeholders in fact increased in several regions among PES, youth centers, and schools, to better support youth at risk and motivate their studies online (Paabot and Kõiv 2021).

The Youth Guarantee action plan for 2022–2027[3] provided a more dedicated intervention for young people's first job experience and access to work, in particular for more disadvantaged groups. Alongside consulting services, the PES has developed training and apprenticeships, but their take-up is low; mostly wage subsidies are used by youth and employers.

In Spain, although investment in ALMPs is also below the EU average, since 2018 a number of new training and internship initiatives have been developed. The 2018 National Plan for Decent Work (*Plan Director por un Trabajo Digno 2018–2020,* MITRAMISS 2018) aimed to tackle misuses with specific measures such as an anti-fraud program in the field of training, along with more training for labor and social security inspectors and sub-inspectors. However, Ibáñez et al. (2021) suggest that some of these measures have been criticized for not being sufficiently systematic, and their impacts have not been closely monitored.

The Spanish government also launched several programs to increase young people's digital skills as part of the national implementation of the European Youth Guarantee initiative. This includes (1) digital skills training programs for young professionals in 2017; (2) digital training for young people provided by the EOI (Industrial Organization School), with support from the European Social Fund and in collaboration with Google; and

---

[3] https://www.sm.ee/sites/default/files/noortegarantii_tugevdamise_tegevuskava_2022-2027.pdf

(3) The 2019–2021 Action Plan for Youth Employment (*Plan de Choque por el Empleo Joven 2019–2021*). The latter was approved in 2018 by the center-left government to foster young people's access to training and decent stable jobs, with a focus on digital skills and adaptation to technological change (Ibáñez et al. 2021; EC DESI 2021, Corti et al. 2021[4]).

Policies to Support Youth at Risk of Poverty

Alongside policies to enhance young peoples' education and skills, we turn to examine policies to protect youth at risk of poverty that have traditionally varied between our four countries and their responses during the pandemic. A raft of unprecedented measures was introduced during the COVID-19 pandemic (2020) to provide an income buffer to the predicted economic downturn, but young people often did not particularly benefit from these.

The United Kingdom

Relative poverty for young people has increased over the last decade (Williams et al. 2021), although severe material deprivation is below the EU average and has been decreasing slightly. The family provides an important buffer, as the poverty rate for young people not living with their parents is 43%, compared to 25% for those that do (Born and Aldridge 2015, 3). However, the most significant increase of the risk of poverty has been for working youth (Table 6.2). Increases in IWP can be seen within the context of austerity measures and declining generosity of working-age benefits.

Protection systems are now less generous than for previous generations and older adults (Gardiner 2019; Williams et al. 2021). While in 1995–1996, 23% of young people's income derived from benefits, it had dropped to 14% by 2017–2018 (Gardiner and Rahman 2019). Despite increasing minimum wages, the wider context of benefit reform and increased housing costs mean households on low incomes have suffered the biggest losses, with rising levels of IWP for young people. The diversity of cohorts within the age group means

---

[4] https://www.ceps.eu/wp-content/uploads/2021/09/RRRP-No-5_NRRPs-comparison-IT-DE-ES-FR-PT-SK.pdf

this is experienced in variable ways, reflecting intersectional inequalities, and is prone to fluctuations (Born and Aldridge 2015).

Exploration of youth IWP highlights their prominence in low-paid sectors and industries. Young women in the United Kingdom represent one-quarter of those employed in the wholesale and retail sector (28%), followed by the accommodation and food sector (13.8%), then health and social work (13.1%). A quarter of young men are employed in the wholesale and retail sector (25.5%), followed by construction (16.3%) and manufacturing (14.3%) (O'Reilly et al. 2019). Youth unemployment will therefore inevitably be impacted by trends within these sectors (Williams et al. 2021). Furthermore, the growth of zero-hour contracts and increased precariousness in labor market contracts exacerbate trends in household poverty rates.

The UK policy approach used to legitimize welfare reform is the drive for work first. The main policy instruments have included "in work benefits" such as tax credits, and comparatively low levels of out-of-work social protection measures to incentivize making work pay. At the same time there have been a range of universal measures to raise wage rates marginally at the lower end of the income scale, for example with the introduction of the National Minimum Wage (1997) and the more recent increase to the Living Wage (2016). There have been significant efforts to reduce inequality. for example with the Equality Act (2010) synthesizing anti-discrimination legislation and encouraging the use of Equality Impact Assessments for a range of protected characteristics.

Despite youth in the United Kingdom being more independent from their parental households in terms of being able to claim social support, there are several limitations that prevent them from having the same social rights as older age groups. The United Kingdom has one of the highest minimum wage schemes in developed nations, but within this regulatory landscape there are lower statutory minimums for young people (Dube 2019). These differentials are reflected across work welfare support schemes. Limitations and restrictions for young people extend beyond work related benefits. In terms of housing, UC had initially removed the housing cost entitlement for 18- to 21-year-olds. But as a result of sharp criticism, this was reinstated in October 2018 during rollout. The Shared Accommodation Rate was introduced in 1996 and limits the level of housing benefit young people can receive. The benefit was frozen from 2016 to 2020. In 2018–2019, housing benefit was found to be inadequate for 92% of rents (Crisis 2019).

Norway

Norwegian social policy has tended to be supply-oriented and to emphasize the person's qualifications, skills, or "human capital," and focused on
how to strengthen these to improve the person's job chances and employability. Obstacles to employment as expressed in social maladjustment, distance from the labor market, and lack of work experience, along with issues
of work capacity, individual accommodation, accessibility at the work place,
and discrimination in employment have been given more limited attention,
as has the potential contribution of demand-oriented approaches. However,
informed by reforms in the United Kingdom and the EU, Norway has
introduced more nondiscrimination regulations in working life since 2000.

The Norwegian income maintenance system has aimed to enable people
to maintain about the same standard of living during periods of unemployment or insufficient income from paid work. From the 1990s, Norway has
tightened up their income maintenance systems for persons of expected
working age. They have introduced stricter qualification criteria and reduced
or frozen compensation rates (generosity) or duration of benefits (Dalgaard
2011; Harsløf 2005; Hultqvist and Nørup 2017; Hvinden 2003; Hvinden
et al. 2001; Johansson and Hvinden 2007; Thorén 2008). To maintain control over the spending of money on welfare and help young adults achieve
employment, Norwegian governments have introduced or reinforced several obligations ("conditionalities") for welfare beneficiaries. They require
recipients to document that they are actively seeking job opportunities, accept offers to participate in labor-market qualification courses, vocational
training, and job placements, to account for their economic situation, family
relationships, and responsibilities in detail, and verify they do not have undeclared work. This orientation toward activation has however not been reflected in increased investments in training or active employment programs.
Also, the priority to 'activation' among national policymakers has not always
been implemented or followed up very enthusiastically by local staff, due to
competing local priorities (e.g., Scharle et al. 2015) and relatively autonomous street-level professionals in the social services (Gjersøe et al. 2019).

Political concern has revolved around the rising proportion of young
people on incapacity-related benefits. In spite of reforms since the mid-
1990s, the rate of young adults in receipt of incapacity-related benefits has
continued to increase. Mental health problems have become a main reason
for benefit receipt among young adults (Bragstad 2018; Halvorsen, Hvinden,

and Schoyen 2019). In 2016 more than half of the NEET youth aged 15–19 received incapacity-related benefits. The distribution illustrates the significant medicalization of early job insecurity in Norway (OECD 2018b).

Young adults who have not gained entitlements to unemployment benefits administrated at the national level usually have been referred to residual and means-tested social assistance provided by the local authorities. These are often more conditional on participation in active labor market policy measures, unlike those for persons with an employment record who have been entitled to social insurance benefits. Beneficiaries of tested social assistance have typically included newly arrived immigrants and young adults with insufficient labor market experience to be entitled to rights-based social security benefits.

Estonia

Poverty rates of young people aged 18–24 are slightly above the average; however, severe material deprivation is marginal in Estonia, affecting only 3.5% of young in 2019. Yet, IWP has increased from 7.4% to 10.5% for youth compared to a decade earlier (Table 6.2). Due to minimal social welfare (apart from in-kind subsidies such as school and health care), employment is essential for protection from poverty. Overall employment levels have been very high in Estonia during boom periods, but due to the consequences of the pandemic they have been decreasing. Being unemployed puts people at great risk of poverty—53% of unemployed were at risk of poverty in 2019.

According to analysis by Ministry of Social Affairs in 2018, 14% of the working-age population (approx. 120,000 people) do not have continuous health insurance in Estonia. Females with children have the highest risk of not being covered during the period after a child turns 3 years of age and they are unable to find a job. Men's risk is high if they are employed in fixed-term jobs with fragmentary social insurance coverage. Young people are overrepresented among those who have irregular, platform work or are unemployed.

Estonia has a rather generous contribution-based unemployment insurance benefit (UIB) (60% of previous salary for first 100 days, 40% thereafter). Young people often do not qualify for UIB, but are entitled to an unemployment allowance which has less strict conditions and is considerably less generous (SB €189 in 2020). There have been discussions at various levels about how to increase the coverage of unemployment insurance payments and/or increase the generosity of the unemployment allowance to alleviate the risk of poverty among the unemployed. From 2021, the unemployment allowance was increased to €220. If enrolled in higher education, a student allowance can be claimed if the parental household is in need, tying youth to their parental homes even if they are living on their own.

The main wage-setting policy in Estonia that is relevant for the young is the statutory national minimum wage. Changes in the statutory national minimum wage have a stronger impact for youth, as a larger proportion of them are in low-wage work (Taru et al. 2021). Although the ratio of the minimum wage to the national median wage has increased annually, moving from 44% in 2012 to 49% in 2019 (Customs and Tax Board 2020), this is still below the relative poverty threshold (60% of median wage).

Wage setting in Estonia mostly takes place at company level through bipartite negotiations between the employer and individual employees. Collective bargaining coverage is low, with only 3.9% of companies and 19% of employees covered in 2015. Minimum wage agreements only exist in health care and transport (Masso et al. 2019). Only 12% of 15- to 24-year-olds worked in these sectors in 2019 (Statistics Estonia 2020), with young people more likely to be affected by company-level wage setting.

During the pandemic the importance of the family grew, as schools and state support systems moved online. Access to high-speed internet, digital devices, and digital skills became essential to participate in learning or to access social services. External support for most vulnerable groups decreased, and no youth-specific measures were launched during the pandemic.

Spain

As a result of Great Recession, children and working-age adults have been facing some of the highest risks of poverty and social exclusion. Although by 2019 all Spanish regions had recovered to a certain extent, poverty indicators were still higher than in 2008. Severe material deprivation was higher in 2019 than 2008 (6.4% vs 4.9%) and comparable with that in the United Kingdom (Table 6.2) The lack of funding for social protection (other than pensions for older adults) is aggravated by regional disparities, inter-territorial coordination problems, and bureaucratic procedures.

The persistence of income inequalities, even when employment rates started to rise after the economic recession, help to explain why IWP rates have increased in households with a medium to high work intensity. The risk of IWP is much higher for fixed-term workers than those with permanent jobs (21.3% and 7.3% in 2018 respectively) (EC 2020b). The rise in IWP in the 16–24 age group between 2012 and 2015 was particularly rapid: in three years the rate doubled from 12.3% to 24.7%. A combination of policies associated with exiting the crisis, and labor market reforms between 2010 and 2014, encouraged the growth of low-paid, temporary, and part-time employment among young workers (Ibáñez et al. 2021). Since the 1990s, Spanish labor market policies (implemented by both center-left and center-right governments) have had little effect in modifying this precariousness for young people.

Many young workers are more likely to be in low-income jobs and poverty (20% in 2019), but the situation is even worse for the unemployed. Family benefits and income-guarantee schemes have a weak effect on poverty reduction. As young people do not usually qualify for contributory unemployment benefits, they are dependent on a low level of fragmented schemes.

Nevertheless, a recent development to provide for households' minimum level of income was introduced in May 2020 with the "Vital Minimum Income" (IMV). While not a universal basic income, this measure supplanted a highly diverse range of regional schemes for the economically vulnerable (Monereo 2020) with a more homogeneous and coherent, non-contributory national solution. This policy was part of a package of activation measures where recipients must be registered as job seekers and participate in social inclusion strategies.

Alongside supply-side training and skill measures, successive national governments have introduced demand-side measures over the past years to tackle youth unemployment. Spain launched a new wage subsidy program for 10,000 unemployed 18- to 29-year-olds in 2018. It also adopted a reduction in the social security contributions for three years for firms that transformed training contracts into open-ended ones, and introduced new wage subsidies for first-time hires by young entrepreneurs (up to 35 years) (EC 2019c). However, the impact of 2010–2016 hiring subsidies for quality youth employment seem to be limited (EC 2020). By 2020, the EC 2020 Country Report still found that hiring subsidies absorbed about 40% of ALMP resources, and they were not very effective.

The measure with the highest impact in reducing IWP has been the increase in the Interprofessional Minimum Wage, which has been raised by

47% over the last five years, with minimum salaries increasing from 736€ a month in 2018 to 1,080€ a month in 2023, and reaching the 60% of the Spanish average wage. While the youth unemployment rate has not risen after the minimum wage increases, contrary to some experts' opinions, the return of high inflation is eroding the most recent increases in the minimum wage. Recovery from the pandemic will be challenging, as young people are more likely to work in low-paying and precarious jobs.

The Consequences of COVID for Youth Transitions

The impact of the pandemic on young people has been evident in several ways. Here we provide a broad overview of three key areas of impact for those aged 15–24: first, for those who were still enrolled in formal education; second, for those transitioning into the labor market; and finally, the psycho-social aspects related to both.

The first wave of the COVID-19 crisis in 2020 was partially cushioned by strong fiscal responses from the EU and national governments (Eurofound 2020; ILO 2020). The subsidized employment programs initially supported the employment of permanent workers, while the support for temporary workers and self-employed people varied considerably across countries. Young people, who are more likely to hold a temporary contract and more likely to engage in various new forms of work with less or no social protection, such as gig work, benefitted proportionally less from these employment programs. Furthermore, young people's employment opportunities have been affected by the series of lockdowns in 2020 and 2021, reducing mobility between workplaces. The increasing trend toward teleworking in professional and other jobs has put newcomers, many of whom are youth, in a less favorable situation, as well as making it difficult for them to transition smoothly to working life due to decreased opportunities for spontaneous and informal networking and on-the-job informal learning.

School Closures

First, when considering the effect of lockdown on young people, a significant factor was the closure of schools and the cancellation of exams, although this varied by country and parental occupations. For example in the United

Kingdom and Spain, approximately half a year of face-to-face teaching was lost; in Estonia the impact was less dramatic, as schools were only fully closed during the first wave; in Norway this full closure lasted between six to eight weeks, with some local adaptations.

The degree of variability in school closures was affected by phased reopening for different age groups, variable local restrictions, and the initial lack of compulsory attendance. In all four countries, children of essential workers, along with some vulnerable children, were allowed to attend; others were dependent on remote learning and family resources to support school attendance. The effect was to enhance existing inequalities between those with sufficient devices and internet connections and those without. In Norway some teachers have expressed concern that the option of coming to school in person did not reach all the children and youth who could not cope very well with home schooling (Andersen et al. 2021; Federici and Vika 2020).

During later waves of the pandemic, there has been considerable variation in the extent and organization of home schooling, with more digital online teaching for older students and in areas with higher infection rates. In subsequent periods of online learning, classes were typically split into smaller cohorts, alternating between home schooling and regular attendance to avoid extended periods at home. Since September 2020 most schools remained open to support face-to-face teaching (OECD 2021).[5]

The variability in outcomes relates to factors such as resources, learning environments at home, and those provided by schools that further embedded intersectional inequalities such as socioeconomic status, race, and gender. For example in the United Kingdom, where there are data on these differences (Andrew et al. 2020), the availability of a digital device to work on and adequate connectivity have been decisive factors in the ability to transition to online learning (Ayllon et al. 2021; DfE 2020; YouthEmploymentUK 2021). In the United Kingdom, 9% of households with children did not have access to a device, including one in five of those eligible for free school meals (Baker et al. 2020). While some broadband providers offer a "social tariff" (i.e., lower costs), the cost of connectivity remains a significant barrier (Lloyds 2021). In Estonia, there is no representative data on availability of necessary digital tools for all pupils. There were ad hoc responses to the crisis from the nonprofit sector—for example, there was a volunteering initiative in Estonia,

---

[5] OECD (2021) *The state of education during the COVID pandemic.*

"Computer to Every Schoolchild,"[6] and comparable measures in other countries to support those who lacked household devices to enable online home learning. This included, for example, Estonian university students providing support for children's home schooling.[7] In the United Kingdom, football players campaigned for such children to receive free school meals during the summer holidays.[8]

Intersectional differences were evident not just in terms of socioeconomic inequalities, which were not always recorded in each country, but other factors that could be measured in regional differences within countries. Broadband infrastructure is built mainly in cities; children living in remote places faced problems with connectivity quality while using such alternatives as hotspots via mobile phones. Estonia already had in place a well-developed and widely used digital environment e-school,—for instance, it was a common practice for teachers to post homework online before the pandemic, and this facilitated a smoother transition to remote learning. Several dedicated non-representative studies (Paabot and Kõiv 2021) mention that both children and young people respond differently to distant learning: a third thrive, a third fail, and a third cope.

In Norway, connectivity and access to necessary equipment for both students and teachers were quite good when students had to switch to online learning in March 2020. Among upper secondary school students full coverage was provided for personal computers even before the pandemic. However, since students could choose whether to use private laptops or publicly procured devices, there was some variation in the quality of the available equipment. Lower secondary school children had been given devices from their schools (Fjørtoft 2020). A perhaps greater challenge was that many teachers felt they had inadequate digital skills to meet the demands of online teaching, and they also experienced that many students had insufficient skills. In many cases, inadequate digital skills have been a greater challenge than digital infrastructure as such (Andersen et al. 2021).

Across all ethnic groups in the United Kingdom, those with Pakistani and Bangladeshi backgrounds spent the least amount of time studying at home, while those with Black Caribbean or Black African students spent the highest

[6] https://www.lastekaitseliit.ee/et/igale-koolilapsele-arvuti/,
[7] https://opleht.ee/2021/02/tudengid-kooli/
[8] https://www.bbc.co.uk/newsround/54862230

average hours on schoolwork (Leahy et al. 2021; Newton 2021). Secondary school students in the highest earning families spent an average of 5.1 hours per day studying compared to 3.9 hours in lowest earning groups. Girls typically spent more time than boys, and the level of parental education marked a further differential.

Plans to address gaps in learning have been implemented in the United Kingdom, such as the National Tutoring Programme, catch-up funding, and proposed extensions to the school day (DFE 2021; DFE 2022). However, schemes have suffered from poor performance that resulted in funds being re-diverted (Shearing 2022). The evidence concerning the experience of online learning and the emergence of potential educational gaps is somewhat mixed in Norway. In a student survey carried out in late 2020, 60% of the respondents report a decline in perceived learning, even if many also stated that they spent as many hours as before, or more, on school work. As far as general satisfaction with the school day is concerned, there is great variation in perceptions. While about one in five stated that they were "far less satisfied," nearly the same share felt happier with school during lockdown. Just over half the respondents stated that they felt a lower learning motivation in this period. Many teachers were especially worried about the negative effects of lockdown and online learning, and consequently a widening learning gap for the weakest students. At the same, teachers also experienced that some students seemed to find it easier to excel academically when they did not have to worry about being socially accepted in the class (Andersen et al. 2021).

School to Work Transitions

Alongside these gaps in learning, young people transitioning from education to work were adversely impacted given the sectors they work in and the insecure contracts they entail (Brewer et al. 2020; Joyce and Xu 2020). Plans to offset these effects in the United Kingdom include expansion of post-18 education and training for young people (PM'sOffice 2020). Recovery in terms of employment has been strong for young people, though more are now economically inactive than pre-pandemic, and poor job quality remains an issue (Powell et al. 2022; Adcock 2022; YouthEmploymentUK 2021). Less than half of young people had access to career advice during the pandemic (YouthEmploymentUK 2021).

In Estonia, unemployment increased among young people especially in services and sales (EAS 2021). Young people were not benefitting from public policies to support employers to keep workers in employment. The financial situation of the young has not been easy: 55% of those aged 18–29 worry about their financial situation and general welfare, and the 15- to 24-year-olds are more than twice as likely (7% vs 3%) than those aged above 25 to turn to their local government for support with problems related to COVID (see Haugas et al. 2021). During the pandemic, a pension reform gave contributors the opportunity to terminate their retirement plans and take out their pension savings.

If we compare youth aged 15–24 to the general population in Norway, we see that unemployment increased more for this group both in March 2020 and during the second round of lockdown measures about a year later. A study of the Norwegian labor market in the period March 1–22, 2022 showed that in the first days after coronavirus control measures were first imposed, workers on low pay and short employment tenure dominated among the applicants for unemployment benefits. Not surprisingly, younger workers were overrepresented in this group (Bratsberg et al. 2022).[9] This picture is partly confirmed in an analysis performed by Statistics Norway and covering a more extended period from the beginning of the pandemic until May 2021. Sectors employing individuals with low education and a low mean age were disproportionately affected (Grini et al. 2021). In terms of policy, from April 2020 the government temporarily changed eligibility rules to allow job seekers to be enrolled in education or training without losing their benefits (Dahl et al. 2021). This made it possible for workers to move into education as an alternative to inactivity while furloughed or fully unemployed. Moreover, the minimum prior earnings requirement to be eligible for unemployment benefits had been temporarily lowered already in March 2020. This benefitted workers in part-time and low-income jobs, including many young people. However, it is worth noting that most students who were furloughed from a (typically part-time) job were still excluded from the unemployment benefit scheme, since most Norwegian students receive a student loan, which disqualifies them from unemployment benefits granted to persons with job-seeker status (Dahl et al. 2021; Danielsen and Sørbø 2021).

[9] English summary of the report available here: https://www.frisch.uio.no/om-oss/Nyheter/pdf/oppsummering-engelsk.pdf.

Psychosocial Factors and Youth Well-being

Finally, and related to both education and the transition to work, are the associated psychosocial factors and young people's well-being. Even before the pandemic there was increased awareness of mental health issues in public debate in the United Kingdom. Inequalities have been marked for single-parent households, those with low-educated parents, larger families, and those in poorer households. During the pandemic there have been increased reports of violence, child abuse, and neglect (Romanou and Belton 2020; BBC 2021). The incidence of poor mental health among children and young people has also been disproportionately affected (Lally 2020). The disruptive effect this has on young people's capacity to transition from education to employment has been highlighted by Youth Employment UK (YouthEmploymentUK 2021). Post-lockdown recovery outcomes appear to be worse for those with special educational needs, disabilities, and those from poorer families (Raw et al. 2021). These findings highlight how the pandemic has intensified existing inequalities for young people in disproportionate ways across many intersecting dimensions.

Even if, at least short-term, the labor market position of young people deteriorated as a consequence of the pandemic, results from the annual Ungdata survey of Norwegian youth show that Norwegian secondary school pupils (approximately aged 13–19) remained fairly optimistic about their long-term labor market prospects and life chances. In 2021, about one year into the pandemic, only 16% believed they would ever experience unemployment. This was identical to the (pre-pandemic) result of surveys carried out in the years 2018–2020. Only 3% answered no when asked whether they thought they would have a "good and happy life." There was no change from the result recorded prior to the pandemic. Conversely, the share of respondents that answered yes to this question was high, and only marginally different from the preceding years (68% in 2021 compared to 69% 2018–2020) (Bakken 2021).[10]

The combination of the two dimensions—rethinking vulnerability and experiencing practical hardships—has had immense and direct impact on the mental health status of young people. There were several campaigns about availability of mental health support, but real support has not been

---

[10] 28% answered "don't know." For an English-language summary of these results, see https://www.oslomet.no/en/research/featured-research/norwegian-youth-handled-pandemic-well.

easily available due to understaffing, long waiting times in public as well as private health care facilities, and low affordability of the latter for the young. Furthermore, in Estonia a young person is not legally entitled to see a therapist without parental consent, and this might become a problem in a sociocultural context where mental health issues are not generally discussed. During the pandemic, the regular interaction with other adults away from home—such as at school, at youth work sites, at work, and so on—was made inaccessible, and the need for support remained undetected. Of those aged 15–24, 55% experience depression or other mental health issues, 38% have anxiety disorders, and 68% feel mentally exhausted (Käger et al. 2021)—and while this has been explained by lack of access to peer communication related to the lockdown of schools, non-formal education, and entertainment, this is of critical relevance, especially for the young to develop self-awareness and become independent adults.

Conclusion

This chapter set out to understand to what extent short-term effects created by the pandemic disrupted path-dependent policy regimes for youth in four European countries. It also sought to understand if there has been a perceptible change attributable to longer-term developments in digitalization. The consequences of the pandemic have only exacerbated some of the challenges that young people have faced since the financial crisis of 2007–2008. Young people were among the hardest-hit groups after the financial crisis, with unemployment rising three times faster than for other groups (Wilson et al. 2020). The high levels of unemployment they suffered and the scarring effects this can have, particularly if it continues longer term, are significant (Mascherini et al. 2017; Zuccotti and O'Reilly 2018; Unt et al. 2021). Despite some labor market recovery from 2013 onward, the pandemic has particularly affected sectors where young people were more likely to work. They are more likely to be employed in sectors associated with low pay and precarious work; combined with rising housing costs and limited welfare support, this makes them increasingly vulnerable.

For most young people the pandemic has been more about all the restrictive measures governments have taken to contain the spread of coronavirus than direct risks to their own health. That is, the lives and opportunities of young people have been greatly affected by school closures, measures to reduce mobility, and restrictions on activities that involve (nonessential) contact between people. In all countries the economic sectors that employ many young people, such as the hospitality industry, have been particularly hard hit by lockdown policies. However, there has been considerable variation across countries in the timing, duration, and strictness of public policies to combat the pandemic.

Intersectional differences position young people according to multiple social categories. The variegated outcomes for them are dependent on factors such as class, education, gender, and ethnicity, highlighting how the risks of poverty interact with welfare reforms and work-first policy initiatives (O'Reilly et al. 2019a, 2019b). Pre-pandemic challenges have only become more heightened. Educational inequalities are enhanced as a result of school closures that have further entrenched the socioeconomic inequalities faced by young people. Key moments of transition will inevitably be frustrated as opportunities for work experience and career guidance will be limited.

One of the key features this analysis reveals is that while governments have been quick to respond to cushioning the effect of the pandemic with financial packages, not all young people could access these. More significant long-term consequences of the pandemic are likely to create significant challenges to previous underlying structural inequalities related to forms of education, training, and the quality of employment offered to young people. We identified how these policies simultaneously reinforce some element of social policy path dependency, while also creating significant disruption in addressing the pandemic in the context of the emerging digital economy, a reinforcement of reliance on the family in some cases, and an increasing level of polarization between different types of households.

There is a pressing need to ensure that social protection systems afford a safety net relevant to the needs and difficulties faced by young people. Our four-country comparison illustrates how the United Kingdom combines individualized youth welfare citizenship, relatively selective skill systems with high overall average level of skills, dual labor markets with expanding zero-hour contracts, and a potential expansion of the welfare state as policies of austerity are abandoned. But the extent to which these will address structural inequalities in plans to build back remains a significant challenge. The Norwegian case also shared an individualized concept of youth welfare citizenship. There was a more comprehensive skill system with high overall average level of skills, and only very marginal share of precarious work. However, students who maintained themselves on part-time jobs were not entitled to furlough. The Estonian case illustrated a distinctive familiarized conception of youth welfare citizenship along with early home-leaving and a comprehensive skill system with very high overall average level of skills. But young people were also more exposed to risks of poverty and the expansion of "no clear employment status" work. The Spanish case includes a familiarized youth welfare citizenship, a comprehensive education system with limited impacts on correcting embedded social inequalities or improving young people's working conditions, and a combination of a rigidly segmented labor market with structural productivity gaps in the economy that traps many young people into low-paid jobs. Additionally, unaffordable accommodation and little access to social benefits also help to explain why many young people leave the parental home well past the age of 30.

Analysis from the economic crisis and the pandemic suggests that the ability for these regimes to significantly shift is marred by the challenges of policy coordination and macroeconomic factors (Hadjivassiliou et al. 2019). These cases illustrate the distinctive and comparable challenges that arise as a result of the pandemic with regard to how social policy addresses the issues of income maintenance and skill development in the digital age.

Acknowledgments

Research for this chapter has received funding from the European Union's Horizon 2020 research and innovation program under grant agreement No. 870698. The opinions published in this chapter only reflect the authors' views. The Research Executive Agency and the European Commission are not responsible for any use that may be made of the information it contains.

As part of the ESRC Digital Futures at Work Research Centre (Digit), this work was also supported by the UK Economic and Social Research Council (grant number ES/S012532/1), which is gratefully acknowledged.

We want to acknowledge the authors of EUROSHIP country reports. In addition, we want to thank Epp Reiska for her research assistance.

References

Andersen, Rolf K., Mona Bråten, Ester Bøckmann, Marianne Takvam Kindt, Torgeir Nyen, and Anna Hagen Tønder. 2021. *Håndtering og konsekvenser av koronautbruddet for videregående opplæring*. FAFO-rapport 2021:09. Fafo. https://www.fafo.no/images/pub/2021/20776.pdf.

Andrew, Alison, Sarah Cattan, Monica Costa Dias, et al. 2020. *Family time use and home learning during the COVID-19 lockdown.* IFS Report R178. The Institute for Fiscal Studies. https://ifs.org.uk/publications/15038.

Bakken, Anders. 2021. *Ungdata 2021. Nasjonale resultater.* NOVA Rapport 8/21. *NOVA Norwegian Social Research.* https://hdl.handle.net/11250/2767874.

Born, Theo Barry, and Hannah Aldridge. 2015. *Poverty among young people in the UK.* New Policy Institute. https://www.npi.org.uk/files/7114/2892/2456/Poverty_among_y oung_people_in_the_UK_FINAL.pdf.

Bratsberg, Bernt, Simen Markussen, Knut Røed, and Oddbjørn Raaum. 2022. *Hvem tar støyten? Arbeidsmarkedet under Koronakrisen.* Frisch Centre, Statistics Norway and NAV. https://www.frisch.uio.no/om-oss/Nyheter/pdf/rapportdagpengesoknader.pdf.

Dahl, Espen, Jorunn Furuberg, Ingunn Heide, et al. 2021. "Ett år med Korona. Utvikling og utsikter for NAVs ytelser og brukere." *Arbeid og Velferd* 2021 (1): 21–43.

Danielsen, Mia Wallgren, and Johannes Sørbø. 2021. "Hvem tok utdanning i kombinasjon med dagpenger under koronapandemien?" *Arbeid og Velferd* 2021 (3): 59–72.

Dølvik, Jon Erik, and Kristin Jesnes. 2018. *Nordic labour markets and the sharing economy: Report from a pilot project.* Nordic Council of Ministers. https://norden.diva-portal.org/smash/get/diva2:1182946/FULLTEXT01.pdf.

Efuribe, Chinwe, Madisen Barre-Hemingway, Evangelina Vaghefi, and Ahna Ballonoff Suleiman. 2020. "Coping with the COVID-19 crisis: A call for youth engagement and the inclusion of young people in matters that affect their lives." *Journal of Adolescent Health* 67: 16–17.

Eurofound. 2020. *Youth in a time of covid.* Luxembourg: Publications Office of the European Union. https://www.eurofound.europa.eu/publications/blog/youth-in-a-time-of- covid.

European Commission. 2020. *Maintenance obligations. National information and online forms concerning Regulation No. 4/2009.* https://e-justice.europa.eu/355/EN/maintena nce_obligations.

European Commission/EACEA/Eurydice. 2018. *National student fee and support systems in European higher education—2018/19. Eurydice—Facts and Figures.* Publications Office of the European Union.

Eurostat. 2019a. Database. Early leavers from education and training by sex and degree of urbanization (EDAT_LFSE_30). Luxembourg, Eurostat.

Eurostat. 2019b. Database. Estimated average age of young people leaving the parental household (YTH_DEMO_030). Luxembourg, Eurostat.

Eurostat. 2021a. Database. Young people neither in employment nor in education and training (EDAT_LFSE_23). Luxembourg, Eurostat.

Eurostat. 2021b. Database. Individuals who have basic or above basic overall digital skills by sex (TEPSR_SP410).

Federici, Roger André, and Karl Solbue Vika. 2020. *Spørsmål til Skole-Norge. Analyser og resultater fra Utdanningsdirektoratets spørreundersøkelse til skoleledere, skoleeiere og lærere under korona-utbruddet 2020.* Rapport 2020:13. Nordisk institutt for studier av innovasjon, forskning og utdanning (NIFU). https://nifu.brage.unit.no/nifu-xmlui/bitstr eam/handle/11250/2656248/NIFU-rapport2020-13.pdf?sequence=1andisAllowed=y.

Fernández-Macías Enrique, Cesira Urzí Brancati, et al. 2018. *Platform workers in Europe: Evidence from the COLLEEM Survey.* Publications Office of the European Union. https://op.europa.eu/en/publication-detail/-/publication/fe8c6fdf-79b8-11e8-ac6a-01aa75ed71a1/language-en.

Fjørtoft, Siw Olsen. 2020. *Nær og fjern. Læreres erfaringer med digital hjemmeskole våren 2020.* 19 August. https://hdl.handle.net/11250/2676094.

Garritzmann, Julian, Silja Häusermann, and Bruno Palier. 2017. *WoPSI—the World Politics of Social Investment: An International research project to explain variance in social investment agendas and social investment reforms across countries and world regions*. LIEPP Working Paper no. 64, 1–68. https://spire.sciencespo.fr/notice/2441/5rob5aq5l98ll9et3sg8meehvg#_ga=2.239407495.549146100.1590477965-2018747 383.1590477965.

Grini, Knut Håkon, Magnus Berglund Johnsen, Ervis and Konci. 2021. *Arbeidslivet og smitteverntiltak—hva har skjedd etter 12. mars 2020*. Rapporter 2021/38, December 17. Statistics Norway. https://www.ssb.no/arbeid-og-lonn/sysselsetting/artikler/arbeidsli vet-og-smitteverntiltak/_/attachment/inline/f20dfb92-d7bc-465e-bb82-84684095b af4:59a9ee43590df0a2d940ce4e138794833b44ecae/RAPP2021-38.pdf.

Hadjivassiliou, Kari P., Arianna Tassinari, Werner Eichhorst, and Florian Wozny. 2019. "How Does the Performance of School-to-Work Transition Regimes Vary in the European Union?" In *Youth Labor in Transition: Inequalities, Mobility, and Policies in Europe*, edited by Jacqueline O'Reilly, Janine Leschke, Renate Ortlieb, Martin Seeleib-Kaiser, and Paolo Villa, 71–103. Oxford: Oxford University Press.

Halvorsen, Rune, and Bjørn Hvinden. 2018. "Introduction: Youth, Diversity and Employment—an Analytic Framework." In *Youth, Diversity and Employment: Comparative Perspectives on Labour Market Policies*, edited by Rune Halvorsen and Bjørn Hvinden, 1–31. Cheltenham: Edward Elgar.

Halvorsen, Rune, Caterina Arciprete, Mario Biggeri, Federico Ciani, and Mi Ah Schoyen. 2021. *D2.2. Analyzing gaps in European social citizenship. The interaction of capabilities, active agency and social resilience*. EUROSHIP working paper.

Halvorsen, Rune, Ivan Harsløf, Bjørn Hvinden, and Mi Ah Schoyen. 2021. *Country report on national social protection systems. Norway*. EUROSHIP unpublished material.

European Parliament, Directorate-General for Internal Policies of the Union Karolien Lenaerts, Willem Wayaert, Harald Hauben, The platform economy and precarious work, Hauben, H. (editor), European Parliament. 2020. *The platform economy and precarious work*. Committee on Employment and Social Affairs (EMPL). https://data.eur opa.eu/doi/10.2861/041400.

Hemerijck, Anton. 2015. "The quiet paradigm revolution of social investment." *Social Politics* 22 (2): 242–56.

Hvinden, Bjørn, Jacqueline O'Reilly, Mi Ah Schoyen, and Christer Hyggen. 2019. *Negotiating Early Job Insecurity. Well-being, Scarring and Resilience of European Youth*. Cheltenham: Edward Elgar.

Ibáñez, Zyab, Margarita León, and LLorenç Soler. 2021. *Country report on national social protection systems. Spain*. EUROSHIP unpublished material.

ILO. 2020. *Youth and COVID-19: Impacts on jobs, education, rights and mental well-being*. https://www.ilo.org/global/topics/youth-employment/publications/WCMS_753026/lang--en/index.htm.

ILO. 2020. *ILO monitor: COVID-19 and the world of work* (2nd ed.). International Labour Organization. https://www.oitcinterfor.org/en/node/7770.

Joint Research Centre (European Commission), Enrique Fernández-Macías, Cesira Urzí Brancati, et al. 2018. *Platform Workers in Europe: Evidence from the COLLEEM Survey*. LU: Publications Office of the European Union. https://op.europa.eu/en/publication-detail/-/publication/fe8c6fdf-79b8-11e8-ac6a-01aa75ed71a1/language-en.

Karamessini, Maria, Maria Symeonaki, Glykeria Stamatopoulou, and Dimitris Parsanoglou. 2019. "Mapping Early Job Insecurity Impacts of the Crisis in Europe." In *Youth Unemployment and job Insecurity in Europe. Problems, Risk Factors and Policies*, edited by Bjørn Hvinden, Christer Hyggen, Mi A. Schoyen, and Tomáš Sirovátka, 24–44. Cheltenham: Edward Elgar.

Kohli, Martin. 1986. "The World We Forgot: A Historical Review of the Life Course." In *Later Life: The Social Psychology of Ageing*, edited by Victor W. Marshall, 271–303. Beverly Hills: Sage.

Lauri, Triin, and Marge Unt. 2021. "Multiple Routes to Youth Well-being: A Qualitative Comparative Analysis of Buffers to the Negative Consequences of Unemployment." In *Social Exclusion of Youth in Europe: The Multifaceted Consequences of Labour Market Insecurity*, edited by Marge Unt, Michael Gebel, Sonia Bertolini, Vassiliki Deliyanni-Kouimtzi, and Dirk Hofäcker, 81–111. Bristol: Policy Press.

Leahy, Fiona, Paul Newton, and Aneesa Khan. 2021. *Learning during the pandemic: quantifying lost time*. The Stationary Office. https://www.gov.uk/government/publications/learning-during-the-pandemic/learning-during-the-pandemic-quantifying-lost-time.

Leisering, Lutz, and Stephan Leibfried. 1999. *Time and Poverty in Western Welfare States: United Germany in Perspective*. Cambridge: Cambridge University Press.

Lewis, Christine, and Ida Tolgensbakk. 2019. "Public Policy on Career Education, Information, Advice and Guidance: Developments in the United Kingdom and Norway." In *Negotiating Early Job Insecurity: Well-Being, Scarring and Resilience of European Youth*, edited by Bjørn Hvinden, Jacqueline O'Reilly, Mi A. Schoyen, and Christer Hyggen Cheltenham, 205–27. Cheltenham: Edward Elgar.

Lister, Ruth, Fiona Williams, Anneli Anttonen. 2007. *Gendering Citizenship in Western Europe: New Challenges for Citizenship Research in a Cross-national Context*. Bristol: Policy Press.

Märtsin, Mariann. 2019. *Identity Development in the Life-Course: A Semiotic Cultural Approach to Transitions in Early Adulthood*. Cham: Palgrave.

Mascherini, Massimiliano. 2019. "Origins and Future of the Concept of NEETs in the European Policy Agenda." In *Youth Labor in Transition: Inequalities, Mobility, and Policies in Europe*, edited by Jacqueline O'Reilly, Janine Leschke, Renate Ortlieb, Martin Seeleib-Kaiser, and Paolo Villa, 503–29. Oxford: Oxford University Press.

Mazzotta, Fernanda, and Lavinia Parisi. 2019. "Stuck in the Parental Nest? The Effect of the Economic Crisis on Young Europeans' Living Arrangements." In *Youth Labor in Transition: Inequalities, Mobility, and Policies in Europe*, edited by Jacqueline O'Reilly, Janine Leschke, Renate Ortlieb, Martin Seeleib-Kaiser, and Paolo Villa, 334–57. Oxford: Oxford University Press.

McDonnell, Ann, Rachel Verdin, and Jacqueline O'Reilly. 2022. *EU citizens' attitudes to digitalisation and the use of digital public services: Evidence from Eurobarometers and eGovernment Benchmark*. EUROSHIP Working Paper No. 12. Oslo Metropolitan University. https://euroship-research.eu/wp-content/uploads/2022/02/Working-Paper-No.-12-EU-Citizens-attitudes-to-digitalisation-and-the-use-of-digital-public-services-Evidence-from-Eurobarometers-and-eGovernment-2.pdf.

Medgyesi, Márton, and Ildikó Nagy. 2019. "Income Sharing and Spending Decisions of Young People Living with their Parents." In *Youth Labor in Transition: Inequalities, Mobility, and Policies in Europe*, edited by Jacqueline O'Reilly, Janine Leschke, Renate Ortlieb, Martin Seeleib-Kaiser, and Paolo Villa, 258–85. Oxford: Oxford University Press.

Ministry of Finance. 2017, March 31. Meld. St. 29 (2016–2017). Retrieved March 6, 2023, from Government.no website: https://www.regjeringen.no/en/dokumenter/meld.-st.-29-20162017/id2546674/?ch=1

MISSOC. 2020. MISSOC database. https://www.missoc.org/missoc-database/comparat ive- tables/. Brussels, European Commission.

Morel, Nathalie, Bruno Palier, and Joakim Palme (eds.) 2012. *Towards a Social Investment Welfare State? Ideas, Policies and Challenges.* Bristol: Policy Press.

Müller, Walter, and Markus Gangl. 2003. *Transition from Education to Work in Europe: The Integration of Youth into EU Labour Markets.* Oxford: Oxford University Press.

O'Reilly, Jacqueline, Raffaele Grotti, and Helen Russell. 2019. "Are some sectors more 'youth friendly' than others? Employment regimes, sectors, and gender disparities in the Great Recession." *Human Resource Management Journal* 29 (3): 490–508.

Neufeind Max, Jacqueline O'Reilly, and Florian Ranft. 2018. *Work in the Digital Age: Challenges of the Fourth Industrial Revolution.* London: Rowman and Littlefield International. https://policynetwork.org/publications/books/work-digital-age/.

Newton, Paul E. 2021. *Learning during the pandemic: quantifying lost learning.* https:// www.gov.uk/government/publications/learning-during-the-pandemic/learning-dur ing-the-pandemic-quantifying-lost-time--2.

O'Reilly, Jacqueline, Werner Eichhorst, András Gábos, et al. 2015. "Five characteristics of youth unemployment in Europe. Flexibility, education, migration, family legacies, and EU policy." *SAGE Open* 5 (1): 1–19.

O'Reilly, Jacqueline, Janine Leschke, Renate Ortlieb, Martin Seeleib-Kaiser, and Paola Villa (eds.) 2019. *Youth Labor in Transition: Inequalities, Mobility, and Policies in Europe.* Oxford University Press. https://academic.oup.com/book/26877?login=false

O'Reilly, Jacqueline, and Rachel Verdin. 2021. "Comparing the digital transformation of welfare delivery in Europe." *EUROSHIP Working Paper No. 8.* Oslo Metropolitan University. https://doi.org/10.6084/m9.figshare.17158028

OECD. 2018. Investing in Youth: Norway | en | OECD. Retrieved March 6, 2023, from www.oecd.org website: https://www.oecd.org/publications/investing-in-youth-nor way-9789264283671-en.htm

OECD. 2018a. *Enrolment rate by age.* https://stats.oecd.org/Index.aspx?DataSetCode= EAG_ENRL_RATE_AGE. Paris, OECD.

OECD. 2018b. *Mathematics performance* (PISA). https://data.oecd.org/pisa/mathemat ics-performance-pisa.htm. Paris, OECD.

OECD. 2018c. *Reading performance* (PISA). https://data.oecd.org/pisa/reading-performa nce- pisa.htm#indicator-chart. Paris, OECD.

OECD. 2020a. *Education at a Glance 2020: OECD Indicators.* OECD Publishing. https:// dx.doi.org/10.1787/69096873-en.

OECD. 2020b. *Youth and COVID-19: Response, recovery and resilience.* https://www.oecd. org/coronavirus/policy-responses/youth-and-covid-19-response-recovery-and-res ilience-c40e61c6/.

Orben, Amy, Livia Tomova, and Sarah-Jayne Blakemore. 2020. "The effects of social deprivation on adolescent development and mental health." *Lancet Child and Adolescent Health* 4: 634–40.

Paabot, Heidi, and Kerli Kõiv. 2021. *Noorte Tugila hetkeseis ja märkamised õppimise ja tööga hõivamata noorte toetamise arengute osas COVID pandeemia olukorras.* https:// ank.ee/uudised/noorte-tugila-hetkeseis-ja-markamised-oppimise-ja-tooga-hoivam ata-noorte-toetamise-arengute-osas-covid-pandeemia-olukorras/. Põltsamaa, Estonia/ The Estonian Association of Open Youth Centers (Eesti ANK).

Passaretta, Giampiero, and Maarten H.J. Wolbers. 2019. "Temporary employment at labour market entry in Europe: Labour market dualism, transitions to secure employment and upward mobility." *Economic and Industrial Democracy* 40 (2): 382–408.

Pohl, Axel, and Andreas Walther. 2007. "Activating the disadvantaged—variations in addressing youth transitions across Europe." *International Journal of Lifelong Education* 26 (5): 533–53.

Puerto Gonzalez, Susana. 2020. *Youth and COVID-19: impacts on jobs, education, rights and mental well-being: survey report 2020.* ILO. https://www.voced.edu.au/content/ngv:87705.

Radiven, Claudia, and Simon Prideaux. 2022. *Boris and Rishi's 2020 'kickstart' for the UK economy: Same old, same old youth employment policies?* https://www.academia.edu/44963256/Boris_and_Rishi_s_2020_Kickstart_for_the_UK_Economy_Same_Old_Same_Old_Youth_Employment_Policies.

Robertshaw, David, and Jo Ingold. 2022. *Barriers to employment service digitalisation?* https://digit-research.org/blog_article/barriers-to-employment-service-digitalisation/.

Rokicka, Magdalena, Marge Unt, Kadri Täht, and Olena Nizalova. 2018. "Youth Labour Market in Central and Eastern Europe." In *European Youth Labour Markets: Problems and Policies*, edited by Miguel Ángel Malo and Almudena Moreno Mínguez, 61–78. Cham: Springer.

Rolf, Steven, Jacqueline O'Reilly, and Marc Meryon. 2022. "Towards privatized social and employment protections in the platform economy? Evidence from the UK courier sector." *Research Policy* 51 (5). https://www.sciencedirect.com/science/article/pii/S0048733322000208

Schleicher, Andreas. 2019. *PISA 2018. Insights and Interpretations.* Paris: OECD Publishing.

Schoyen, Mi Ah, and Janikke Vedeler. 2016. *Deliverable 3.4: Institutional determinants of early job insecurity in nine European countries—Country report NORWAY.* https://uni.oslomet.no/negotiate/wp-content/uploads/sites/746/2015/03/WP-3.4_Country-report-Norway.pdf.

Taru, M., Unt, M., and Täht, K. 2021. *Country report on national social protection systems. Estonia.* EUROSHIP unpublished material.

Thomson, R., R. Bell, J. Holland, S. Henderson, S. McGrellis, and S. Sharpe. 2002. "Critical moments: Choice, chance and opportunity in young people's narratives of transition." *Sociology* 36 (2): 335–54.

Trussell Trust. 2021. *State of Hunger.* https://www.trusselltrust.org/wp-content/uploads/sites/2/2021/06/State-of-Hunger_Exec-Summary.pdf. Available at: https://www.trusselltrust.org/state-of-hunger/. London/The Trussell Trust.

Unt, Marge. 2007. *Transition from school-to-work in enlarged Europe.* Tallinna Ülikooli kirjastus.

Unt, Marge, and Michael Gebel. 2018. "Synthesis of the main empirical findings of EXCEPT project." *EXCEPT Working Paper, 57.* Tallinn University. http://www.except-project.eu/working-papers.

Unt, Marge, and Ellu Saar. 2016. "Determinants of Retirement and Late Career in Estonia." In *Delaying Retirement: Progress and Challenges of Active Ageing in Europe, the United States and Japan*, edited by Dirk Hofäcker, Moritz Hess, and Stefanie König, 53–72. London: Palgrave Macmillan.

Unt, Marge, Kazjulja, Margarita, and Viivi Krönström. 2020. "Estonia." In *Extended Working Life Policies*, edited by Ní Léime, Jim Ogg, Martina Rašticová, Debra Street, Clary Krekula, Monika Bédiová, and Ignacio Madero-Cabib, 241–49. Cham: Springer.

Unt, Marge, Michael Gebel, Sonia Bertolini, Vassiliki Deliyanni-Kouimtzi, and Dirk Hofäcker. 2021. *Social Exclusion of Youth in Europe: The Multifaceted Consequences of Labour Market Insecurity.* Bristol: Policy Press.

Verdin, Rachel, and Jacqueline O'Reilly. 2021. "The digital transformation of work and associated risks." *EUROSHIP Working Paper No. 9.* Oslo Metropolitan University. https://euroship-research.eu/wp-content/uploads/2021/12/EUROSHIP-Working-Paper-No-9-The-digital-transformation-of-work-and-associated-risks.pdf.

Walther, Andreas. 2006. "Regimes of youth transitions: Choice, flexibility and security in young people's experiences across different European contexts." *Young* 14 (2): 119–39.

Walther, Andreas, and Axel Pohl. 2005. *Thematic Study on Policies for Disadvantaged Youth in Europe: Final Report to the European Commission.* Institute for Regional Innovation and Social Research. http://ec.europa.eu/employment_social/social_in clusion/docs/youth_study_en.pdf.

Williams, Joy, Kate Alexander, Tony Wilson, and Becci Newton. 2021. *A better future: Transforming jobs and skills for young people post-pandemic.* https://www.emp loyment-studies.co.uk/resource/better-future-transforming-jobs-and-skills-young-people-post-pandemic.

7

Enforcement of Minimum Labor Standards and Institutionalized Exploitation of Seasonal Agricultural Workers in the EU

Cecilia Bruzelius and Martin Seeleib-Kaiser

Introduction

The COVID-19 pandemic has exposed the dependence of modern societies on certain vital public services and essential economic sectors. As agricultural producers in several Member States faced severe labor shortages due to border closures and travel restrictions at the beginning of the pandemic (Samek Lodovici et al. 2022), it was not surprising that national governments and the European Union classified mobile seasonal agricultural workers as "critical" or "essential workers" very early on during the pandemic (EC 2020a). Several Member States arranged exceptions to their very restrictive entry regulations; for instance, Germany allowed seasonal workers to travel from Eastern Europe by plane, making them the only "frequent flyers" during the height of mobility restrictions (Weisskircher et al. 2020).

Some of the essential public services and economic sectors, such as agriculture, are dependent on internationally mobile and migrant labor. Even though EU citizens have the right to reside and work across the EU and are protected by the core principle of non-discrimination, seasonal workers from EU Member States are often discriminated against and exploited. During the height of the first infection wave in the early summer of 2020, one such incidence of exploitation was exposed by the Romanian Labor Minister, who—due to the travel restrictions—traveled by car from Bucharest to Bornheim, a small village near the German city of Bonn, to show her support

Cecilia Bruzelius and Martin Seeleib-Kaiser, *Enforcement of Minimum Labor Standards and Institutionalized Exploitation of Seasonal Agricultural Workers in the EU* In: *European Social Policy and the COVID-19 Pandemic.* Edited by: Stefanie Börner and Martin Seeleib-Kaiser, Oxford University Press. © Oxford University Press 2023. DOI: 10.1093/oso/9780197676189.003.0007 for Romanian seasonal agricultural workers who had not received their wage (Hummel 2020). This incident highlighted the vulnerabilities and exploitation of highly mobile EU workers and the lack of enforcement of labor rights for seasonal workers. While the importance of enforcement of employment and social rights has been highlighted in the literature on posted workers (cf. Arnholtz and Lillie 2020a), surprisingly little research focuses on rights enforcement and its consequences for migrant, non-posted seasonal workers. However, as Arnholtz and Lillie (2020b, 14) state: "Enforcement actors make up the first line of defence against the labour standard erosion."

Against this background, we analyze recent policy changes regulating seasonal workers at the EU level and the enforcement of labor and social rights by EU Member States. Specifically, we focus on the enforcement of minimum wages in the agricultural and forestry sectors of Austria, Germany, Sweden, and the United Kingdom,[1] which employ large numbers of seasonal workers. Research has shown that enforcement of labor standards through industrial relations is normally more effective than administrative or judicial enforcement. Therefore, we expect enforcement also in the agricultural sectors to be more effective in countries characterized by enforcement through social partners (Austria and Sweden in our selection) than in countries where enforcement is carried out by administrative agencies (Germany and the UK). Contrary to our expectation, however, the analysis of enforcement practices in the four countries suggests that irrespective of the different enforcement regimes, minimum labor rights of seasonal workers are poorly enforced in the agriculture and forestry sector. This also did not change significantly in the wake of the pandemic. The conditions, we argue, justify speaking of institutionalized exploitation. Recently discussed or introduced measures at the EU level, such as the establishment of the European Labour Authority and various specific initiatives for seasonal workers, have so far not had a game-changing impact, especially as national authorities continue to be responsible for enforcement.

The chapter is structured as follows: First, we first consider the particularities of EU migrant and seasonal agricultural workers in relation to social and labor rights and discuss some of the policies developed at the EU level in face of the COVID-19 pandemic. In the following section, we

---

[1] We include the UK despite no longer being an EU Member State, as the transition arrangements governing Brexit ended only on December 31, 2020, and farmers were able to recruit EU seasonal workers without any immigration restrictions up until then. UK agriculture has for more than a decade depended heavily on seasonal workers from Central and Eastern Europe.

review the literature on different enforcement methods and regimes with a focus on the enforcement of minimum wages. The remainder of the chapter then examines enforcement of seasonal workers' rights in Austria, Germany, Sweden, and the United Kingdom. We conclude by summarizing the findings and emphasizing the need for more effective enforcement by national authorities. Furthermore, we highlight how the EU was promoting seasonal workers' rights at the discursive level in Brussels, while at the same time demanding that the Swiss government abolish its comparatively more effective enforcement regime for migrant and seasonal workers. Methodologically, we rely on document analysis, expert interviews, and secondary research.

EU Mobile Workers and the Agricultural Sector

Many contemporary political economies are characterized by dual labor markets, which are distinguished by a primary sector providing secure jobs with relative high wages and generous social protection, and a secondary labor market sector with a predominance of precarious employment contracts, low wages, poor working conditions, and no or very rudimentary social protection. Migrant workers are disproportionally employed in the secondary sector (Piore 2008; Emmenegger et al. 2012). In the EU, mobile or migrant workers from poorer Member States disproportionally take up employment in the secondary labor market sector of the more affluent Member States for a lack of other opportunities. Within the agriculture and forestry sector a significant proportion, and in some countries even a majority, of dependent workers are mobile seasonal workers from other Member States. Although exact numbers of the extent of seasonal work within the EU are not available, the EU Commission estimates that between 650.000 to 850.000 EU citizens work as seasonal workers in the agri-food sector (Samek Lodovici et al. 2022, 48).

Seasonal employment of EU workers is governed by the laws of the respective Member State, based on the principle of non-discrimination. Intra-EU seasonal workers enjoy the same rights as nationals regarding working conditions (including remuneration). Nevertheless, economically inactive EU mobile and migrant citizens can be excluded from accessing social assistance benefits—that is, benefits that ensure a minimum floor of protection—in another Member State for the duration of up to five years of lawful residence (Directive 2004/38/EG). Although EU law provides the opportunity for unemployment benefits to be exported by mobile or migrant workers to another Member State, exportable unemployment benefits of EU mobile and migrant workers from Central Eastern European countries are often below the level of subsistence in the country of destination and therefore do not provide any substantive social protection (Bruzelius et al. 2017).

In other words, mobile and migrant EU citizens from poorer Member States have extremely low reservation wages and are therefore fully commodified and dependent on market income. Seasonal workers without sufficient financial means are consequently inclined to accept whatever terms an employer offers, as in the absence of a minimum social protection benefit, the only alternative these workers often have is to return to their country of origin. The possibility of returning to the same employer in subsequent years can make workers reluctant to demand better terms and conditions, as such demands may reduce their chances of re-engagement (Davies 2014, 80). Seasonal work can also make it difficult for mobile workers to build up periods of long-term continuous residence to acquire a more secure residence status and associated social rights. Hence, it is no surprise that a report on seasonal workers issued by the European Parliamentary Research Service states: "Labour inspectors repeatedly report violations of seasonal farm workers' rights as regards working hours, remuneration, living conditions, and health and safety standards in the workplace. . . . EU citizenship does not protect migrant workers from exploitation or abuse" (Augère-Granier 2021, 6).

In recent years, the EU Commission has placed increasing emphasis on minimum social standards as part of an overall strategy of strengthening "Social Europe" and moving beyond "negative integration" (Vanhercke et al 2020; Vesan et al 2021). The European Pillar of Social Rights can be characterized as its flagship approach and includes the establishment of the European Labour Authority (ELA). ELA was founded in 2019 and is meant to "contribute to ensuring fair labour mobility across the Union" (ELA 2020, 9) and a "more effective enforcement of rules" (ibid., 6). More specifically, ELA will assist national authorities by *facilitating coordination* of national enforcement efforts. Among its more concrete tasks, the authority is meant to establish and maintain a framework for enabling Member States to carry out joint cross-border inspections (ELA 2020, 26). Shortly after its establishment, ELA, in partnership with the European Commission and other national and European actors, launched the information campaign "Rights for all seasons" to highlight the rights of seasonal workers (ELA 2021).

Irrespective of such initiatives, national authorities continue to be responsible for inspections. Moreover, ELA has only limited resources to coordinate and facilitate enforcement: in 2021 it had a total budget of 30 million Euros and 150 employees for a European labor market with more than 197 million workers (2020).

Relatively quickly after the onset of the pandemic, other EU institutions also acknowledged the precarious situation of many seasonal agricultural workers. In May 2020, the EU Commission issued a "communication" entitled *A Farm to Fork Strategy for a Fair, Healthy and Environmentally-friendly Food System* as part of its *Green Deal*. The document stated:

> The COVID-19 pandemic has also made us aware of the importance of critical staff, such as agri-food workers. This is why it will be particularly important to mitigate the socio-economic consequences impacting the food chain and ensure that the *key principles enshrined in the European Pillar of Social Rights are respected, especially when it comes to precarious, seasonal and undeclared workers.* The considerations of workers' social protection, working and housing conditions as well as protection of health and safety will play a major role in building a fair, strong and sustainable food system (EC 2020c, Sec. 2.2; emphasis added).

In June 2020, the European Parliament adopted a resolution regarding the situation of cross-border and seasonal workers. The resolution calls for better protection and equal labor as well as social rights for all workers (EP 2020). Responding to the EU Parliament's motion, the Commission issued additional guidelines for seasonal workers, who were identified as workers more vulnerable to precarious employment. The Commission highlighted that the COVID-19 pandemic had exposed, and in some cases exacerbated, the poor working conditions (EC 2020d). Finally, in June 2021, the Council reached an agreement that the Common Agricultural Policy (CAP) will include a form of social conditionality in the future, whereby labor authorities in EU countries will need to inform agricultural paying agencies at least once a year on the results of their controls. If violations have been identified, the paying agency will apply a reduction to the farmer's payment (EC 2021).

Although these initiatives to promote social and labor rights of seasonal workers can be interpreted as a move in the direction of strengthening the rights of seasonal workers, they have not changed the enforcement competencies within the multilevel governance arrangement. Member States continue to be responsible to enforce EU as well as national policies. It remains the case that although the EU is "a formidable law-making machine. It is not, however, a law enforcing one" (Bernard cited by Kullmann 2015, 6).

Enforcement Methods and Regimes of Selected EU Member States

How minimum labor conditions are enforced varies across Member States, sectors, and types of rules (there is for example often a difference between how minimum wages and health and safety standards are enforced within countries). Three kinds of enforcement strategies (Malmberg 2004) or "methods" (Kullman 2015, 1) are normally employed—*industrial relations, administrative,* and *judicial* enforcement. The industrial relations enforcement method involves supervision and enforcement of rules by trade unions, works councils, or other workers' representatives and employers. The administrative method entails that supervision and enforcement is a task for public authorities, such as labor inspectors or equality agencies. The judicial method of enforcement entails enforcement through judicial procedures, such as in courts or other arbitration institutions, initiated by either individual employees or their representatives. These methods are often intertwined in rather complex ways; they can be applied alongside or replace each other (Malmberg 2004, 222). Insofar as one method tends to predominate within a country, we may speak of a national enforcement regime (Bosch et al. 2019).

Research suggests that enforcement through an industrial relations regime, involving trade unions or works councils, tends to lead to the highest degree of rule compliance (Malmberg 2004, 223). In countries and sectors in which wages are primarily set through collective agreements, enforcement mostly happens through industrial relations enforcement, whereas in countries or sectors where (minimum) wages are determined through legislation, they are predominantly enforced administratively. There is, in other words, "a strong interrelationship between the source of the norm regulating a substantive issue and the kind of enforcement process used" (Malmberg 2004, 223). In line with the literature on enforcement strategies, we could expect countries with an industrial relations enforcement regime to be more effective in enforcing wages *across* sectors. To assess this assumption, we conduct a small-n comparison of the enforcement of wages in the agriculture and forestry sector in Austria, Germany, Sweden, and the United Kingdom,

Table 7.1 Enforcement Methods by Country

Enforcement Methods	Country*
Industrial relations	**Austria**, Germany, Sweden
Administrative	Austria, **Germany, United Kingdom**
Judicial	Austria, Germany, Sweden, United Kingdom

* Bold font indicates the dominance of a specific enforcement method.

countries which belong to different enforcement regimes (see Table 7.1). For each country, we consider key features of the economic sector, in particular the share of mobile seasonal workers and associated vulnerabilities (nature of work and access to social protection), and examine how enforcement is carried out in principle and in practice.

Austria

Agriculture and forestry employ the highest proportion of migrants among all economic sectors in Austria. According to official figures, almost 60% of workers in agriculture do not hold Austrian citizenship (Sezioneri 2020, 8). Approximately 14,000–15,000 seasonal workers come to Austria each year to work in agriculture, mainly from Eastern Europe (Kainrath 2020a; Sezioneri 2020, 7). Romanians constitute the biggest group (4,800), followed by Hungarians (2,800) and Poles (1,600) (Möchel und Schreiber 2021). Formally, EU seasonal workers are not exempt from social security contributions and are therefore principally covered by the Austrian social insurance system (ÖG 2018).

Austria does not have a *statutory* minimum wage; moreover, wages, including minimum wages, are determined through collective bargaining agreements, which cover 95% of all employees and apply to seasonal workers. It is well known that farmers undercut these collective agreements, for example by underreporting hours worked and not providing holiday payments (Sezioneri 2020). As minimum wages are not set by the state, the enforcement of wages should in principle be achieved through an industrial relations enforcement regime. In theory, employees are asked to report problems with remuneration to works councils and the Chamber of Labour (*Arbeiterkammer*), and the trade unions are subsequently responsible to enforce respective rights.

The agricultural and forestry sector deviates from the general enforcement regime, as in this sector inspection by the so-called Agriculture and Forestry Inspectorates of the Austrian *Länder* (*Land- und Forstwirtschaftsinspektionen*) are the main method of enforcement. These state inspectorates are however severely under-resourced: for example in Styria, which is a key agricultural region, there are only two inspectors for every 3,000 farms. In 2019, eight inspections were carried out in Tyrol across 16,215 businesses (Tirol 2020). And in Carinthia the number was 195 inspections across 17,475 agricultural employers (2018)—observers have identified a steady decline of inspections in Carinthia since around 2000 (Kainrath 2020a). As there are only very few controls, it is not surprising that no minimum wage violations have been identified in some regions. Lower Austria officially reported zero cases of noncompliance regarding wages and holiday rights in 2019 (Bachmayr-Heyda 2021). The Finance Police, in accordance with the "Wage and Social Dumping Law" of 2016 (BGBl. I Nr. 44/2016), carries out random controls of establishments employing posted workers, including in the agricultural sector (BMF 2021). Although the Finance Police only carry out controls of wages for posted workers and is not responsible for monitoring other workers or working conditions, it frequently identifies cases of gross minimum wage violations and can confirm increased wage dumping practices across sectors (Bachmayr-Heyda 2021).

Officially identified violations of collective bargaining agreements do not automatically lead to enforcement of the payment of the underpaid wages to the employee. If the employer does not "voluntarily" pay the outstanding sums, the worker must individually sue the employer (with free legal support by the Chamber of Labour).[2] Although workers have the right to take up the judicial method or pathway to enforce their rights through courts, this method is chosen only very rarely, especially by seasonal workers, as it is very common for court proceedings to last for many months if not years (Sezioneri 2020, 29).

As exploitative conditions in seasonal agriculture came to the fore during the 2020 COVID-19 pandemic, the opposition in the Austrian parliament formally requested information from the Federal Ministry of Labour regarding controls, penalties, and future measures to avoid exploitation (BR 2020a). The Federal Ministry responded that it was not responsible for

---

[2] Correspondence with the Austrian Health Insurance Fund, who refer cases of underpayment to local authorities, if detected by the Finance Police.

controls, as these are within the competence of the states (BR 2020b, 115–121). Moreover, it highlighted a forthcoming federal law (*Landarbeitsgesetz 2021*) that in 2021 replaced the multitude of state laws regulating labor standards (other than wages) in the agricultural sector as an effort to simplify information for workers and to combat exploitation. Yet, even with the adoption of this law, the regional agricultural inspectorates remain responsible for administrative enforcement of the minimum wage in the agricultural and forestry sector; efforts to improve the administrative inspection capacities seemingly are not high on the agenda.

Germany

Seasonal work predominates dependent employment within the German agriculture sector. According to data by the German Statistics Office from 2020, agricultural establishments employed approximately 271,500 seasonal workers, which amounted to approximately 60% of all dependent employees in agriculture (DESTATIS 2020a). The overwhelming majority of these workers comes from other EU Member States in Central and Eastern Europe (Bundesagentur für Arbeit 2021). Hence, the comprehensive travel restrictions imposed to mitigate the spread of the COVID-19 pandemic immediately threatened the harvest of certain crops in summer 2020. To avoid crops rotting on the fields, the German Federal Minister for Agriculture arranged a special "airlift" and exceptions to the strict entry regulations for seasonal workers from Central and Eastern European countries within days of the general travel ban (Initiative Faire Landarbeit 2021).

Seasonal workers in Germany are often in especially precarious employment, as they tend to be employed at or below the minimum wage and can be fired very easily, often with a notice period of only one day (Initiative Faire Landarbeit 2020, 10). Also, they are largely excluded from social security protection. Until 2020 employers could hire seasonal workers for up to 70 days per year and be exempt from having to pay contributions to the various social insurance schemes. In wake of the COVID-19 pandemic, the duration for exemptions from paying social security contribution were extended to 115 days per year for 2020 and to 102 days for 2021. As these workers are exempt from social insurance coverage, they are evidently also not entitled to social insurance benefits, be it the export of unemployment insurance benefits to the country of origin or the accrual of pension entitlements within the regulations of EU Social Security Coordination. As many of these workers migrate to Germany for the harvest season on an annual basis, they are very likely to end up on in old-age poverty (DGB 2021).

Since 2015 Germany has a general statutory minimum wage, which also applies to the agricultural sector. To ensure appropriate remuneration, employers are legally obliged to document the hours worked on a regular basis; the amount of money that can be deducted from wages for food and accommodation is limited by law. However, it is well known and evidenced that employers circumvent these regulations by not properly documenting hours of work, demanding a certain degree of minimum productivity of the workers before paying the minimum wage, and deducting unreasonable amounts for food and accommodation, and thereby evade paying the minimum wage (Mindestlohnkommission 2020, 65; Initiative Faire Landarbeit 2020, 14–15).

Enforcement of the minimum wage is the responsibility of a special unit (*Finanzkontrolle Schwarzarbeit*) of the German Customs Authority. This unit is notoriously understaffed (including staff without specific training, and former civil servants from the Deutsche Telekom and Post as well as from the German Weather Service) and not well coordinated (Bosch 2019; Deutscher Bundestag 2020). In 2020, the unit had a staff of approximately 7,000 employees to enforce the minimum wage across all economic sectors in Germany, while about 1,400 posts remained unfilled (Mindestlohnkommission 2020, 61). The unit of the Customs Authority inspected 710 agricultural workplaces (ibid., 62) out of a total of approximately 299,000 farms in 2019 (DESTATIS 2020b); *ceteris paribus*, the likelihood of an individual farm being inspected is once in every 421 years. These numbers demonstrate the very low priority of inspections within the agricultural sector, despite most workers being precariously employed seasonal workers.

A core element of inspections by the German Customs Authority is to check whether the employer has paid the correct amount of taxes or social security contributions; officially determined violations of the minimum wage do not automatically lead to the enforcement of the payment of back pay to the employee. Rather, the employee must sue the employer individually to receive the back pay, should the employer not voluntarily agree to the payment (Weinkopf 2020). In most determined cases, noncompliance constitutes a misdemeanor—in 2019 the average fine amounted to €2,752 for nonpayment of the minimum wage or violations in documenting hours worked.[3] Despite a greater awareness of the precarious situation of many seasonal workers during the pandemic, the conditions did not improve: reports of severe minimum wage violations continued (Dribbusch 2021); many posts within the Customs Authority's unit to enforce the minimum wage remained unfilled (Doll 2021), and the actual number of inspections declined by one-fifth in 2020 compared to 2019 due to health and safety precautions during the pandemic (Greive et al. 2021).

Sweden

Recruitment of foreign workers in forestry started on a large scale in 2005 after two big storms suddenly increased the demand for short-term workers (Interview GS). Some 5,000 seasonal workers come to work in the Swedish forestry sector annually (Röstlund and Lundborg 2021). A study from 2019 showed that 97% of workers in the 10 largest forestry companies (by revenue) were migrant workers, of which 82% were EU citizens (dominated by Latvian, Polish, and Romanian workers) (Forsmark and Johannesson 2020, 9–11).

Wages in Sweden are determined by collective bargaining agreements and therefore, there is no statutory minimum wage. Most collective agreements do not stipulate a specific minimum wage: only about 250 of the circa 700 Swedish collective agreements contain specified minimum wage levels. A worker is covered by collective agreements even if s/he is not a trade union member, granted that the employer has signed the respective agreement (Herzfeld Olsson 2019, 643). Based on the industrial relations enforcement regime, social partners are responsible for enforcing agreed wages with no involvement of public authorities. The grievance procedure is as follows: workers turn to their trade union for support should they not receive the agreed wage, and the trade union in turn deals with the employer. However, if a worker is not a union member, s/he will individually have to pursue the judicial method of enforcement through court proceedings or by consulting a judicial ombudsperson. In principle, employees can receive financial support from the state to partially cover the costs of this process,

---

[3] Own calculations based on the total amount of fines of €12.1 million divided by the total number of misdemeanors of 4,394 in 2019 (Mindestlohnkommission 2020, 64).

but foreign workers need "specific reasons" to be eligible for the financial support.[4]

Trade unions point to the very low level of union membership among seasonal mobile workers as one of the main challenges (Röstlund and Lundborg, 2021; Riksrevisionen 2020; Interview GS). Concluding collective bargaining agreements with the employers in the sector is said not to constitute a problem; yet if few or none of the seasonal workers are organized in trade unions, it can be difficult to control compliance with these agreements (Riksrevisionen 2020, 48–50). For instance, a representative from the GS Union, the union representing forestry workers, reported that the Green Employers' Federation refuses GS "every possibility to exercise any control over compliance with the collective agreement" (Interview GS). The GS Union tries to reach out with information to migrant and mobile workers and offers cheaper seasonal membership; yet, of the approximately 5,000 migrant workers that come to Sweden to work in forestry each year, only very few become union members. Moreover, the very nature of work makes it difficult for unions to carry out controls, as the Swedish forest area is vast and covers some 22 million hectares of land, and the location of work is mobile—tree seedlings are sown in the southern part of the country and then planted in the north (Interview GS).

However, exploitation in the forestry industry is rife, and underpayment and outstanding payments are a systemic problem (Röstlund and Lundborg 2021; Fröberg and Mahmoud 2020; Norberg 2009). Employers often misuse piecework salaries: planting a minimum number of plants is often a precondition to receive the contractually agreed wage (Interview GS; Röstlund and Lundborg 2021). The GS trade union reports that they deal with several cases of exploitation each month and maintain that "systematic wage dumping is occurring," but that most cases of exploitation would remain unreported.[5] Workers are often threatened not to speak to others or contact the union (Interview GS).

While the trade unions' ability to control many workplaces with a known risk for exploitation is effectively limited, Swedish public authorities have no legal competence to control wages. The Swedish government has not initiated any efforts that directly target labor exploitation; recent efforts have

---

[4] 12 § Rättshjälpslagen (1996,1619).
[5] Email exchange with representative from GS, the Swedish union representing workers in forestry and woodworking industries.

been aimed at human trafficking and exploitation but not wage enforcement, and inspectors have argued that more controls would be necessary to identify labor exploitation (Riksrevisionen 2020, 43). Finally, judicial enforcement does not seem to be effective in fighting labor exploitation in Sweden, as only two cases since 2004 have resulted in convictions for the crime of trafficking human beings for the purpose of forced labor (Riksrevisionen 2020, 36). The Swedish National Audit Office concludes upon a review of relevant Swedish law that "at present, the risk of being punished for human exploitation or trafficking is almost non-existent for the employer who exploits the worker" (Riksrevisionen 2020, 36).

United Kingdom

The agricultural sector in the United Kingdom is dependent on approximately 75,000 seasonal workers; before Brexit, an estimated 98% of these workers were recruited from EU Member States, mainly from Romania and Bulgaria (HC 2017, 6). This high dependency on mobile seasonal farm workers has a long tradition through the continuous recruitment via the Seasonal Agricultural Worker Scheme (SAWS) since 1945. SAWS allowed workers from Bulgaria and Romania to work in the United Kingdom on a temporary basis before they had full freedom of movement as EU citizens (HC 2017; Davis 2014).

Exploitative practices by employers in agriculture are well known. Nonpayment or underpayment of wages is remarkably common, hours are often deducted from the actual numbers of hours worked, and large sums are withheld for the provision of accommodation (Barnard 2014, 203–4; MCA 2014). Employers have also often requested EU citizens to register as self-employed in attempts to avoid employment protection legislation, as self-employed workers generally enjoy no employment protection (Barnard 2014, 202).

The United Kingdom has a national minimum wage that also applies to agricultural workers. The minimum wage is enforced administratively as part of an enforcement regime that involves many agencies and is "severely fragmented" (HM Government 2018, 19). A government report explains that "[w]ith a plethora of organisations operating in this space, it can be difficult for individuals experiencing employment violations to know where to go for help" (HM Government 2018, 19). The minimum wage is enforced by at least three different bodies: the National Minimum Wage Inspectorate (NMWI) of the Income Tax Authority (HMRC); the Gangmaster and Labour Abuse Authority (GLAA, previously GLA), which is the key agency dealing with labor exploitation; and the Employment Agency Standards that enforces regulations covering employment agencies.

Controls are however rare. On average the NMWI conducts approximately 5,000 inspections annually, a rate at which it would take 250 years to inspect every employer. Correspondingly, between 2007 and 2013, nine prosecutions were carried out, which amounted to the probability of employers being prosecuted under the national minimum wage legislation as *once in a million years* (MAC 2014, 164–65). Data by the tax authority shows that just 33 businesses were investigated in the agricultural, forestry, and fishing sectors in 2017–2018. Of the inspected businesses, 11 were found to be in arrears with employees (Meredith 2019). The GLAA's remit extended dramatically with the 2016 Immigration Act, when its powers were extended to investigate severe exploitation across the entire UK labor market. It went from covering about 0.5 million workers in the food-related economic sectors to technically being responsible for approximately 30 million workers of the entire economy. However, the GLAA's resources continued to be extremely limited, as it was only provided with 40 additional staff—in addition to a previous workforce of 70 staff (Craig 2017, 22; Noble 2020).

Due to this very residual administrative enforcement regime, enforcement seems to depend mainly on the willingness of workers, intermediary labor providers, or farm businesses to contact the authorities (cf. Davies 2014, 89). In the unlikely event that employers are inspected, they generally do not face harsh consequences. Procedures to prosecute violators can be very lengthy; since 2008–2009 only 84 prosecutions have been pursued (HM Government 2020, 64).

Discussion and Conclusion

The EU has placed stronger emphasis on seasonal agricultural workers' rights during the pandemic, as evidenced in the information campaigns by ELA, the EU Commission's Strategy *From Farm to Fork*, the resolution by the EU Parliament that was also supported by the Council, and the inclusion of social conditionality in CAP. Nevertheless, as our analysis shows, the issue at stake is not necessarily a lack of regulations and norms at the EU level, but a lack of enforcement by Member States. In fact, our analysis demonstrates that countries with industrial relations enforcement regimes (Austria and Sweden) appear not to be more effective in enforcing seasonal workers' rights than those with administrative enforcement regimes (Germany and UK). Inspections are very infrequent, the risk of labor violations being identified very low, and penalties for exploitations and underpayment often low or un-likely, irrespective of enforcement regime.

In this regard, the EU Commission's objection to the seemingly more effective Swiss model of enforcement is noteworthy. The latter was to be abolished at the request of the EU as part of the negotiations of the new Framework Agreement governing the relations of the non–Member State Switzerland with the EU, precisely at a time when various EU actors were emphasizing the social and labor rights of mobile seasonal workers at the discursive level in Brussels. In May 2021, the Swiss national government uni-laterally ended the negotiations with the EU on the Framework Agreement, a key reason being the demand by the EU for the abolition of the existing Swiss wage-protection policy (also called flanking measures) (Gafafer et al. 2021). The flanking measures were initially set up ahead of the 2000 Swiss referendum on the Agreement on the Free Movement of Persons (AFM), when the pro–free movement Swiss government and business commu-nity garnered the unions' support to foster a majority among the electorate (Fischer 2003, Afonso 2010). According to the flanking measures, bipartite wage control units regularly inspect workplaces to ensure that mobile and migrant workers receive collectively agreed wages. In economic sectors with a high risk of wage dumping, companies are required to deposit a specified sum of money with the authorities to ensure workers can be compensated for unpaid work, even if the company declares bankruptcy or changes its legal status (Rechsteiner 2021). The policy is overseen at the national level by tripartite labor commissions (Erne and Imboden 2015). When the flanking measures were initially introduced, hardly any labor inspections were carried out; however, approximately 40,000 inspections are carried out annually in sectors considered high risk, including the agricultural sector, since 2013 (Huwiler and Maron 2019). According to observers of organized labor, the "bundle of measures, agreed and implemented by trade unions and employer organisations, ensure effective wage protection in Switzerland" (Rechsteiner 2021).

The EU Commission seems to perceive the Swiss flanking measures to distort competition, cause administrative barriers, and constitute a protectionist instrument, rather than as an effective policy to protect wage compliance and workers' rights (Wixforth and Wiehler 2021). In other words, simultaneously to setting up ELA to support enforcement, agreeing on resolutions and statements supporting labor rights of seasonal workers, the EU Commission has sought to end the existing comparatively effective enforcement measures for mobile and migrant workers' rights in Switzerland.

To sum up: Our analysis leads us to conclude that for most part the policies adopted by the EU in the wake of the pandemic regarding the labor and social rights of seasonal workers constitute cheap talk, as Member States' enforcement of minimum labor rights remains lacking. Effective enforcement by social partners within a public or tripartite framework, as demonstrated by the Swiss example, or an effective national administrative enforcement regime with sufficient resources would seem potentially effective means to ensure mobile seasonal workers' rights in the agriculture and forestry sector. Continuing with the current practices amounts to a continuation of institutionalized exploitation of seasonal workers. Ending institutionalized exploitation of seasonal workers would require leadership by politicians and policy change within Member States.

Acknowledgments

We thank Michelle Franke for her excellent research assistance and Roland Erne for pointing us to the Swiss case. Furthermore, we gratefully acknowledge the financial support by the German Federal Ministry of Labor and Social Affairs for the Research Group "Freedom of Movement and Social Policy in Historical and International Comparison."

References

Afonso, Alexandre. 2010. "Europeanisation, new political cleavages and policy concertation in Switzerland." *European Journal of Industrial Relations* 16 (1): 57–72.

Arnholtz, Jens, and Nathan Lillie (eds.). 2020a. *Posted Work in the European Union: The Political Economy of Free Movement.* Abingdon/New York: Routledge.

Arnholtz, Jens, and Nathan Lillie, N. (eds.). 2020b. "European Integration and the Reconfiguration of National Industrial Relations: Posted Work as a Driver of Institutional Change." In Arnholtz, Jens, and Nathan Lillie, *Posted Work in the European Union: The Political Economy of Free Movement.* Abingdon/New York: Routledge, 1–30.

Augère-Granier, Marie-Laure. 2021. "Migrant seasonal workers in the European agricultural sector." Briefing, PE 689.347, *European Parliamentary Research Service*, February 2021. Available at https://www.europarl.europa.eu/RegData/etudes/BRIE/2021/689 347/EPRS_BRI(2021)689347_EN.pdf.

Aumayr-Pintar, Christine. 2021. "Minimum wages in 2021: Most countries settle for cautious increase." *EUROFOUND*, 3 February 2021, EF21061. Available at https://www. eurofound.europa.eu/publications/article/2021/minimum-wages-in-2021-most-countries-settle-for-cautious-increase.

Bachmayr-Heyda, A. 2021. "Ausbeutung am Feld: 'Made in Austria' ist kein Garant für faire Arbeitsbedingungen", *Kontrast*, March 26, 2021. Available at https://kontrast.at/ erntehelfer-jobs-erfahrungsberichte/

Barnard, Catherine. 2014. "Enforcement of Employment Rights by Migrant Workers in the UK." In *Migrants at Work*, edited by Cathryn Costello and Mark Freedland, 193–215. Oxford: Oxford University Press.

BMF. 2021. Antwort auf parlamentarische Anfrage Nr. 7961/J. Bundesministerium der Finanzen, Republik Österreich, November 22, 2021.

Bogoeski, Vladimir. 2021. "Harvesting Injustice." *Verfassungsblog*, April 20, 2021. Available at https://verfassungsblog.de/harvesting-injustice/

BR. 2020a. "Anfrage: Missstände im Bereich der Erntearbeit." 3794/J-BR/2020, *Bundesrat, Republik Österreich*, July 16, 2020.

BR. 2020b. "Plenarsitzung des Bundesrates." Stenographisches Protokoll, 911. Sitzung des Bundesrates der Republik Österreich, July 16, 2020.

Bruzelius, Cecilia, Constantin Reinprecht, and Martin Seeleib-Kaiser. 2017. "Stratified social rights limiting EU citizenship." *Journal of Common Market Studies* 55 (6): 1239–53.

Bundesagentur für Arbeit. 2021. "Kurzfristig Beschäftigte nach Wirtschaftszweigen WZ 2008 und Staatsangehörigkeit." Nuremberg: Bundesagentur für Arbeit.

Corrado, Alessandra, and Letizia Palumbo. 2022. "Essential Farmworkers and the Pandemic Crisis: Migrant Labour Conditions, and Legal and Political Responses in Italy and Spain." In *Migration and Pandemics: Spaces of Solidarity and Spaces of Exception*, edited by Anna Triandafyllidou, 145–66. IMISCOE Research Series. Cham: Springer. https://doi.org/10.1007/978-3-030-81210-2.

Craig, Gary. 2017. "The UK's modern slavery legislation: An early assessment of progress." *Social Inclusion* 5 (2): 16–27.

Davies, A.C.L. 2014. "Migrant Workers in Agriculture—A Legal Perspective." In *Migrants at Work*, edited by Cathryn Costello and Mark Freedland, 79–97. Oxford: Oxford University Press.

DESTATIS. 2020a. "Arbeitskräfte in landwirtschaftlichen Betrieben." Statistisches Bundesamt.

DESTATIS. 2020b. "Landwirtschaftszählung—Betriebe Insgesamt und im Zeitvergleich." Statistisches Bundesamt.

Deutscher Bundestag. 2020. "Antwort der Bundesregierung auf die Kleine Anfrage der Abgeordneten Sven-Christian Kindler, Lisa Paus, Beate Müller-Gemmeke, weiterer Abgeordneter und der Fraktion BÜNDNIS 90/ DIE GRÜNEN." BT-Drucksache 19/ 21481.

DGB. 2021. "Beispiellose Aushöhlung des Sozialstaates." Available at https://www.dgb.de/ themen/++co++2655bafe-a371-11eb-a42d-001a4a160123.

Doll, Nikolaus. 2021. "Ausgerechnet bei den Zollfahndern spart Scholz Hunderte Millionen ein." In *Die Welt*, July 10, 2021. Available at https://www.welt.de/politik/deut

schland/article232414713/Haushaelter-empoert-Ausgerechnet-bei-den-Zollfahnd
ern-spart-Scholz.html.

Dribbusch, B. 2021. "Lohndumping und Erntearbeit: Vier Euro Akkordlohn." *die
tageszeitung*, October 22, 2021. Available at https://taz.de/Lohndumping-und-Ernt
earbeit/!5810228/.

EC. 2020a. "Coronavirus: Commission presents practical guidance to ensure the free
movement of critical workers." Press release, March 30, 2020. Available at: https://
ec.europa.eu/commission/presscorner/detail/en/ip_20_545.

EC. 2020b. "Proposal for a Directive of the European Parliament and of the Council
on adequate minimum wages in the European Union." COM/2020/682 final,
Brussels: European Commission, October 28, 2020.

EC. 2020c. "Communication from the Commission to the European Parliament, The
Council, The European Economic and Social Committee and The Committee of the
Regions. A Farm to Fork Strategy for a fair, healthy and environmentally-friendly food
system." Brussels: European Commission, May 20, 2020 COM(2020) 381 final.

EC. 2020d. "Communication from the Commission: Guidelines on seasonal workers
in the EU in the context of the COVID-19 outbreak." (2020/C 235 I/01) Available at
https://eur-lex.europa.eu/legal-content/EN/TXT/PDF/?uri=CELEX:52020XC0
717(04)&from=EN.

EC. 2021. "Key Reforms in the New CAP." Available at https://ec.europa.eu/info/food-
farming-fisheries/key-policies/common-agricultural-policy/new-cap-2023-27/key-
reforms-new-cap_en.

ELA. 2021. "Rights for all seasons: European Labour Authority supports fair work for
seasonal workers." Available at https://www.ela.europa.eu/en/news/rights-all-seasons-
european-labour-authority-supports-fair-work-seasonal-workers.

Emmenegger, Patrick, Silja Häusermann, Bruno Palier, and Martin Seeleib-Kaiser. 2012.
The Age of Dualization. New York/Oxford: Oxford University Press.

EP. 2020. "European Parliament resolution on European protection of cross-border and
seasonal workers in the context of the COVID-19 crisis" (2020/2664(RSP)), B9-0172/
2020/REV. Available at https://www.europarl.europa.eu/doceo/document/B-9-2020-
0172_EN.pdf.

EP. 2021. "Briefing: Migrant Seasonal Workers in the European Agricultural Sector."
EPSR, European Parliament Research Service, PE 689.347—February 2021.

Erne, Roland, and Natalie Imboden. 2015. "Equal pay by gender and by nationality: a
comparative analysis of Switzerland's unequal equal pay policy regimes across time."
Cambridge Journal of Economics 39: 655–74.

Fischer, Alex. 2003. "Vetospieler und die Durchsetzbarkeit von Side-Payments. Der
schweizerische innenpolitische Entscheidungsprozess um flankierende Massnahmen
zur Personenfreizügigkeit mit der Europäischen Union," *Swiss Political Science Review*
9 (2): 27–58.

Forsmark, Victoria, and Tomas Johannesson. 2020. *Skogsvårdsföretagens rekrytering—
förusättningar, nuläge och konsekvenser*. Skogsforsk, Arbetsrapport 1030, 2020.

FRA. 2018. *Protecting migrant workers from exploitation in the EU: Boosting workplace
inspections*. European Union Agency for Fundamental Rights. Luxembourg: Publications
Office of the European Union.

Gafafer, Tobias, Christoph G. Schmutz, and Daniel Steinvorth. 2021. "Ein Geheimtreffen
zwischen der Schweiz und der EU sorgt bis heute für Verstimmung—was 2018 in
Zürich passiert ist." *Neue Zürcher Zeitung*, June 22, 2021. Available at https://www.nzz.

ch/schweiz/was-beim-geheimtreffen-zwischen-bern-und-der-eu-2018-passiert-ist-ld.1630710.

Greive, Martin, Jan Hildebrand, Silke Kersting, and Frank Specht. (2021) "Die Schwarzarbeit in Deutschland nimmt zu," *Handelsblatt,* February 9, 2021. Available at https://www.handelsblatt.com/politik/deutschland/schattenwirtschaft-die-schwarzarbeit-in-deutschland-nimmt-zu/26899426.html.

HC. 2017. "Migrant Workers in Agriculture." Commons Library, Briefing Number 7987, 4 July 2017, London: House of Commons.

Herzfeld Olsson, Petra. 2019. "Konsten att inkludera arbetskraftsmigranter i den svenska arbetsrättsliga modellen." *Juridisk Tidskrift*, 2019/20 (3).

HM Government. 2018. *United Kingdom Labour Market Enforcement Strategy 2018/19.* Director of Labour Market Enforcement, HM Government, David Metcalf, May 2018.

Hummel, Thomas. 2020. "Grausige Unterkünfte, kaum Lohn und dann auch noch Corona." *Süddeutsche Zeitung,* May 21, 2020. Available at https://www.sueddeutsche.de/politik/migration-werkvertraege-landwirtschaft-rumaenien-1.4913656.

Huwiler, Ursina Jud, and Valentine Mauron. 2019. "Flankierende Massnahmen: 15 Jahre Lohnschutz." *Die Volkswirtschaft*, 20.06.2019. Available at https://dievolkswirtschaft.ch/de/2019/06/jud-huwiler-mauron-07-2019/.

Interview GS. 2021. Representative from the GS Trade Union, September 9 2021

Initiative Faire Landarbeit. 2020. *Bericht 2019: Saisonarbeit in der Landwirtschaft.* Available at: https://igbau.de/Binaries/Binary13929/2019-Bericht-Saisonarbeit-Landwirtschaft-Online.pdf.

Initiative Faire Landarbeit. 2021. *Bericht 2020: Saisonarbeit in der Landwirtschaft.* Available at https://igbau.de/Binaries/Binary15315/InitiativeFaireLandarbeit-Bericht2020.pdf.

Kaelin, Lukas. 2011. "The political making of health worker migration." *Journal of Public Health Policy* 32 (4): 489–98.

Kaernten. 2019. *Tätigkeitsbericht der Land- und Forstwirtschaftsinspektion. Berichtsjahr 2018.* Klagenfurt am Wörthersee, im Mai 2019.

Kainrath, Verena. 2020. "Schwere Kost: Hat die Ausbeutung von Erntehelfern in Österreich System?" *Der Standard,* September 17, 2020. Available at: https://www.derstandard.at/story/2000120057690/schwere-kost-hat-die-ausbeutung-von-erntehelfern-in-oesterreich-system

Kullman, Miriam. 2015. *Enforcement of Labour Law in Cross-border Situations.* Deventer: Wolters Kluwer Legal Publishers.

MAC. 2014. *Migrants in Low Skilled Work.* Migration Advisory Committee, July 2014, London. Available at: https://www.gov.uk/government/publications/migrants-in-low-skilled-work.

Malmberg, Jonas. 2004. "Effective Enforcement of EC Labour Law: A Comparative Analysis of Community Law Requirements." *European Journal of Industrial Relations* 10 (2): 219–29.

Meredith, Andrew. 2019. "Agricultural workers at risk from minimum wage violations." *Farmers Weekly,* May 1, 2019. Available at https://www.fwi.co.uk/business/business-management/staff/agricultural-workers-at-risk-from-minimum-wage-violations=.

Mindestlohnkommission. 2020. *Dritter Bericht zu den Auswirkungen des gesetzlichen Mindestlohns Bericht der Mindestlohnkommission an die Bundesregierung nach § 9 Abs. 4 Mindestlohngesetz.* Berlin.

Möchel, Kid, and Dominik Schreiber. 2021. "Spargelernte: Hunderte Erntehelfer fehlen." *Kurier*, 15.04.2021, https://kurier.at/chronik/oesterreich/spargelernte-hunderte-ernt ehelfer-fehlen/401351855.

Noble, Victoria. 2020. "Revealed: How the UK's agriculture sector relies on modern slavery." *Open Democracy*, September 16, 2020. Available at https://www.opendemocr acy.net/en/oureconomy/revealed-how-the-uks-agriculture-sector-relies-on-modern-slavery/.

ÖG. 2018. *Erntehelfer*. Veröffentlichung: NÖDIS Nr. 16/20.12.2018, Österreichische Gesundheitskasse. Available at https://www.gesundheitskasse.at/cdscontent/?conten tid=10007.818955.

Piore, Michael. 1979. *Birds of Passage: Migrant Labour and Industrial Societies*. Cambridge: Cambridge University Press.

Rechsteiner, Paul. 2021. "Switzerland: defending workers' rights." *Social Europe Blog Post*, July 7, 2021. Available at https://socialeurope.eu/switzerland-defending-workers-rights.

Riksrevisionen. 2020. "Statens insatser mot exploatering av arbetskraft—regelverk, kontroller samt information och stöd till de drabbade." rir 2020:27, Riksdagens Intertryckeri: Stockholm.

Röstlund, L., and B. Lundborg. 2021. Migrantarbetare berättar: Vi utnyttjas av skogsbolag. *Dagens Nyheter*, May 15, 2021. Available at: https://www.dn.se/sverige/migrantarbet are-berattar-vi-utnyttjas-av-skogsbolag/.

Samek Lodovici, Manuela, Elena Ferrari, Emma Paladino, Flavia Pesce, Nicoletta Torchio, and Alessandra Crippa. 2022. *Revaluation of working conditions and wages for essential workers*. European Parliament. Available at https://www.europarl.europa.eu/thinkt ank/en/document/IPOL_STU(2021)695491.

Sezioneri. 2020. "Willkommen bei der Erdbeerernte! Ihr Mindestlohn beträgt ... Gewerkschaftliche Organisierung in der migrantischen Landarbeit—ein internationaler Vergleich." *Sezonieri-Kampagne für die Rechte von Erntehelfer_innen*. Available at https://www.sezonieri.at/wp-content/uploads/2018/02/Willkommen_b ei_der_Erdbeerernte.pdf.

Vesan, Patrik, Francesco Corti, and Sebastiano Sabato. 2021. "The European Commission's entrepreneurship and the social dimension of the European Semester: from the European Pillar of Social Rights to the Covid-19 pandemic." *Comparative European Politics* 19: 277–95.

Wagner, Bettina, and Anke Hassel. 2016. "Posting, subcontracting and low wage employment in the German meat industry." *Transfer: European Review of Labour and Research* 22 (2): 145–46.

Weinkopf, Claudia. 2020. "Zur Durchsetzung des gesetzlichen Mindestlohns in Deutschland." *Aus Politik und Zeitgeschichte*. Available at https://www.bpb.de/apuz/315577/zur-durchsetzung-des-gesetzlichen-mindestlohns-in-deutschland.

Weisskircher, Manès, Julia Rone, and Mariana S. Mendes. 2020. "The only frequent flyers left: Migrant workers in the EU in times of Covid-19." *Open Democracy*, April 20, 2020. Available at: https://www.opendemocracy.net/en/can-europe-make-it/only-frequent-flyers-left-migrant-workers-eu-times-covid-19/.

Wixforth, Susanne, and Lukas Wiehler. 2021. "Darf's etwas weniger sein?" *IPG Journal*, 12.07.2021. Available at https://www.ipg-journal.de/regionen/europa/artikel/darfs-etwas-weniger-sein-5304/.

8

Is the Recession a "Shecession"? Gender Inequality in the Employment Effects of the COVID-19 Pandemic in Germany

Katja Möhring, Maximiliane Reifenscheid,
Andreas Weiland, and Klara Kuhn

Introduction

In early research on the employment consequences of the COVID-19 pandemic, implications for gender inequality were widely discussed. Several early studies showed that the effects of the pandemic recession differ from those of previous recessions, as especially women are expected to be disproportionally affected (Alon et al. 2020a; Collins et al.2020). However, most research on the consequences of the pandemic for gender inequality focused on the sharing of child care and home-schooling tasks in couples facing school and day care closures, and its implications for parents' and especially mothers' well-being (Hank and Steinbach 2020; Hipp and Bünning 2020; Möhring et al. 2020; Yerkes et al. 2020). Less research has been devoted to exploring gender inequality within employment risks induced by the pandemic. The few existing studies point out that working women have been highly affected by job loss and reduction of working hours in the pandemic recession (Alon et al. 2020a; Collins et al. 2020; Möhring et al. 2021). Therefore, the current pandemic recession is described as "Shecession" (Alon et al. 2020b). In contrast, women are also overrepresented among essential workers, especially in the health and care sector (Blundell et al. 2020). However, previous studies operate either with projections based on data that were gathered before the onset of the pandemic (e.g., Alon et al. 2020a) or are based on descriptive analysis of cross-sectional data (e.g., Blundell et al. 2020). Furthermore, existing research on the employment consequences of

Katja Möhring, Maximiliane Reifenscheid, Andreas Weiland, and Klara Kuhn, *Is the Recession a "Shecession"? Gender Inequality in the Employment Effects of the COVID-19 Pandemic in Germany* In: *European Social Policy and the COVID-19 Pandemic*. Edited by: Stefanie Börner and Martin Seeleib-Kaiser, Oxford University Press.
© Oxford University Press 2023. DOI: 10.1093/oso/9780197676189.003.0008

the COVID-19 pandemic mostly focuses on liberal market economies such as the United States of America. These countries, with their comparatively flexible labor markets, experienced a sharp rise in unemployment (OECD 2021). In the United States, job loss among women was indeed much more severe than in previous recessions (Alon et al. 2020b). In more regulated welfare states, unemployment did not sharply rise immediately after the onset of the pandemic because governments implemented new or existing job retention schemes, as the "furlough scheme" in the UK and the "short-time work" benefit in Germany (Adams-Prassl et al. 2020; Konle-Seidl 2020; OECD 2021). The consequences of these approaches for gender inequality at the labor market are not clear and have not been investigated so far.

With this background, the present study focuses on the situation in Germany, which has a highly regulated labor market and provides a generous social security net for the core work force, but is also characterized by a high gender-based dualization of employment (Emmenegger et al. 2012). We address two research questions related to gender inequality in employment during the pandemic recession. What gender differences can be identified in the risks of short-time work, job loss, and having to work on-site in the early phase and in the further course of the crisis? Which factors related to socioeconomic status and employment explain these differences? To the best of our knowledge, this study is the first using detailed panel data to analyze how gender inequalities in employment have evolved during the COVID-19 pandemic in Germany. Our data provide weekly information on the employment status over a time span of 16 weeks ranging from March 20 to July 9, 2020. We combine this weekly data with further longitudinal information for January 2021, thereby covering the first COVID-19 lockdown and the period after containment measures were eased, as well as the second lockdown in winter 2020–2021. The data come from the German Internet Panel, a longitudinal survey representative of the German population (Blom, Gathmann, and Krieger 2015), and a special COVID-19 study carried out as part of the GIP (Blom et al. 2020).

This chapter is organized as follows: in the next section we describe gender inequality on the German labor market and the design and targeting of governmental crisis measures. Our data, sample, operationalizations, and methods are explained in the "Materials and Methods" section. Afterward, we present descriptive results on gender differences in employment between March and July 2020, and in January 2021. We then turn to our multivariate results for the risks of short-time work, being out of work, and working on-site; first we look at *changes in work statuses for men and women during* the first wave of the pandemic in spring and summer 2020, and second at the situation in 2021. We close with a discussion of the results and conclusion.

Background

Gendered Dualization of the German Labor Market

Germany is a conservative welfare state with a coordinated market economy and corporatist structure (Esping-Andersen 1990; Hall and Soskice 2001). In the post-war decades, West Germany represented a male-breadwinner society promoting a traditional gendered division of tasks in couples (Struffolino, Studer, and Fasang 2016). The traditional division of paid work and unpaid care work between men and women was underpinned by central elements of the social security system, taxation, and wage structure (Schäfer and Gottschall 2015; Trappe, Pollmann-Schult, and Schmitt 2015). Family policy focused on cash benefits and long leave periods for mothers, and public child care remained largely underdeveloped in the pre-millennial decades (Gangl and Ziefle 2015). The marriage tax premium generally disincentivizes the increase of employment hours or the uptake of employment by the part-time or non-working spouse, thereby supporting inequality in labor market participation among married couples (Bach, Haan, and Ochmann 2013). Especially during the economic upturn in the immediate post-war decades, wage levels of industrial workers were sufficient to provide a livelihood for a family without the necessity of a second earner (Schäfer and Gottschall 2015). Men's employment careers of the post-war decades were characterized by an exceptional homogeneity and stability (Lersch, Schulz, and Leckie 2020; Möhring 2016).

This traditional arrangement has been changing for about three decades. First, changes induced by the economic crises of the 1970s and the stalled economic development of the 1980s led to mass unemployment and an increasing de-standardization of men's employment histories. At the same time, women's attachment to the labor market steadily increased. Second, with German reunification, East Germany was integrated into the Western institutional setting, which was at odds with the predominant dual-earner model in the former socialist German Democratic Republic. Today, eastern German women's labor force participation is still higher than that of western

German women, albeit converging to western German level, especially with respect to part-time work (Trappe et al. 2015). Finally, reforms in family policy since the mid-2000s toward a Scandinavian model, including the expansion of public child care in western Germany, led to a further increase in the labor market participation of women. Despite these developments, central elements of the institutional structure that supports a male breadwinner model, such as the marital wage premium, are still in place. As a consequence, the incentives for labor market participation of women, and especially mothers, are contradictory. Thus, the change in women's employment occurred mainly through higher labor market involvement of women in the form of part-time and marginal employment, the so-called mini-jobs, with the latter not being subject to social security payment and protection (Bergmann, Scheele, and Sorger 2019).

Labor market inequality intensified after the labor market reforms of the early 2000s, which included the flexibilization of the low-wage sector through incentives for employers and employees to generate and take up low-wage employment (Bosch and Weinkopf 2008; Eichhorst and Marx 2011). These changes implied an increased dualization of the labor force, including a polarization between full-time and part-time employees with employment contracts based on the regulations of the "mini-job" scheme in terms of wages and job security (Brülle et al. 2019; Emmenegger et al. 2012). This coincides with both a pronounced vertical and a horizontal segregation of the labor market in Germany. Vertical segregation in terms of underrepresentation of women in upper hierarchical positions is more pronounced in the private sector and tends to intensify with the size of the enterprise (Holst, Busch-Heizmann, and Wieber 2015). At the same time, women are overrepresented in those sectors of the economy, which are often accompanied by less favorable working conditions in terms of pay, social insurance, and job security; some examples include social and personal services, education, hotel and catering, and the beauty business (Eichhorst, Marx, and Tobsch 2015). In the traditional core sectors of the German economy, such as manufacturing, full-time employment with permanent contracts based on collective agreements and employee representation are generally prevalent. Here, the share of men among employees is also much higher. In the tertiary sector, however, where women are much more represented, part-time employment (in the social and personal services sector), marginal part-time employment (in the hotel and restaurant sector), temporary employment (in education) or solo self-employment (in the beauty industry) are much more common (Eichhorst and Marx 2009). As a consequence, gender represents a main division in the dualized German labor market with predominantly women working part-time and in the low-wage sector (Hassel 2014; Häusermann and Schwander 2012). Although female labor force participation in Germany is above the EU average, with 72.8% of women in employment in 2019 compared to the EU average of 64.1%, a more nuanced look shows that women in Germany are often still on the margins of the labor market: 46.7% of women worked part-time, compared to the EU average of 31.3%, and just 9.9% of men in Germany (data for 2019; Eurostat 2020a). Furthermore, 26.2% of women in Germany are in low-wage employment, compared to the EU average of 18.8%; this is one of the highest shares in Europe (data for 2018; Eurostat 2020b).

Gender Bias of Government Crisis Measures

The German social security system buffers income shortfalls, providing earnings-related benefits in case of unemployment or health-related loss of work ability. These benefits are supposed to secure the previous living standard instead of just preventing poverty, and thereby serve as an automatic stabilizer of lifetime earnings and consumption (Gangl 2004; Hall and Soskice 2001). During economic crises, further instruments compensate for negative consequences. Short-time work is the main instrument of social policy to avoid mass lay-offs during economic crises in Germany. It allows companies to reduce working hours and wages of employees in times of economic hardship. The employer can then apply for a government earnings replacement that compensates for the wage loss of up to 60% based on the previous net wage, and 67% for employees with dependent children (Konle-Seidl 2020; Wachter 2020).

Generally, governmental crises measures are designed for the usual cyclic economic recessions that first and foremost hit the export-oriented German industrial sector, such as the automotive industry, as well as the construction industry. Especially during the Great Recession, these measures were successful in preventing mass unemployment. Usual economic recessions affect men's employment much more than women's: the average working hours of men are reduced more than those of women because the male-dominated industry and construction sectors are more strongly affected from job losses, making men's employment much more volatile and dependent on economic circumstances (Doepke and Tertilt 2016). This was generally also the case for Germany during the Great Recession, but job losses here were much fewer and rather short-term, due to the rapid recovery of the German economy compared to many other countries (Rinne and Zimmermann 2012). During the Great Recession, the short-time work policy was applied and, in conjunction with direct state subsidies, mass lay-offs were prevented in the export-oriented industrial sectors, such as the automotive industry (Burda and Hunt 2011). On the contrary, the service sector had an increase in employment even in the core crisis years of 2008–2009. This led to an increase in the employment rate of women in part-time, and especially atypical, employment during this period (Kirchmann and Rosemann 2010). Hence, the fact that crisis measures are mostly targeted at male-dominated sectors of the economy did not become noticeable at that time.

During the COVID-19 pandemic, the German federal government has extended existing crisis measures and adopted several new subsidies to mitigate the negative consequences. From January 2021, the government has extended the possible duration of the short-time work status to up to 24 months and decided on a temporary top-up of the short-time work benefit to up to 70% (77% for parents) of the net wage loss after four months of receipt, and to 80% (87% for parents) after seven months of receipt. These extensions of the usual short-time work framework applied until the end of 2021 (BMAS 2020). A government aid package, including direct payments for companies that had lost revenues, was launched during the spring lockdown and repeated several times thereafter (BMWI 2021). Nevertheless, the economic aid package is still largely focused on male-dominated sectors of the economy. Wiesner (2020) presents the only study to date on the distribution of aid funds in Germany from a gender perspective. According to their calculations, the largest share of the package consists of direct government subsidies for affected companies in the private sector, while payments for the social and cultural sector, including care, health, education, and art/culture, are smaller. Even investments in sectors with a high female share of the workforce, such as public child care and health, focus on construction and infrastructure measures and thus mainly benefit the largely male-dominated construction sector (Wiesner 2020).

Furthermore, gender differences also exist in the eligibility and level of the short-time work benefit. Most importantly, jobs that are not subject to social security payments are exempted from short-time work, hence the impact of the pandemic on employment among the marginally employed became very quickly apparent on the labor market. By the end of March 2020 there were

300,000 jobs less in marginal employment than three months before, while from March 2020 to March 2021 a total of 800,000 jobs in marginal employment had vanished (Deutsche Rentenversicherung 2020; 2021). As a result, many female employees working in sectors heavily affected by the pandemic crisis such as retail and hospitality, which account for almost one-third of the total marginal employment in Germany (Deutsche Rentenversicherung 2020), were excluded from receiving the short-time work earning's replacement and thus could not bridge pandemic-related closures and restrictions. Furthermore, the short-time work benefit must be applied for by the employer, which requires administrative effort that small firms in the service sector might be less capable of than large manufacturing companies. Therefore, one response to the pandemic has been to temporarily suspend employees. These furloughed employees represent a highly heterogeneous group: for some, especially civil servants in the public sector, salary is continued, while others neither receive pay from their employer, nor any government earnings replacement to compensate for their loss of income (unlike Britain's temporary furlough scheme; Adams-Prassl et al. 2020). Those in precarious employment ineligible for short-time work benefits mostly compose the latter group (Grabka, Braband, and Göbler 2020). Even for those eligible to receive short-time work benefits, gender differences exist. Sectors with collective agreement coverage grant an upscaling of the short-time work benefit of up to 90% of the previous wage. Women, however, mostly work in areas that are not subject to collective agreements (Hammerschmid, Schmieder, and Wrohlich 2020; Wiesner 2020). In contrast, women are overrepresented in the social and care professions with 83.7% of employees being female, and in nursing professions with 81.8%, as well as in retail with 71.5% (Bundesagentur für Arbeit 2021). Therefore, they represent a large share of the so-called key or essential workers during the pandemic (Koebe et al. 2020). Normally they work close to patients or customers and do not have autonomy over their work location, which is potentially related to a higher risk of COVID-19 infection (Vlachos, Hertegård, and Svaleryd 2021; Möhring et al. 2021).

Data and Method

We use data from the German Internet Panel, a bimonthly voluntary online survey, which is based on an offline-recruited random probability sample of the general population of Germany aged 16 to 75 (Blom et al. 2015, 2020). On

March 20, 2020, the GIP launched a special survey to gather data about the COVID-19 pandemic, where GIP respondents were invited to take surveys every week. We merge this weekly information for the early phase of the pandemic with further information from the survey months September 2020 and January 2021. In the descriptive analysis we use GIP weights to extrapolate participants' characteristics to those of Germany's general population. In all analyses, we include only individuals who were in dependent employment in January 2020 and are below 68 years old.

With respect to the employment situation, we are interested in the risks of short-time work, being out of work, and working on-site. For the risks of short-time work we have direct information from the respondents at each weekly interview on whether they are in short-time work and receive governmental short-time work benefits. We form a common category for being out of work, in which we group the unemployed and those suspended without pay, as the latter is de facto equal to being temporarily unemployed. Working on-site is operationalized using information on the work location and summarizing those who always or mainly work on-site, with those who work always, mainly, or half of the time from home as reference category.

We complement descriptive analyses of gender differences in employment risks with multivariate regression analyses controlling for educational degree, occupational sector, personal net income in January 2020, partner, and number of children. For the weekly data of March 20 (week 1) and July 9 (week 16), we use logit random effects growth curve models; for the data of January 2021, we use cross-sectional logit regressions. All analyses include only those individuals who have been in gainful employment in January 2020, to focus on if and how they are affected by the changes induced by the pandemic (see also Tables 8.1, 8.2, 8.3, 8.4 and 8.5 in the Appendix).

Results

Gender Differences in Employment Risks During the Early Phase of the Pandemic

Figure 8.1 illustrates the development of the employment situation of individuals who have been employed in January 2020, over the first phase of the pandemic, separated by gender and complemented with indices on the intensity of non-pharmaceutical interventions (NPI, Hale et al. 2021). We use

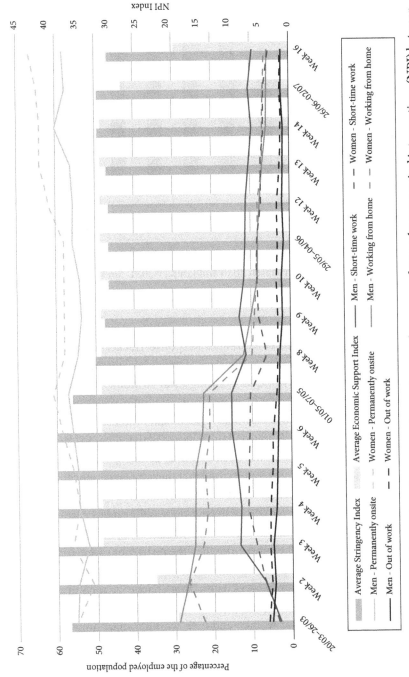

Figure 8.1 Weighted shares of employment statuses of men and women and non-pharmaceutical interventions (NPI) between March and July 2020. Source: German Internet Panel (2020) and Oxford Government Response Tracker (Hale et al. 2021), author estimation.

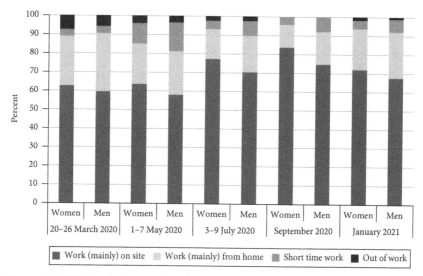

Figure 8.2 Weighted shares of employment statuses of men and women for selected time-points between March 2020 and January 2021. Source: German Internet Panel, author estimations.

two indices from the Oxford Government Response Tracker OxCGRT: the Average Stringency Index refers to a variety of potential containment measures, including school and workplace closings, stay-at-home-requirements, and travel controls; the Average Economic Support Index scales generosity and availability of state-funded earnings replacements and debt-relief measures for households (ibid). We adjusted the scales of both indices to a possible maximum of 50 scale points. In the week of March 20 to 26, 2020, under 5% of both male and female employees reported that they were receiving the government short-time work allowance; this number increased for both groups until early May 2020, however with a steeper increase for men. Also, men's share in short-time work was almost twice as high as women's in early July 2020 after the first wave of the pandemic when the restrictions were eased.

From the sixth to the seventh week, stringency of the government measures was reduced, and again a week later. This change in measures also coincides with a sharp drop in the share of women and men working from home, and a smaller share of women and men working short hours. A less steep but considerable decline in those working permanently on-site also follows the first relaxation in week seven, but subsequent increases in on-site work (for example, for women from week 12 on, and men from weeks 13 to 14) are not accompanied by changes in NPI. Overall, women had higher shares working on-site from mid-April 2020 to early July 2020.

In terms of working from home, men and women had their highest share in week one and week two, respectively. As mentioned above, a sharp decline in home-working can be observed from week seven to eight for both groups, where numbers almost reduced by half and mostly continued to decline until July 2020. In January 2021, during the peak of the second pandemic wave, rates of employees working from home were similarly high as in early May 2020. Overall, the development of working from home was similar for men and women; however, especially in the first eight weeks, fewer women than men worked from home. Also, the trend in short-time work was similar across groups, but with almost continuously higher rates among men. Furthermore, more women than men worked on-site, especially in the second half of the observation window.

To further investigate gender differences in the probabilities of short-time work, being out of work, and working on-site controlling for socioeconomic characteristics, we use logistic growth curve models as described above. The regression results are depicted in Figure 8.3 (detailed regression results are included in Table 8.6 in the Appendix). In terms of short-time work, men and women follow a similar trajectory. The probability for short-time work only slightly increases across weeks, and more so for men than for women. At first, the probability increases until week three and week four (April 10 to 16) for men and women, respectively. From this point on, men's probability of experiencing short-time work remains relatively stable and is generally slightly higher than women's, which drops lower than men's in week eight; yet these differences are not significant (see Figure 8.3; first row). We will now turn to the analysis of risk of being out of work.

Men's and women's predicted probabilities of being out of work both start out at around 4%. Whereas men's probability decreases only slightly until week eight (May 8–14), women experience a visible drop between week three and eight (April 3rd– May 14), until both trajectories converge again. From week nine until the end of the observation window (May 15– July 9), trajectories of men and women diverge visibly. Here, men experience a slight increase in their predicted probabilities of being out of work, back to their initial level. Women's trajectories, in contrast, exhibit a visible decline and decrease to a probability of about 1% by week 15 (June 26– July 2), which is significantly lower than men's (see Figure 8.3; second row). To sum up, men are at a significantly higher risk of being out of work between the end of June

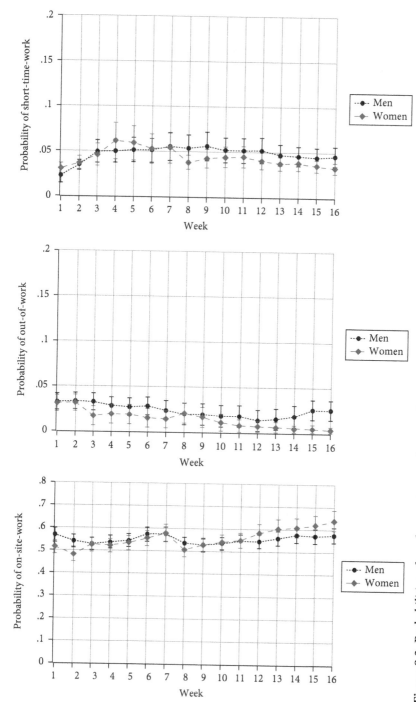

Figure 8.3 Probabilities of employment state of men and women between March and July 2020. Notes: Adjusted predictions with 95% confidence intervals. Full regression results.

and mid-July, while women's risk of being out of work seems to follow the stringency of containment measures more strongly.

Consulting predicted probabilities of working on-site at the means of covariates (Figure 8.3; bottom row), we see that men have a slightly higher likelihood than women to work on-site in week one. By week two (March 27–April 2), the likelihood of workplace presence declines more strongly for women, leaving men with a significantly higher probability of on-site work. From week three throughout week seven (April 3–May 7), probabilities slightly increase again and converge, which is followed by another substantial drop in week eight. From week nine throughout week 16 (May 15–July 9), probabilities for both men and women increase again, albeit at a higher rate for the latter. Consequently, by week 12, women's probability of on-site work becomes higher than men's, however differences are not significant. Overall, we can observe a slight increase in on-site work for both men and women between weeks 3 and 7, and 8 and 16, respectively.

Gender Differences in Employment Risks in the Second Wave of the Pandemic

Figure 8.2 complements the developments in employment risks over the early phase of the pandemic with information for September 2020, when COVID-19 case numbers were low and restrictions were eased, and January 2021 during the second wave of the pandemic. As in July 2020, women's share in short-time work was lower than men's, and their shares of on-site work and being out of work were slightly higher, although gender differences decreased as compared to the first phase of the pandemic.

This picture is confirmed in a further multivariate analysis. We again use logistic regression models to further investigate the probability of short-time work and being out of work in January 2021 (detailed regression results are included in Table 8.7 in the Appendix). There are no significant gender differences in the odds of short-time work or being out of work. Generally, higher incomes are associated with lower odds of short-time work and being out of work, whereas a higher educational attainment is only associated with lower odds of the out-of-work risk. With regard to sector, we only find that those in the public or educational sector are significantly less likely to engage in short-time work.

Discussion and Conclusion

We investigated gender differences in the risks of short-time work, job loss and unpaid furlough, and having to work on-site during the COVID-19 pandemic in Germany. Given the inherent challenges of the dualized German labor market, we were particularly interested in inequalities in the experience of crisis-related disadvantages that occurred in the early phase of the pandemic, beginning in March 2020. This early phase was characterized by high uncertainty about what the pandemic would bring in the future in terms of the health of the population but also, precisely, the robustness of the economy. During this time, governments were looking for benchmarks and blueprints that simply did not exist, making it difficult to predict which constraints and for how long would be needed, and how the economy and employment would be affected by these. In the early months of the pandemic, this was exacerbated by the fact that protective measures that can be used today to open stores or businesses did not exist at the time, due to the sheer lack of basic protective materials and appropriate technology. Our weekly data covering the time span March 20 until July 9, 2020, is suited to capture the high pace of changes that occurred.

Our results show no particularly high exposure of women to pandemic-related labor market risks. Women are not significantly less or more likely to be in short-time work; in other words, accessibility to a crisis measure that serves as buffer for risks of income loss and job loss does not differ between genders. Furthermore, we did not observe an increased likelihood of job loss and unpaid furlough among women, and women did not show a significantly higher probability than men of working on-site during the early phase of the pandemic. Regarding the unemployment risk in the first and second wave of the pandemic, our results rather suggest that individual characteristics such as low income and education are important drivers. This also applies to the likelihood of short-time work during the second wave of the pandemic. The risk for short-time work is significantly lower, both in the service sector and in public administration, education, and health than in manufacturing, but the risk of being out of work is only increased in the service sector; that fact confirms in general the dualization of the labor market and the higher protection in the traditional key industries.

Turning back to our initial question—is the pandemic recession a "Shecession"? —our results point in the direction that challenges for women were rather heterogeneous among women. Depending on the profession and employment contract, lay-offs especially in the hospitality sector might have quickly led to hiring in other sectors of the economy, where persons who lost their jobs might have had to quickly adapt to new jobs. Women in care and health professions continued to work, due to their considerable overrepresentation in occupations classified as essential during the pandemic. In the long term, the COVID-19 pandemic could exacerbate the existing shortage of qualified health workers, especially in hospitals, where workloads have been continuously very high since the beginning of the pandemic. Our results apply to the first and second wave of the pandemic; with a view to the further course of the crisis, it must be closely monitored here how changes in the markets affect employment, especially if job opportunities that have now experienced a strong upswing as a result of the pandemic, or have even only arisen at all because of it, are reduced again.

The non-significant gender differences show that women in Germany were far more affected by the pandemic crisis than by the Great Recession, when job loss was concentrated among men (Kirchmann and Rosemann 2010). Yet, this does not manifest in widespread job loss among women as in the United States (Alon et al. 2021). Rather, it is the case in Germany that men and women are much more equally affected by negative employment consequences during the pandemic recession than they have been in previous recessions. Reasons for that might be the higher level of labor market regulation, which prevents immediate lay-offs for the majority of the workforce, as well as the high share of part-time work among women in Germany, which lessens the necessity for quitting a job to assume child care. However, while mothers in the pandemic have largely compensated for the loss of institutional child care (Jessen, Spieß, and Wrohlich 2021), the exit of mothers from part-time and marginal employment is made more difficult, seeing that the child care infrastructure in Germany has repeatedly collapsed due to COVID-19.

While the data used for this study does not allow to control for mothers with small children who require adult care most of the time, for this group the incompatibility of care work and gainful employment, even on part-time basis, may have contributed to short-time work or lay-offs. As Bujard et al. (2020) show using data from the Mannheim Corona Study, the average working time of mothers decreased by 0.8 hours, comparing working hours in 2018 with those from April 2020. This decrease seems moderate when considering that not only schools and child care facilities were closed, but also support from persons outside the household was not possible. It can be assumed that gainful employment and child care often had to take place simultaneously, or that working hours were shifted to the late evening and night hours (ibid). This indicates that there was a considerable double burden on all working mothers, especially in the first months of the pandemic, while local closures and quarantine regulations in the months that followed repeatedly made it necessary to perform care duties and work at the same time.

Table 8.1 Gender Differences Employment in January 2020 (weighted)

Employed in January 2020	Men	Women	Total
Full-time	91.71	50.97	72.52
Part-time	6.42	42.04	23.2
Marginally/occasionally employed	1.87	6.99	4.28
Personal net income	**Men**	**Women**	**Total**
<1.000 Euro	5.02	21.23	12.55
1.000 - 2.500 Euro	47.26	60.2	53.27
>2.500 Euro	47.72	18.57	34.18
Employment situation	**Men**	**Women**	**Total**
Permanently on-site	15.33	15.39	15.36
Ever working from home	39.70	35.88	37.89
Ever short-time work	24.12	14.22	19.41
Ever out of work	8.7	7.59	8.17
Sector of employment	**Men**	**Women**	**Total**
Manufacturing	39.96	15.42	28.3
Service	36.13	34.89	35.54
Public administration, education, and health	20.36	43.09	31.16

Source: German Internet Panel, own estimations, based on 2385 observations, applying GIP rake weights.

Note: All numbers referring to individuals in gainful employment in January.

Table 8.2 Short-time Work Summary Statistics for All Variables (unweighted)

	Women		Men		Total			
	Mean	Stand. Dev.	Mean	Stand. Dev	Mean	Stand. Dev.	Min	Max
Employment status: short-time work	0.04	0.19	0.03	0.16	0.03	0.17	0	1
Age	46.05	11.34	46.92	10.94	46.92	10.94	20	67
Education								
Low	0.02	0.14	0.01	0.12	0.02	0.13	0	1
Medium	0.60	0.49	0.60	0.49	0.60	0.49	0	1
High	0.38	0.49	0.39	0.49	0.38	0.49	0	1
Personal net income								
< 1.000 Euro	0.14	0.35	0.03	0.17	0.08	0.27	0	1
1.000-2.500 Euro	0.60	0.49	0.38	0.48	0.47	0.50	0	1
> 2.500 Euro	0.25	0.44	0.59	0.49	0.45	0.50	0	1
Sector								
Manufacturing	0.14	0.35	0.35	0.48	0.26	0.44	0	1
Service	0.34	0.47	0.41	0.49	0.38	0.48	0	1
Public administration / education / health	0.52	0.50	0.24	0.43	0.36	0.48	0	1
Observation weeks per individual	-	-	-	-	12.9	-	2	16

Source: German Internet Panel, own estimations.

Table 8.3 Out of Work Summary Statistics for All Variables (unweighted)

	Women		Men		Total			
	Mean	Stand. Dev.	Mean	Stand. Dev	Mean	Stand. Dev.	Min	Max
Employment status: out of work	0.04	0.21	0.03	0.18	0.04	0.19	0	1
Age	46.05	11.34	46.92	10.94	46.92	10.94	20	67
Education								
Low	0.02	0.14	0.01	0.12	0.02	0.13	0	1
Medium	0.60	0.49	0.60	0.49	0.60	0.49	0	1
High	0.38	0.49	0.39	0.49	0.38	0.49	0	1
Personal net income								
< 1.000 Euro	0.14	0.35	0.03	0.17	0.08	0.27	0	1
1.000-2.500 Euro	0.60	0.49	0.38	0.48	0.47	0.50	0	1
> 2.500 Euro	0.25	0.44	0.59	0.49	0.45	0.50	0	1
Sector								
Manufacturing	0.14	0.35	0.35	0.48	0.26	0.44	0	1
Service	0.34	0.47	0.41	0.49	0.38	0.48	0	1
Public administration / education / health	0.52	0.50	0.24	0.43	0.36	0.48	0	1
Observation weeks per individual	-	-	-	-	13	-	2	16

Source: German Internet Panel, own estimations.

Table 8.4 On-site Work Summary Statistics for All Variables (unweighted)

	Women		Men		Total			
	Mean	Stand. Dev.	Mean	Stand. Dev	Mean	Stand. Dev.	Min	Max
Employment status: on-site work	0.51	0.50	0.52	0.50	0.04	0.19	0	1
Age	46.05	11.34	46.92	10.94	46.92	10.94	20	67
Education								
Low	0.02	0.14	0.01	0.12	0.02	0.13	0	1
Medium	0.60	0.49	0.60	0.49	0.60	0.49	0	1
High	0.38	0.49	0.39	0.49	0.38	0.49	0	1
Personal net income								
< 1.000 Euro	0.14	0.35	0.03	0.17	0.08	0.27	0	1
1.000-2.500 Euro	0.60	0.49	0.38	0.48	0.47	0.50	0	1
> 2.500 Euro	0.25	0.44	0.59	0.49	0.45	0.50	0	1
Sector								
Manufacturing	0.14	0.35	0.35	0.48	0.26	0.44	0	1
Service	0.34	0.47	0.41	0.49	0.38	0.48	0	1
Public administration / education / health	0.52	0.50	0.24	0.43	0.36	0.48	0	1
Observation weeks per individual	-	-	-	-	13	-	2	16

Source: German Internet Panel, own estimations.

Table 8.5 Gender Composition of Service Sector Fields

	Men	Women	Total
Wholesale and Retail Trade	45.98	54.02	100
Transportation and Storage	67.29	32.71	100
Accommodation and Food Service	40.9	59.1	100
Information and Communication	72.89	27.11	100
Financial and Insurance Activities	46.68	53.32	100
Real Estate	33.12	66.88	100
Professional, Scientific and Technical Activities	55.31	44.69	100
Other Service Activities	15.53	84.47	100
Arts, Entertainment and Recreation	50.61	49.39	100

Source: German Internet Panel, own estimations, based on 2385 observations, applying GIP rake weights. Notes: All numbers referring to individuals in gainful employment in January 2020.

Table 8.6 Logit Random Effects Regressions on the Risk of Employment State between March and July 2020 (odds Ratios displayed)

	Short-time-work		Out of work		On-site-work	
	Baseline b(se)	Gender differences b(se)	Baseline b(se)	Gender differences b(se)	Baseline b(se)	Gender differences b(se)
Week (ref. week 1)						
2	1.45***	1.89***	0.087	0.12	−0.46**	−0.38*
	(0.31)	(0.44)	(0.40)	(0.52)	(0.14)	(0.19)
3	2.68***	3.38***	−0.69	0.017	−0.24	−0.57**
	(0.30)	(0.43)	(0.45)	(0.58)	(0.14)	(0.19)
4	2.98***	3.40***	−0.85	−0.47	−0.17	−0.42*
	(0.31)	(0.43)	(0.46)	(0.61)	(0.14)	(0.20)
5	3.01***	3.50***	−0.95*	−0.62	−0.026	−0.32
	(0.30)	(0.43)	(0.46)	(0.62)	(0.14)	(0.19)
6	2.88***	3.46***	−1.13*	−0.47	0.34*	0.081
	(0.31)	(0.43)	(0.47)	(0.63)	(0.15)	(0.20)
7	3.06***	3.71***	−1.45**	−1.00	0.50***	0.084
	(0.31)	(0.43)	(0.48)	(0.65)	(0.15)	(0.20)
8	2.59***	3.62***	−1.21*	−1.45*	−0.33*	−0.48*
	(0.31)	(0.43)	(0.50)	(0.73)	(0.15)	(0.20)
9	2.81***	3.74***	−1.55**	−1.49*	−0.22	−0.60**

Table 8.6 Continued

	Short-time-work		Out of work	On-site-work		
	Baseline b(se)	Gender differences b(se)	Baseline b(se)	Gender differences b(se)	Baseline b(se)	Gender differences b(se)
	(0.31)	(0.43)	(0.51)	(0.72)	(0.15)	(0.20)
10	2.73***	3.53***	−2.01***	−1.69*	−0.058	−0.48*
	(0.31)	(0.43)	(0.52)	(0.73)	(0.15)	(0.20)
11	2.73***	3.51***	−2.35***	−1.69*	0.089	−0.30
	(0.31)	(0.43)	(0.54)	(0.73)	(0.15)	(0.20)
12	2.62***	3.53***	−2.69***	−2.24**	0.30*	−0.31
	(0.31)	(0.44)	(0.56)	(0.80)	(0.15)	(0.20)
13	2.32***	3.24***	−2.73***	−2.04**	0.53***	−0.081
	(0.31)	(0.43)	(0.57)	(0.77)	(0.15)	(0.20)
14	2.28***	3.13***	−2.79***	−1.67*	0.67***	0.12
	(0.31)	(0.44)	(0.57)	(0.74)	(0.15)	(0.20)
15	2.10***	3.06***	−2.20***	−0.78	0.70***	0.055
	(0.31)	(0.43)	(0.54)	(0.68)	(0.15)	(0.20)
16	2.00***	3.14***	−2.39***	−0.81	0.84***	0.12
	(0.31)	(0.44)	(0.55)	(0.67)	(0.15)	(0.20)
Week*female						
2*female		−0.89		−0.033		−0.16
		(0.64)		(0.75)		(0.29)
3*female		−1.53*		−1.62		0.75*
		(0.63)		(0.87)		(0.29)
4*female		−0.74		−0.87		0.58*
		(0.63)		(0.89)		(0.29)
5*female		−0.94		−0.75		0.67*
		(0.62)		(0.88)		(0.29)
6*female		−1.18		−1.38		0.59*
		(0.63)		(0.90)		(0.29)
7*female		−1.38*		−0.96		0.94**
		(0.63)		(0.93)		(0.30)
8*female		−2.44***		0.31		0.35
		(0.63)		(0.98)		(0.30)
9*female		−2.15***		−0.19		0.85**
		(0.63)		(1.00)		(0.30)
10*female		−1.80**		−0.72		0.95**
		(0.63)		(1.02)		(0.30)
11*female		−1.75**		−1.36		0.88**

(continued)

Table 8.6 Continued

	Short-time-work		Out of work		On-site-work	
	Baseline b(se)	Gender differences b(se)	Baseline b(se)	Gender differences b(se)	Baseline b(se)	Gender differences b(se)
		(0.63)		(1.05)		(0.30)
12*female		−2.11***		−0.91		1.37***
		(0.63)		(1.10)		(0.30)
13*female		−2.16***		−1.36		1.40***
		(0.63)		(1.10)		(0.30)
14*female		−1.96**		−2.26*		1.26***
		(0.64)		(1.11)		(0.31)
15*female		−2.29***		−3.07**		1.47***
		(0.63)		(1.08)		(0.30)
16*female		−2.78***		−3.55**		1.65***
		(0.65)		(1.13)		(0.31)
Female	−0.27	1.29*	−1.02	−0.20	−0.051	−0.84*
	(0.38)	(0.64)	(0.56)	(0.66)	(0.28)	(0.35)
Education (ref. low)						
medium	0.064	0.13	−4.18***	−2.45*	1.74	1.74
	(1.14)	(1.15)	(0.54)	(1.00)	(0.93)	(0.95)
high	−0.68	−0.65	−4.11	−2.46*	−2.16*	−2.21*
	(1.17)	(1.19)	(.)	(1.05)	(0.95)	(0.97)
Sector (ref. manufacturing)						
service	−1.17***	−1.16***	2.73***	2.08***	−1.48***	−1.51***
	(0.35)	(0.35)	(0.73)	(0.55)	(0.32)	(0.32)
public administration / education / health	−8.14*** (0.57)	−8.07*** (0.58)	1.08 (0.82)	1.04 (0.60)	0.44 (0.33)	0.45 (0.33)
Income (ref. < 1.000 Euro)						
1.000 – 2.500 Euro	0.30	0.35	−7.04***	−3.18***	0.76	0.78
	(0.64)	(0.63)	(0.75)	(0.55)	(0.46)	(0.47)
> 2.500 Euro	−0.38	−0.35	−9.13***	−4.63***	−0.50	−0.49
	(0.69)	(0.69)	(0.88)	(0.63)	(0.51)	(0.51)
Constant	−8.97***	−9.67***	−8.65***	−8.20***	−1.52	−1.19
	(1.48)	(1.51)	(1.77)	(1.53)	(1.17)	(1.19)
n	20017	20017	20185	20185	20185	20185
N	1557	1557	1,557	1,557	1,557	1,557

Notes: Controlled for number of children, partner in household, self-employment; t statistics in parentheses; + p < .1, * p < .05, ** p < .01, *** p < .001.

Source: German Internet Panel, own estimations.

Table 8.7 Logit Regressions for the Risk of Short-time Work and Out of Work in January 2021 (odds ratios displayed)

	(1)	(2)	(3)	(4)
	Short-time work	Short-time work	Unemployed/ furlough w/o pay	Unemployed/ furlough w/o pay
Female	0.703	0.452	1.783	1.874
	(−1.23)	(−1.40)	(1.03)	(0.66)
Education (ref. low)				
medium	1.109	1.121	0.0911**	0.0845***
	(0.14)	(0.15)	(−3.25)	(−3.34)
high	1.024	1.058	0.145*	0.129*
	(0.03)	(0.07)	(−2.44)	(−2.54)
Income (ref. <1000)				
1000-2500	0.481+	0.498+	0.0812***	0.0795***
	(−1.84)	(−1.75)	(−3.78)	(−3.78)
>2500	0.314**	0.324*	0.150**	0.149**
	(−2.62)	(−2.54)	(−2.90)	(−2.85)
Sector (ref. manufacturing)				
service	1.100	0.914	0.767	0.507
	(0.36)	(−0.29)	(−0.44)	(−0.72)
public administration / education / health	0.174*** (−3.70)	0.210* (−2.49)	0.469 (−1.09)	1.052 (0.05)
Age	0.996	0.997	1.009	1.011
	(−0.32)	(−0.30)	(0.42)	(0.47)
Number of children (ref. no children)				
1	1.189	1.186	0.498	0.522
	(0.51)	(0.50)	(−0.84)	(−0.79)
2	0.922	0.903	0.548	0.535
	(−0.19)	(−0.23)	(−0.55)	(−0.57)
3+	0.916	0.923	0.434	0.448
	(−0.26)	(−0.24)	(−1.03)	(−0.99)
Partner in household	1.501	1.469	0.952	0.921
	(1.13)	(1.06)	(−0.08)	(−0.13)
Female*sector (Ref. female* manufacturing)				
female*service		2.031		1.782
		(1.09)		(0.45)
female* public administration / education / health		0.973 (−0.03)		0.312 (−0.85)
N	1513	1513	1513	1513
Pseudo-R sq.	0.0715	0.0742	0.137	0.147

Notes: t statistics in parentheses; + p < .1, * p < .05, ** p < .01, *** p < .001.

Source: German Internet Panel, own estimations.

References

Adams-Prassl, Abi, Teodora, Boneva, Marta, Golin, and Christopher Rauh. 2020. "Furloughing*." *Fiscal Studies* 41(3): 591–622. https://doi.org/10.1111/1475-5890.12242

Alon, Titan, Matthias Doepke, Jane Olmstead-Rumsey, and Michèle Tertilt. 2020a. "The impact of COVID-19 on gender equality." *NBER Working Paper Series*, Working Paper Nr. 26947: 1–37. National Bureau of Economic Research, Cambridge. https://doi.org/10.3386/w26947

Alon, Titan, Matthias Doepke, Jane Olmstead-Rumsey, and Michèle Tertilt. 2020b. "The shecession (she-recession) of 2020: Causes and consequences." Retrieved from https://voxeu.org/article/shecession-she-recession-2020-causes-and-consequences

Alon, Titan, Sena Coskun, Matthias Doepke, David Koll, and Michèle Tertilt. 2022. "From mancession to shecession: Women's employment in regular and pandemic recessions." *NBER Macroeconomics Annual* 36.

Bach, Stefan, Peter Haan, and Richard Ochmann. 2013. "Taxation of married couples in Germany and the UK: One-earner couples make the difference." *International Journal of Microsimulation* 6(3): 3–24. https://doi.org/10.34196/IJM.00086

Banerjee, Rupa. 2009. "Income growth of new immigrants in Canada: Evidence from the Survey of Labour and Income Dynamics." *Relations Industrielles / Industrial Relations* 64(3): 466–88. https://doi.org/10.7202/038552ar

Bergmann, Nadja, Alexandra Scheele, and Claudia Sorger. 2019. "Variations of the same? A sectoral analysis of the gender pay gap in Germany and Austria." *Gender, Work and Organization* 26(5): 668–87. https://doi.org/10.1111/gwao.12299

Blom, Annelies G., Catherine Gathmann, and Ulrich Krieger. 2015. "Setting up an online panel representative of the general population: The German Internet Panel." *Field Methods* 27(4): 391–408. https://doi.org/10.1177/1525822X15574494

Blom, Annelies G., Jessica M. Herzing, Carina Cornesse, Joseph W. Sakshaug, Ulrich Krieger, and Dayana Bossert. 2017. "Does the recruitment of offline households increase the sample representativeness of probability-based online panels? Evidence from the German Internet Panel." *Social Science Computer Review* 35(4): 498–520. https://doi.org/10.1177/0894439316651584

Blom, Annelies G., Carina Cornesse, Sabine Friedel, Ulrich Krieger, Marina Fikel, Tobias Rettig, Alexander Wenz, Sebastian Juhl, Roni Lehrer, Katja Möhring, Elias Naumann, and Maximiliane Reifenscheid. 2020. "High frequency and high quality survey data collection." *Survey Research Methods* 14(2): 171–78. https://doi.org/10.18148/srm/2020.v14i2.7735

Blundell, Richard, Monica Costa Dias, Robert Joyce, and Xiaowei Xu. 2020. "COVID-19 and inequalities*." *Fiscal Studies* 41(2): 291–319. https://doi.org/10.1111/1475-5890.12232

Bosch, Gerhard, and Claudia Weinkopf. 2008. *Low-wage Work in Germany.* New York: Russell Sage Foundation. https://doi.org/10.1111/j.1467-8543.2009.00745_3.x

Brülle, Jan, Markus Gangl, Asaf Levanon, and Evgeny Saburov. 2019. "Changing labour market risks in the service economy: Low wages, part-time employment and the trend in working poverty risks in Germany." *Journal of European Social Policy* 29(1): 115–29. https://doi.org/10.1177/0958928718779482

Bujard, Martin, Inga Laß, Sabine Diabaté, Harun Sulak, and Norbert F. Schneider. 2020. "Eltern während der Corona-Krise: Zur Improvisation gezwungen." BiB.Bevölkerungs.

Studien 1/2020: 1–56. Federal Institute for Population Research. https://doi.org/10.12765/bro-2020-01.

Bundesagentur für Arbeit. 2021. Anteil von Frauen und Männern in verschiedenen Berufsgruppen in Deutschland am 30. Juni 2020 (sozialversicherungspflichtig und geringfügig Beschäftigte) [Graph]. In *Statista*. Retrieved from https://de.statista.com/statistik/daten/studie/167555/umfrage/frauenanteil-in-verschiedenen-berufsgruppen-in-deutschland/

Bundesministerium für Arbeit und Soziales (BMAS). 2020. Erfolgsmodell Kurzarbeit wird verlängert. Retrieved from https://www.bmas.de/DE/Presse/Pressemitteilungen/2020/erfolgsmodell-kurzarbeit-wird-verlaengert.html

Bundesministerium für Wirtschaft und Energie (BMWI). 2021. Corona-Hilfen für Unternehmen. Retrieved from https://www.bmwi.de/Redaktion/DE/Infografiken/Wirtschaft/corona-hilfen-fuer-unternehmen.html

Burda, Michael C., and Jennifer Hunt. 2011. "What explains the German labor market miracle in the Great Recession?" *NBER Working Paper Series*, Working Paper Nr. 17187: 1–37. National Bureau of Economic Research, Cambridge. https://doi.org/10.3386/w17187

Collins, Caitlyn, Liana Christin Landivar, Leah Ruppanner, and William J. Scarborough. 2020. "COVID-19 and the gender gap in work hours." *Gender, Work and Organization* 28: 101–12. https://doi.org/10.1111/gwao.12506

Deutsche Rentenversicherung Knappschaft-Bahn-See, 2. Quartalsbericht 2020. "Aktuelle Entwicklungen im Bereich der Mini-Jobs." 2020. Retrieved from https://www.minijob-zentrale.de/DE/02_fuer_journalisten/02_berichte_trendreporte/quartalsberichte_archiv/2020/2_2020.pdf?__blob=publicationFile andv=4

Deutsche Rentenversicherung Knappschaft-Bahn-See, 1. Quartalsbericht 2021. "Aktuelle Entwicklungen im Bereich der Mini-Jobs." 2021. Retrieved fromhttps://www.minijob-zentrale.de/DE/02_fuer_journalisten/02_berichte_trendreporte/quartalsberichte_archiv/2021/1_2021.html?nn=700302

Doepke, Matthias, and Michèle Tertilt. 2016. "Families in Macroeconomics." In *Handbook of Macroeconomics*, edited by J. B. Taylor and H. Uhlig, 1798–891. Saint Louis: Elsevier Science and Technology. https://doi.org/10.1016/bs.hesmac.2016.04.006

Eichhorst, Werner, and Paul Marx. 2009. "From the dual apprenticeship system to a dual labor market? The German high-skill equilibrium and the service economy." *IZA Discussion Paper*, No. 4220: 1–27. Retrieved from https://ssrn.com/abstract=1423336

Eichhorst, Werner, and Paul Marx. 2011. "Reforming German labour market institutions: A dual path to flexibility." *Journal of European Social Policy* 21(1): 73–87. https://doi.org/10.1177/0958928710385731

Eichhorst, Werner, Paul Marx, and Verena Tobsch. 2015. "Non-standard employment across occupations in Germany: the role of replaceability and labour market flexibility." In *Non-Standard Employment in Post-Industrial Labour Markets*, edited by Werner Eichhorst and Paul Marx, 29–51. Edward Elgar Publishing. https://doi.org/10.4337/9781781001721.00008

Emmenegger, Patrick, Silja Häusermann, Bruno Palier, and Martin Seeleib-Kaiser, eds. 2012. *The Age of Dualization: The Changing Face of Inequality in Deindustrializing Societies*. Oxford and New York: Oxford University Press. https://doi.org/10.1093/acprof:oso/9780199797899.001.0001

Esping-Andersen, Gøsta. 1990. *The Three Worlds of Welfare Capitalism*. Princeton, NJ: Princeton University Press.

Eurostat. 2020a. Employment by sex, age and economic activity (from 2008 onwards, NACE Rev. 2) [LFSQ_EGAN2] Retrieved from https://ec.europa.eu/eurostat/data browser/view/lfsq_egan2/default/table?lang=en

Eurostat. 2020b. Low-wage earners as a proportion of all employees (excluding apprentices) by sex [earn_ses_pub1s]. Retrieved from https://ec.europa.eu/eurostat/databrowser/view/earn_ses_pub1s/default/table?lang=en

Gangl, Markus. 2004. "Welfare states and the scar effects of unemployment: A comparative analysis of the United States and West Germany." *American Journal of Sociology* 109(6): 1319–64. https://doi.org/10.1086/381902

Gangl, Markus, and Andrea Ziefle. 2015. "The making of a good woman: Extended parental leave entitlements and mothers' work commitment in Germany." *American Journal of Sociology* 121 (2): 511–63. https://doi.org/10.1086/682419

Grabka, Markus M., Carsten Braband, and Konstantin Göbler. 2020. "Beschäftigte in Minijobs sind VerliererInnen der coronabedingten Rezession." *DIW Wochenbericht* 45/2020: 841–47. Deutsches Institut für Wirtschaftsforschung (DIW), Berlin. https://doi.org/10.18723/diw_wb:2020-45-1

Hale, Thomas, Noam Angrist, Rafael Goldszmidt, Beatrix Kira, Anna Petherick, Toby Phillips, Samuel Webster, Emily Cameron-Blake, Laura Hallas, Saptarshi Majumdar, and Helen Tatlow. 2021. "A global panel database of pandemic policies (Oxford COVID-19 Government Response Tracker)." *Nature Human Behaviour* 5: 529–38. https://doi.org/10.1038/s41562-021-01079-8.

Hall, Peter A., and David Soskice. 2001. *Varieties of Capitalism: The Institutional Foundations of Comparative Advantage.* Oxford: Oxford University Press.

Hammerschmid, Anna, Julia Schmieder, and Katharina Wrohlich. 2020. "Frauen in Corona-Krise stärker am Arbeitsmarkt betroffen als Männer." *DIW aktuell*, No. 42: 1–7. Deutsches Institut für Wirtschaftsforschung (DIW), Berlin. http://hdl.handle.net/10419/222873.

Hank, Karsten, and Anja Steinbach. 2020. "The virus changed everything, didn't it? Couples' division of housework and childcare before and during the Corona crisis." *Journal of Family Research* 33 (1): 99–114. https://doi.org/10.20377/jfr-488.

Hassel, Anke. 2014. "The paradox of liberalization—Understanding dualism and the recovery of the German political economy." *British Journal of Industrial Relations* 52 (1): 57–81. https://doi.org/10.1111/j.1467-8543.2012.00913.x.

Häusermann, Silja, and Schwander, Hanna. 2012. "Varieties of Dualization: Identifying Insiders and Outsiders across Regimes." In *The Age of Dualization. The Changing Face of Inequality in Deindustrializing Societies,* edited by Patrick Emmenegger, Silja Häusermann, Bruno Palier, and Martin Seeleib-Kaiser, 27–51. Oxford and New York: Oxford University Press. https://doi.org/10.1093/acprof:oso/9780199797 899.001.0001.

Hipp, Lipp, and Mareike Bünning. 2020. "Parenthood as a driver of increased gender inequality during COVID-19? Exploratory evidence from Germany." *European Societies* 23 (1): 658–73. https://doi.org/10.1080/14616696.2020.1833229.

Holst, Elke, Anne Busch-Heizmann, and Anna Wieber. 2015. "Führungskräfte-Monitor 2015: Update 2001-2013." *DIW Berlin: Politikberatung kompakt*, No. 100. Deutsches Institut für Wirtschaftsforschung (DIW), Berlin. Retrieved from http://nbn-resolving.de/urn:nbn:de:0084-diwkompakt_2015-1005.

Jessen, Jonas, C. Katharina Spieß, and Katharina Wrohlich. 2021. "Sorgearbeit während der Corona-Pandemie: Mütter übernehmen größeren Anteil-vor allem bei schon zuvor ungleicher Aufteilung." *DIW Wochenbericht* 09/2021: 131–39. Deutsches Institut für Wirtschaftsforschung (DIW), Berlin. https://doi.org/10.18723/diw_wb:2021-9-1

Kirchmann, Andrea, and Martin Rosemann. 2010. "Wer sind die Betroffenen der Krise? Parallelen und Unterschiede zur vorangegangenen Krise." *WSI-Mitteilungen* 63 (11): 560–68. https://doi.org/10.5771/0342-300X-2010-11-560.

Koebe, Josefine, Claire Samtleben, Annekatrin Schrenker, and Aline Zucco. 2020. "Systemrelevant, aber dennoch kaum anerkannt: Entlohnung unverzichtbarer Berufe in der Corona-Krise unterdurchschnittlich." *DIW aktuell*, No. 48: 1–9. Deutsches Institut für Wirtschaftsforschung (DIW), Berlin. Retrieved from https://www.diw.de/de/diw_01.c.792754.de/publikationen/diw_aktuell/2020_0048/systemrelevant__aber_dennoch_kaum_anerkannt__entlohnung_unverzichtbarer_berufe_in_der_corona-krise_unterdurchschnittlich.html.

Konle-Seidl, Regina. 2020. "Short-time Work in Europe: Rescue in the Current COVID-19 Crisis?" *IAB-Forschungsbericht*, 4/2020: 1–18. Institute for Employment Research (IAB), Nuremberg. Retrieved from https://doku.iab.de/forschungsbericht/2020/fb0420_en.pdf.

Lersch, Philipp M., Wiebke Schulz, and George Leckie. 2020. "The variability of occupational attainment: How prestige trajectories diversified within birth cohorts over the twentieth century." *American Sociological Review* 85 (6): 1084–116. https://doi.org/10.1177/0003122420966324.

Möhring, Katja. 2016. "Life course regimes in Europe: Individual employment histories in comparative and historical perspective." *Journal of European Social Policy* 26 (2): 124–39. https://doi.org/10.1177/0958928716633046.

Möhring, Katja, Elias Naumann, Maximiliane Reifenscheid, Annelies G. Blom, Alexander Wenz, Tobias Rettig, et al. 2020. "Inequality in employment during the Corona lockdown: Evidence from Germany." *Jesp European Social Policy Blog*. Retrieved from: https://www.uni-mannheim.de/media/Einrichtungen/gip/Corona_Studie/JESP-Blog_Mo__hring_et__al_2020.pdf.

Möhring, Katja, Elias Naumann, Maximiliane Reifenscheid, Alexander Wenz, Tobias Rettig, Roni Lehrer, Sebastian Juhl, et al. 2020. "The COVID-19 Pandemic and subjective well-being: Longitudinal evidence on satisfaction with work and family." *European Societies*, 23(S1): 601–617. https://doi.org/10.1080/14616696.2020.1833066.

OECD. 2021. Unemployment rate (indicator). https://doi.org/10.1787/52570002-en.

Rinne, Ulf, and Klaus F. Zimmermann. 2012. "Another economic miracle? The German labor market and the Great Recession." *IZA Journal of Labor Policy* 1 (1): 3. https://doi.org/10.1186/2193-9004-1-3.

Schäfer, Andrea, and Karin Gottschall. 2015. "From wage regulation to wage gap: How wage-setting institutions and structures shape the gender wage gap across three industries in 24 European countries and Germany." *Cambridge Journal of Economics* 39 (2): 467–96. https://doi.org/10.1093/cje/bev005.

Singer, Judith D., and John B. Willett. 2003. *Applied Longitudinal Data Analysis: Modeling Change and Event Occurrence*. Oxford: Oxford University Press. Retrieved from http://www.loc.gov/catdir/enhancements/fy0612/2002007055-d.html.

Struffolino, Emanuela, Matthias Studer, and Anette Eva Fasang. 2016. "Gender, education, and family life courses in East and West Germany: Insights from new sequence analysis techniques." *Advances in Life Course Research* 29: 66–79. https://doi.org/10.1016/j.alcr.2015.12.001.

Trappe, Heike, Matthias Pollmann-Schult, and Christian Schmitt. 2015. "The rise and decline of the male breadwinner model: Institutional underpinnings and future expectations." *European Sociological Review* 31 (2): 230–42. https://doi.org/10.1093/esr/jcv015.

Vlachos, Jonas, Edvin Hertegård, and Helena B. Svaleryd. 2021. "The effects of school closures on SARS-CoV-2 among parents and teachers." *Proceedings of the National Academy of Sciences* 118 (9): 1–7. https://doi.org/10.1073/pnas.2020834118

Wachter, Till von. 2020. "Lost generations: Long-term effects of the COVID-19 crisis on job losers and labour market entrants, and options for policy." *Fiscal Studies* 41 (3): 549–90. https://doi.org/10.1111/1475-5890.12247.

Wiesner, Claudia 2020. "Das Konjunkturpaket der Bundesregierung und seine Auswirkungen auf Frauen und Männer." *i3—Kasseler Diskussionspapiere—Ideen, Interessen und Institutionen im Wandel*, No. 9, 12/2020. Retrieved from https://www.uni-kassel.de/fb05/fileadmin/datas/fb05/i3DiskussionsPapiere_9-2020_Wiesner_03 1220_02.pdf.

Yerkes, Mara A., Stéfanie André, Debby Beckers, Janna Besamusca, Peter Mathieu Kruyen, Chantal Remery, et al. 2020. "Intelligent lockdown, intelligent effects? The impact of the Dutch COVID-19 'intelligent lockdown' on gendered work and family dynamics among parents." *PloS ONE* 15 (11): e0242249. https://doi.org/10.1371/journal.pone.0242249.

PART III
EU SOCIAL POLICY

9

Toward a Real Green Transition?

Triple Constraints Holding Back EU Member States' "Greening" Industrial Strategies

Zhen Jie Im, Caroline de la Porte, Elke Heins, Andrea Prontera, and Dorota Szelewa

Introduction

Against the backdrop of the COVID-19 pandemic, the EU launched its flagship "European Green Deal" in 2021 to usher in a Green Transition—namely a climate-neutral Europe by 2050—by boosting the uptake of renewable energy resources, reducing household, transport, and industrial emissions, and creating new green jobs (European Commission 2021). Funding for this Green Transition would come partly from the EU's post-pandemic recovery program, the NextGenerationEU (NGEU), which has been described by some scholars as a groundbreaking and "Hamiltonian" moment as it allows the EU to "borrow significant resources from the financial markets and use them to fiscally support national economies severely hit by the pandemic" for the first time (Lionello 2020, 22). Others argue that the NGEU decision is a response to past imbalances and question the likelihood of major changes (Armingeon et al. 2022). Irrespective of these interpretations, its design is new. By operating through "expansionary oriented conditionality" where reforms and investments must conform to the key aims of the EU, the NGEU is not just about helping Member States recover from the financial shock of the pandemic. Instead, it is also about investing in a green future. Thirty-seven percent of funding for Member States from the NGEU is earmarked for the Green Transition. The Commission's first annual report on the Recovery and Resilience Facility (RRF), which is the lion's share of the NGEU, shows that on average, Member States have spent 50% of their allocated funding on the Green Transition (European Commission 2022). Additionally, Member States' RRF plans, which are needed to unlock funding from the

Zhen Jie Im, Caroline de la Porte, Elke Heins, Andrea Prontera, and Dorota Szelewa, *Toward a Real Green Transition?* In: *European Social Policy and the COVID-19 Pandemic*. Edited by: Stefanie Börner and Martin Seeleib-Kaiser, Oxford University Press. © Oxford University Press 2023. DOI: 10.1093/oso/9780197676189.003.0009

EU's post-pandemic recovery fund (NGEU), were positively evaluated by the European Commission.

However, to truly achieve a Green Transition requires a shake-up of Member States' industrial strategies. We focus here on industries because they are the major source of carbon emissions (European Environment Agency 2020; Intergovernmental Panel on Climate Change 2015, 743). Hence, decarbonization to achieve a green future would require Member States to change their industrial make-up by shifting away from heavy carbon-emitting industries toward green industries that emit less carbon. Yet, such industrial reforms may impose burdens on workers in fossil fuel–intensive and carbon-polluting industries. Member States may alleviate these burdens by strengthening labor market policies that support a socially fair transition in their RRFs. If social investment policies—education and activation policies—are earmarked in the RRF plans and targeted at workers who may become redundant as carbon-polluting industries where they work are being downscaled, this transition could be both green and socially fair. Social policies are thus crucial to facilitate a transition that is both just and inclusive. For instance, training enables workers who find themselves disadvantaged during the Green Transition to reskill and hence overcome job and wage loss in the long run. Employment support would also smooth their reentry into a much-transformed labor market (European Commission 2020a).

Overall, the European Green Deal presents an opportunity to pursue environmental sustainability, economic growth, and social cohesion (Mandelli and Sabato 2018). It appears as a win–win strategy that promotes green industries to fuel economic growth, decrease dependence on fossil fuels, and maintain social cohesion through its funding instruments like the NGEU (European Commission 2019, 2021). The European Green Deal also highlights the role of coordinated industrial, environmental, and social policies in meeting economic, social, and industrial decarbonization objectives concurrently.

Despite the opportunity presented by NGEU to pursue these three objectives, it remains to be seen whether Member States will take it up. Specifically, it is uncertain if Member States are willing to enact wide-ranging but necessary industrial decarbonization reforms. A green future requires Member States to embark on both "low-hanging" and uncontroversial reforms as well as "deep-seated" and divisive reforms. "Low-hanging" reforms promise a win–win situation because they are unlikely to yield clear winners and losers. Thus, these reforms resemble valence issues with low political costs, making them expedient for governments to embark on them. For instance, improving energy efficiency is advantageous to both industry and consumers, and thus governments are unlikely to encounter substantial pushback with this reform. By contrast, "deep-seated" reforms that reduce dependence on fossil fuels or target carbon emissions in major industries could create stark winners and losers. For instance, some industries may become less competitive with these reforms, which may lead to job losses. These types of reforms resemble positional issues with high political costs, making them challenging for governments to embark on them even if they are critical to meet decarbonization objectives.

Therefore, it remains to be seen which types of industrial decarbonization reforms Member States will pursue, and if there will be substantial variations across Member States because such reforms may be more costly to some than to others. To examine such variation, we analyze the types of reforms Member States have planned in their RRF. We go beyond the European Commission's (2022) declaration that Member States have spent 50% of their allocated funding on the Green Transition on average. We disaggregate this figure to see if this allocation comprises mostly "deep-seated" industrial decarbonization reforms or "low-hanging" ones. As there is no hard conditionality (Crnčec 2021; Schulz 2020) in the RRF, there is no incentive for Member States to earmark spending on "deep-seated" industrial decarbonization reforms, even though they are critical to avert a climate crisis (Intergovernmental Panel on Climate Change).[1]

We develop a conceptual framework to account for variations in countries' willingness to pursue deep-seated industrial decarbonization reforms. We postulate that three constraints reduce Member States' willingness to pursue these difficult and politically costly reforms, even when they have EU funding to kick-start them. The three constraints are (a) Member States' macroeconomic vulnerability, (b) reliance on carbon-polluting industries, and (c) the degree to which social policy institutions are geared toward social investment to enable a country's workforce to transit and meet the new labor market demands of the Green Economy. We expect Member States to pursue these reforms only if they are macroeconomically stable, have low reliance

---

[1] Although governments are required to budget at least 37% of the fund to green growth, the Commission's examples of policies supporting such growth are very broad. They cover various aspects of the Green Transition ranging from increasing the use of renewables, sustainable and efficient transportation, waste management, greener agriculture, and biodiversity investments (European Commission 2021a, 25–26). These examples are not exhaustive. https://ec.europa.eu/info/sites/default/files/document_travail_service_part1_v2_en.pdf

on carbon-polluting industries, and have strong social investment–oriented social policy institutions.

Our contributions are two-fold. First, we provide a framework that explains differences in governments' readiness to adopt costly deep-seated industrial decarbonization reforms, which brings to the fore the need to consider the role of politics in understanding environmental reforms (Burns 2008; Ćetković et al. 2017; Mandelli and Sabato 2018; Prinz and Pegels 2018; Turn 2014; Wood et al. 2020). Here, we focus on how comparative political economy can help understand environmental (industrial decarbonization) reforms. Second, we fill a gap within the social policy literature which has thus far overlooked the Green Transition (for a few exceptions, see Kaasch and Waltrup 2021, 321; Koch 2021, 2; Markova 2021). Social policy institutions oriented to the challenges of the Green Transition can enable the adoption of green reforms and alleviate the fallout that afflicts displaced workers. Thus, social policy institutions are crucial to enable an economy that is simultaneously green and inclusive (e.g., Meckling et al. 2015). In sum, this chapter provides a conceptual framework that links environmental policymaking to social policy and politics.

In the following, we first present our conceptual framework. We next empirically map where EU Member States are located within this triangle of constraints. Using cross-national data, we then assess the degree to which Member States have budgeted policies targeted at reforming carbon-polluting industries in their RRF plans. Thereafter, we delve deeper into four country cases which are confronted by the triangle of constraints to different degrees—Denmark, Germany, Spain, and Poland—to examine variations in their RRF plans. Last, we evaluate our conceptual framework based on these two sets of empirical analyses.

Conceptual Framework

With the climate emergency, Member States' policymaking aims to meet three objectives (Mandelli and Sabato 2018). The first objective is *macroeconomic stability*. Owing to the Stability and Growth Pact (SGP) as well as permanent austerity, macroeconomic stability has become a relevant policy objective for Member States (see De la Porte and Heins 2016). Member States are expected to pursue growth and keep unemployment, public debt, and deficit rates low to avoid massive fluctuations and downward pressure on their macroeconomy. Next, governments are keen to maintain *social stability*. Third, Member States have come under growing pressure to ensure *environmental stability* by pursuing decarbonization within industry and among private consumers.

As these three policy objectives may conflict with each other, governments face trade-offs. For instance, governments are unlikely to pursue industrial decarbonization if it worsens the macroeconomic outlook and reduces social stability. Thus, while Mandelli and Sabato's (2018) framework shows the three overriding policy objectives that Member States face today, it does not underline the conditions under which these conflicting objectives may be reconciled. In short, the framework does not show when Member States can and are willing to pursue costly "deep-seated" decarbonization industrial reforms. To this end, we put forward a conceptual framework consisting of three constraints to show when such reforms are likely to occur.

The first is Member States' reliance on these industries. While some industries can readily adopt available technology or work practices that reduce their emissions significantly, others may struggle to do so because such technologies and practices are unavailable or expensive (Fischer and Heutel 2013). If Member States can afford it, they may subsidize the research and adoption of such expensive technologies and practices to meet the EU's carbon targets of being climate neutral by 2020. If they cannot afford it, these industries are left with the costly tab to decarbonize, or risk being phased out so that Member States can meet these climate targets. Either way, industries which struggle to decarbonize or find decarbonization too costly will struggle to be competitive, with negative labor market consequences for their workers. By contrast, industries like the automotive industry, which can adapt to decarbonization through technological innovations, would be able to avoid large-scale unemployment increases or dramatic wage losses. Hence, the risk of unemployment or wage loss incurred by workers is greatest among Member States which rely on carbon-polluting industries that cannot adapt, such as the coal industry (see Dechezleprêtre and Kruse 2018).[2] These consequences may trigger opposition from affected trade unions, industry lobby groups, and employer associations (see Mildenberger 2020), as well as electoral backlash from afflicted workers (for related see Ballard-Rosa et al. 2021; Im et al. 2019; Kurer 2020). Owing to the likelihood of deterioration in

---

[2] Research on industrial transformations show that these they often yield unemployment or wage loss (e.g. Goos et al. 2014).

macroeconomic and social stability, Member States that rely heavily on non-adaptable carbon-polluting industries are unlikely to pursue deep-seated reforms.

The second constraint is whether Member States' social policy institutions are sufficiently geared toward social investment to help affected workers adapt to the demands of the Green Economy. Social policy institutions are often sticky and resistant to change (Hall and Gingerich 2009; Pierson 1996; Pontusson 2006). Therefore, existing configurations of Member States' social policy institutions affect how well they can help disadvantaged workers adapt to the Green Economy and thus avoid backlash arising from these transformations. While existing research shows that enacting environmental reforms is easier in Coordinated Market Economies than in Liberal Market Economies because of the latter's limited welfare state (e.g., MacNeil 2016), it does not account for the role of social investment and enabling active labor market policies (ALMPs). Therefore, we provide a finer-grained analysis of the role of variations in national social policy institutions. Some Member States spend more on compensatory policies like unemployment benefits, early retirement policies, and pensions, whereas others spend more on social investment policies like training, education, and employment support (Bengtsson et al. 2017; Hemerijck 2017; Morel et al. 2012). Within the social investment framework, enabling ALMPs like training and reeducation are crucial to reskill and shift structurally unemployed workers into new and better jobs in the Green Economy (see European Commission, 2021). Likewise, employment support facilitates labor market reentry of disadvantaged workers and prevents long-term structural unemployment and skill atrophy. Although unemployment benefits and early retirement policies mitigate affected workers' income loss, they do not of themselves enable workers to benefit from the Green Economy. Such compensation is also expensive and may act as a downward drag on macroeconomic stability. Furthermore, without adequate social investment institutions, affected workers may feel that they have been left behind, which worsens social stability.

The third is Member States' macroeconomic vulnerability. With the SGP and permanent austerity, Member States suffering from low economic growth, high public debt and deficit, and high unemployment may seek to avoid huge short-term economic costs from decarbonizing industry (for related, see Armingeon et al. 2022; Walter et al. 2020). Decarbonizing industries may entail subsidies to incentivize industries to research and adopt new technologies and work practices to decarbonize, or compensation

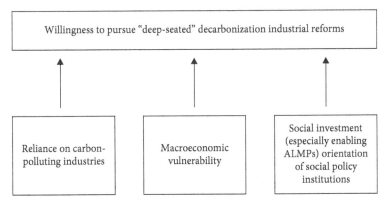

Figure 9.1 Triple constraints limiting governments' willingness to pursue "deep-seated" decarbonization industrial reforms.

for phasing out unadaptable carbon-polluting industries. If deep-seated decarbonization industrial reforms lead to a rise in unemployment (such as when these industries are phased out), public expenditure on compensatory and social investment policies will also rise. Hence, deep-seated decarbonization industrial reforms will require Member States to have deep pockets or be able to absorb temporary macroeconomic and labor market shocks.

Therefore, we expect Member States' willingness to pursue deep-seated decarbonizing industrial reforms to depend on these three constraints (Figure 9.1). A government is most likely to pursue these reforms if it is macroeconomically stable, does not rely on carbon-polluting industries, and has social investment–oriented social policy institutions that enable workers to adapt to the labor market demands of the Green Economy. By contrast, a government is least likely to pursue such reforms if it is macroeconomically vulnerable, relies heavily on these industries, and does not have social policy institutions that help workers adapt to the labor market demands of the Green Economy. Failing to meet any one of these constraints will reduce governments' willingness to pursue reforms to achieve the green and inclusive transition called for by the European Green Deal.

Member States' Profiles Based on the Three Constraints

Using indicators taken from Eurostat and the World Bank, we mapped and categorized EU Member States based on their positions relative to the three constraints over a 10-year period (2009 to 2018). First, we operationalized Member States' macroeconomic vulnerability based on Armingeon et al. (2022) and Walter et al.'s (2020) measure—a summary index of a country's unemployment rate, its public debt expressed as a percentage of gross domestic product, its public deficit expressed as a percentage of gross domestic product, and private debt. However we omitted private debt, as we are primarily concerned with the aspect of governments' macroeconomic stability that influences their ability to allocate resources to social expenditures and subsidies for industrial decarbonization, as well as the ability to absorb macroeconomic shocks from such industrial reforms. To make these three variables' scales comparable, we inversed the variable measuring governments' public deficit and then standardized all of them. We then combined them into a single index (Cronbach's Alpha = 0.69).[3] Higher values indicate greater macroeconomic vulnerability.

Second, we measured reliance on carbon-polluting industries as the weighted share of workers employed in greenhouse gas (GHGs) polluting industries in each Member State. We consider a country to be more reliant on carbon-polluting industries if there are more workers employed in such industries. We first identified industries that are most responsible for carbon emissions based on the Intergovernmental Panel on Climate Change's report on industry (2015)—mining and quarrying, food production, leather and textiles, paper and pulp, chemicals, metals, and cements.[4] We next calculated the annual share of workers employed in these sectors as a proportion of all sectors in each country. To account for differences in carbon emissions across countries and years owing to technological or work-practice improvements, as well as electricity and heat from renewable energy sources (Intergovernmental Panel on Climate Change 2015), we multiplied this value by the air emissions intensity of the respective sector per country-year and the share of renewable energy used for producing electricity and heat. Reliable estimates on air emissions intensity, which measures the amount of GHGs emissions produced per value added, runs from 2009 to 2018 for most Member States, which explains the timespan of our analysis. In short, this

---

[3] We crosschecked the validity of this index with exploratory factor analysis (EFA). EFA detects a single dimension with which all three variables have factor loadings greater than 0.5, which suggests the suitability of this index.

[4] Food production here does not include agriculture. It is considered separately by the Intergovernmental Panel on Climate Change (2015) . The NACE-2 categories are B (mining), C10-C12 (food production), C13-C15 (leather and textiles), C17 (paper), C20 (chemicals), C23 (cement), C24 (metals).

index captures the share of workers employed in GHGs-emitting industries weighted by variations in air emission intensity and use of renewable energy. To ease comparison, we standardized the variable for which higher values would indicate a higher share of workers employed in these GHGs-emitting industries which suggests greater reliance on these industries.

Third, we used public expenditure on training and employment support as a proxy for the social investment orientation of Member States' social policy institutions. This expenditure approach is commonly used in previous studies in comparative political economy and social policy (e.g., Bengtsson et al. 2017). We chose public expenditure on these two social policy instruments because they are the most direct and relevant pathways through which affected workers can improve their labor market prospects in the Green Economy (European Commission, 2021). Training reskills disadvantaged workers, and employment support smooths their reentry into the labor market and green jobs. Public expenditure on both is measured as percentages of countries' gross domestic product (GDP). As expenditure on both policies varies as unemployment levels fluctuate, we divided them by the respective country's annual unemployment rate (Bengtsson et al., 2017). Higher values indicate that a Member State has social policy institutions that are more social investment–oriented.

Our estimation strategy relies on latent profile analysis (LPA) to identify latent profiles or unobserved "subgroups" in a population that share similar characteristics on relevant dimensions included in the model (Nylund-Gibson and Choi 2019, 441). It is commonly used in psychology, labor market, and education research (e.g., Lindblom-Ylänne et al. 2018; Nylund-Gibson and Choi 2018). A strength of LPA over other classification techniques such as a cluster analysis relying on k-means clustering is that it is model-based and permits a mathematical evaluation of how well a proposed LPA model, and hence its profiles, represent the data (Nylund-Gibson and Choi 2019, 442) through a battery of fit indices. We elaborate on our analytic and identification strategy in the supplementary material, available in the online edition of this book.

We identified four different profiles (clusters) that differ in their three constraints (Table 9.1). We postulate that willingness to pursue deep-seated but difficult reforms to carbon-polluting industries varies by these profiles. Profile 1 contains Member States with moderate reliance on carbon-polluting industries and social policy institutions are moderately high in their social investment orientation to enable their workforce to adapt to the

Table 9.1 Profiles (clusters) of Member States by the Position on the Three Constraints

---

Profile 1: Moderate reliance on carbon-polluting industries and moderately high social investment orientation

Characteristics	Description	Countries (55.55%)
Macroeconomic vulnerability	Statistically insignificant	Belgium, Cyprus, Germany, Estonia, France, Croatia, Hungary, Ireland, Italy, Lithuania, Latvia, Malta, the Netherlands, Portugal, Slovenia
Reliance on carbon-polluting industries	Moderate reliance+	
Social investment orientation	Moderately high*	

Profile 2: Low macroeconomic vulnerability, low reliance on carbon-polluting industries, and high social investment orientation

Characteristics	Description	Countries (18.52%)
Macroeconomic vulnerability	Low vulnerability***	Austria, Denmark, Finland, Luxembourg, Sweden
Reliance on carbon-polluting industries	Low reliance***	
Social investment orientation	High***	

Profile 3: High macroeconomic vulnerability, moderately low reliance on carbon-polluting industries, and low social investment orientation

Characteristics	Description	Countries (7.41%)
Macroeconomic vulnerability	High vulnerability***	Spain, Greece
Reliance on carbon-polluting industries	Moderately low reliance***	
Social investment orientation	Low***	

Profile 4: Moderately low macroeconomic vulnerability, high reliance on carbon-polluting industries, and low social investment orientation

Characteristics	Description	Countries (18.52%)
Macroeconomic vulnerability	Moderately low vulnerability***	Bulgaria, Czech Republic, Poland, Romania, Slovakia
Reliance on carbon-polluting industries	High reliance***	
Social investment orientation	Low***	

Notes: + p < 0.10, * p < 0.05, ** p < 0.01, *** p < 0.005

labor market demands of the Green Economy. They are statistically indistinct ($p>0.1$) on macroeconomic vulnerability, which means some of them are macroeconomically stable whereas some are macroeconomically vulnerable. It is the largest profile and includes Belgium, Cyprus, Germany, Estonia, France, Croatia, Hungary, Ireland, Italy, Lithuania, Latvia, Malta, the

Netherlands, Portugal, and Slovenia. We expect this profile to be mixed in terms of pursuing deep-seated decarbonization industrial reforms. Member States which are macroeconomically stable may pursue limited reforms, whereas those which are macroeconomically vulnerable may not.

The second profile comprises Member States with low macroeconomic vulnerability, low reliance on carbon-polluting industries, and social policy institutions that have high social investment orientation. It consists of Austria, Denmark, Finland, Luxembourg, and Sweden. We expect these Member States to have the greatest likelihood of pursuing these reforms. They are least tied down by the three constraints and may thus face the least cost from deep-seated decarbonization industrial reforms. Consequently, they may also face the least political blowback.

The third profile contains Member States with high macroeconomic vulnerability, moderately low reliance on carbon-polluting industries, and social policy institutions that have low social investment orientation. It consists of a smaller group of countries, namely Spain and Greece. Finally, the fourth profile includes Member States that have moderately low macroeconomic vulnerability, high reliance on carbon-polluting industries, and social policy institutions that have low social investment orientation. They consist of Bulgaria, Czech Republic, Poland, Romania, and Slovakia. We consider it unlikely that Member States in both the third and fourth profiles will pursue deep-seated decarbonization industrial reforms.

Comparative Overview of Member States' Willingness to Pursue Decarbonization Industrial Reforms

We used the dataset provided by Bruegel—a European think tank—to explore if RRF budget allocations to decarbonization industrial reforms varied across Member States according to their identified profiles.[5] Through this comparative overview, we examine if these variations vary according to our identified profiles. Bruegel classified budget allocations for programs in 20 Member States' RRFs based on the six pillars listed in the EU's plans for the RRF (European Commission 2021c).[6]

---

[5] See: https://www.bruegel.org/publications/datasets/european-union-countries-recovery-and-resilience-plans/

[6] Bruegel classified the budget allocations in several ways. However, this one based on the pillars is most relevant for us.

We focused on budget allocations for programs that correspond with the pillar on the Green Transition. We next filtered for programs with descriptions indicating industrial reforms related to decarbonization, climate neutrality, or circular economy. As our interest is in industry, we then narrowed our search to programs that related to manufacturing or the energy sector that produces heat and energy for manufacturing activities.[7] Decarbonization industrial reforms can relate to direct changes to industry, or indirect changes from their energy and heat inputs. Finally, we classified Member States based on whether or not they included these decarbonization industrial reform programs.

We cannot distinguish between additive or new programs in the RRF with the Bruegel dataset (see also Armingeon et al. 2022). Regardless of whether programs are additive or new, they nevertheless reflect a Member State's broader policy approach toward decarbonization industrial reform. Hence, the RRF plans are useful indicators of Member States' willingness to undertake such reforms.

Table 9.2 presents Member States by their profiles but splits them by their (non)inclusion of decarbonization industrial reforms. There is an observable difference in the percentage of Member States that have budgeted for programs reflecting such reforms. As we had posited, profile 2 has the highest percentage of Member States which have budgeted for such reforms. By contrast, profiles 3 and 4—Member States with social policy institutions that are not social investment–oriented and are macroeconomically vulnerable or dependent on these industries respectively—have the lowest percentage of Member States that have budgeted such reforms. Finally, and as expected, the picture is evenly split for Member States in profile 1. Although we expected this split to depend on Member States' macroeconomic vulnerability, it seems to resemble a divide between the EU-15 and the EU-11. Overall, the descriptive results suggest that Member States' willingness to pursue deep-seated decarbonization industrial reforms depends on their ability to overcome the three necessary constraints.

Danish, German, Spanish, and Polish RRF Plans

We explore the RRF plans of one Member State from each profile in greater detail. We focus on the extent to which deep-seated decarbonization industrial

---

[7] Manufacturing industries have NACE classifications B and C. Energy industries have classification D.

Table 9.2 Breakdown of Member States by Profiles and Allocation for Decarbonization Industrial Reforms in the RRF

Profiles	Characteristics	Countries with allocations for decarbonization industrial reforms in RRF	Count	Countries without allocations for decarbonization industrial reforms in RRF	Count	Percentage of countries with allocations for decarbonization industrial reforms in RRF
Profile 1	Moderate reliance on carbon-polluting industries, and moderately high social investment orientation	Belgium, Estonia, France, Germany, Portugal, Slovenia	5	Cyprus, Croatia, Hungary, Italy, Latvia, Lithuania	5	50.00
Profile 2	Low macroeconomic vulnerability, low reliance on carbon-polluting industries, and high social investment orientation	Austria, Finland, Sweden	3	Luxembourg	1	75.00
Profile 3	High macroeconomic vulnerability, moderately low reliance on carbon-polluting industries, and low social investment orientation		0	Spain, Greece	2	0.00
Profile 4	Moderately low macroeconomic vulnerability, high reliance on carbon-polluting industries, and low social investment orientation	Slovakia	1	Czech Republic, Poland, Romania	3	25.00
Total			9		11	45.00

Notes: Member states that are missing were not included in the Bruegel dataset.

reforms are budgeted in their plans submitted to the European Commission. We triangulated our analysis of the plans with the Commission's evaluation reports, and assessment reports from relevant think tanks.

Denmark

Among our country cases, Denmark is the best prepared to deal with the Green Transition based on the three constraints. Regarding social investment orientation, Denmark is considered a leader in active labor market policies. Its labor market is considered flexible but also adaptable due to the focus on reinvestment in skills in case of job redundancy. Key indicators, when controlled for unemployment, show that ALMP expenditure has been increasing between 2010 and 2019. Expenditure increased from 0.178% to 0.272% of GDP for each percent of unemployment. Also, the unemployment rate decreased from 7.7% to 5.0% between 2010 and 2019, and it was it was 5.6% in 2020. Regarding macroeconomic vulnerability, Denmark has a low level of accumulated public debt (33.6% of GDP), which means that the economy is very robust and can handle short-term economic costs derived from phasing out carbon-polluting industries. Denmark has a relatively low reliance on carbon-polluting industries, with only a small proportion of the economy depending on manufacturing.[8] Yet, as it will be demonstrated through the case of Aalborg Portland below, there are still substantial political costs which Danish governments will face when they embark on decarbonization industrial reforms, even if they are well-placed to pursue them.

Denmark has become the first country globally to constitutionalize the Green Transition with a climate law whereby the Danish government commits to reduce carbon emissions by 70% in 2030 (1990s emissions as reference) and to be climate neutral by 2050. It ties present and future governments to these benchmarks and requires fundamental changes in some industries to achieve the aims. While the minority Social Democratic (SD) government (2019 onward) has adopted various measures to meet these aims, critics—especially green nongovernmental organizations—argue that they are insufficient. In line with the collective bargaining tradition in Denmark, more specific agreements to reach the aims of the climate

---

[8] We rely on Eurostat on industrial composition and macroeconomic data when describing the case studies.

law are made sectorally. For instance, there is a concrete agreement to decrease carbon emissions by 55%–65% by 2030 in agriculture, which implies reducing the territory used in agriculture and converting it to forest and other nature areas (Politiken 2021). In other areas, there is hesitation to make binding political commitments, especially on carbon tariffs. For instance, the cement industry is symbolically and economically important, especially Aalborg Portland. The company stands out because it is the largest single carbon emitter in Denmark (4% of total carbon emissions). It has agreed to reduce its carbon emissions by one-third by 2023 through investments in a new form of cement which is less carbon-polluting. However, in line with the climate law, there are still plans to levy a new national tariff, which Aalborg Portland opposes. It argues that it would then become too difficult to compete internationally (Politiken 2022), which led to the SD prime minister Mette Frederiksen (2019–present) proclaiming on several occasions that she will support Aalborg Portland and its 350 workers. Consequently, there are political deliberations about reconsidering these carbon tariffs for Aalborg Portland. This case shows that the Danish government faces a dilemma due to large companies' concerns about cost competitiveness as well as adverse labor market effects on their specialized workforce, even if Denmark is not severely limited by the three constraints.

Denmark's Recovery and Resilience Plan invests 59% of the allocated expenditure on climate objectives through six reforms and 33 investments. Most of the investments are channeled toward energy efficiency and reduction of carbon emissions, which reflects the fact that Denmark's climate law has constitutionalized carbon reductions with two clear benchmarks. The largest initiative is a green tax reform, which reorients energy taxation to encourage reducing carbon emissions and rewrites the tax code by introducing a broad tax on GHGs. Almost one-third of Denmark's RRF resources is devoted to this reform, which indicates commitment to the national climate law. This substantial earmark shows that Denmark's government was able to plan these reforms because they are not heavily restricted by the three constraints. Nevertheless, the case of Aalborg Portland suggests that compromises may have been made to ensure that symbolically and economically important industries keep their production in Denmark. The second largest commitment in the RRF is toward energy effectiveness (including the shift to green heating sources). Part of this investment is already ongoing, such as replacement of oil burners and gas furnaces, and the RRF further supports this. Other components include energy efficiency in industry, energy renovation of public buildings, and energy efficiency of private households. Thus, the RRF here supports reforms that are less contentious and more acceptable to citizens and industries but nevertheless has an impact on the climate. The third largest financial commitment in Denmark's RRF is dedicated to sustainable road transport, with plans to boost the current practice of improving the linkage of the car registration tax to carbon emissions, in order to incentivize buyers to buy hybrid or electric cars. It is also notable that the Danish plan has allocated a considerable amount of funds—the fourth largest component in its RRF—to research and development in green solutions as along with incentives to boost such research in companies.

Altogether, the green ambitions in Denmark's RRF are substantial but perhaps watered down to meet the concerns of important large companies. Some reforms are low-hanging fruit in that they are uncontroversial with voters, such as energy efficiency in housing and public buildings. However, Denmark also proposes several reforms that are deep-seated and contentious, such as taxation on carbon emissions that will impose substantial economic costs to carbon-polluting industries if they fail to reform, It remains to be seen if special deals will be made with major polluters such as Aalborg Portland, or even with agriculture. Separately, there is no plan to boost social investment or enabling ALMPs in the RRF, as the infrastructure, policies, and financial commitments are already high and the system functions well.

Germany

Germany, the EU's biggest economy, is in profile 1, which is characterized by moderate reliance on carbon-polluting industries. There is also considerable reliance on fossil fuels for power, especially after the withdrawal from nuclear energy after the 2011 Fukushima disaster. Its social policy institution has a moderately high social investment orientation and is thus relatively prepared to help workers negatively affected by the Green Transition. Traditionally, the German welfare state relied heavily on social compensation via generous social insurance systems. However, the Hartz reforms in the mid-2000s brought about far-reaching labor market and unemployment policy reforms that strengthened activation policies (Manow 2020; Seeleib-Kaiser 2002). ALMP spending in 2019 stood at 0.087% of GDP for each percent of unemployment. While this spending level in 2019l is greater than in Spain and

Poland, it is lower than in Denmark. Unlike some other countries in profile 1, Germany is on solid macroeconomic footing in 2019. Unemployment is at a historical low of 3.0%, and public debt stood at 58.9% of GDP in 2019. GDP is forecasted in April 2022 to recover at a growth rate of around 3% by the end of 2022 when compared to before the pandemic. Germany's pursuit of decarbonization industrial reforms is therefore limited by its reliance on carbon-polluting industries rather than by the other two constraints.

Despite Germany's reliance on such industries, carbon-polluting industries already faced a raft of decarbonization reforms prior to the submission of the German RRF plan. In August 2020, the government decided to incrementally phase out coal by 2038 (*Kohleausstiegsgesetz*) to meet Germany's climate targets. Energy companies will receive subsidies of €4.35 billion for the demolition of coal production facilities, and affected regions will be supported with investments in infrastructure and countryside conservation. An additional act makes funding of up to €14 billion available for investment in former coal production regions. A further package of up to €26 billion will support research, transport infrastructure, and job creation programs (Bundesministerium für Wirtschaft und Klimaschutz 2020). Finally, industries relying heavily on fossil fuels for their production—notably the steel, chemicals, cement, and metal working sectors—have been supported financially with a €3 billion decarbonization program so that Germany can meet its aim of a 65% greenhouse gas reduction by 2030 (Bundesumweltministerium 2020).

The German RRF plans mirror the government's prior policies on the Green Transition. The German RRF amounts to around €28 billion. Climate protection and energy transition is a core of the plan, with an earmark of around 40% of overall spending (Bruegel 2021). The most important measures are massive investments in hydrogen power comprising research, capacity, and infrastructure (€1.5 billion). A second set of instruments relates to climate-friendly transport (investments into fuel cells, incentives for private and public electric vehicles, and improvements to the charging infrastructure—€2.4 billion). A third broad package of measures relates to increasing the energy efficiency of residential buildings (€2.5 billion) (Bundesministerium der Finanzen 2021), thus supporting the construction sector. Furthermore, unlike the coal, steel, or cement industries, the important German car industry—although not explicitly mentioned—has also been earmarked for decarbonization in the RRF through investments in fuel cell research and e-vehicles infrastructure.

While industry reforms indicate a move toward a green economy and there is capacity to use enabling ALMPs to reskill the workforce in this direction, the German RRF plan is silent about the use or strengthening of enabling ALMPs, even if it has earmarked social policies to improve social resilience. By contrast, early retirement schemes—not used since the 1990s—seem to have been reactivated as a tool to compensate workers who would become redundant due to the Green Transition. Following recommendations by the European Commission, social cohesion measures are put in place to support the energy transition (Bundesministerium der Finanzen 2021): 5,000 jobs are planned to be created via the relocation of federal agencies, and coal industry workers will be supported through a long-term financial compensation scheme to smooth their transition into early retirement (Bundesministerium der Justiz 2020). Although the government plans to expand job creation programs to help the long-term unemployed and other vulnerable labor market groups, there appears to be little focus on providing enabling ALMPs to support the transition to the Green Economy, despite the solid footing of Germany's macroeconomy and social policy. Crucially, there is very little in the plan on upskilling or retraining workers—apart from a mention of furthering education in timber construction—and nothing in relation to those who might lose their jobs in carbon-polluting industries. Instead, the government appears keen to foster future workers' economic opportunities in the Green Economy through a general commitment to early education and further training.

Overall, the plans tally with expectations that governments in profile 1 would pursue some degree of comprehensive reform to carbon-polluting industries. The German plan contains a mix of both "low-hanging fruit" as well as "deep-seated" decarbonization reforms targeted at some of the carbon-polluting industries, especially in terms of reducing polluting energy sources. It is however uncertain if the transition will be supported by enabling ALMPs, as there is policy momentum to compensate affected workers rather than reskill them.

Spain

Spain is in profile 3, which is characterized by moderately low reliance on carbon-polluting industries but high macroeconomic vulnerability and social policy institutions that have low social investment orientation. Spanish macroeconomic vulnerability was particularly high even before the COVID-19 pandemic crisis, which only made it worse. In 2020, GDP fell massively by 10.8%, unemployment rose considerably to 15.5%, and public debt grew to 120.0% of GDP. Concurrently, Spanish spending on ALMPs dropped from 0.71% in 2010 to 0.563% in 2019, despite the stubbornly high unemployment rate. This spending level trails that of Denmark and Germany, as well as Poland. Hence, Spain may be less equipped to help workers to adapt to the new demands of the Green Economy in comparison to these other countries. Unlike Germany and Poland, Spain is less reliant on carbon-polluting industries.

Since the early 2010s, the socioeconomic transition of coal mining regions has been prominent within the political agenda. In 2018, the government led by Pedro Sánchez of the Spanish Socialist Workers' Party was able to finalize a deal for the closure of several coal mines after long negotiations with trade unions, employer associations, and local authorities.[9] This deal provided €250 million of investment in affected regions, early retirement schemes for workers, local re-employment in environmental restoration works, and reskilling programs for green industries. Furthermore, in 2019 the Sánchez government adopted a "Strategic Framework for Energy and Climate" based on three components: the (then-draft) Integrated National Energy and Climate Plan 2021–2030; a draft law on climate change; and the Just Transition Strategy, which provided for additional compensation measures for the coal mining sector (Barreira and Ruiz-Bautista 2020).

The Spanish RRF plan builds on these earlier governmental initiatives. It allocates €28 billion to the Green Transition (about 40% of the total amount). Of this €28 billion, the plan devotes a substantial share to accelerating energy transition and climate targets with important investments in the areas of renewables (€3.9 billion) and energy efficiency (€3.4 billion). However, the plan lacks specific decarbonization reforms directly targeted at carbon-polluting industries. The lack of specificities may be traced to splits within industry actors (Green Recovery Tracker 2021). A large group, which covers over 50% of the IBEX35-listed companies, advocated for a green recovery, whereas a separate industry alliance—"La Alianza por la Competitividad de la Industria Española"—did not advocate for a green recovery and instead emphasized compensations for carbon emission charges and tax reductions.

---

[9] See "Spain's National Strategy to Transition Coal-Dependent Communities," available at https://www.wri.org/just-transitions/spain.

This latter alliance comprises industries from carbon-polluting sectors such as paper, chemicals, food production, cement, and metal, as well as the automotive industry. This debate therefore gets at the core of difficult deep-seated decarbonization industrial reforms: affected industries seek support to compensate for costs incurred by changing practices, adopting new technologies, or being phased out. If a government is macroeconomically constrained like Spain, it may avoid such reforms that may impose further economic burden on itself. This may explain why Spanish reforms are targeted in a limited way at carbon-polluting industries that have already been earmarked for transition (shift from coal to renewable energy) or are "low-hanging" valence reforms like energy efficiency. Additionally, cost concerns may also explain why the Spanish RRF earmarks funding for public–private cooperation projects to fund the green restructuring of strategic industries (*Proyectos Estratégicos para la Recuperación y Transformación Económica*: PERTE). The first of these projects targeted the automotive industry, focusing on electric vehicles and the related supply chain.

Additionally, the Spanish RRF seeks to reinforce social resilience by allocating €300 million to social policies including those of the social investment mold. The Spanish government appears to belatedly realize the need to devote a sizable sum to modernizing its vocational education training and invest in upskilling and reskilling of its workers. Although Spain starts from a weaker point in terms of its social policy institutions' readiness to enable workers to adapt to the demands of the Green Transition, spending from the RRF may improve these institutions to better support such workers than they do today.

Overall, it seems that the Spanish RRF is largely consistent with expectations of a low willingness to pursue deep-seated decarbonization industrial reforms. Yet, it is important to highlight that spending on the RRF lays an overdue groundwork for more socially fair labor market outcomes in the future, whenever the Spanish government decides to pursue similar economic transformations. Beyond willingness, the tradition of state-led corporatism may affect the success of decarbonization industrial reforms. Spain has a tradition of "state-led corporatism" in which the state steps in to help collaboration between employers, unions, and government (Schmidt 2009, 524). The coal phase-out and the PERTE concept are successful examples of this corporatism, which enables the government to enact these reforms. However, the lack of support from employers may also mean that implementing these reforms will be challenging, as shown in the lack of targeted action on the most carbon-polluting industries that have demanded compensation for reforms. Finally, Spain has a regionalized institutional structure which makes effective cooperation between the national government and regional and local actors a key challenge for the implementation of the recovery plan.

Poland

Poland represents profile 4, with a high reliance on carbon-polluting industries. It is the country with the second highest number of coal power plants (37) in the EU (Joint Research Centre 2018), and 72% of its energy mix is based on coal. Social policy in Poland has been dominated by compensatory schemes—cash transfers/compensatory measures including early retirement schemes, severance pay, or transferring workers into disability payment schemes have been easily available for even small disability payments (Żukowski 2011). Spending on ALMPs is still much lower than countries in profile 2. Spending on ALMPs between 2010 and 2019 declined from 0.589% to 0.253% of GDP respectively. Concurrently, unemployment fell from 10% to 3.3% in the same period. Thus, when ALMP spending is divided by the unemployment rate, it increases from 0.059% to 0.077% of GDP for each percent of unemployment, which remains small compared to compensatory schemes (see also Szelewa and Polakowski 2022). With Poland's social policy institutions being unable to help displaced workers adapt to the Green Economy, any deep-seated decarbonization industrial reforms will yield high social costs. Additionally, Poland has moderately low economic vulnerability currently. It has not suffered as much from the economic crisis or the pandemic in comparison to some other Member States. Public debt amounts to 45.6% of GDP, and unemployment was 3.3% in 2019. After the pandemic, public debt has grown to 57.4% of GDP, and unemployment remained stable at 3.2% in 2020.

Decarbonization reforms to industry have been limited. GHGs in Poland decreased by more than 15% since 1990. Poland also managed to improve the energy efficiency of industry significantly, reduce the consumption of hard coal and lignite, and increase the share of energy generated from renewable sources (Engel et al. 2020). However, consecutive governments refrained from setting any ambitious goals for decarbonization due to a long tradition of protests and strikes organized by trade unions from the coal mining industry. The unions repeatedly demanded extension of state aid and longer time horizons for full decarbonization, as well as for generous compensatory measures for labor market costs arising from decarbonization. Likewise, although more than half of the power plants that existed since the 1990s have been closed, further green transformation has been repeatedly blocked by the coal mining industry and remains a politically difficult issue. These circumstances have contributed to a slow departure from dependence on carbon-polluting industries.

The Polish RRF has a budget of €36 billion, of which 57.36% is earmarked to finance the Green Transition, 13.61% on digital transformation, 13.07% on smart, sustainable, and inclusive growth, and 12.63% on health, economic, social, and institutional resilience (Bruegel 2021). The plan aims to reduce the consumption of natural resources, strengthen the science sector through improvements in science and innovation, develop renewable energy sources and zero-emissions transport, and improve smart mobility. Among others, the plan promises substantial support for developing the renewable energy industry through investment in the offshore wind industry: port infrastructure for offshore wind will be supported through grants (€437 million) and the development of offshore wind farms— through loans (€3,250 million). However, the RRF is predominantly focused on energy policy and less on decarbonization of industry. Hard coal mines will be phased out gradually only by 2049 (Ministerstwo Funduszy i Polityki Regionalnej 2021) because of a need for energy security and to limit the negative socioeconomic effects related to the decline in the number of jobs in the mining sector. Decarbonization of industries will require social security measures and changes to the economic structure. The changes are characterized as "evolutionary" that facilitate social and territorial cohesion in post-mining areas (Ministerstwo Funduszy i Polityki Regionalnej 2021).

Concurrently, the RRF acknowledges the need to adjust skills and qualifications to the requirements of the labor market with "effective" labor market policies, investment in child care services for children under the age of three, and supporting employment of persons who are aged 55 or more. It even devotes 12.63% of the RRF on health, economic, social, and institutional resilience. However, it stops short of a coherent plan to fund and improve social investment policies and enabling ALMPs to help displaced workers adapt to the Green Economy. While the RRF frequently refers to these existing policies, it does not offer concrete targets to improve availability levels or coverage of the policies that are required to avoid the worst of the economic fallout that workers in affected sectors and regions would suffer.

Crucially, Poland's RRF took a long time to be approved by the European Commission because of concerns about the rule of law in Poland and a series of political decisions that interpret the Polish legal system as superior to EU hard law. Regardless of these political circumstances, a critical appraisal indicates that Poland will only implement deep-seated, contentious decarbonization industrial reforms to a limited extent, even though the Polish macroeconomic situation would be able to absorb short-term macroeconomic shocks, increase substantial investment to fund decarbonization of industries, and develop social investment and ALMPs that can help displaced workers adapt to a green economy. Furthermore, the Polish RRF appears to "lack teeth," as it does not emphasize strategic planning or benchmarking of key decarbonization goals. As such, implementation of more contentious aspects of the RRF could be lacking. Additionally, as decarbonization is only treated briefly as a domestic (regional) issue and framed around energy efficiency, the Polish government's strategy seems to reflect a pursuit of low-hanging, uncontentious reforms rather than deep-seated reforms to decarbonize industry.

Finally, there is a clear orientation toward compensation rather than social investment and enabling ALMPs to deal with the labor market fallout from the Green Transition. This focus on compensation is supported by the government's orientation toward traditional "old" welfare policies, and is favored by key political actors who rely on the coal industry and who have thus mobilized to defend the status quo.

Discussion

This chapter provides a framework to understand the willingness of countries, but especially EU Member States, to pursue 'deep-seated' decarbonization industrial reforms. Such reforms are critical to avoid the worst effects of climate change and maintain environmental stability, but they frequently entail substantial costs that may threaten economic, social, and political stability. With the European Commission's pledge toward a carbon-neutral EU by 2050 and the "Fridays for Future" climate marches, these reforms have become even more salient and are pushed onto the political agenda of Member States. We suggest that three constraints shape governments' willingness to take on such reforms: (a) their reliance on carbon-polluting industries, (b) the social investment orientation of social policy institutions to enable displaced workers to cope with the labor market demands of the Green Economy, and (c) their macroeconomic vulnerability. Based on these three constraints, we categorized Member States into four groups that faced these constraints to different degrees, and then compared whether the incidence of decarbonization industrial reforms of Members States' RRF plans varies across the four groups. Based on the Bruegel dataset, we indeed find that groups of Member States that are less restricted by the three constraints had a greater incidence of decarbonization industrial reforms in their RRF plans. Crucially, the European Commission's own breakdown of Member States' RRF plans regarding expenditure on the Green Transition also demonstrates the low incidence of such costly and difficult reforms. Most plans target improving energy efficiency and strengthening renewable energy and networks rather than tackling the most polluting industries (European Commission 2022, 15). Hence, both findings suggest that embarking on deep-seated decarbonization industrial reforms is less prevalent than "low-hanging fruit" reforms, even though both types of reform are equally necessary.

We then unpacked the RRF plans of four Member States from each group. We observe that these plans are additive in the sense that they generally build on prior national plans or strategies to address climate change. Corroborating findings from the comparative overview and the European Commission's report, the case studies show that Member States allocate more of their RRFs to easier and less contentious "low-hanging" reforms like energy efficiency. Reforms affecting industrial carbon-pollution tend to occur at the level of energy sources. However, Member States are more likely to decarbonize industry themselves if they are less limited by all three constraints, as in Denmark and Germany. Nevertheless, Member States still face resistance and political costs even when they are less limited by all three constraints, as shown in the case of Aalborg Portland in Denmark. Thus, if Member States like Denmark are compelled to make exceptions to decarbonization industrial reforms due to such political costs, Member States that are more constrained, like Poland, where coal mining is a major source of employment in several cities, may face even greater pressure to water down such reforms or sidestep them in favor of low-hanging and politically uncontentious reforms.

When Member States are able and willing to reform carbon-polluting industries, they allocate funding to reform sectors with better economic prospects and that can easily decarbonize, such as the automotive sector in Germany. Otherwise, they give leeway to such industries in terms implementing green reforms, like the cement sector in Denmark. While this is an efficient allocation of scarce economic resources, it leaves workers with uncertain labor market futures in industrial sectors that cannot easily decarbonize. Sectors that will struggle without legislative or financial help to find ways to decarbonize are faced with the choice of spending heavily on their own behalf to decarbonize, or to wind down operations. These sectors will struggle to remain competitive and thus go into decline, which may reflect a deliberate strategy by governments to have them phased out gradually on their own accord, rather than forcing them out and then having to compensate them. Regardless of the motivation, these policy choices will have negative labor market consequences for workers employed in these sectors. For differing reasons, neither Denmark nor Germany have allocated substantial parts of their RRF to social investment policies that may help workers in these industrial sectors adapt to the Green Economy. Denmark did not do so because its social policy institutions are already better equipped to retrain such workers than Germany's. Hence, the labor market futures of such workers are more uncertain in Germany than Denmark.

Beyond spending allocations, the case studies also show that the four cases vary in their approaches to deal with labor market challenges from industrial decarbonization for the Green Transition. Denmark is committed to using social investment–oriented ALMPs like training and reeducation to help its current workforce adapt, whereas Germany focuses on easing the fallout by compensating them with early retirement, even if it has adequately functioning social investment instruments. With its weaker social investment starting point, Spain uses the RRF to lay the groundwork for a social investment–oriented approach that may help affected workers transit into new green jobs in the future. Separately, Poland remains wedded to a compensatory approach rather than one that enables affected workers to adapt. In short, Member States differ both in their greening and adjustment strategies. In the long run, however, Member States that have robust social investment–oriented social policy institutions may encounter less political resistance if they pursue more difficult decarbonization industrial reforms. If displaced workers can be offered better economic prospects, there may be less political resistance to such reforms. Member States that face less resistance are better able to adapt to the Green Economy and benefit from it. Since the social investment orientation of Member States' social policy institutions often reflects the North–South and East–West divide, there is a concern that the Green Transition may lead to a two-speed Europe. In this context, the European Commission launched the Just Transition Mechanism (JTM) alongside the European Green Deal that aims to "promote economic renewal, new skills and new job opportunities . . . [so that] no one is left behind and all regions and all Europeans are able to tap the benefits of a greener, fairer more digital future" (European Commission 2020, 1). However, its funding is only a fifth of the sum dedicated to the climate and environment earmarked in the EU's budget. While the JTM is an important signal from the European Commission, it remains to be seen if it is sufficient to overcome social instability that may limit Member States' willingness to pursue deep-seated decarbonization industrial reforms that will be needed to bring about a European-wide Green Economy.

This chapter contributes by bridging social policy and comparative political economy to environmental reform. Until now, the nexus between social policy and environmental reforms remains underexplored (for exceptions, see Kaasch and Schulze Waltrup 2021). As the salience and need for comprehensive environmental reforms grows with the climate emergency, policymakers will increasingly face severe opportunity costs when they adopt structural reforms to decarbonize and green their economies. We offer a conceptual framework to understand some of the key considerations and challenges that will need to be overcome before policymakers will be incentivized to embark on such reforms. Concurrently, we highlight the role that social policy institutions will play, especially social investment and enabling ALMPs, in ensuring that these structural reforms will not adversely compromise social stability among European welfare states. Although compensating displaced workers mitigates short-term economic loss from structural reforms associated with decarbonization and the Green Transition, it does not offer them a means of improving their long-term economic prospects. When such prospects stagnate, displaced workers may feel left behind and politically disillusioned. Since political disillusionment and feelings of stagnation drive protests and support for radical parties (Ballard-Rosa et al. 2021; Im et al. 2021; Kurer 2021), social policy is critical to ensure that solidarity is maintained in European welfare states while painful but necessary reforms are made to avert the worst of the climate emergency. Future studies could explore which combinations of social policies—both compensation and social investment—ensure a fairer Green Transition by dampening unequal distributive effects from green-related structural transformations. Additionally, while we focus on how these conditions constrain Member States' RRF plans regarding decarbonization industrial reforms, future studies could also explore how they affect other green reforms. Finally, future studies could examine the impact of geopolitical shocks like the Ukrainian war on Member States' move away from fossil fuels as well as industrial decarbonization.

References

Armingeon, Klaus, Caroline De La Porte, Elke Heins, and Stefano Sacchi. 2022. "Voices from the Past: Economic and political vulnerabilities in the making of Next Generation EU." *Comparative European Politics* 20 (2): 144–65. https://doi.org/10.1057/s41 295-022-00277-6.

Ballard-Rosa, Cameron, Mashail A. Malik, Stephanie J. Rickard, and Kenneth Scheve. 2021. "The economic origins of authoritarian values: Evidence from local trade shocks in the United Kingdom." *Comparative Political Studies* 54 (13): 2321–53. https://doi.org/10.1177/00104140211024296.

Barreira, Ana., and Carlota Ruiz-Bautista. 2020. *El Comité De Cambio Climático De Reino Unido, ¿Un Modelo Para España?* IDMA (Madrid: 2020). https://www.iidma.org/atta chments/Publicaciones/Informe_IIDMA_CCC.pdf.

Bundesamt für die Sicherheit der nuklearen Entsorgung. 2021. "Der Atomausstieg in Deutschland." (June 29). https://www.base.bund.de/DE/themen/kt/ausstieg-atomkr aft/ausstieg_node.html.

Bengtsson, Mattias, Caroline de la Porte, and Kerstin Jacobsson. 2017. "Labour market policy under conditions of permanent austerity: Any sign of social investment?" Social Policy & Administration 51 (2): 367–88. https://doi.org/10.1111/spol.12292.

Bundesumweltministerium. 2021. "Dekarbonisierung in Der Industrie." (April 27). https://www.bmu.de/programm/dekarbonisierung-in-der-industrie.

Bundesministerium für Wirtschaft und Klimaschutz. 2020. "Strukturstärkungsgesetz Kohleregionen." (September 24). https://www.bmwi.de/Redaktion/DE/Textsammlun gen/Wirtschaft/strukturstaerkungsgesetz-kohleregionen.html.

Bundesministerium der Finanzen. 2021. "Deutscher Aufbau- Und Resilienzplan (Darp)." (April 27). https://www.bundesfinanzministerium.de/Content/DE/Standardartikel/ Themen/Europa/DARP/deutscher-aufbau-und-resilienzplan.html.

Bundesministerium der Justiz. 2020. "Gesetz Zur Reduzierung Und Zur Beendigung Der Kohleverstromung Und Zur Änderung Weiterer Gesetze (Kohleausstiegsgesetz)." *Bundesministerium der Justiz und für Verbraucherschutz* 37: 1818–1867. https://www. gesetze-im-internet.de/kohleausg/BJNR181800020.html.

Burns, Steven. 2008. "Environmental policy and politics: Trends in public debate." *Natural Resources & Environment* 23 (2): 8–12.

Ćetković, Stefan, Aron Buzogány, and Miranda Schreurs. 2017. "Varieties of Clean Energy Transitions in Europe: Political-Economic Foundations of Onshore and Offshore Wind Development." In *The Political Economy of Clean Energy Transitions*, edited by Douglas Arent, Channing Arndt, Mackay Miller, Finn Tarp, Owen Zinaman, 103–122. Oxford: Oxford University Press.

Crnčec, Danijel. 2021. "Covid-19 crisis: More EU integration and a step forward for EU energy policy and climate action?" *Teorija in Praksa* 57: 1105–23.

De La Porte, Caroline, and Elke Heins. 2016. "Introduction: Is the European Union More Involved in Welfare State Reform Following the Sovereign Debt Crisis?" In *The Sovereign Debt Crisis, the EU and Welfare State Reform*, edited by Caroline De La Porte and Elke Heins, 1–13. London: Palgrave Macmillan.

Dechezleprêtre, Antoine., and Tobias Kruse. 2018. *A Review of the Empirical Literature Combining Economic and Environmental Performance Data at the Micro-Level.* Paris: OECD. https://www.oecd-ilibrary.org/content/paper/45d269b2-en.

Engel, Hauke, Marcin Purta, Eveline Speelman, Gustaw Szarek, and Po van der Pluijm. 2020. *Neutralna Emisyjnie Polska 2050.* Jak Wyzwanie Zmienić W Szansę. McKinsey & Company. https://www.mckinsey.com/pl/our-insights/carbon-neutral-poland-2050. McKinsey & Company w Polsce.

European Commission. 2019. Communication from the Commission to the European Parliament, the European Council. The Council, the European Economic and Social Committee and the Committee of the Regions. The European Green Deal. European Commission. Brussels. https://eur-lex.europa.eu/resource.html?uri=cellar:b828d165-1c22-11ea-8c1f-01aa75ed71a1.0002.02/DOC_1&format=PDF.

European Commission. 2020. The European Green Deal Investment Plan and Just Transition Mechanism Explained. European Commission. Brussels.

European Commission. 2021. European Green Deal. Delivering on Our Targets. European Commission. (Luxembourg: Publications Office of the European Union). https://ec.europa.eu/commission/presscorner/detail/en/fs_21_3688.

European Commission. 2021a. A Socially Fair Transition. European Commission. Brussels. https://ec.europa.eu/commission/presscorner/detail/en/fs_21_3677.

European Commission. 2021b. Commission Staff Working Document Guidance to Member States. Recovery and Resilience Plans. Part 1/2. European Commission. Brussels. https://commission.europa.eu/system/files/2021-01/document_travail_service_part2_v3_en.pdf.

European Commission. 2021c. "Regulation (EU) 2021/241 of the European Parliament and of the Council of 12 February 2021 Establishing the Recovery and Resilience Facility." *Regulation. Official Journal of the European Union 2021*, 241.

European Commission. 2021d. Analysis of the Recovery and Resilience Plan of Spain. Brussels.

European Commission. 2022. Report from the Commission to the European Parliament and the Council on the Implementation of the Recovery and Resilience Facility. European Commission.

European Environment Agency. 2020. "Industrial Pollution." In *The European Environment—State and Outlook 2020. Knowledge for Transition to a Sustainable Europe*, 268–87. Luxembourg: Publications Office of the European Union.

Intergovernmental Panel on Climate Change. 2015. "Industry." In *Climate Change 2014: Mitigation of Climate Change: Working Group III Contribution to the IPCC Fifth Assessment Report*, edited by IPCC, 739–810. Cambridge: Cambridge University Press.

Fischer, Carolyn, and Garth Heutel. 2013. "Environmental macroeconomics: Environmental policy, business cycles, and directed technical change." *Annual Review of Resource Economics* 5 (1): 197–210. https://doi.org/10.1146/annurev-resource-091912-151819.

Goos, Maarten, Alan Manning, and Anna Salomons. 2014. "Explaining job polarization: routine-biased technological change and offshoring." *American Economic Review* 104 (8): 2509–26. https://doi.org/10.1257/aer.104.8.2509.

Green Recovery Tracker. Spain. 2021. https://www.greenrecoverytracker.org/country-reports/spain.

Hall, Peter A., and Daniel W. Gingerich. 2009. "Varieties of capitalism and institutional complementarities in the political economy: An empirical analysis." *British Journal of Political Science* 39 (3): 449–82. https://doi.org/10.1017/S0007123409000672.

Hemerijck, Anton. 2017. "Social Investment and Its Critics." In *The Uses of Social Investment*, edited by Anton. Hemerijck, 3–40. Oxford: Oxford University Press.

Im, Zhen Jie, Nonna Mayer, Bruno Palier, and Jan Rovny. 2019. "The 'losers of automation': A reservoir of votes for the radical right?" *Research & Politics* 6 (1): 1–7. https://doi.org/10.1177/2053168018822395.

IPCC. 2021. "Summary for Policymakers." In *Climate Change 2021: The Physical Science Basis. Contribution of Working Group I to the Sixth Assessment Report of the Intergovernmental Panel on Climate Change*, edited by V. Masson-Delmotte, P. Zhai, S.L. Pirani, C. Connors, S. Péan, N. Berger, Y. Caud, et al., 3–34. Cambridge: Cambridge University Press.

Joint Research Centre. 2018. *EU Coal Regions: Opportunities and Challenges Ahead*. Joint Research Centre, Brussels.

Kaasch, Alexandra, and Robin Schulze Waltrup. 2021. "Introduction: Global eco-social policy: Contestation within an emerging policy era?" *Global Social Policy* 21 (2): 319–22. https://doi.org/10.1177/14680181211019152.

Kurer, Thomas. 2020. "The declining middle: Occupational change, social status, and the populist right." *Comparative Political Studies* 53 (10-11): 1798–835. https://doi.org/10.1177/0010414020912283.

Lindblom-Ylänne, Sari, Anna Parpala, and Liisa Postareff. 2019. "What constitutes the surface approach to learning in the light of new empirical evidence?" *Studies in Higher Education* 44 (12): 2183–95. https://doi.org/10.1080/03075079.2018.1482267.

Lionello, Luca. 2020. "Next Generation EU: Has the Hamiltonian moment come for Europe?" EUROJUS 4: 22–42.

MacNeil, Robert. 2016. "Death and environmental taxes: Why market environmentalism fails in liberal market economies." *Global Environmental Politics* 16 (1): 21–37. https://doi.org/10.1162/GLEP_a_00336.

Mandelli, Matteo, and Sebastiano Sabato. 2018. The EU's Potential for Promoting an Eco-Social Agenda. European Social Observatory, Brussels.

Manow, Philip. 2020. *Social Protection, Capitalist Production: The Bismarckian Welfare State in the German Political Economy, 1880–2015*. Oxford: Oxford University Press.

Meckling, Jonas, Nina Kelsey, Eric Biber, and John Zysman. 2015. "Winning coalitions for climate policy." *Science* 349 (6253): 1170–71. https://doi.org/10.1126/science.aab1336.

Mildenberger, M. Carbon 2020. *Captured: How Business and Labor Control Climate Politics*. Cambridge, MA: MIT Press.

Ministerstwo Klimatu i Środowiska. 2021. Polityka Energetyczna Polski Do 2040 R. Ministerstwo Klimatu i Środowiska, Warsaw.

Ministwo Funduszy I Polityki Regionalnej. 2021. "Krajowy Plan Odbudowy I Zwiększania Odporności." https://www.gov.pl/web/planodbudowy/kpo-wyslany-do-komisji-europejskiej. Warsaw: Ministertwo Funduszy I Polityki Regionalnej.

Morel, N., and B. Palier. 2011. *Towards a Social Investment Welfare State?: Ideas, Policies and Challenges*. Bristol: Policy Press.

Nowak, Kamil. 2015. "Polska Po 1989 R. Doświadczyła Katastrofy Przemysłowej. Czy Możemy Odbudować Nasz Potencjał?" Forsal. https://forsal.pl/artykuly/888899,sor oka-polska-po-1989-r-doswiadczyla-katastrofy-przemyslowej-musimy-odbudowac-nasz-potencjal.html.

Nylund-Gibson, Karen, and Andrew Choi. 2018. "Ten frequently asked questions about latent class analysis." *Translational Issues in Psychological Science* 4 (4): 440–61. https://doi.org/10.1037/tps0000176.

Pierson, Paul. 1996. "The new politics of the welfare state." *World Politics* 48 (2): 143–79. https://doi.org/10.1353/wp.1996.0004.

Politiken. 2022. "Danmarks Største Udleder Af Drivhusgasser: »Det Er Ikke Sådan, at Vi Elsker at Være Sorte«." *Politiken.* http://politiken.dk/8615584.

Politiken. 2021. "»Det Er En Rigtig God Nyhed«, Siger Klimarådet Om Ny Aftale." *Politiken.* http://politiken.dk/8409313.

Pontusson, Jonas. 2006. *Inequality and Prosperity: Social Europe vs. Liberal America*. Ithaca: Cornell University Press.

Porter, Michael E., and Claas van der Linde. 1995. "Toward a new conception of the environment-competitiveness relationship." *The Journal of Economic Perspectives* 9. (4): 97–118. http://www.jstor.org/stable/2138392.

Prinz, Lukas, and Anna Pegels. 2018. "The role of labour power in sustainability transitions: insights from comparative political economy on Germany's electricity transition." *Energy Research & Social Science* 41: 210–19. https://doi.org/https://doi.org/10.1016/j.erss.2018.04.010.

Reuters. 2020. "Factbox: Spain's \$4.2 billion aid plan to support the auto industry." *Coronavirus explainers.* https://www.reuters.com/article/us-health-coronavirus-spain-autos-factbo-idUSKBN23M2EZ.

Rykowski, Rafal, and Francesa Canali. 2021. *Assessment of Poland's Recovery and Resilience Plan*. CEE Bankwatch Network, Prague.

Schmidt, Vivien A. 2009. "Putting the political back into political economy by bringing the state back in yet again." *World Politics* 61 (3): 516–46. https://doi.org/10.1017/S0043887109000173.

Schulz, Florence. 2020. "Meps warn of insufficient control over EU climate spending." *Euractiv* (Online), https://www.euractiv.com/section/energy-environment/news/meps-warn-of-insufficient-control-over-eu-climate-spending/.

Seeleib-Kaiser, Martin. 2002. "A dual transformation of the German welfare state?" *West European Politics* 25 (4): 25–48. https://doi.org/10.1080/713601641.

Sokołowski, Jakub, Frankowski, Jan, Mazurkiewicz, Joanna, Antosiewicz, Marek, Lewandowski, Piotr.2021. Dekarbonizacja a Zatrudnienie W Górnictwie Węgla Kamiennego W Polsce. Institute for Structural Research (Warsaw: 2021).

Szelewa, Dorota, and M. Polakowski. 2022. "Explaining the Weakness of Social Investment Policies in the Visegrád Countries: The Cases of Childcare and Active Labor Market Policies." In *The World Politics of Social Investment, Volume II*, edited by Julian L. Garritzmann, Silja. Häusermann and B. Palier, 185–208. Oxford: Oxford University Press.

Turin, Dustin R. 2014. "Environmental problems and American politics: Why is protecting the environment so difficult?" *Inquiries Journal/Student Pulse* 6 (11): 1.

Walter, S., A. Ray, and N. Redeker. 2020. *The Politics of Bad Options: Why the Eurozone's Problems Have Been So Hard to Resolve*. Oxford: Oxford University Press.

Wood, Geoffrey, Jared J. Finnegan, Maria L. Allen, Matthew M. C. Allen, Douglas Cumming, Sofia Johan, et al. 2019. "The Comparative Institutional Analysis of Energy Transitions." *Socio-Economic Review* 18 (1): 257–94. https://doi.org/10.1093/ser/mwz026.

Wupperal Institut. 2021. *Green Recovery Tracker: Poland*. https://assets.website-files.com/602e4a891047f739eaf5dfad/60dee83d7aecbeea61dedf0c_Poland_Green%20Recovery%20Tracker%20Analysis_updated.pdf.

Żukowski, Maciej. 2011. "Ekonomiczne Uwarunkowania Zmian W Polskim Systemie Emerytalnym W Latach 1989-2011." In *Ewolucja Ubezpieczeń Społecznych W Okresie Transformacji Ustrojowe*, edited by Wagner Barbary and Malaki Antoniego. Bydgoszcz: Polskie Stowarzyszenie Ubezpieczenia Społecznego.

10

COVID-19: An Accelerating Force for EU Activity in Health?

Mary Guy

Introduction

Interest in the development of EU-level activity in health is not new, with attention arguably being focused on concerns relating to respective EU and Member State competence in this area and mapping expansion, inter alia in terms of both hard and soft law mechanisms (Greer et al. 2019; Guy and Sauter 2017).[1] Establishing a precise location for health within wider EU law and policy may appear elusive, insofar as health ". . . is either non-existent as an autonomous policy area, given that it is mainstreamed into all other policies, or that it is basically everything, in that all EU public policy is also health policy" (de Ruijter 2019, 52). However, successful attempts have been made by lawyers and political scientists to delineate—and develop—a field of EU health law and policy (Hervey and McHale 2004, 2015; Greer et al. 2014 and 2019; Brooks and Guy 2021). It is increasingly acknowledged that development of EU-level interest in health care is determined in terms of politics, both in terms of EU–Member State interaction, but also at EU level, in view of Commissioner Kyriakides' expanded mandate for health relative to the space afforded under the previous Juncker Commission (Brooks 2019; Brooks and Guy 2021). However, what is also starting to emerge is that the dynamism of EU law in the health context may have much to offer (Hervey and de Ruijter 2020).

EU-level responses to COVID-19 might be considered not only to highlight or amplify existing EU competence in this area, but also to galvanize

---

[1] Email: M.J.Guy@ljmu.ac.uk. I am grateful for feedback from audiences at workshops associated with this collected volume in April and September 2021, the EU Health Governance panel at UACES 2021 on September 6, 2021, and to Dr. Eleanor Brooks for comments on an earlier draft.

Mary Guy, *COVID-19: An Accelerating Force for EU Activity in Health?* In: *European Social Policy and the COVID-19 Pandemic.* Edited by: Stefanie Börner and Martin Seeleib-Kaiser, Oxford University Press.
© Oxford University Press 2023. DOI: 10.1093/oso/9780197676189.003.0010

or accelerate EU activities in the health field. What emerged in early 2020 was that EU competence in health was not well understood and was in need of elaboration (Purnhagen et al. 2020), and perceptions that health care system organization as a Member State competence inhibited wider EU-level responses (Greer 2020). The combining of both public health and health care in the "hard law" mechanism of Article 168 Treaty on the Functioning of the European Union (TFEU), and the delicate interplay between EU and Member State competence perhaps suggested a level of nuance unhelpful for a crisis response. Indeed, where a long-standing distinction between "public health" and "health care" exists, with EU competence being focused on the former and Member State competence on the latter, the multifaceted effects of, and responses to, COVID-19 perhaps suggest that this distinction is increasingly less clear. Or at least that EU-level policy interventions may no longer separate as easily along seemingly clear lines such as "public health," "internal market," and "fiscal policy" (Greer 2014).

It is therefore unsurprising that the initial EU-level responses led to calls for greater powers at EU level and for these to take a demonstrably concrete form, as evidenced by framings such as "a Europe for health" (Huffington Post 2020; Fortuna 2020) and calls for "Treaty change" (Nielsen 2020; Euractiv 2021). What has persisted since approximately May 2020 are calls for the development of a European Health Union. Initially proposed at EU level by the Socialists and Democrats in the European Parliament (Socialists and Democrats 2020a and 2020b), the concept gained traction by reference in Commission President von der Leyen's State of the Union address in September 2020 (von der Leyen 2020), with elaboration by the Commission following in November 2020 (European Commission 2020a). Further support for a European Health Union can be found with the elaboration of EU4Health, the latest EU health program, which incorporates (financial) commitment to "[m]ak[ing] the European Health Union a reality . . ." (European Commission, 2020b).

A concurrent movement outside of the EU institutions—the European Health Union (EHU) initiative—has gone further in elaborating a manifesto and proposals for Treaty change (European Health Union Initiative 2020/2021). Furthermore, consensus appeared to be building around the extent of a European Health Union, specifically that this should extend beyond the confines of the immediate pandemic response to other aspects of health (Luena 2021).

So, it appears that defining the contours of a European Health Union in response to the COVID-19 pandemic may be difficult. Indeed, this echoes earlier conceptions of a "European Health Community" (Ribeyre 1952 cited in Parsons 2003); a "new compound European healthcare state" (Lamping 2005), and a "European healthcare union" (Vollaard, van de Bovenkamp and Sindbjerg Martinsen 2016). The complexity of defining the contours of these visions appears attributed primarily to the political sensitivities attaching to EU Member State competence interactions regarding national health care (Vollaard, van de Bovenkamp, and Sindbjerg Martinsen 2016), and the effects of this dynamic on global health visions (Steurs et al. 2018), although comparisons are inevitably drawn with "unions" in other sectors, notably banking (Bazzan 2020; Bartlett 2020).

The wide-ranging implications of the COVID-19 pandemic may suggest that there was sufficient impetus to operationalize implementation of a European Health Union by means of Treaty change, a higher threshold than introducing other legislation or soft law initiatives that characterize a notable part of EU health law and policy. This impetus can be tested by reference to wider questions of what enables policy change. The fluctuating budget granted initially in response to COVID-19 and latterly to the EU4Health program[2] might indicate that answers are by no means straightforward, insofar as the rarity of radical policy change may be linked with variations in public policy budgets (Jones and Baumgartner 2012). The role of crisis in shaping EU integration is well documented (Jones, Kelemen, and Meunier 2021; Nicoli 2019) and is also acknowledged in the development of EU health policy (Brooks and Geyer 2020). Furthermore, the conception of a European Health Union has been deemed a post-Westphalian health governance framework, in light of the unique window of opportunity presented by the failure of Westphalian governance responses to the COVID-19 pandemic (Fraundorfer and Winn 2021).

In September 2021, 18 months on from the initial EU responses to COVID-19, the European Health Union appeared to occupy a prominent place on the Commission's agenda, albeit with skepticism emerging (Deutsch 2021). This, and the restated commitment at national and EU levels both within and outside the EU institutions, would seem to indicate policy change (Kingdon 2014). However, just how far implementation of the European Health Union

---

[2] Initially €9.4 billion in May 2020, scaled back to €1.7 billion following the Council summit in July 2020, then agreed at €5.1 billion in December 2020.

can go—to extend beyond the realms of crisis response or to prompt Treaty change to refocus EU and national competence in health—remained moot. These questions can be examined by reference to Kingdon's Multiple Streams Framework to analyze whether windows of opportunity were opened, have remained open, or may yet open. In broad terms, the problem stream represents COVID-19 responses but also encompasses wider issues, such as weaknesses in national health care systems and whether more or less EU-level activity is needed. The politics stream can comprise the European Commission and Member States. The policy stream is represented by the proposals for a European Health Union of both the Commission and the EHU initiative, but may also extend to the Conference on the Future of Europe, in view of the reservation of discussions of competence to this by Commission President von der Leyen in the State of the Union address in September 2020. Potential confluence of these streams (or of associated tributaries) can be identified at different points in the period May 2020 to September 2021.

This chapter therefore examines how COVID-19 can be said to accelerate EU-level activity in health by reference to the implementation of a European Health Union and proposals for Treaty change. This examination is framed by Kingdon's Multiple Streams Framework and "windows of opportunity" model to explore the chances for success for the European Health Union proposals. This can help highlight answers to questions of how change occurs with regard to EU health policy, and more specifically whether COVID-19 can be said to accelerate change in this area. The second section considers how the Treaty provision governing EU competence in health has developed and outlines how "Europeanization" can affect Member State competence (Sindbjerg Martinsen 2012; Vrangbaek and Sindbjerg Martinsen 2008). The third section sets out the calls for a European Health Union and how this has developed—to include proposals for Treaty change—between approximately May 2020 and September 2021 (European Health Union Initiative 2021). The fourth section outlines Kingdon's model and explains how it can help answer the questions posed by the current discussion. The final section offers some concluding remarks.

The Development of EU Competence in Health and "Europeanization" of Health Care

The development (and expansion) of EU competence in health has been traced both in chronological terms (Hervey and McHale 2015, ch. 3; Guy and Sauter 2017; Greer et al. 2019, ch. 1), and as concepts such as the "three faces" of EU health policy, encompassing public health, the internal market, and fiscal policy (Greer 2014). A persistent theme has been the extent to which EU and Member State competence regarding health is delineated, and the extent to which the former may encroach on the latter. This section first considers briefly the inclusion of the public health Treaty provision as the prime example of health—and the delineation of respective national and EU-level competence—being incorporated into EU hard law. It then engages with the consideration that health represents a "least likely candidate" for integration but has nevertheless undergone "Europeanization" (Sindbjerg Martinsen 2012) by reference to the examples of the Patients' Rights Directive,[3] EU competition policy, and the inclusion of country-specific recommendations in the European Semester fiscal policy assessment framework.

Development of the Public Health/Health Care Treaty Provision

The interaction between the EU and Member State levels initially assumed a "complementary" character, but has evolved to balance this with a clear delineation between national and EU competence with regard to public health matters on the one hand (where overlap can have clear benefits), and health care system organization and policy on the other (which may be considered contained within individual Member States for a variety of reasons including historical and cultural).

A public health competence was outlined with Article 129 EEC, and subsequently Article 152 TEU (Hervey and McHale 2004, 72–84) which allowed for "Community action" to "complement" national policies directed toward improving public health (Article 152(1) TEU), "encourage cooperation between Member States (Article 152(2) TEU) and foster cooperation between Member States and with third countries (Article 152(3) TEU). A subsidiarity element was first incorporated in Article 152(5) TEU, and specified that:

---

[3] Directive 2011/24/EU of the European Parliament and of the Council of 9 March 2011 on the application of patients' rights in cross-border health care.

Community action in the field of public health shall fully respect the responsibilities of the Member States for the organisation and delivery of health services and medical care . . .

Subsequent to this, the current provision—Article 168 TFEU—includes the aforementioned focus for "Union action" on complementing and encouraging/fostering cooperation (Article 168(1),(2),(3) TFEU), but has also expanded in both implicit and explicit ways. Article 168(5) TFEU enables the European Parliament and the Council to adopt incentive measures designed to protect and improve human health, combat cross-border health scourges and threats, and protect human health regarding tobacco and alcohol abuse. However, Article 168(5) TFEU is clear that the adoption of incentive measures excludes harmonization of the laws and regulations of the Member States—a distinction illustrated by EU-level activity regarding tobacco advertising (now a formal power specified by Article 168(5) TFEU) and the Patients' Rights Directive (based on the harmonization provision of Article 114 TFEU) (Hancher and Sauter 2012, 15–16). Prior to considerations in connection with COVID-19 responses (discussed below), an illustration of incentive measures adopted in connection with Article 168(5) TFEU had been the example of the successive EU health programs in operation since 2003[4] (Hancher and Sauter 2012).

Article 168(7) TFEU was expanded relative to Article 152(5) TEU to offer a renewed framing of EU-level/Member State competence thus:

Union action shall respect the responsibilities of the Member States for the definition of their health policy and for the organisation and delivery of health services and medical care. The responsibilities of the Member States shall include the management of health services and medical care and the allocation of the resources assigned to them.

Article 168(7) TFEU underwent four subtle, but ultimately significant, amendments by reference to its predecessor: a decoupling of the subsidiarity focus on health care from "public health"; a change in Union focus from

---

[4] Decision No 1786/2002/EC of the European Parliament and of the Council of 23 September 2002 adopting a programme of Community action in the field of public health (2003-2008); Decision No 1350/2007/EC of the European Parliament and of the Council of 23 October 2007 establishing a second programme of Community action in the field of health (2008-13); Regulation (EU) No 282/2014 of the European Parliament and of the Council of 11 March 2014 on the establishment of a third Programme for the Union's action in the field of health (2014-2020).

"fully respecting" to merely "respecting" Member State responsibilities; explicit stipulation of "health policy" alongside these; and elaboration, in a new second sentence, of what the responsibilities include (Guy 2020). While Article 168(7) TFEU can be read as a clarification of the extent of Member State competence in the wider context of the TFEU (Piris 2010, 321), with the second sentence representing "statements of national autonomy" (Garben 2018), it has also been considered to introduce a "a delicate and sophisticated balance" in the context of EU competition policy and health care (van de Gronden and Szyszczak 2011, 486).

It is considered next how this "hard law" Treaty provision for health has been used to shape contours of "Europeanization" of health care, but the ambiguity of this should not be overlooked. On the one hand, "from the point of view of EU health lawyers, this Treaty recognition set health law on the road to becoming a recognised aspect of EU law" (Hervey and McHale 2015, 39). However, on the other hand, Article 168 TFEU has been depicted as a gate in a field around which sheep of EU policies as diverse as competition, the European Semester, the internal market, and agriculture are free to roam (Comic House/Floris Oudshoorn, cited in Greer et al. 2019, 176). This has led to suggestions that the separation of health from other policies, and consequently the interaction between EU and national levels, represents a porous barrier (Guy 2020).

How Far Does "Europeanization" in Health Care Go in Reframing the National/EU Competences in Health Care?

Despite seeming a "less likely" candidate, health care has undergone a process of integration and "Europeanization" as evidenced by the example of patient mobility and cross-border health care (Sindbjerg Martinsen 2012). In contrast to public health initiatives, the linking of patient mobility and the overarching objective of achieving the internal market can be seen as perhaps the strongest example of "Europeanization" in health care, given the involvement of the courts in case law underpinning the subsequent Patients' Rights Directive and harmonization providing the legal basis for this. If the Patients' Rights Directive can be described as "explicit harmonization," then it appears also possible to identify "implicit harmonization" in other policy areas absent recourse to the harmonization provision amid concerns about the pervasiveness of EU-level influence regarding competition and fiscal policy. This appears consistent with the view that "the degree of coerciveness and thus the imperative to Europeanize may vary considerably from one EU regulatory area to the other" (Sindbjerg Martinsen 2012).

The influence of EU competition policy on national health care systems, although acknowledged to be emerging, proves difficult to categorize (Morton 2021). The applicability of the EU antitrust and state aid rules (Articles 101; 102; 107–109 TFEU) would appear to circumvent national power regarding national policies to experiment with marketization reforms in health care (Prosser 2010; Andreangeli 2016). However, the ultimate influence on national competition reforms in health care may be evidenced more by the development of "EU-national competition rules for health care" with terminology reflecting the wider EU competition law framework (van de Gronden 2011; van de Gronden and Szyszczak 2014; Guy 2019). National health care policies may be considered strengthened by recourse to the Services of General Interest exemption or by designating specific activities as Services of General Economic Interest (another example of Member State competence—Protocol No. 26), but here too concerns emerge that the latter proves too cumbersome for engagement at a national level (Nikolić 2021).

The development of the European Semester fiscal policy annual assessment program has been considered a further expansion of EU-level influence over Member State responsibility for national health policy and health care system organization, particularly in view of the country-specific recommendations (CSRs) issued by the European Commission (Greer, Jarman and Baeten 2016). However, here too the parameters of the "incursion" of EU-level influence are less clear-cut than may first be thought. On the one hand, CSRs can be considered to represent a "particularly coercive form of soft law" (Garben 2018) and exercising clear influence over national health care systems (Azzopardi-Muscat et al. 2015). On the other hand, the process involved in elaborating the CSRs would seem to suggest a sense of "circularity" in the respective inputs of the national and EU levels, such that the focus shifts to the differing interactions between the EU and national levels as determined by the extent of fiscal restraints imposed (Guy 2020).

These broader considerations of the interactions regarding health care between the national and EU levels across diverse aspects of EU law and policy, and the wider expansion of EU health law and policy as a "patchwork" (Hervey and Vanhercke 2010), show that there has been clear expansion of EU-level influence over health care despite Treaty limits regarding national health care policy and system organization. Indeed, it has been considered that the expansion is such as to amount to a "European health care union," a system of cooperative federalism, albeit one of limited robustness due to the limited loyalty to the EU it generates (Vollaard et al. 2016).

The Development of a European Health Union in Response to COVID-19 (May 2020–September 2021)

What emerged in the first months of response to COVID-19 was that EU competence in health was not well understood, and that the salience of Article 168(7) TFEU as a constraining feature may be primarily political rather than legal (Purnhagen et al. 2020), given that it is considered to add little to the formal division of powers elsewhere in the Treaties (Greer et al. 2019, 63). It has also been considered that what was more notable than perceptions of a disappointing response at EU level was the support and solidarity which Member States showed one another (Brooks, de Ruijter and Greer 2020), although solidarity between Member States was also found wanting at various points.

The idea for a "European Health Union" can be traced back to calls by Emmanuel Macron for a *Europe de la santé* during a joint press conference with Angela Merkel in May 2020 outlining a health strategy for Europe (Huffington Post 2020; Fortuna 2020). This outlined a "health strategy" for a strategically positioned European health care industry which would upgrade the European dimension of health care and reduce EU dependency, while fully respecting Member State responsibility for health care systems.

At the same point, the Socialists and Democrats (S&D) party in the European Parliament outlined a vision for a European Health Union (Socialists and Democrats 2020a, 2020b). This call proved wide-ranging, encompassing aspects as diverse as access to pharmaceuticals, health research, and health and safety in the workplace, arguably consistent with the EU's diversity of powers which might be considered related to health. The S&D's call appeared premised on a fundamental need for more (or more explicit) EU-level cooperation because health care systems remain the responsibility of Member States (Guy 2020), and this respect for Member State competence has been prominent in setting the parameters for constructing a European Health Union.

A further development in May 2020 was the publication of the initial proposals for the fourth EU health program, EU4Health, to run between

2021 and 2027. This provided for an ambitious health strategy encompassing not only more coordinated COVID-19 responses and key action areas for the improvement of the resilience of national health care systems, but also emphasizing strong embedding in the "One Health" approach, recognizing the interconnection between human health, animal health, and the environment. The ambition of this program may be considered recognized by the initial budget assigned to it in May 2020—€9.4 billion. However, this was dramatically cut to €1.7 billion following the EU summit in July 2020 under pressure from the so-called frugal countries —Austria, Denmark, Netherlands, and Sweden (Fortuna 2020b).

Calls for a European Health Union were given significant reinforcement in Commission President von der Leyen's inaugural State of the Union address in September 2020, with the words "For me, it is crystal clear—we need to build a stronger European Health Union" (von der Leyen 2020). This commitment was accompanied by recognition of the need to "future proof" the EU4Health program. The vision for a European Health Union outlined by von der Leyen in 2020 focused on strengthening crisis preparedness and managing cross-border health threats in a three-fold approach: reinforcing and empowering the European Medicines Agency (EMA) and the European Centre for Disease Control (ECDC); building a European Biomedical Advanced Research and Development Agency; and discussing the question of health competences. Indeed, the latter was confirmed by von der Leyen as a "noble and urgent task" for the Conference on the Future of Europe (von der Leyen 2020). Further impetus to calls for a European Health Union came from Angela Merkel in December 2020 (Stone 2020).

In November 2020, the Commission published a range of proposals to extend the mandate of the ECDC and the EMA and for a regulation on serious cross-border threats to health, as well as outlining a pharmaceutical strategy for Europe and a Communication on Building a European Health Union—preparedness and resilience. The Communication confirmed that it proposed the first building blocks for a European Health Union and that these were envisaged within the current Treaty provisions, particularly Article 168(5) TFEU:

> By upgrading the EU framework for cross-border health threats, these first building blocks of the European Health Union will bring greater overall impact while fully respecting the Member States' competence in the area of health (European Commission 2020a).

This appears consistent with the initial calls for a European Health Union—as focused around an apparently immutable core of Member State competence in health care. However, the Communication is notable for its portrayal of EU–Member State interaction, in recognizing the need to work together and use the EU's potential to improve the health response and to support Member States to fulfill their responsibilities, and particularly with the concluding sentence: "The European Health Union will be as strong as its Member States' commitment to it."

The EU4Health program was subsequently elaborated as paving the way to a European Health Union[5] by investing in urgent health priorities, namely, responding to the COVID-19 crisis and improving EU-level resilience for cross-border threats, Europe's Beating Cancer Plan, and the Pharmaceutical Strategy for Europe. Just as the scope for the EU4Health program evolved, so too did the budget associated with it. In September 2020 von der Leyen had indicated support for the European Parliament's fight for more funding following the cutting of the budget to €1.7 billion in July 2020 by the European Council. In December 2020, the European Council and European Parliament agreed a budget of €5.1 billion for the EU4Health program, a move acknowledged by Commissioner Schinas as a vote of confidence in making a European Health Union a reality (Commission December 2020). The entry into force of EU4Health in March 2021 has been highlighted by Commissioner Kyriakides as meeting EU citizens' expectations of a European Health Union (Commission March 2021).

November 2020 also saw the launch of the aforementioned European Health Union Initiative, facilitated by the European Health Forum Gastein[6] and comprising a diverse group of academics and policymakers.[7] The initiative's independence means it has scope to outline a vision for a European Health Union which can be considered more ambitious than that proposed by the Commission, while stating its support for the Commission's action and Commission President von der Leyen's commitment to building a European Health Union. The European Health Union Manifesto is anchored around two aims: to call on the political leaders of Europe in the framework of the Conference on the Future of Europe to commit to creating a European Health Union, and to invite the people of Europe to engage in building a

---

[5] EU4Health 2021-2027—a vision for a healthier European Union | Public Health (europa.eu)
[6] European Health Forum Gastein (ehfg.org)
[7] Including Vytenis Andriukaitis former Commissioner for Health and Food Safety (2014–2019) and former president of the European Parliament, Klaus Hänsch.

health policy that contributes to the EU's long-term sustainable development. Signatories of the Manifesto comprise an impressive array of health care practitioners, politicians at national and international levels, policymakers, civil society actors, and academics from across the EU and beyond.[8]

The connection of developing a European Health Union with treaty change has emerged in different ways and has received both cautious welcomes and more skeptical reception (Hervey and de Ruijter 2020; Guy 2020), amid recognition that expectations of EU citizens had changed (Alemanno 2020). Treaty change had already been hinted at by Commissioner Schinas in May 2020: "if the moment is right, it will happen" (Nielsen 2020). Although not referenced by Commission President von der Leyen in September 2020, the openness to reviewing EU and Member State competence was reiterated and linked again with the Conference on the Future of Europe. Angela Merkel outlined her support for Treaty change in connection with strengthening coordination of EU-level responses as recently as April 2021 (Euractiv 2021). While the Commission's proposals are clearly framed within the existing Treaty competences, the European Health Union Initiative was clear about its support for a Treaty change from the outset and have since published proposed amendments (European Health Union Initiative 2021). These amendments relate both to Article 168 TFEU and elsewhere in the Treaty, for example, by stipulating the European Health Union as an instance of a shared competence between the EU and the Member States under Article 4 TFEU.

The Initiative's vision for amending Article 168(7) TFEU sees the Member State–EU interaction regarding national health competence being linked explicitly with the principle of subsidiarity. As the Initiative notes, this may create a rebalancing of the EU–Member State dynamic such that a counterintuitive effect of stronger EU power in health might be that national health ministries and the attached health communities will have a more powerful role in determining whether or not EU legislation meets the test of subsidiarity.

However, the amendments to Article 168(7) TFEU are notable for two further reasons. First, they envisage the removal of "health policy" such that Member States would only be responsible for the organization and delivery of health services and medical care. Second, they elaborate the EU's role as "support[ing] the capabilities of Member States to promote health equality, reduce unmet medical needs, and strengthen the interoperability of their health systems." While the first amendment has echoes of a curious return to

---

[8] As of October 31, 2021, there were 1,265 signatures. https://europeanhealthunion.eu/#signatures

the original formulation of Member State competence (Article 152(5) TEU), the second indicates a decisive change in focus which could provide a useful reframing of the interaction between the EU and Member States regarding national health care, insofar as "health policy" may be considered to be concerned with aspects such as health inequalities and responses to these.

In view of the foregoing, it is useful to focus the present discussion around the broad questions of whether the COVID-19 pandemic has opened a window to accelerate EU-level activity in health, but to amend the Treaty to reflect this and refocus EU-level and Member State–level interaction.

Kingdon's Multiple Streams Framework—"Window(s) of Opportunity" in the EU Health Context and COVID-19 Responses

Whether or not the COVID-19 pandemic provides a "window of opportunity" to accelerate EU-level activity in health care, and more specifically to put Treaty change on the agenda to extend the EU's competence in this area, can be examined using Kingdon's Multiple Streams Framework. While this has been widely used in the context of empirical research (Herweg, Zahariadis, and Zohlnhöfer 2018), its serviceability is widely acknowledged insofar as it has been considered ". . . not only [to] travel well to different policy areas and stages of the policy cycle, but also to different units of analysis" (Zohlnhöfer, Herweg, and Rüb 2015). While the use of this in a health care context may seem uncontroversial, given Kingdon's own focus on US health care (Kingdon 2014), the relevance of the Multiple Streams Framework to the present discussion, and indeed EU health law more generally, may be less immediately self-evident. However, the Multiple Streams Framework has increasingly been applied to policymaking at the European level since the late 2000s (for example, Zahariadis 2008; Ackrill et al. 2013). It has also been used to examine legislative changes, such as connections between negotiations prior to the Single European Act providing a "window of opportunity which the Commission required to launch a renewed offensive on the social dimension" (Cram 1997 cited in Zahariadis 2008), and the Dassonville[9] and Cassis de Dijon[10] cases, which proved decisive in shaping

---

[9] Case 8/74 *Procureur du Roi v. Dassonville and Others* [1974] ECR 837. ECLI:EU:C:1974:82.
[10] Case 120/78 *Rewe-Zentral AG v. Bundesmonopolverwaltung fuer Branntwein* [1979] ECR 649. ECLI:EU:C:1979:42

the law governing freedom of movement to indicate interactions between EU institutions (Nowak 2010). The particular relevance of the Multiple Streams Framework to the calls for a European Health Union in response to COVID-19 can be linked to the view that it offers a good starting point for understanding what decisions are made and why by reference to who pays attention to what and when, and since it offers a lens of policymaking that assumes ambiguity and stresses a temporal order (Zahariadis 2008).

From the foregoing discussion, it might be considered that the politics stream comprises primarily the Commission and the European Parliament, but also national politicians who have called for Treaty change (notably Angela Merkel). The policy stream may appear to be populated primarily by the Commission and the European Health Union Initiative, given their focus on proposing solutions and alternatives, and the latter's entrepreneurial spirit. The importance accorded to the Conference on the Future of Europe for the discussion of competences would seem to suggest it may occupy a space both within the policy stream and the politics stream—such that it may make more sense to identify tributaries (and potential confluence of these) within the wider streams. While the outbreak of the COVID-19 pandemic appears clearly the main component of the problem stream, it provides a focusing event, as well as highlighting a problem–solution sequence, pointing out glaring deficiencies in health systems across the EU and prompting a search for specific solutions and policy coordination in a similar example to bird flu (Zahariadis 2008).

Before considering the potential coupling of these streams into windows of opportunity, it is useful to recall the sequence of events surrounding calls for a European Health Union:

What emerged over the course of successive events of the 18 months between March 2020 and September 2021 are two related but arguably ultimately diverging propositions: extending EU competence in health, and Treaty change. In keeping with the "streams" imagery, it may be possible to conceptualize the extension of EU powers in a health crisis response as a tributary flowing into a larger stream of extending EU powers, or reformulating EU and Member State interaction regarding health more generally. Similarly, Treaty change might be considered to represent a sea beyond the confluence of politics and policy streams. This can be explained by the complexities inherent in effecting Treaty change—including the requirement for approval from all Member States meeting in an intergovernmental conference and unanimous ratification at national level (Article 48 TEU)—and illustrated

Table 10.1 Timeline overview of events May 2020—September 2021 connected with the development of a European Health Union

Month	Event
May 2020	Calls for a European Health Union by Macron and Merkel; S&D • Indication of Treaty change – link with Conference on Future of Europe by Commissioner Schinas Initial proposal for EU4Health (budget €9.4 billion)
July 2020	EU4Health budget cut to €1.7 billion
September 2020	Von der Leyen's inaugural State of the Union address
November 2020	Commission proposal for building EHU EHU Initiative manifesto launched
December 2020	Merkel call for EHU Agreement of EU4Health budget at €5.1 billion
March 2021	Entry into force of the EU4Health programme
April 2021	Merkel call for Treaty change EHU Initiative outline Treaty amendments
September 2021	Comments by Commissioner Kyriakides Von der Leyen's second State of the Union address

by the experience of implementing the Lisbon Treaty (Peers 2012). The convoluted inputs that combine to give effect to Treaty change should not be underestimated, with the implication that Treaty change is best understood as a process with different levels (Christiansen, Falkner and Jørgensen 2002). Demonstrations of the dynamism of EU law (Hervey and de Ruijter 2020) can also indicate that Treaty change represents a significant step, or a hurdle which is difficult to cross, leading to the suggestion that calls for Treaty change as a necessary mechanism for implementing a European Health Union should be treated with caution (Guy 2020).

With this in mind, how the problem/policy/politics streams couple, and at what point(s), becomes important in assessing whether (and where) windows of opportunity have opened, and the prospects for success of the different visions for constructing a European Health Union. There are also questions of the size of window that opens and the extent to which it opens (Natali 2004; Keeler 1993, cited in Nugent and Saurugger 2002). Thus, while the rapid spread of COVID-19 in the first part of 2020 may be seen as a severe crisis and an unpredictable "window," causal mechanisms are needed to link this to window-opening (Nugent and Saurugger 2002). One such mechanism may be the refocusing of health within the von der Leyen

Commission relative to the Juncker Commission, and the mandate extended to Commissioner Kyriakides in December 2019. The evolution of the pandemic response, determined in part by the passage of time, may also prove instructive. Where "more Union" may be desirable in connection with an initial, short-term crisis response, it may be the case that "less Union" is called for over the longer term, even if activity can be linked ultimately with pandemic response (Guy 2020). In other words, windows may open only slightly, or for a short period of time.

EHU Vision 1: Extending the EU's Competence/Raising the EU's Profile in Health Crisis Responses

The first vision for a European Health Union—based primarily around facilitating EU-level response to health crises—provides the clearest instances of a coupling of the streams, as illustrated by Figure 10.1.

In this coupling, we saw the initial COVID-19 outbreak in the problem stream combining with the political will (at national and EU levels) to extend

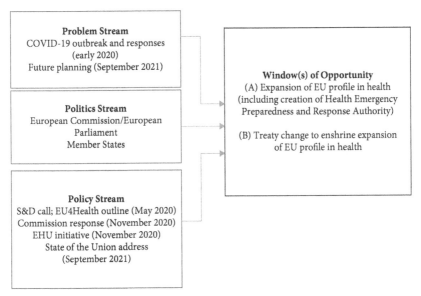

Figure 10.1 Coupling of the streams creating window(s) of opportunity for EHU Vision 1: strengthening EU competence/raising EU profile in health crisis responses.

EU-level competence to respond. Thus, a window appeared to open in May 2020 with the confluence of the problem stream with the politics stream (EU institutions and Member States) and the policy stream (including the Socialists and Democrats' call). The initial proposal for EU4Health's conception as EU-level response to the pandemic, along with the initial commitment of a significant budget (€9.4 billion), can be understood as commitment within the political stream as well as a proposed solution in the policy stream. Although connections have been drawn between the implementation of policy and the funding available (Jones and Baumgartner 2012), the dramatic cut in the budget (to €1.7 billion) in July 2020, perhaps counterintuitively, appears not to have "undone" the coupling of the three streams. Rather, the window appears to have been kept open by the renewed commitment in September 2020 by Commission President von der Leyen to build a European Health Union, reinforced by Commission proposals in November 2020, and subsequent agreement by the Council and the Parliament to increase the budget (to €5.1 billion) and calls by Angela Merkel for a European Health Union, both in December 2020. Indeed, this window might be considered to still be open as at September 2021, albeit with a refocusing of the problem stream in view of Commission President von der Leyen's outline of proposals for "a new health preparedness and resilience mission for the whole of the EU . . . backed up by Team Europe investment of €50 billion by 2027" in her second State of the Union address (von der Leyen 2021).

A secondary window for Treaty change to enshrine this extension of EU-level competence in crisis responses has perhaps been less certain. As hinted at above, Treaty change would require any windows to be wide open, and for a relatively long period of time. Treaty change with regard to raising the EU profile in health crisis responses (as distinct from refocusing EU and Member State competence interaction) was indicated by Commissioner Schinas' comments in May 2020, and already at that stage was linked with debates in the Conference on the Future of Europe (Nielsen 2020). If this can be seen as a confluence of the three streams, then it may have generated a window of opportunity that received subsequent reinforcement by the outlining of the EHU initiative manifesto and Treaty amendment proposals (EHU Initiative 2020/2021), and by Angela Merkel's call in April 2021 for Treaty change, seemingly specifically with regard to the EU-level competence (such as extending the mandate of different agencies). However, as of September 2021, the extent to which this window could still be said to be open was moot.

EHU Vision 2: Extending the EU's Competence
by Reframing the EU–Member States Competence in Health
(Beyond Crisis Responses)

It has been noted that it is much easier to tell when coupling and a window of opportunity have happened after the fact (Greer 2018). This can be illustrated well by the vision of a European Health Union which extends beyond crisis responses, insofar as the chance to refocus EU and Member State competence regarding health may be seen as a "missed opportunity" if no attempt was made to align this with the COVID-19 crisis response. In this sense, parallels and distinctions can be drawn between COVID-19 responses and responses to the economic downturn of 2008–2009, insofar as the latter prompted more EU-level interest (and influence) in health care via fiscal policy. However, an obvious impetus for Treaty change regarding health competence was lacking.

As noted above, the threshold for Treaty change affecting EU–Member State competence in health appears higher than for crisis response: a more unambiguous coupling of the streams would be needed for a window of opportunity to be open both to a larger extent and for a certain (longer) period of time. The three streams within this EHU vision are set out in Figure 10.2.

The problem stream within this vision would comprise both the crisis responses to COVID-19 and the inevitable continuity responses as Member States ensure delivery of non–COVID-19 related health services (and treatment of "long COVID" might be considered here, too). This can be seen to couple with the politics and policy streams not only in connection with the May 2020 Franco-German and S&D calls, but also the elaboration of EU4Health to incorporate policy aspects such as the Europe Beating Cancer Plan. While the entrepreneurship evident in the EHU Initiative's outlining of possible Treaty amendments lends notable definition to the policy stream, it may also be seen to contribute to the politics stream, in view of the range of supporters (including both national and EU-level politicians).

The reservation of discussion of competences to the Conference on the Future of Europe offers an interesting dimension to both the policy and politics streams, because this would seem to play a decisive role in determining the window for Treaty change, both in terms of the extent to which it is open and the length of time it remains open. While there is some skepticism about the Conference's ability to effect change (Nguyen 2021), the novelty of the Conference initiative—relying on a different logic, format,

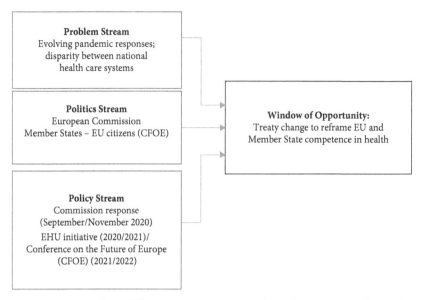

Figure 10.2 Coupling of the streams creating window of opportunity for EHU Vision 2: extending the EU's competence by reframing the EU–Member State competence in health (beyond crisis responses).

and legal basis (consultative, deliberative, and deliberative-constituent) (Alemanno 2021)—may give tentative grounds for optimism, or at least justify a more neutral stance. The effect of the Conference on the extent to which a window opens is difficult to assess, but if it is seen as a mechanism to engage actively with EU citizens, this may have notable implications for the constituency of the politics stream insofar as calls for a European Health Union have emanated not only from (national and EU-level) politicians but also medical professionals and civil society actors. The ability of medical professionals to influence national health policy can be significant, but is perhaps less evident at EU level. The ability of the Conference to affect the length of time any window remains open appears increasingly limited in view of the reduction in time allocated to it (from an original timeline of two years between May 2020 and May 2022, to approximately nine months to wind down in spring 2022 with approval of its conclusions—Alemanno 2021).

The extent to which there can be said to be a of the three streams might be considered undermined by the potential for the European Commission being present in both the politics and policy streams. The Commission's outline for a European Health Union in November 2020 was unequivocal that the legal basis for the initial proposals would be Article 168(5) TFEU, and that Member State competence in health would be fully respected (Commission November 2020). Indeed, scope for divergence—rather than confluence—may have been hinted at by the closing comment of the proposals: "The European Health Union will be as strong as Member States' commitment to it" (Commission November 2020). Further support for a lack of joining the three streams may be found in comments by Commissioner Kyriakides at the start of September 2021: "[a] strong European Health Union is not about redrawing the competences of Member States" would seem to underline this (Kyriakides cited in Deutsch 2021).

Concluding Remarks

September 2021 provided an important moment to reflect on the development of calls for a European Health Union in response to the COVID-19 pandemic. Approximately 18 months after the initial lockdowns across Europe, it became possible to start to identify further the parameters of a European Health Union—whether this as simply an extended EU-level crisis response device or a more robust mechanism to reconceptualize EU-level and Member State interaction regarding health (an issue of long-standing political sensitivity). The linking of the concept of a European Health Union with treaty change, perhaps with hindsight, appeared inevitable since the latter would represent a significant level of commitment, and a suitable rebuttal to the perceptions and misunderstandings of EU-level competence in health which accompanied the initial pandemic responses in spring 2020.

By juxtaposing some of the activities of the first 18 months of pandemic response with the expansion of EU-level interest in health across diverse policy areas, it is possible to contribute to the discussion of the need for a European Health Union. Making use of Kingdon's Multiple Streams Framework and identification of "windows of opportunity" enables us to start to identify what may be needed for (or missing from) ambitions for establishing a European Health Union. This has generated at least two main insights.

First, that the confluence of the problem, politics, and policy streams with regard to legislation intended merely to enshrine an extended EU-level mechanism for responding to health crises needs only to meet a certain threshold. Furthermore, the confluence is arguably unaffected by fluctuating factors that may prove more detrimental elsewhere (such as a notable reduction in budget).

Second, and conversely, that the confluence of the three streams needs to be more certain when attempting a more ambitious aim—such as Treaty change to reconceptualize respective EU and Member State competence in health. This confluence needs to support a window of opportunity which can open to a larger extent and for a longer period of time, given the complexity inherent in Treaty change.

Finally, the problem stream linked to the COVID-19 pandemic might be seen as comprising tributaries, both of crisis (hence unpredictable windows) and identifying underlying weaknesses in EU Member State health care systems—which are highlighted, but not caused, by a pandemic. This can have significant implications for the confluence of the problem stream with the politics and policy streams, and thus windows of opportunity and what can realistically be achieved with regard to "hard law" amendment.

Despite these different insights, if taken together, it might be considered that COVID-19 does represent an accelerating force for EU-level activity in health. This is clearly most evident in connection with EHU Vision 1, and it has yet to be seen how the more tentative confluence of the streams in connection with EHU Vision 2 may provide further opportunity to revisit EU and Member State competence interaction in the future. Certainly, it has been noted that in view of the political sensitivities that attach to health care, even a seemingly small change can actually prove significant (de Ruijter cited in Deutsch 2021).

References

Ackrill, Robert, Adrian Kay, and Nikolaos Zahariadis. 2013. "Ambiguity, multiple streams, and EU policy" *Journal of European Public Policy* 20 (6): 871–87.

Alemanno. Alberto. 2021. "Unboxing the Conference on the Future of Europe: A preliminary view on its democratic raison d'être and participatory architecture." HEC Paris Research Series, September 2021. https://papers.ssrn.com/sol3/papers.cfm?abstract_id=3925065.

Alemanno, Alberto. 2020. "Towards a European Health Union: Time to level up." *European Journal of Risk Regulation—Beyond COVID-19: Towards a European Health Union* 11 (4): 721–25

Andreangeli, Arianna. 2016. "Healthcare services, the EU single market and beyond: Meeting local needs in an open economy—How much market or how little market?" *Legal Issues of Economic Integration* 43 (2):145–72.

Azzopardi-Muscat, Natasha, Timo Clemens, Deborah Stoner, and Helmut Brand. 2015. "EU Country-Specific Recommendations for health systems in the European Semester process: Trends, discourse and predictors." *Health Policy* 119 (3): 375–83.

Bartlett, Oliver. 2020. "COVID-19, the European Health Union and the CJEU: Lessons from the case law on the banking union." *European Journal of Risk Regulation* 11 (4): 781–89.

Bazzan, Giulia. 2020. "Exploring integration trajectories for a European Health Union" *European Journal of Risk Regulation* 11 (4): 736–46.

Brooks, Ellie. 2019. "A new European commission for health?" *Global Health Policy Unit Blog*, December 20, 2019. https://ghpu.sps.ed.ac.uk/a-new-european-commission-for-health/.

Brooks, Eleanor, and Robert Geyer. 2020. "The development of EU health policy and the Covid-19 pandemic: trends and implications." *Journal of European Integration* 42 (8): 1057–76.

Brooks, Eleanor, and Mary Guy. 2021. "EU health law and policy—shaping a future research agenda." *Health Economics, Policy and Law*, 16 (1): 1–7.

Brooks, Eleanor, Anniek de Ruijter, and Scott L. Greer. 2021. "COVID-19 and EU health policy: From crisis to collective action." In *Social Policy in the European Union: State of Play 2020*, edited by Bart Vanhercke, Slavina Spasova, and Boris Fronteddu, 33–52. Brussels: ETUI.

Christiansen, Thomas, Gerda Falkner, and Knud Erik Jørgensen. 2002. "Theorising treaty reform: Beyond diplomacy and bargaining." *Journal of European Public Policy* 9 (1): 12-32.

Deutsch, Jillian. 2021. "Europe's 'health union' prepares for its first feeble steps." *Politico*, 1 September 2021. https://www.politico.eu/article/european-health-union-coronavirus-ema-hera-barda/.

Euractiv. 2021. "Merkel open to Treaty change to boost health powers." *Euractiv*, April 22, 2021. https://www.euractiv.com/section/future-eu/news/merkel-open-to-eu-treaty-change-to-boost-health-powers/.

European Commission. 2020a. "Communication from the Commission to the European Parliament, the Council, the European Economic and Social Committee and the Committee of the Regions, Building a European Health Union: Reinforcing the EU's resilience for cross-border health threats." COM/2020/724 final. November 11, 2020. https://eur-lex.europa.eu/legal-content/EN/TXT/PDF/?uri=CELEX:52020DC0724&from=EN.

European Commission. 2020b. "Commission welcomes political agreement on EU4Health." Press Release, Brussels, December 15, 2020. https://ec.europa.eu/commission/presscorner/detail/en/IP_20_2420.

European Commission. 2021. "Commission welcomes entry into force of EU4Health programme." Press Release, Brussels, March 26, 2021. https://ec.europa.eu/commission/presscorner/detail/en/ip_21_1344.

European Health Union Initiative, European Health Union. 2021. https://europeanhealthunion.eu/.

European Health Union Initiative, Manifesto for a European Health Union. 2021. https://europeanhealthunion.eu/#manifest.

Fortuna, Gerardo. 2020. "Franco-German couple set eyes on EU health sovereignty." *Euractiv*, May 19, 2020. https://www.euractiv.com/section/health-consumers/news/franco-german-couple-sets-eyes-on-eu-health-sovereignty/.

Fortuna, Gerardo. 2020. "Council meets Parliament halfway on EU health budget." *Euractiv*, November 11, 2020. https://www.euractiv.com/section/health-consumers/news/council-meets-parliament-halfway-on-eu-health-budget/.

Fraundorfer, Markus, and Neil Winn. 2021. "The emergence of post-Westphalian health governance during the COVID-19 pandemic: the European Health Union." *Disasters* 45 (11): 5–25. https://doi.org/10.1111/disa.12511.

Garben, Sacha. 2018. "Supporting Policies." In *The Law of the European Union* (5th ed,), edited by PJ Kuiper, F Ambtenbrink, D Curtin, B De Witte, A McDonnell, and S Van den Bogaert, ch 38. Alphen aan den Rijn: Wolters Kluwer.

Greer, Scott L. 2014. "The three faces of European Union health policy: Policy, markets and austerity." *Policy and Society* 33 (1): 13–24.

Greer, Scott L. 2015. "John W. Kingdon, Agendas, Alternatives, and Public Policies." In *The Oxford Handbook of Classics in Public Policy and Administration* edited by Martin Lodge, Edward C. Page, and Steven J. Balla, 417–32. Oxford: Oxford University Press.

Greer, Scott L. 2020. "How did the EU get the Coronavirus so wrong? And what can it do right next time?" *New York Times*, April 6, 2020.

Greer, Scott L., Nick Fahy, Heather A. Elliott, Matthias Wismar, Holly Jarman, and Willy Palm. 2014. *Everything You Always Wanted to Know about European Union Health Policies but Were Afraid to Ask*. Copenhagen: WHO Regional Office for Europe.

Greer, Scott L., Nick Fahy, Heather A. Elliott, Matthias Wismar, Holly Jarman, and Willy Palm. 2019. *Everything You Always Wanted to Know about European Union Health Policies but were Afraid to Ask*. (2nd edition). Copenhagen: WHO Regional Office for Europe.

Greer, Scott L., Holly Jarman, and Rita Baeten. 2016. "The new political economy of health care in the European Union: The impact of fiscal governance." *International Journal of Health Services* 46 (2): 262–82.

van de Gronden, Johan W. 2011. "The Treaty Provisions on Competition and Health Care." In *Health Care and EU Law*, edited by Johan W. van de Gronden, Erika Szyszczak, Ulla Neergaard, and Markus Krajewski, 265–94. Utrecht: TMC Asser Press.

van de Gronden, Johan W., and Erika Szyszczak. 2011. "Conclusions: Constructing a 'Solid' Multi-Layered Health Care Edifice" In *Health Care and EU Law*, edited by Johan W. van de Gronden, Erika Szyszczak, Ulla Neergaard, and Markus Krajewski, 481–96. Utrecht: TMC Asser Press.

van de Gronden, Johan W., and Erika Szyszczak. 2014. "Introducing competition principles into healthcare through EU law and policy: A case study of the Netherlands" *Medical Law Review* 22 (2): 238–54.

Guy, Mary. 2019. *Competition Policy in Healthcare—Frontiers in Insurance-Based and Taxation-Funded Systems*. Cambridge: Intersentia

Guy, Mary. 2020. "Towards a European health union: What role for member states?" *European Journal of Risk Regulation* 11 (4): 757–65.

Guy, Mary, and Wolf Sauter. 2017. "The History and Scope of EU Health Law and Policy." In *Research Handbook on EU Health Law and Policy*, edited by Tamara k. Hervey, Calum Alasdair Young, and Louise E. Bishop, 17–35. Cheltenham: Edward Elgar.

Hancher, Leigh, and Wolf Sauter. 2012. *EU Competition and Internal Market Law in the Healthcare Sector*. Oxford: Oxford University Press.

Hervey, Tamara K., and Jean V. McHale. 2004. *Health Law and the European Union*. Cambridge: Cambridge University Press.

Hervey, Tamara K., and Jean V. McHale. 2015. *European Union Health Law: Themes and Implications*. Cambridge: Cambridge University Press.

Hervey, Tamara K., and Bart Vanhercke. 2010. "Health Care and the EU: The Law and Policy Patchwork." In *Health Systems Governance in Europe: The Role of European Union Law and Policy*, edited by Elias Mossialos, Govin Permanand, Rita Baeten, and Tamara K. Hervey, 84–133. Cambridge: Cambridge University Press.

Hervey, Tamara K., and Anniek de Ruijter. 2020. "The dynamic potential of European Union health law." *European Journal of Risk Regulation* 11 (4): 726–35.

Herweg, Nicole, Nikolaos Zahariadis, and Reimut Zohlnhöfer. 2018. "The Multiple Streams Framework: Foundations, Refinements and Empirical Applications." In *Theories of the Policy Process*, 4th Edition, edited by Cristopher M. Weible and Paul A. Sabatier, 17–54. New York: Routledge.

Le HuffPost, "Qu'est-ce que "l'Europe de la santé dont parle Macron?" May 18, 2020. https://www.huffingtonpost.fr/entry/macron-europe-de-la-sante-coronavirus_fr_5 ec2cff1c5b6e323a3b9cebb.

Jones, Bryan D., and Frank R. Baumgartner. 2012. "From there to here: Punctuated equilibrium to the general punctuation thesis to a theory of government information processing." *Policy Studies Journal* 40 (1): 1–20.

Jones, Erik, R. Daniel Kelemen, and Sophie Meunier. 2021. "Failing forward? Crises and patterns of European integration." *Journal of European Public Policy*, 28 (10): 1519–36.

Kingdon, John W. 2014. *Agendas, Alternatives, and Public Policies*, 2nd Edition. Harlow: Pearson.

Lamping, Wolfram. 2005. "European integration and health policy: a peculiar relationship." In *Health Governance in Europe: Issues, Challenges and Theories*, edited by Monika Steffen, 18–48. London: Routledge.

Luena, Cèsar. 2021. "European Health Union: Strengthening Europe's post-pandemic competencies." *The Parliament Magazine*, July 27, 2021.

von der Leyen, Ursula. 2020. State of the Union Address by President von der Leyen at the European Parliament Plenary, September 16, 2020. https://ec.europa.eu/commission/presscorner/detail/en/SPEECH_20_1655.

von der Leyen, Ursula. 2021. State of the Union Address by President von der Leyen, Strasbourg, September 15, 2021. https://ec.europa.eu/commission/presscorner/detail/en/SPEECH_21_4701.

Morton, Andrew J.B. 2021. "European healthcare systems and the emerging influence of European competition policy." *Journal of Health Politics, Policy and Law* 46 (3): 467–86.

Natali, David. 2004. "Europeanization, policy arenas, and creative opportunism: the politics of welfare state reforms in Italy." *Journal of European Public Policy* 11 (6): 1077–95.

Nicoli, Francesco. 2019. "Crises, path dependency, and the five trilemmas of European integration: Seventy years of "failing forward" from the Common Market to the European Fiscal Union." The Amsterdam Centre for European Studies SSRN Research Paper 2019/05.

Nielsen, Nikolaj. 2020. "EU Commission aspires for Treaty change on health." *Euobserver*, May 29, 2020. https://euobserver.com/institutional/148503.

Nikolić, Bruno. 2021. "Applicability of EU competition law to healthcare providers: The dividing line between economic and noneconomic activities." *Journal of Health Politics, Policy and Law* 46 (1): 49–70.

Nowak, Tobias. 2010. "Of garbage cans and rulings: Judgments of the European Court of Justice in the EU legislative process." *West European Politics* 33 (4): 753–69

Nugent, Neill, and Sabine Saurugger. 2002. "Organizational structuring: the case of the European Commission and its external policy responsibilities." *Journal of European Public Policy* 9 (3): 345–64.

Parsons, Craig. 2003. *A Certain Idea of Europe*. New York: Cornell University Press.

Peers, Steve. 2012. "The future of EU treaty amendments." *Yearbook of European Law* 31 (1): 17–111.

Piris, Jean-Claude. 2010. *The Lisbon Treaty—A Legal and Political Analysis*. Cambridge: Cambridge University Press.

Prosser, Tony. 2010. "EU Competition Law and Public Services." In *Health Systems Governance in Europe: The Role of European Union Law and Policy*, edited by Elias Mossialos, Govin Permanand, Rita Baeten, and Tamara K. Hervey, 315–36. Cambridge: Cambridge University Press.

Purnhagen, Kai P., Anniek de Ruijter, Mark L. Flear, Tamara K. Hervey, and Alexia Herwig. 2020. "More competences than you knew? The web of health competence for European Union Action in response to the COVID-19 outbreak." *European Journal of Risk Regulation* 11 (2): 297–306.

de Ruijter, Anniek. 2019. *EU Health Law & Policy—the Expansion of EU Power in Public Health and Health Care*. Oxford: Oxford University Press.

Sindbjerg Martinsen, Dorte. 2012. "The Europeanization of Healthcare: Processes and Factors." In *Research Design in European Studies: Establishing Causality in Europeanization*, edited by Theofanis Exadaktylos and Claudio M. Radaelli, ch. 8, 141–159. Basingstoke: Palgrave MacMillan.

Sindbjerg Martinsen, Dorte, and Karsten Vrangbæk. 2008. "The Europeanisation of health care governance—implementing the market imperatives of Europe." *Public Administration* 86 (1): 169–84.

Socialists and Democrats. 2020a. Letter from I. García Pérez, H. Fritzon, and J. Gutteland to President von der Leyen, President Michel, and Prime Minister Plenkovic. May 7, 2020. https://www.socialistsanddemocrats.eu/sites/default/files/2020-05/european-health-union-letter-200507.pdf.

Socialists and Democrats. 2020b. "A European Health Union—Increasing EU Competence in Health—Coping with COVID19 and Looking to the Future." S&D Position Paper. May 12, 2020. https://www.socialistsanddemocrats.eu/sites/default/files/2020-05/european_health_union_sd_position_30512.pdf.

Steurs, Lies, Remco Van de Pas, Sarah Delputte, and Jan Orbie. 2018. "The global health policies of the EU and its member states: a common vision?" *International Journal of Health Policy and Management* 7 (5): 433–42.

Stone, Jon. 2020. "Angela Merkel calls for creation of European Health Union." *The Independent*, December 11, 2020.

Vollaard, Hans, Hester van der Bovenkamp, Dorte Sindbjerg Martinsen. 2016. "The making of a European healthcare union: A federalist perspective." *Journal of European Public Policy* 23 (2): 157–76.

Zahariadis, Nikolaos. 2008. "Ambiguity and choice in European public policy." *Journal of European Public Policy* 15 (4): 514–30.

Zohlnhöfer, Reimut, Nicole Herweg, and Friedbert Rüb. 2015. "Theoretically refining the multiple streams framework: An introduction." *European Journal of Political Research* 54 (3): 412–18.

11

Non-centralized Coordination during a Transboundary Crisis

Examining Coronavirus Pandemic Responses in Four Federal Systems

Natalie Glynn

Introduction

Governments must increasingly deal with issues that bridge jurisdictional and functional boundaries, such as climate change (Blondin and Boin 2020; Boin 2019), with the coronavirus pandemic of 2020 being yet another example of a crisis spanning multiple borders and policy areas. Presented with a crisis that could potentially impact their entire population and territorial reach, leaders of municipalities, regions, and nations around the world sought solutions for their constituents while their counterparts elsewhere did likewise for the same threat. From an emergency management (EM) perspective, this presented a unique challenge because EM is normally predicated on the assumption that the lowest level of government as possible should manage an emergency response, calling on higher levels of government or horizontal partnerships only once they become overwhelmed (Henstra 2013). Yet, when governments (of all levels) reached out during this crisis, there was little help to be found as everyone sought the same resources and expertise for themselves (Boffey et al. 2020). In this way, the coronavirus pandemic presented the world with a major issue that required collective action to appropriately address.

There are a variety of ways in which governments can respond to the coordination challenge that collective action problems present, but in the

Natalie Glynn, *Non-centralized Coordination during a Transboundary Crisis* In: *European Social Policy and the COVID-19 Pandemic.* Edited by: Stefanie Börner and Martin Seeleib-Kaiser, Oxford University Press.
© Oxford University Press 2023. DOI: 10.1093/oso/9780197676189.003.0011

context of a crisis, governments have tended to prioritize administrative co-ordination or centralization (Boin 2019; Bolleyer 2009). Perhaps because of this fundamental need to assign responsibility and accountability to spe-cific government actors, it has been argued that crises demonstrate where sovereignty truly lies in a federal system (Palermo 2020). In administrative coordination, bureaucrats aim to clarify boundaries by stipulating the roles and responsibilities of the varied affected stakeholders, which takes place within and between ministries or agencies rather than at a political level (Bolleyer 2009). Centralization, on the other hand, seeks to transcend the boundary issue by raising the responsibility for decision-making to another jurisdictional level that encompasses and applies to all the affected lower-level jurisdictions. Therefore, by requiring collective action, crises test plans, systems, and institutions such that they assist in clarifying the roles and responsibilities of different governments and may even lead to policy or in-stitutional change.

In contrast to both traditional administrative coordination and centralization, there is another style of horizontal coordination that prioritizes joint decision-making in the political, not just the bureau-cratic sphere, while avoiding a transfer of authority to another juris-dictional level. Called non-centralization, this type of coordination supports policy harmonization across diverse jurisdictions (Csehi 2017) rather than simply clarifying which government (or agencies or ministries) is responsible for what aspect(s) of the issue. Among a variety of activities, governments were tasked with engaging in three key aspects of management during the COVID-19 pandemic: information and com-munication, provision of care, and outbreak containment.[1] As such, the coronavirus pandemic provides an opportunity to investigate the coor-dination challenges and solutions faced by different polities. Examining the first nine months of the pandemic, this chapter investigates the decision-making and coordination of freedom-of-movement policies that arose during the responses in four different federal systems. The chapter asks: *How did collective action develop in different federal systems during the COVID-19 crisis?*

---

[1] This list does not include issues of economic fallout or financial stabilization, which are not within the scope of this chapter. See Caravita et al. (2021) for an overview of the fiscal response to the pandemic crisis in the European Union.

Responding to the Crisis: Horizontal Coordination in Federal Systems

Throughout 2020 there were variously calls for powers to be centralized in different federal systems and pieces lauding the value of decentralization in the form of localized and responsive measures (Palermo 2020). So, was this the hour of centralization or decentralization? Looking at the responses in different federal systems seems to contradict both stances. Instead, this chapter evidences coordinated decision-making and activities among lower-level governments and between the lower levels and the federal level, rather than transfers of authority to higher levels or significant unilateral decision-making at lower levels. Thus, one might instead see this as the hour of non-centralization, where lower-level governments avoided ceding any sovereignty while also recognizing the necessity *and value* of working together.

There are three different conceptual issues to clarify in order to examine this phenomenon of intergovernmental coordination: decision-making in federal systems, non-centralized coordination, and the intergovernmental council (IGC). While there are several different activities governments needed to engage in throughout the pandemic, decision-making was a key predecessor to other activities, which is why this analysis focuses on the decision-making arrangements that arose during the crisis period. Adding to the distinction between decentralized and centralized decision-making, the concept of non-centralization differentiates between two types of sub-unit decision-making: unilateral versus coordinated. Finally, the IGC illustrates one of the ways in which intergovernmental arrangements can be modified to suit non-centralization. The following section explains these points further.

Making Decisions in Federal Systems

Of the seven key activities in any crisis response (namely detection, sense-making, decision-making, coordination, meaning-making, communication, and accountability) (Backman and Rhinard 2018), this work focuses on decision-making. There are two dimensions to decision-making in a federal system that are on a continuum from (1) centralized to decentralized and from (2) unilateral to coordinated (Hegele and Schnabel 2021), as shown in Figure 11.1. The first dimension is about the "location" of the decision.

Centralized
Decision-Making

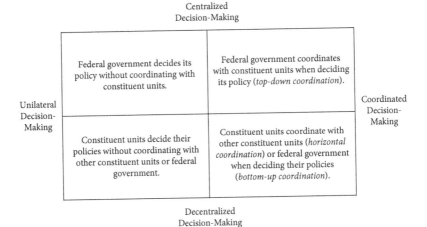

	Federal government decides its policy without coordinating with constituent units.	Federal government coordinates with constituent units when deciding its policy (*top-down coordination*).
Unilateral Decision-Making		Coordinated Decision-Making
	Constituent units decide their policies without coordinating with other constituent units or federal government.	Constituent units coordinate with other constituent units (*horizontal coordination*) or federal government when deciding their policies (*bottom-up coordination*).

Decentralized
Decision-Making

Figure 11.1 Federal approaches to decision-making (modified from Hegele and Schnabel 2021, p. 6).

That is, is the decision-making occurring at the level of the central government or at the level of the constituent units? The second dimension describes the nature of the decision-making, which indicates whether it was taken without collaboration with other governments (unilateral) or in collaboration with other governments (coordinated). To better understand where the power and legitimacy to make decisions was situated and the extent to which governments coordinated with one another, this chapter asks where decision-making was situated and how it was characterized.

Non-centralization as a Strategy to Retain Sub-unit Authority

As previously noted, there is often pressure for and argument made in favor of centralization during a crisis. It is assumed that this will ensure uniformity in the response, clarify decision-making during the crisis, and increase accountability in the aftermath of the crisis. On the other hand, crises can be the critical juncture that precipitates decentralization or disintegration. In this case, the argument is that lower levels of government can more effectively respond to the local pressures and context, which may lead to the strengthening of their political position vis-à-vis the central government (Dosenrode 2012).

However, both scenarios fall onto the unilateral decision-making side of the possible federal styles outlined above. Looking to the coordinated decision-making side, we see three other possible scenarios: top-down coordination (of federal policies), bottom-up coordination, and horizontal coordination. The lower-right corner of Figure 11.1, which includes the horizontal coordination of constituent units by a central entity and bottom-up coordination from constituent units themselves, represents a third form of intergovernmental relations (IGR) called *non-centralization*.

Hence, centralization and decentralization do not account for all the ways that sub-federal and federal-level governments can relate to one another (Csehi 2017). Centralization describes an arrangement whereby the central government has unilateral policymaking authority of a given policy area; for example, the federal government in the United States of America (US) has the sole power to initiate wars. Centralization can also describe a scenario where the sub-units enact the policy, so long as it was the central government that passed the legislation outlining the policy (thereby ensuring uniformity of policy throughout the federal system) (Hegele and Schnabel 2021). Decentralization, on the other hand, describes effectively the opposite—the sub-federal governments have the primary policymaking authority of a given policy area. For example, education policy is typically a devolved power in federations. In this case, constituent units decide unilaterally on policy for their territory, which applies only in their territory (Hegele and Schnabel 2021). Decentralized decision-making is often associated with differences and localized variation throughout the federal system. However, this need not necessarily be the case if coordination is pursued.

As such, non-centralization is distinct in that *horizontal coordination* is promoted in a given policy area without transferring policymaking authority. Csehi (2017) notes that in this decision-making arrangement "the major function of intergovernmental relations is not to assist a formal transfer of competences from one jurisdiction to another but rather to substitute it with horizontal coordinating mechanisms" (Csehi 2017, 566). In this case we see policy uniformity arising not because the central government has created a policy that applies uniformly throughout the federation, but because sub-units converge on similar policies through intentional coordination. That is, we see constituent units cooperating in a policy area to produce net benefits for all involved, without the policy authority being transferred to a higher order of government.

Csehi (2017) argues that there are two different conditions that promote or facilitate the development of non-centralization compared to centralization. First, constituent units find it increasingly difficult to act alone in the policy area. This development is best understood through "a closer look at the character of policy challenges (i.e., the complexity and interdependence of the matter)" (Csehi 2017, 566), but it is easy to see how the coronavirus pandemic fits such a condition. Second, these incentives for horizontal coordination are matched by a preference for vertical autonomy, which is to say that the constituent units do not want to give up their policymaking authority in this field (again, noticeably relevant for EM and public health [PH] during the pandemic). When these two conditions exist, there are two possible solutions for the governments involved: (1) reform existing institutions to meet the new demands, or (2) create new institutions (Csehi 2017).

Intergovernmental Relations and Intergovernmental Councils

This is the point where the classification of IGR and issues of intergovernmental venues arises. Csehi (2017) asserts that this phenomenon shifts the role of the federal government from that of "law-maker to that of an honest broker and administrator" (Csehi 2017, 574), where its "main purpose will be to administer, support and facilitate horizontal coordination" (Csehi 2017, 566). However, this work identifies another IGR that could develop to support such activities: an IGC (which may or may not include federal actors). A bottom-up coordination arrangement in which constituent governments within a federation form a council absent any federal actors, such as the Council of the Federation (CoF) in Canada or the National Governors Association (NGA) in the United States, could serve to facilitate horizontal policy coordination without participation from the federal government.[2]

This chapter uses the development (or not) of such IGCs to distinguish between other forms of IGR and IGCs. Employing the framework developed by Behnke and Mueller (2017), a distinction is made between traditional vertical and horizontal relations and the new relationships that are established

---

[2] It may also serve a joint lobbying function with the federal level of government, which is particularly true of IGR in the US, where horizontal policy coordination between states is limited by separation of powers between the executive and legislative branches (Bolleyer 2009).

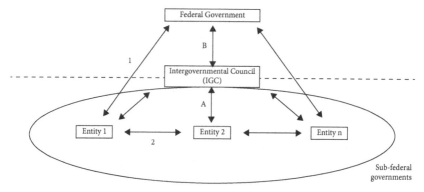

Figure 11.2 Patterns of IGR (modified from Behnke and Mueller 2017).

by the existence of an IGC. Figure 11.2 illustrates the distinct nature of IGCs compared to other kinds of IGR, namely that a new entity, the council, is created to mediate relations. The arrows labeled 1 and 2 describe the traditional direct vertical and horizontal relationships between governments. An example of horizontal relationships depicted by arrow 2 would be state compacts in the United States. The arrows labeled A and B, on the other hand, describe the relationship between the different levels of government with the new entity, the IGC.

The creation of such a council is an important distinction because it creates a new political actor in the intergovernmental system. Such councils have varying levels of institutionalization, but at a minimum they have defined membership, specifications regarding the convening of meetings, and document their proceedings. Thus, we can see how the IGC is a new political entity that acts in the space between the federal government and the sub-federal governments. The IGC's unique interest in the development of successful IGR creates an incentive for the IGC to advocate for new policy bargains that may not have been propositioned in a traditional intergovernmental arrangement (Bolleyer 2009).

Methodology

Examining the pandemic responses in federal systems is useful for investigating non-centralization because PH and EM are both policy areas whose policymaking authority are typically reserved to lower levels of government in federal systems (Henstra 2013; Steytler 2021). Even in the cases where national health care systems exist, there is usually a delegating of management and organization to the state or even in some instances the local authority levels of government. In terms of PH, the federal government often acts in an advisory capacity or support function to subsidize efforts that are controlled or managed by the states. In the case of EM, a similar subsidiarity of responsibility and management exists. Local entities take the lead in responding, and only if they are overwhelmed or unable to respond effectively are they supported by state governments. Then, typically, only if the state level is overwhelmed may the federal level of government intervene, usually at the specific request of the state. Notably, when higher levels of government begin assisting in a relief effort, there is not necessarily a change in the command structure (Henstra 2013). Thus, examining a crisis in the areas of PH and EM provides a good opportunity to better understand non-centralization as a specific phenomenon in IGR, because the sub-federal units generally have authority in these areas that they likely prefer to keep, yet the crisis demands collective action.

A comparative analysis of the COVID-19 responses in four federal systems spanning the period from February 1, 2020 to October 31, 2020 (a timeframe that captures the first wave in its entirety in all cases and the second wave in part or in whole) is presented. Using a qualitative case study approach (Gerring 2006), the analysis relies on a diversity of documentary evidence, including publicly available data such as news media accounts, government announcements and meeting minutes, and recently published research (i.e., journal articles and gray literature) to develop the case profiles.

Case selection was guided by commonalities in federal system development and differences and commonalities regarding aspects of the pandemic response that would affect the development of collective action. While the EU to some extent defies traditional polity definitions, it is most similar to the concept of a "coming-together" federation in which constituent units choose to pool their resources and sovereignty to act as a single unit in some respects (Stepan 1999). Drawing on Blondin and Boin's (2020) review of crisis and collective action literature, there are four important points of comparison to consider during this crisis when investigating variation in the development of collective action: level of politicization of the pandemic, size of the affected group (i.e., number of constituent units of the federal system), extent and type of preexisting IGR (in this case, especially experience with IGCs), and leadership.

Along these lines and as coming-together federal systems, Australia, Canada, and the United States stand out as useful comparison cases to the EU in this crisis. Australia has historically relied heavily on IGCs to facilitate decision-making within the federation (Phillimore and Fenna 2017), and there was a general political consensus on the key aspects of the pandemic response (Aroney and Boyce 2021). Canada, on the other hand, has mixed experience with IGCs and a reputation for decentralization (Bolleyer 2009), but there was also little politicization of the pandemic and high levels of cross-party consensus on potential responses (Schertzer and Paquet 2020). Similar to Australia, the EU has a strong level of institutionalization and in some respects is constitutionally required to be intergovernmental in terms of decision-making (Coman 2018). The United States, in contrast, has numerous IGCs that serve primarily a policy-learning or lobbying function, rather than supporting the development of coordinated decision-making among states (Bolleyer 2009, 114–15). Perhaps most importantly, the pandemic was heavily politicized in the United States compared to the other federal systems, with the two main parties taking drastically different stances on the nature of the problem as well as potential solutions (Downey and Myers 2020; Rozell and Wilcox 2020). As such, we can expect that coordination might be highest in Australia and the EU, moderate in Canada, and least likely in the United States.

Case Studies

In the following section, the case studies for Australia, Canada, and the United States precede the EU case. Each case includes a description of the decision-making arrangements that arose in the federal system (focusing on those for freedom of movement policies) followed by an overview of key freedom of movement related decisions that occurred during the study period.

Australia

While several preexisting institutional arrangements were utilized for the crisis response, they were adapted to fit the need by increasing their frequency of occurrence and sometimes the scope of their authority to make decisions (as predicted by Csehi, 2017).

Decision-making Arrangements

Two main institutions have been the primary sources of decision-making during the crisis in Australia: The Australian Health Protection Principal Committee (AHPPC) and the National Cabinet. The National Cabinet is the primary decision-making body for the federation and is the main innovation in terms of IGR during the crisis. As the primary decision-making body, it is being advised by a number of commissions and committees, such as the COVID-19 Coordination Commission, which focuses on business and economic issues. During the COVID-19 pandemic response, the AHPPC has acted as the primary health policy body advising the National Cabinet, providing up-to-date information on matters such as incidence and prevalence of the virus in Australia and making suggestions for preventive PH measures to implement (Aroney and Boyce 2021).

The National Cabinet is responsible for standard-setting and coordination of policies within the Australian federation. It was initially convened by the Australian Prime Minister in March 2020 and included all but one of the members of a preexisting institution, namely the Council of Australian Governments (COAG). Historically, COAG was an infrequent organizing body that met perhaps once a year at the discretion of the Australian prime minister, but as part of the crisis response the convened members agreed to hold the meetings weekly (Downey and Myers 2020; Elphick 2020). Originally composed of the heads of government of the Commonwealth and states[3] and the president of the Australian Local Government Association (Phillimore and Fenna 2017), the head of the Local Government Association was not included in the initial invitation, and the new body was quickly named the National Cabinet. Notably, this new IGC has since replaced the old COAG and has been branded as the future of Australian federalism. That is, it will be the primary IGC managing federal–state relations moving forward (Aroney and Boyce 2021). As such, the National Cabinet is now a body that meets monthly to discuss federation-level issues and policymaking, even outside of pandemic related topics (Department of the Prime Minister and Cabinet 2020). The choice to remove local government from the IGC, which has become much more consequential and influential in state–federal relations than the former COAG, is both notable and interesting but not within

---

[3] In addition to state and provincial governments, there are territorial and tribal governments in Australia, Canada, and the US, all of which were involved in responding to the COVID-19 pandemic. This work refers collectively to the states and territories as "states" and the provinces and territories as "provinces" for reasons of parsimony.

the scope of this work to consider further. It should be noted, however, that it was criticized for creating a coordination problem between the local and state levels in terms of tailoring responses. That is, states were criticized for being too centralized in their responses and not allowing tailoring to local conditions at lower levels (Aroney and Boyce 2021).

Managing Freedom of Movement

The first decision was unilaterally made by the prime minister of Australia on February 1, 2020, to restrict entry for individuals traveling from China. Tasmania would be the first state to introduce policies regarding movement of individuals into its territory, namely the suspension of cruise ships into its ports on March 15, 2020 (Worthington 2020). Reporting does not clearly indicate that this was a decision taken in concert with other governments, but the decision did come two days after the first meeting of the National Cabinet on March 13, 2020. Subsequently, between March 20 and March 25, four of the eight state governments implemented border restrictions limiting the freedom of movement within the Australian federation, with most requiring 14-day quarantine periods for people entering (Brown 2020). Reporting (as well as the similarity in guidance, restrictions, and timing) indicates these were coordinated efforts. After this initial period, decisions regarding movement within the federation were clearly discussed in the National Cabinet meetings and announced by National Cabinet press releases (in addition to state website updates). While some variance from National Cabinet preferences remained, the decision-making was taken in this venue, even when it was characterized by dissent from the majority (such as Queensland, Western Australia, and Tasmania declining to join the Agricultural Worker Movement Code in September 2020 when the other states chose to do so) (Verley and Hermann 2020). Thus, notwithstanding what appeared to be a unified approach to the pandemic, there was considerable variation in the implementation of policies that were agreed upon in the National Cabinet in a coordinated-decentralized fashion.

Despite the obvious discussions and coordination, the maintenance of internal borders varied somewhat throughout the pandemic and was frequently characterized in the media as a patchwork of restrictions that were confusing for travelers. Even as criteria for labeling areas "low-risk" or "high-risk" were established, the states continued to set their own thresholds for allowing travelers to enter their domain, and set their own requirements (or not) for quarantine. That said, throughout the pandemic, all of the Australian governments remained consistent in their advisement that individuals avoid travel to remote areas or Aboriginal communities, as these are considered particularly vulnerable should the coronavirus be introduced. Finally, while there were at least four court cases challenging the legality of the restrictions on freedom of movement, only two were brought during the February to October 2020 period, and all have since been rejected by the courts (Karp 2020, 2021; Trask 2020; Whitbourn et al. 2020).

In summary, the federal government convened an archetypal IGC, the National Cabinet (itself an *adaptation* of a preexisting IGC), where the heads of the federal and state governments, consulting one another, acted as the primary decision-making body for the federation. Through this IGC, the states made decisions with the federal government in a primarily coordinated-decentralized fashion, with some coordinated-centralized decisions also taking place. In areas with federal primacy, some unilateral decisions were taken early on, such as the restriction on travel with China, but once the IGC was established, even policies for which the federal government has primacy were discussed within this venue (a strategy that may have increased good faith between participating governments and increased the perceived legitimacy of decisions). In this respect, the Australian case falls neatly within the scenario predicted by Csehi (2017) in which existing institutions are adapted and the federal government may act as an honest broker of cooperation among the sub-units.

Canada

In the Canadian case study, there was a reliance on technical positions and bodies to drive policy development and cross-provincial arrangements,

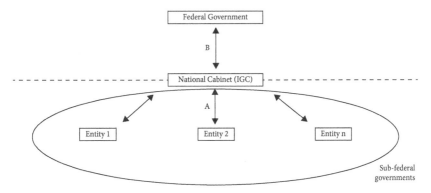

Figure 11.3 IGR Patterns during the Australian COVID-19 response.

highlighting how long-standing, dense administrative coordination can substitute for political coordination (Poirier and Michelin 2021; Segatto et al.
2021). Chief public health officers of every province and the federal government were regularly debriefing the public and advising on the latest PH advice (Adeel et al. 2020; Schertzer and Paquet 2020).

Decision-making Arrangements
The provincial and federal governments communicated regularly throughout
the pandemic but did not invest heavily in the development of intergovernmental venues. For example, Prime Minister Trudeau held an informal weekly
call with the heads of the provinces, and, as the nature and scale of the coronavirus crisis became more apparent, the preexisting annual event—called
the First Ministers' Meeting (March 12–13, 2020)—which was originally
scheduled to "address the political alienation of Alberta and Saskatchewan,"
was updated to include the pandemic (Tasker 2020). However, in contrast
to the Australian case, the weekly calls remained informal throughout the
study period, and while similar to the original Australian COAG in that it
was an annual event that facilitated IGR (Bothwell 2014), the First Ministers'
Meeting did not become more frequent nor more institutionalized in response to the pandemic. In fact, the next summit did not take place again
until the middle of September 2020 (Burston 2020). Publicly available documentation indicates that both the regular phone calls and the First Ministers'
Meetings were primarily information-sharing sessions rather than decision-
making venues, which remained the case for the duration of the study period.

Thus, while there were some intergovernmental venues for cooperation
in the Canadian case, the federal and provincial governments largely organized themselves separately from one another, as expected in a dualist federal
arrangement (Poirier and Michelin 2021; Segatto et al. 2021). For example,
the federal government focused on forming federal-level committees that
were meant to liaise with and organize intergovernmental coordination.
However, official documentation and reporting indicate that there were no
provincial representatives included in the membership of these bodies, two
of which were particularly prominent in the federal response: the Cabinet
Committee and the Incident Response Group. Both explicitly stated a purpose of facilitating intergovernmental coordination, though they did not
include non-federal members. On March 4, 2020, the Trudeau government
announced the creation of a Cabinet Committee that would "meet regularly
to ensure whole-of-government leadership, coordination, and preparedness

for a response to the health and economic impacts of the virus," including "coordination of efforts with other orders of government" (Prime Minister of Canada 2020a). The Incident Response Group is a federal-level decision-making body that is convened to respond to serious incidents. The group of relevant ministers began meeting in late January 2020 to assess the threat of a pandemic and begin considering policy responses. It was regularly briefed by the Chief Public Health Officer of Canada and other Government of Canada officials (Prime Minister of Canada 2020b).

Meanwhile, the provincial governments largely organized their own interests independent of the federal government. To this end, the provincial governments turned to existing relationships and intergovernmental venues, such as the CoF and the Council of Atlantic Premiers, to organize horizontally during the crisis. The CoF is an existing intergovernmental body that represents the provincial governments and acts as a bargaining venue to consolidate horizontal interests in advance of meetings with the federal government. Initially, the CoF wrote to the federal government in April to discourage it from invoking the Emergencies Act (Council of the Federation 2020a). Then, later in April, the heads of the provinces released another statement through the CoF outlining the principles they had agreed on in terms of opening up the economy and easing restrictions on public life (Council of the Federation 2020b 2020c). Additionally, the Council of Atlantic Premiers was instrumental in the development of a freedom-of-movement agreement between its member provinces in July 2020 (The Council of Atlantic Premiers 2020).

In terms of decision-making, the PH apparatus of Canada came to the fore. Throughout the pandemic, the Public Health Agency of Canada (PHAC) acted as a primary coordinator of intergovernmental actions at the federal level and promoted information sharing. By activating the Emergency Operations Centre on January 15, 2020, the PHAC became engaged in planning and coordination of the federal-level PH response efforts, in collaboration with international, federal, and provincial partners (Canadian Public Health Association 2021). This dense administrative coordination was supported by a strong preexisting network for collaboration in the PH apparatus of Canada, which included weekly coordinating calls and the Pan-Canadian Public Health Network, which have both existed for more than a decade (Bolleyer 2009; Segatto et al. 2021). As such, the PHAC and the provincial health departments were key actors involved in the aggregation of data and the formulating of policy. In fact, nearly 40% of policies enacted at the provincial level in the first four months of the crisis originated in the regional

PH agencies (Adeel et al. 2020). In terms of organizing cross-border issues, these agencies largely interacted with their nearest neighbors, though there was also ongoing communication between the regional PH departments and PHAC for federation-wide situational awareness. It was through Canada's Chief Public Health Officer that PHAC remained in close contact with provincial Chief Medical Officers of Health to share information, coordinate response efforts, and support informed vigilance as the situation evolved (Prime Minister of Canada 2020a). However, the PHAC role, similar to that of the US Centers for Disease Control and Prevention (CDC), remained advisory throughout the pandemic, offering guidelines and recommendations rather than having the power to issue mandates (Adeel et al. 2020).

Managing Freedom of Movement

Similar to the Australian case, the federal government took unilateral action early in the pandemic to limit movement of people from outside of Canada. On January 22, 2020, the federal government implemented screening for passengers coming back from China in airports in Toronto, Vancouver, and Montreal, which was expanded to all international passengers at 10 airports on February 20 (Canadian Public Health Association 2021). Moreover, the Canadian provinces began unilaterally implementing restrictions on freedom of movement within the federation from mid-March 2020 (CBC News 2020). However, there appeared to be more horizontal efforts in Canada than in Australia to organize "travel bubbles" whereby the residents of a few cooperating provinces could freely travel within their borders but not outside of them. The so-called "Atlantic Travel Bubble" was the first to be formalized, and the negotiations for it were centered in the IGC called the Council of Atlantic Premiers, which does not include any federal representatives (The Council of Atlantic Premiers 2020; Vigliotti 2020). While seen as largely successful for these provinces, there were legal challenges to the restrictions on freedom of movement (English and Murphy 2020). However, similar to the Australian case, the challenges were generally struck down by the courts. Notably, though, in at least one case the court found that the restriction of freedom of movement is generally outside of the purview of the provinces but that the power of PH, which is theirs, could override this in a genuine emergency, such as the pandemic (Cooke 2020).

In summary, Canada used some preexisting IGCs to facilitate lobbying between levels of government and information sharing, but these IGCs were not converted to decision-making bodies for the federation like the National

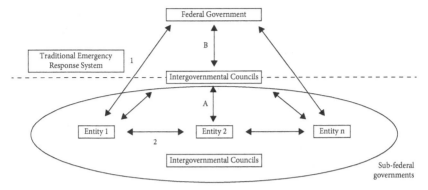

Figure 11.4 IGR Patterns during the Canadian COVID-19 response.

Cabinet in Australia. Instead, these IGCs primarily acted as venues for information sharing, policy learning and transfer, and lobbying of the federal government. The notable exception to this trend was the Council of the Atlantic Premiers that facilitated the development of uniform inter-provincial travel policy (Poirier and Michelin 2021), which is likely related to the fact that this IGC is more institutionalized than other Canadian IGCs and has a longer history of coordinated decision-making (Bolleyer 2009). As Bolleyer (2009) has explained, the nature of the power-concentrating, majoritarian parliamentary system in Canadian provinces discourages them from engaging in both horizontal coordination against the federal government and horizontal–vertical coordination with the federal government.

United States of America

The United States has many intergovernmental organizations, but these IGR venues are not typically used for coordinated or joint decision-making (Bolleyer 2009). Instead, these organizations act as policy learning and transfer venues and sources of joint lobbying of the federal government. This function continued to be the norm throughout the pandemic, and traditional horizontal and vertical relationships predominated in the development of IGR during the US pandemic response.

Decision-making Arrangements
While a number of different intergovernmental organizations exist (e.g., the NGA, National Conference of State Legislatures, National Association of

Counties, and The Council of State Governments), there was little evidence that these intergovernmental venues were used for policy coordination or decision-making (as opposed to sharing and learning) during the study period (Kincaid and Leckrone 2021). In fact, the US response was largely characterized by governors declaring states of emergency that empowered them with broad police powers, which they used to enforce things like "lockdowns," mask mandates, and quarantines. According to Adeel et al. (2020), fully 90% of the policies enacted between January 24 and April 24, 2020 in states originated with governors (p. 575).

The US response was consistently described as chaotic and lacking coordination between states and the federal government. The federal government was criticized early on (April) for not having a national strategy, a criticism which continued well into the pandemic (July and August) (Dilanian and De Luce 2020; Ruoff 2020; Tanne 2020). The federal response was also characterized by disagreements between, and political grandstanding from, the president and prominent Democrats in the congress and Democratic governors of several states. While there were calls for a more coordinated national approach, the federal-level executive branch generally avoided acting as a convener or administrator of coordination between the states. Notably absent from the US response in comparison to the other cases was regular communication between the heads of the federal and state governments, in the form of conference calls or meetings, for example.

In lieu of national coordination, governors sought to establish regional cooperations on key issues, such as interstate travel restrictions and personal protective equipment (PPE) purchasing (Kincaid and Leckrone 2021; Peters 2021). For example, in the Northeast, governors of seven states (New York, Connecticut, Delaware, Massachusetts, New Jersey, Pennsylvania, and Rhode Island) created a council to manage a regional supply chain for acquiring PPE and a shared framework for reopening their economies (Cohen 2020b; Governor, New York State 2020a). Some of these negotiations do appear to have been supported by or started in calls organized by the NGA, but the NGA appeared to be an initiation venue rather than a decision-making body. Ultimately, states with historically strong economic or cultural ties developed regional partnerships through the established state compact process (Rogers 2020).

At the federal level, the response remained primarily advisory in the domain of preventive PH measures, instead focusing on financial support for states, businesses, and individuals. In terms of coordination, the US response relied primarily on the traditional emergency response architecture that entails a standard incident command structure which, among other things, organizes the gathering of information from and dissemination to state and tribal officials. This National Response Coordination Center was activated on January 31, 2020, when President Trump declared a state of emergency (Aubrey 2020). Having no legal authority to impose policy decisions, the CDC maintained its advisory role throughout the pandemic, issuing guidelines for individual behavior and advice for states regarding safe reopening plans. This information was disseminated directly from the CDC through its website and Health Alert Network and through the national associations of PH professionals, including the Association of State and Territorial Health Officials and the National Association of County and City Health Officials (Centers for Disease Control and Prevention 2020).

Managing Freedom of Movement

Similar to Australia and Canada, the federal government took early unilateral action to limit travel of individuals from outside of the country into the United States, with the president issuing an executive order restricting the travel of individuals to and from China on January 31, 2020 (Aubrey 2020). This unilateral action on external border control arose again later when travel from Europe was restricted (Baker et al. 2020). However, as community transmission became increasingly evident, states also took unilateral actions to limit freedom of movement into their territories. Typically, these orders involved the requirement for entering individuals to quarantine for a mandatory 14-day period, which was enforced by state National Guard members in some cases (National Conference of State Legislatures [NCSL] 2020; Palmer 2020). At the end of March, Florida was the first state to implement such restrictions on interstate travel by requiring a mandatory 14-day quarantine for travelers from New York, New Jersey, and Connecticut (Holcombe 2020; LeBlanc 2020).

There were, however, examples of coordinated action at the state level. For example, the governors of New York, New Jersey, and Connecticut issued a joint travel advisory in June for individuals traveling from areas of high transmission (defined as "a positive test rate higher than 10 per 100,000 residents over a 7-day rolling average or a state with a 10% or higher positivity rate over a 7-day rolling average") to quarantine if entering their jurisdictions (Governor, New York State 2020b). Additionally, the Western States Compact was announced in mid-April after governors of California, Oregon, and Washington negotiated an agreement on policies such as common travel restrictions and "opening up" policies (Governor, State of California 2020). A similar compact was created around the same time in the Northeast (Cohen 2020a). These compacts typically arose between states that had long-standing compact agreements in other areas, such as the Port Authority between New York and New Jersey (Rogers 2020; Tatum 2020).

In summary, the United States relied on traditional horizontal and vertical IGR, with preexisting IGCs playing only limited lobbying and information-sharing roles for state governments. This is consistent with the history of interstate relations in the United States, where states have compulsory power sharing that divides the legislature and executive, which undermines their ability to consolidate interests as a collective and then represent them in an intergovernmental setting (Bolleyer 2009). In short, there is not one government interest but at least two interests for every state, namely the governor's interests versus the legislature's, which inhibits the use of IGCs for policy coordination. Notably, no new intergovernmental institutions were developed during the crisis, nor were preexisting ones reconfigured to meet the new coordination challenges. Rather, states turned to established interstate relations to coordinate and develop intergovernmental agreements at the regional level. Thus, the US response was dominated by unilateral centralized and decentralized decision-making with some regional horizontal coordination.

European Union

Initially, the EU's response was criticized as devolving into nation states fending for themselves and as demonstrating a distinct lack of solidarity

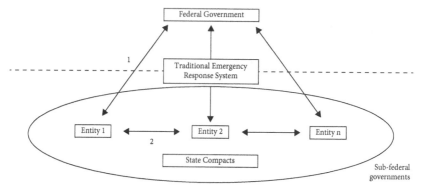

Figure 11.5 IGR Patterns during the US COVID-19 response.

(Brattberg 2020). However, both the institutional arrangements and sub-unit behaviors were remarkably similar to those seen in the other case studies, where unilateral decision-making by sub-unit governments did not call into question the very existence of the federal governments. Significantly, the ability of the EU institutions to serve a coordinating and supportive function for Member States increased as the pandemic unfolded (Caravita et al. 2021). Despite this early criticism, the overall impression was that EU citizens wanted more, not less, coordination and support from the EU throughout the crisis (Butler 2020).

Decision-making Arrangements

Comparing the decision-making arrangements of the EU to the federal states makes explicit the institutionalized intergovernmental nature of some EU decision-making. For example, except in the case of non-legislative acts that have been delegated to the Commission, decisions at EU level require inter-governmental consultation and agreement in the form of comitology committee deliberation and/or Council approval. While the Commission has the sole authority to draft and propose legislation, this legislation can only come into effect with the explicit approval of the Council and the Parliament together, both of which have the right to amend or reject the legislation. This process is referred to as the "Community Method" and is part of the ordinary legislative procedure of the EU (Coman 2018). Reviewing the legally binding activities of the EU during the study period, many of the activities pertained to issues of the single market and financial assistance, which are outside the scope of this chapter. Instead, the focus here is on the issue of freedom of movement, which was generally handled through the second method of decision-making in the EU, the intergovernmental method. The intergovernmental method centers the European Council and the Council of Ministers as the agenda-setters and decision-makers, whereas the Parliament and the Commission provide consultative and supporting roles, respectively (Coman 2018).

Despite the intergovernmental method being the primary method of decision-making (in policies concerning freedom of movement), the Commission was tasked by the European Council with producing documents, research, and guidelines for its review and approval (General Secretariat of the Council 2020a, 2020c). Thus, as the pandemic unfolded, a core function of the Commission was the drafting of guidelines to promote fairly uniform decision-making within the bloc. During the crisis, the freedom-of-movement policy area was dominated by non-binding activities at the EU level, such as communications, recommendations, and guidelines issued by both the Commission and the Council. For example, guidelines were issued in April for resuming travel and rebooting the tourism industry, and another set of guidelines were published in July to advise on the protecting of seasonal workers during the pandemic (European Commission 2020f). The Commission was the primary drafter, and the Council approved/ amended these drafts before publishing. On the whole, revisions were limited and the final documents were primarily the original text proposed by the Commission. Especially at the beginning of the crisis, the Council characterized the negotiations among its members or with the European Parliament as taking place as "a matter of urgency" (General Secretariat of the Council 2020b, 2020d, 2020e), with the turnaround between Commission proposal and Council approval being relatively short, on the order of days or weeks.

Consequently, the European Council provided significant leeway for the Commission to steer the coordination efforts by initially drafting and proposing recommendations and guidelines. Thus, in many ways, the Commission took the lead in ensuring a successful response throughout the bloc, intending to support policy coordination across the Member States despite the primacy of the Council as the final decision-maker in the inter-governmental method. For example, on March 2, 2020, the Commission indicated that the European response would focus on three pillars: the medical field, mobility (i.e., transport, travel advice, and Schengen-related questions), and the economy. These pillars were announced at the same time that the Commission created a Coronavirus Response Team (CRT) with five commissioners, each in charge of one of the following areas: crisis management, health, border-related issues, mobility, and macroeconomics (European Commission 2020a). The CRT was set up to act as a high-level decision-making body that would take aggregate information and make recommendations for EU action.

In addition to establishing the new CRT, the existing EU crisis and EM mechanisms were activated and implemented early on in the pandemic. For example, the Directorate-General for Health and Safety created an alert notification in the Early Warning and Response System (EWRS) about the novel coronavirus on January 9, 2020. This EWRS acts as a space for Member States to share information on response and communication measures (Directorate-General for Communication, European Commission 2021).

Then, the Health Security Committee first met to discuss the novel coronavirus on January 17, 2020. Unfortunately, only 12 Member States and the United Kingdom were in attendance. Notably, the Italian health minister, among several others, was not in attendance (Boffey et al. 2020). On January 28, 2020, the EU Civil Protection Mechanism was activated, which made available funds and organizing capacity for things like repatriation and procurement of PPE. While IGCs like the Health Security Committee had a rocky start, these institutions became more relevant for decision-making after March 2020, when the presidents of the Commission and the Council jointly encouraged the use of these venues (especially the Health Security Committee) and Member States began prioritizing attendance at such IGCs and coordination of activities (European Commission 2020e).

Managing Freedom of Movement

Unlike the three federal states, the EU did not take unilateral action on external border control because this is not a delegated competency. Additionally, the measures limiting travel into the Schengen Zone were taken in mid-March compared to late January and early February for the other three cases. By mid-March, however, the necessity to restrict international travel was acknowledged by the Commission issuing a Communication to the Council and Parliament advising on restrictions to travel into the EU Schengen Zone (European Commission 2020c). The Communication was not a binding legal document but rather an advisory one. The next day, the Council supported the Commission's recommendations. On June 30, 2020, the Council made a recommendation that included the Commission's guidelines and established criteria for lifting travel restrictions, which were again noted to be at the discretion of individual Member States (European Council 2020).

A primary criticism of the early EU response to the pandemic was related to the unilateral introduction of internal borders within the Schengen Zone (Brattberg 2020; Butler 2020). The Union was accused of not really existing and breaking into lone nation states, despite this phenomenon also being apparent in the federal case studies presented here (where the regulation of internal movement was challenged legally but did not raise the question of the validity of the federal government itself as a political entity). Perhaps as a consequence of this existential political threat, the Commission began to engage in more concerted effort to provide guidance and rules to the Member States regarding internal borders than took place the United States and Canada, where the federal governments were less visibly involved in these matters. In this respect, Australia is a more comparable federation, as the states engaged with each other and the federal government through the National Cabinet to establish norms around internal restriction of freedom of movement within the federation.

After several Member States took unilateral action to close their borders starting on March 11, the Commission began on March 16 to issue guidelines for the introduction of internal borders in the Schengen Zone, and communications explaining the temporary travel restrictions being advised for non-essential travel from third countries into the EU (European Commission 2020b). The next day (March 17), the European Council convened a conference to discuss coordination on the temporary restriction of non-essential travel into the EU. From this point, the relevant Council of Ministers began working closely with the Commission to develop coordinated approaches to such issues as freight transport (e.g., developing "green lanes"), tourism, and freedom of movement of workers (European Commission 2020d). In addition to these efforts to standardize decision-making throughout the EU, several Member States developed bilateral agreements, such as Germany and Romania, regarding things like the movement of seasonal agricultural workers (Kühnel 2020).

In summary, the EU is constitutionally designed to rely on IGCs for decision-making authority, which distinguishes it from federal states (though Australia prefers this mode of operating, it is not constitutionally required). As such, we see more coordinated decentralized decision-making, especially once the period of unilateral decentralized decision-making passed, and the EU institutions reasserted their coordinating capacities. Nevertheless, there were also several examples of bilateral or coordinated decision-making outside of the EU-provided intergovernmental venues.

Discussion

These cases illustrate how the crisis provoked quite different responses in different federal systems. Though there was a clear need for coordination of activities, such as, *inter alia*, PPE purchasing and restricting freedom of movement, the cases point to different aspects that promote coordination at the federal versus the regional level. For example, political polarization and weak preexisting intergovernmental coordination venues inhibited federation-wide coordination efforts, while strong federal-level

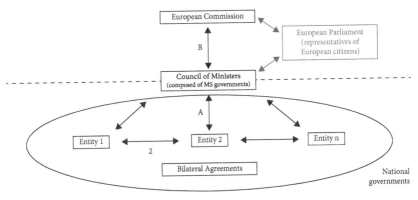

Figure 11.6 IGR Patterns during the EU COVID-19 response.

leadership and established intergovernmental coordination venues supported federation-wide coordination efforts. The United States and to a lesser extent the Canadian cases exemplify dual federalism, with a distinct separation between the constituent units and the federal government, which promoted regionalized coordination over nationwide horizontal coordination or coordination with the federal government. Australia and to a lesser extent the EU provide examples of the organizing capacity of the highest level of government and the added value it can provide to the constituent units during a crisis.

Strength of Regional Governments

If crises are sovereignty detectors, then this crisis has shown the power and value of regional governments. In all cases, the federal government had limited ability to act unilaterally, and the states were clearly the level of government tasked with most decision-making authority. Yet, during the crisis in these federal systems, rather than a transfer of competencies to facilitate centralized decision-making we see a retention of authority coupled with a coordination need among lower levels of government. Coordination was organized variously by the lower levels themselves or a higher jurisdictional authority acting as an administrative support for lower-level coordination. Notably, engagement from the higher jurisdiction in the coordination of lower units was viewed positively when it occurred, and generally missed where it was absent (Peters 2021).

From a European perspective, the power that Member States retain in all areas of policy, but especially those which strongly influence the development of the single market, reinforces the value of institutional coordination arrangements and the Commission as a supportive secretariat. In fact, this work points to the need for more investment in and commitment to EU coordinating mechanisms that are available to Member States in policy areas for which they are the primary authority yet coordination is desirable, such as social and migration policies. Australia, for example, has demonstrated that IGCs and committees can be an effective method for managing IGR in a federal system where sub-units retain significant policymaking authority. Therefore, the initial lack of use of EU coordination committees and "dissolution" of the Union indicates that there is a need for more substantive solidarity among Member States in the form of committing to working together in key policy areas through the established EU mechanisms, even in times of crisis.

Commission as Mediator of Intergovernmental Method

Though scholars have debated whether the increased use of the Intergovernmental Method has weakened the Commission or not (Coman 2018), this study demonstrates that the Commission can retain strong influence even in areas dominated by the Intergovernmental Method. The supportive and at times even directive role of the Commission during this crisis shows how it has the institutional capacity and initiative to provide both the coordination as well as the direction that the Union needs in IGR. While the Council retains the ultimate authority in the Intergovernmental Method, the actual functioning of the method relies heavily on the bureaucracy of the Commission to produce workable positions and documents from which to negotiate within reasonable timeframes, especially during crises (Caravita et al. 2021). Similar to Bolleyer (2009), this work indicates that an independent and institutionalized secretariat has the capacity and often political interest to go beyond an administrative support function to a more substantive role in shaping positions and policy in intergovernmental venues, presenting bargaining positions that were not originally considered (or would not have been proffered) by the governmental parties of their own accord. Thus, the Commission can use its supportive and administrative functions to strongly influence negotiations in the Intergovernmental

Method and steer the development of even those policy areas outside of its domain.

Reflecting on the implications of non-centralized decision-making in the EU and the future of Social Europe, the nature of social policy in Europe is such that it has the characteristics of a policy problem that promotes non-centralization. First, the current state of related issues such as freedom of movement, mutual recognition, and non-discrimination promote coordination in this policy area (Börzel 2010; Scharpf 2002). Second, it remains a jealously guarded and nationally sensitive policy area for Member States, which indicates that they will attempt to retain decision-making authority to the greatest extent possible. This suggests that future social policy negotiations in the EU will take place either in the Intergovernmental Method or through the Open Method of Coordination. However, this work and others (Bolleyer 2009) suggest that the Commission could be an influential actor shaping the nature of those future negotiations, perhaps even proposing previously unconsidered compromises (should it choose to do so). In view of constructing a Social Europe, this is an important governance finding that indicates not just why we might expect to see more Commission engagement in the field of social policy as time passes (though not necessarily more authority) but also why this might also be desired, even as it remains in the purview of the Intergovernmental Method.

Australia: A Promising Comparator to the EU Federal System

Comparing the EU with the other federal systems highlighted the ways in which it is constitutionally unique as a federal system. First, institutional hat-swapping occurs based on policy area. For example, in areas of delegated authority, the Commission is functionally similar to the executive branch of a federal state, but in areas reserved for the Intergovernmental Method of decision-making it functions more similarly to the legislature (drafting policy) or administrative bureaucracy (monitoring implementation), with the role of executive being taken on by the Council and European Council depending on the policy in question. Second, the Member States of the EU have chosen to formalize non-centralization as a mode of governance through both the Intergovernmental Method and the Open Method of Coordination to limit the centralization of sensitive policy areas while also acknowledging that policy coordination is preferable to independent acting (Coman 2018). Consequently, the EU operated in a generally decentralized fashion, initially uncoordinated and later with more intentional coordination on the part of the Commission and the Council.

Despite this unique structure, the present comparison demonstrates the value of comparing the EU with Australia, which has a style of executive federalism and preference for IGCs to manage IGR that could be instructive for future developments in the EU. First, the Australian federation has historically relied heavily on the use of IGCs to manage state–federal relations (Phillimore and Fenna 2017). These IGCs have been important to the development of federation-wide polices in areas that are state powers. Given state-level competencies in relevant policy areas such as public health and health care provision, comparing the EU and Australia could be informative for understanding the role and effectiveness of IGCs to handle horizontal coordination of such policies. Second, the Australian federation created a new IGC (the National Cabinet) during this crisis that is quite comparable to the role that the European Council plays in the Intergovernmental Method. Thus, Australia's long history of using IGCs to facilitate federation-wide policy development, including in a coordinated-centralized and -decentralized fashion (Phillimore and Fenna 2017), makes it a useful comparator to the EU, which relies heavily on similar structures. Therefore, the changes and adjustments that have been made within the Australian federation to these IGR institutions could be instructive for understanding the challenges, pressures, and potential developments that take place when IGCs dominate IGR in a federal system.

Conclusion

The nature of this analysis was such that it focused on areas that fall under the Intergovernmental Method of decision-making in the EU; nevertheless, this is of interest because there has been a marked increase in the use of this style of coordination in the EU alongside an associated decline in the delegation of authority to (and use thereof by) the European Commission (Coman 2018). Moreover, the relative success of the response and the preference of the Member States for limiting the independent authority of the Commission seems to point to a continuation (and potential expansion) of intergovernmental decision-making in the EU. Thus, it is important to study the developing modes of governance in the Intergovernmental Method. Furthermore, comparative studies have the potential to point to other political systems with relevant and instructive developments. Perhaps most notably, this work supports the argument (Coman 2018) that the development of New Intergovernmentalism in recent decades has not simply undermined the role of supranational institutions, but rather the intergovernmental institutions working with the supranational ones have created new dynamics that may be disempowering in one way (e.g., undermining the Commission's right of initiative) and empowering in another way (e.g., relying on the Commission to formulate or implement policy) for supranational institutions.

References

Adeel, Abdul Basit, Michael Catalano, Olivia Catalano, Grant Gibson, Ezgi Muftuoglu, Tara Riggs, Mehmet Halit Sezgin, et al. 2020. "COVID-19 policy response and the rise of the sub-national governments." *Canadian Public Policy*, 46 (4): 565–84. https://doi.org/10.3138/cpp.2020-101.

Aubrey, Allison. 2020. "Trump declares coronavirus a public health emergency and restricts travel from China." NPR, January 31, 2020. https://www.npr.org/sections/health-shots/2020/01/31/801686524/trump-declares-coronavirus-a-public-health-emergency-and-restricts-travel-from-c.

Aroney, Nicolas, and Michael Boyce. 2021. "The Australian Federal Response to the COVID-19 Crisis: Momentary Success or Enduring Reform?" In *Comparative Federalism and Covid-19: Combating the Pandemic,* edited by Nico Steytler, 298–316. London: Routledge.

Backman, Sarah, and Mark Rhinard. 2018. "The European Union's capacities for managing crises." *Journal of Contingencies and Crisis Management* 26 (2): 261–71.

Baker, Mike, Michael Crowley, Peter Eavis, Donald G. McNeil, Choe Sang-Hun, Thomas Fuller, et al. 2020. "Trump calls for calm on virus and expands travel restrictions." *The New York Times*, March 17, 2020. https://www.nytimes.com/2020/02/29/world/coronavirus-news.html.

Behnke, Nathalie, and Sean Mueller. 2017. "The purpose of intergovernmental councils: A framework for analysis and comparison." *Regional and Federal Studies* 27 (5): 507–27.

Blondin, Donald, and Arjen Boin. 2020. "Cooperation in the face of transboundary crisis: A framework for analysis." *Perspectives on Public Management and Governance* 3 (3): 197–209.

Boffey, Daniel, Celine Schoen, Ben Stockton, and Laura Margottini. 2020. "Revealed: Italy's call for urgent help was ignored as coronavirus swept through Europe." *The Guardian*, July 15, 2020. https://www.theguardian.com/world/2020/jul/15/revealed-the-inside-story-of-europes-divided-coronavirus-response.

Boin, Arjen. 2019. "The transboundary crisis: Why we are unprepared and the road ahead." *Journal of Contingencies and Crisis Management* 27 (1): 94–99.

Bolleyer, Nicole. 2009. *Intergovernmental Cooperation: Rational Choices in Federal Systems and Beyond*. Oxford: Oxford University Press.

Börzel, Tanja. 2010. "European governance: Negotiation and competition in the shadow of hierarchy." *JCMS: Journal of Common Market Studies* 48 (2): 191–219.

Bothwell, Robert. 2014. "First Ministers Conferences." In *The Canadian Encyclopedia*. Historica Canada. https://www.thecanadianencyclopedia.ca/en/article/first-minist ers-conferences.

Brattberg, Erik. 2020. "EU Struggling to Overcome Muddled Coronavirus Response [NGO]." *Carnegie Endowment for International Peace*. https://carnegieendowment.org/ 2020/03/18/eu-struggling-to-overcome-muddled-coronavirus-response-pub-81316.

Brown, Natalie. 2020. "Australia's chaotic border rules explained." *News.Com.Au*, October 2, 2020. https://www.news.com.au/travel/travel-updates/australias-covid19-state-bor der-restrictions-travel-rules-explained-statebystate/news-story/8dee56180be0c9a53 fedfac00204b743#.wdr0e.

Burston, Cole. 2020. "Trudeau to hold virtual first ministers meeting on federal health transfers to provinces, territories." *The Globe and Mail*, September 11, 2020. https:// www.theglobeandmail.com/politics/article-trudeau-to-hold-virtual-first-ministers-meeting-on-federal-health/.

Butler, Katherine. 2020. "Coronavirus: Europeans say EU was 'irrelevant' during pandemic." *The Guardian*, June 24, 2020. https://www.theguardian.com/world/2020/jun/ 23/europeans-believe-in-more-cohesion-despite-eus-covid-19-failings.

Canadian Public Health Association. 2021. "Canada's Initial Response to the COVID-19 Pandemic: A Review." *Canadian Public Health Association*, February 16, 2021. https:// www.cpha.ca/review-canadas-initial-response-covid-19-pandemic.

Caravita, Beniamino, Simone Barbareschi, Francesco Severa, Sergio Spatola, and Adriano Dirri. 2021. "Weak Institutions, Positive Results: The European Union's Response to Covid-19." In *Comparative Federalism and Covid-19: Combating the Pandemic*, edited by Nico Steytler, 106–23. London: Routledge.

CBC News. 2020. "Checkpoints go up at N.S. border to prevent spread of COVID-19." *CBC News*, March 23, 2020. https://www.cbc.ca/news/canada/nova-scotia/checkpoi nts-covid-19-borders-public-health-nova-scotia-1.5506621.

Centers for Disease Control and Prevention. 2020. *Health Alert Network (HAN)* [Government Information]. https://emergency.cdc.gov/han/. Atlanta, GA, USA: Centers for Disease Control and Prevention.

Cohen, Rona. 2020a. "Northeastern governors forge coalition to reopen their economies." *The Council of State Governments, Eastern Regional Conference*. https://csg-erc.org/ northeastern-governors-forge-coalition-to-reopen-their-economies/.

Cohen, Rona. 2020b. "Northeast governors announce regional agreement to buy medical supplies." *The Council of State Governments, Eastern Regional Conference*. https:// csg-erc.org/northeast-governors-announce-regional-agreement-to-buy-medical-supplies/.

Coman, Ramona. 2018. "Intergovernmental Method, Community Method, and Open Method of Coordination: The Resilience, Efficiency and Legitimacy of the EU's Modes of Governance." In *The Crisis of the European Union: Challenges, Analyses, Solutions*, edited by A. Grimmel, 173–184. London: Routledge.

Cooke, Ryan. 2020. "N.L. travel ban upheld in provincial Supreme Court ruling." *CBC News*, September 17, 2020. https://www.cbc.ca/news/canada/newfoundland-labrador/ nl-travel-ban-supreme-court-decision-1.5727549.

Council of the Federation. 2020a. *Letter from the Premiers to the Prime Minister of Canada on the Emergencies Act* [Official Communication]. https://www.canadaspremiers.ca/wp-content/uploads/2020/04/Letter_to_PM_from_Canadas_Premiers_Apr_14_2 020.pdf. Ottawa, Ontario, Canada: Council of the Federation.

Council of the Federation. 2020b. *First Ministers' statement on shared public health approach to support restarting the economy* [Press Release]. https://www.canadaspremiers.ca/first-ministers-statement-on-shared-public-health-approach-to-support-restarting-the-economy/.

Council of the Federation. 2020c. *First Ministers' statement on Safe Restart Agreement* [Press Release]. https://www.canadaspremiers.ca/first-ministers-statement-on-safe-restart-agreement/. Ottawa, Ontario, Canada: Council of the Federation.

Csehi, Robert. 2017. "Horizontal coordination in federal political systems – non-centralization in the European Union and Canada compared." *Journal of European Public Policy* 24 (4), 562–79.

Department of the Prime Minister and Cabinet. 2020. *Effective Commonwealth-State Relations* [Government Information]. Australian Government. https://www.pmc.gov.au/domestic-policy/effective-commonwealth-state-relations.

Dilanian, Ken, and Dan De Luce. 2020. "Trump administration's lack of unified corona-virus strategy will cost lives, say a dozen experts." *NBC News*, April 3, 2020. https://www.nbcnews.com/politics/donald-trump/trump-administration-s-lack-unified-coronavirus-strategy-will-cost-lives-n1175126.

Directorate-General for Communication, European Commission. 2021. *Timeline of EU action* [Government Information]. European Commission. https://ec.europa.eu/info/live-work-travel-eu/coronavirus-response/timeline-eu-action_en.

Dosenrode, Søren. 2012. "Crisis and Regional Integration: A Federalist and Neo-Functionalist Perspective." In *Regions and Crises: New Challenges for Contemporary Regionalisms*, edited by L. Fioramonti, 13–30. Palgrave Macmillan.

Downey, Davia Dox, and William. M. Myers. 2020. "Federalism, intergovernmental relationships, and emergency response: A comparison of Australia and the United States." *The American Review of Public Administration*, 50(6–7), 526–35.

Elphick, Karen. 2020. *Australian COVID-19 response management arrangements: A quick guide*. Parliamentary Library, Parliament of Australia. https://www.aph.gov.au/About_Parliament/Parliamentary_Departments/Parliamentary_Library/pubs/rp/rp1920/Quick_Guides/AustralianCovid-19ResponseManagement.

English, Jill, and Tom Murphy. 2020. Support for Atlantic bubble remains strong even as some question its constitutionality. *CBC News*, September 16, 2020. https://www.cbc.ca/news/canada/nova-scotia/atlantic-bubble-covid-19-pandemic-borders-1.5718807.

European Commission. 2020a. *President von der Leyen on the EU's response to COVID-19*. https://ec.europa.eu/commission/presscorner/detail/en/statement_20_368.

European Commission. 2020b. *COVID-19: Guidelines for border management measures to protect health and ensure the availability of goods and essential services* (Information 2020/C 86 I/01; Official Journal of the European Union). https://eur-lex.europa.eu/legal-content/EN/TXT/PDF/?uri=CELEX:52020XC0316(03)andfrom=EN.

European Commission. 2020c. *COVID-19: Temporary Restriction on Non-Essential Travel to the EU* (Communication from the Commission COM(2020) 115 final). https://eur-lex.europa.eu/legal-content/EN/TXT/PDF/?uri=CELEX:52020DC0115andfrom=EN.

European Commission. 2020d. *On the implementation of the Green Lanes under the Guidelines for border management measures to protect health and ensure the availability of goods and essential services* (Communication from the Commission 2020/C 96 I/01; Official Journal of the European Union). https://eur-lex.europa.eu/legal-content/EN/TXT/PDF/?uri=CELEX:52020XC0324(01)andfrom=EN.

European Commission. 2020e. *Joint European Roadmap towards lifting COVID-19 containment measures* [Press Release]. https://ec.europa.eu/info/sites/info/files/communication_-_a_european_roadmap_to_lifting_coronavirus_containment_measures_0.pdf. Brussels, Belgium: European Commission.

European Commission. 2020f. *Guidelines on Seasonal Workers in the EU in the Context of the Covid-19 Outbreak* (Communication from the Commission C(2020) 4813 final; Official Journal of the European Union). https://ec.europa.eu/info/sites/default/files/guidelines_on_seasonal_workers_in_the_eu_in_the_context_of_the_covid-19_outbreak_en.pdf. Brussels, Belgium: European Commission.

European Council. 2020. Council Recommendation (EU) 2020/912 of 30 June 2020 on the temporary restriction on non-essential travel into the EU and the possible lifting of such restriction. In *OJ L* (ST/9208/2020/INIT; Vol. 208I). Official Journal of the European Union; EUR-Lex. http://data.europa.eu/eli/reco/2020/912/oj/eng. Brussels, Belgium: Official Journal of the European Union, 1–7.

General Secretariat of the Council. 2020a. *Video conference of the members of the European Council, 10 March 2020* [Government Information]. Council of the European Union. https://www.consilium.europa.eu/en/meetings/european-council/2020/03/10/.

General Secretariat of the Council. 2020b. *COVID-19: Council agrees its position on helping airlines by suspending slot requirements* (Press Release No. 166/20). Council of the European Union. https://www.consilium.europa.eu/en/press/press-releases/2020/03/20/covid-19-council-agrees-its-position-on-helping-airlines-by-suspending-slot-requirements/.

General Secretariat of the Council. 2020c. *Remarks by President Charles Michel at the press conference on the EU response to the coronavirus crisis* [Press Release]. https://www.consilium.europa.eu/en/press/press-releases/2020/04/15/remarks-by-president-charles-michel-at-the-press-conference-on-the-eu-response-to-the-coronavirus-crisis/.

General Secretariat of the Council. 2020d. *COVID-19: More flexibility for deploying EU budget money* (Press Release No. 245/20). Council of the European Union. https://www.consilium.europa.eu/en/press/press-releases/2020/04/22/covid-19-more-flexibility-for-deploying-eu-budget-money/.

General Secretariat of the Council. 2020e. *COVID-19 transport measures: Council agrees its position on temporary derogations in support of the rail sector* (Press Release No. 556/20). Council of the European Union. https://www.consilium.europa.eu/en/press/press-releases/2020/09/09/covid-19-transport-measures-council-agrees-its-position-on-temporary-derogations-in-support-of-the-rail-sector/.

Gerring, John. 2006. *Case Study Research: Principles and Practices.* Cambridge: Cambridge University Press.

Governor, New York State. 2020a. *Governor Cuomo, Governor Murphy, Governor Lamont, Governor Wolf, Governor Carney, Governor Raimondo Announce Multi-State Council to Get People Back to Work and Restore the Economy.* https://www.governor.ny.gov/news/governor-cuomo-governor-murphy-governor-lamont-governor-wolf-governor-carney-governor-raimondo. Albany, NY, USA: Office of the Governor of New York.

Governor, New York State. 2020b. *Governor Cuomo, Governor Murphy and Governor Lamont Announce Joint Incoming Travel Advisory That All Individuals Traveling from States with Significant Community Spread of COVID-19 Quarantine for 14 Days* [Press

Release].   https://www.governor.ny.gov/news/governor-cuomo-governor-murphy-and-governor-lamont-announce-joint-incoming-travel-advisory-all.   Albany,   NY, USA: Office of the Governor of New York.

Governor, State of California. 2020. *California, Oregon and Washington Announce Western States Pact* [Press Release]. https://www.gov.ca.gov/2020/04/13/california-oregon-washington-announce-western-states-pact/.

Hegele, Yvonne, and Johanna Schnabel. 2021. "Federalism and the management of the COVID-19 crisis: Centralisation, decentralisation and (non-)coordination." *West European Politics* 44 (5–6): 1052–76.

Henstra, Daniel. 2013. *Multilevel Governance and Emergency Management in Canadian Municipalities*. Montreal, Quebec, Canada: McGill-Queen's University Press.

Holcombe, Madeline. 2020. "Here are the states restricting travel from within the US." *CNN*, March 31, 2020. https://www.cbs58.com/news/here-are-the-states-restricting-travel-from-within-the-us.

Karp, Paul. 2020. "High court rejects legal challenge against Victoria's Covid lockdown." *The Guardian*, November 6, 2020. http://www.theguardian.com/law/2020/nov/06/high-court-rejects-legal-challenge-against-victorias-covid-lockdown.

Karp, Paul. 2021. "Clive Palmer v Western Australia: Border ban justified by risks of Covid-19, high court reveals." *The Guardian*, February 24, 2021. http://www.theguardian.com/australia-news/2021/feb/24/clive-palmer-v-western-australia-border-ban-justified-by-risks-of-covid-19-high-court-reveals.

Kincaid, John, and J. Wesley Leckrone. 2021. "American Federalism and COVID-19: Party Trumps Policy." In *Comparative Federalism and Covid-19: Combating the Pandemic*, edited by Nico Steytle, 181–99. London, UK: Routledge. https://doi.org/10.4324/9781003166771-13.

Kühnel, Alina. 2020. "Germany drafts Romanian farm labor for coronavirus pandemic." *Deutsche Welle*, April 8, 2020. https://www.dw.com/en/germany-drafts-romanian-farm-labor-for-coronavirus-pandemic/a-53066735.

LeBlanc, Paul. 2020. "Florida governor mandates self-quarantine for travelers coming from New York, New Jersey and Connecticut." *CNN*, March 24, 2020. https://www.cnn.com/2020/03/23/politics/florida-coronavirus-new-york-new-jersey/index.html.

National Conference of State Legislatures (NCSL). 2020. *National Guard Assists Response to the COVID-19 Pandemic*. https://www.ncsl.org/research/military-and-veterans-affairs/national-guard-activation-in-every-state-assisting-response-to-the-covid-19-pandemic.aspx.

Palermo, Francesco. 2020. "Is there a space for federalism in times of emergency?" *Verfassungsblog*. https://doi.org/10.17176/20200513-133602-0.

Palmer, E. 2020. "The Open Road Calls, but Authorities Say 'Stop.'" *The New York Times*. https://www.nytimes.com/article/coronavirus-driving-restrictions.html.

Peters, B. Guy. 2021. "American Federalism in the Pandemic." In *American Federal Systems and COVID-19: Responses to a complex intergovernmental problem*, edited by B. Guy Peters, Eduardo J. Grin, and Fernando Luiz Abrucio, 23–42. Bingley, UK: Emerald Publishing Limited.

Phillimore, John, and Alan Fenna. 2017. "Intergovernmental councils and centralization in Australian federalism." *Regional and Federal Studies* 27 (5): 597–621.

Poirier, Johanne, and Jessica Michelin. 2021. "Facing the Coronavirus Pandemic in the Canadian Federation: Reinforced Dualism and Muted Cooperation?" In *Comparative Federalism and Covid-19: Combating the Pandemic*, edited by Nico Steytler, 200–19. London: Routledge.

Prime Minister of Canada. 2020a. *Prime Minister creates committee on COVID-19* [Government Information]. https://pm.gc.ca/en/news/news-releases/2020/03/04/prime-minister-creates-committee-covid-19.

Prime Minister of Canada. 2020b. *Prime Minister Justin Trudeau convenes the Incident Response Group to discuss the new COVID-19 variant identified in the United Kingdom* [Press Release]. https://pm.gc.ca/en/news/readouts/2020/12/20/prime-minister-justin-trudeau-convenes-incident-response-group-discuss-new.

Rogers, Adam. 2020. "State Alliances are leading the US Fight against Covid-19." *Wired*, April 16, 2020. https://www.wired.com/story/state-alliances-are-leading-the-us-fight-against-covid-19/.

Rozell, Mark J., and Clyde Wilcox. 2020. "Federalism in a time of plague: How federal systems cope with pandemic." *The American Review of Public Administration* 50 (6–7): 519–25.

Ruoff, A. 2020. "Trump is pressed to set national strategy as covid deaths mount." *Bloomberg Law*. https://news.bloomberglaw.com/zz-bgov/trump-is-pressed-to-set-national-strategy-as-covid-deaths-mount-1.

Scharpf, Fritz W. 2002. "The European social model." *Journal of Common Market Studies* 40 (4): 645–70.

Schertzer, Robert, and Mireille Paquet. 2020. "How well is Canada's intergovernmental system handling the crisis?" *Policy Options | Politiques, The Coronavirus Pandemic: Canada's Response.* https://policyoptions.irpp.org/magazines/april-2020/how-well-is-canadas-intergovernmental-system-handling-the-crisis/.

Segatto, Catarina Ianni, Daniel Béland, and Shannon Dinan. 2021. "Canadian Federalism in the Pandemic." In *American Federal Systems and COVID-19: Responses to a Complex Intergovernmental Problem*, edited by B. Guy Peters, Eduardo Grin, and Fernando Luiz. Abrucio, 89–106. Bingley, UK: Emerald Publishing Limited.

Stepan, Alfred C. 1999. "Federalism and democracy: Beyond the U.S. model." *Journal of Democracy* 10 (4): 19–34.

Steytler, N. (Ed.). 2021. *Comparative Federalism and Covid-19: Combating the Pandemic* (1st edition). London, UK: Routledge.

Tanne, Janice Hopkins. 2020. "Covid-19: US needs a national plan to fight rising infections, experts say." *British Medical Journal* 370: m3072.

Tasker, John Paul. 2020. "Trudeau to meet with premiers, Indigenous leaders Thursday as COVID-19 spreads and oil prices tank." *CBC News*, March 12, 2020. https://www.cbc.ca/news/politics/coronavirus-trudeau-premiers-indigenous-oil-1.5494115.

Tatum, James. 2020. "States form pacts to coordinate economic response to COVID-19." *COVID-19 Resources for State Leaders, Council of State Governments.* https://web.csg.org/covid19/2020/05/13/states-form-pacts-to-coordinate-economic-response-to-covid-19/.

The Council of Atlantic Premiers. 2020. *Atlantic Provinces Form Travel Bubble* [Press Release]. https://cap-cpma.ca/news/atlantic-provinces-form-travel-bubble-amended-version/.

Trask, Steven. 2020. "Pauline Hanson threatens to challenge state coronavirus border closures in the High Court." *SBS News*, May 21, 2020. https://www.sbs.com.au/news/pauline-hanson-threatens-to-challenge-state-coronavirus-border-closures-in-the-high-court.

Verley, Angus, and Bridget Hermann. 2020. "Farmer frustration as national cabinet fails to agree on agricultural worker movement code." *ABC News*, September 4, 2020.

https://www.abc.net.au/news/rural/2020-09-04/national-cabinet-fails-agree-ag-work
ers-code-covid-state-borders/12628600.

Vigliotti, Marco. 2020. "Atlantic premiers announce creation of regional travel bubble."
IPolitics, June 24, 2020. https://ipolitics.ca/2020/06/24/atlantic-premiers-announce-
creation-of-regional-travel-bubble/.

Whitbourn, Michaela, David Crowe, and Anthony Dennis. 2020. "Legal challenges to
border closures 'have legs,' experts say." *The Sydney Morning Herald*, May 25, 2020.
https://www.smh.com.au/national/legal-challenges-to-border-closures-have-legs-
experts-say-20200525-p54w8a.html.

Worthington, Jackson. 2020. "Cruise ships banned from docking in Tasmania until July."
The Examiner, March 15, 2020. https://www.examiner.com.au/story/6678919/cruise-
ships-banned-until-july/.

12

European Integration as Complementary Institution-Building

The Impact of the COVID-19 Pandemic

Georg Vobruba

Introduction

The coronavirus pandemic unfolded as a crisis that hit the European Union (EU) at one of its weakest points. This is not my assessment, its the European Commission's own: "There was a clear shortfall in pandemic preparedness and planning, with few tools already in place to respond swiftly and effectively as soon as the pandemic broke out" (European Commission 2021c). Health is a policy area in which the EU proved to be poorly equipped. In addition, the pandemic policy quickly involved other policy areas. After only a few months in 2020, the EU found itself in a complex crisis situation—another in a series of crises, in particular the international financial and euro crises and the Schengen crisis. How does this complex crisis affect European integration? I focus this question on three policy areas that are central to the pandemic and pandemic policy: mobility, health, and public finances.

This chapter is structured into three parts. In each of these parts, I shall analyze the impact of the pandemic on these three political areas: mobility, health, and public finances. It will turn out that the impact of the pandemic in the three areas differs remarkably. Empirically, this leads to a detailed analysis of the effects of the pandemic on the European integration process in three crucial policy areas. In theory and practice, the pandemic is a dramatic lesson in mutual social interdependencies. Development, manifestations, and consequences of social interdepencies are a domain of social sciences.

Georg Vobruba, *European Integration as Complementary Institution-Building* In: *European Social Policy and the COVID-19 Pandemic.* Edited by: Stefanie Börner and Martin Seeleib-Kaiser, Oxford University Press.
© Oxford University Press 2023. DOI: 10.1093/oso/9780197676189.003.0012

The Logic of Pandemics

Contagion describes an asymmetric causal relationship. It is never certain in individual cases whether it will take place, but it can always be clearly proven in retrospect. Contagion captures the fact that a problem affecting one actor tends to be transferred to other actors via functional interconnectedness or a spatial proximity relationship. Functional interconnectedness lies at the ground of the international financial and Euro crisis, leading to the metaphoric use of the term contagion by executives (Constancio 2011) as well as in social sciences (Missio, Watzka 2011; Vobruba 2012, 72ff.). Spatial proximity[1] is crucial in the case of the medical understanding of contagion (Last 2001, 38); hence, "social distancing," a logical albeit in its consequences a socially rather complex remedy (Patra 2021). Contagion implies a problem, actors as problem bearers, and a social constellation—namely, the establishment of the proximity relationship. Consequences of contagion are interdependencies of problems, whereby mutual dependencies intensify, and therefore individual benefit calculations must include the benefit of others. Contagion thus is an important term in the everyday world as well as in sociology. A "pandemic" is "an epidemic occurring worldwide, or over a very wide area, crossing international boundaries and usually affecting a large number of people" (Last 2001, 131). To this definition should be added the dynamic of contagion, for it is exactly this feature of the pandemic that implies the potential of overburdening institutions, hence creating time pressure for pandemic policies—a core criterion of crises in general. The term *pandemic* denotes a wide-ranging social constellation that arises through contagion, with specific consequences associated (Doshi 2011; Kelly 2011). Talk of a pandemic therefore has a performative effect, and in particular the public declaration of a constellation as a pandemic—for example by the World Health Organization—has political consequences. Pandemic policy is linked to a social constellation declared as a pandemic by relevant actors. This is analogous to the declaration of a constellation as a crisis, including its consequences.

What is the particular difficulty of pandemic policy? Infectious problems are never just individual problems. Pandemics are shaped by the logic of contagion. Sociologically, contagion is an expanding constellation of mutual

---

[1] Either as a "direct and essentially immediate transfer of infectious agents", or via "contaminated inanimate material or objects" (Last 2001: 180).

dependency. Thus, pandemic policy must overcome two problems: (A) the collective-good trap and (B) the prevention paradox.[2]

(A) Mutual dependencies give rise to collective goods. In our case the collective good is the containment of the pandemic. The problem is that this good also benefits those who do not participate in its production, in particular by avoiding inconveniences (masks, distance, etc.). It remains to be analyzed whether in course of mass vaccination, the relation between collective and (perceived) private benefits changes. (B) Pandemics are characterized by cascades of contagions. Problem diagnoses that imply expansion dynamics built in require prevention. But problems that are supposed to be tackled preventively have an uncertain epistemic status: because of the asymmetric causal relationship that contagion implies, it is never quite certain whether they exist or do not exist. The prevention paradox is the result of an exaggeration of the second of these two possibilities. It means that the success of prevention is taken as evidence that the problem was never real. Taking both problems together: pandemic policy must organize collective efforts to produce a non-event. This raises problems for policy at the Member State and European levels.

There is an overwhelming consensus that with the corona pandemic, the European Union is confronted with its most severe crisis so far. "Will Coronavirus kill the European Union?" (Alesina and Giavazzi 2020). Or will it turn into a further push for integration? These questions lead directly to the problem of an appropriate integration theory. The juxtaposition of neofunctionalism and intergovernmentalism is almost a ritual in political science research on European integration.[3] The following analysis of the pandemic and pandemic policy on European integration can be read as the attempt to undermine this opposition. On the one hand, intergovernmentalism is right, for it provides an actor-theoretical approach. Unfortunately, it is based on an inappropriate overgeneralization of a specific historical constellation, namely the early phase of European integration when state governments indeed were the dominant political actors. Nevertheless "real actors" (Scharpf 1997) are indispensable for an open-ended and empirically substantial analysis, but the term "actors" must be understood in a broader sense. This brings my analysis close to actor-centered institutionalism; in

---

[2] See also my sketch: Vobruba 2021.
[3] The dependence of the dominance of the respective approach on the state of the European Union becomes clearly visible in Verdun (2020). For an instructive presentation of alternative theories of European integration without deciding for one, see Hooghe and Marks (2019).

THE IMPACT OF THE COVID-19 PANDEMIC

particular, I share the "basic assumption of the approach . . . that institutions provide opportunities for action and at the same time set limits to action without, however, determining it" (Mayntz 2009, 83; my translation; see also Mayntz and Scharpf 1995). On the other hand, however, the empirical evidence I shall present does, to a certain extent, support neofunctionalism (Sandholtz and Stone Sweet 2012). For some important problems, as we will see, that occurred in the course of the pandemic have indeed already turned out to be impulses for further steps of integration. Crucially, the correlation between problems and their successful solutions does not always hold. But a functionalist approach that is not always confirmed is already refuted, for in a functionalist world every problem causes its solution.[4]

The approach I coined as complementary institution building (Vobruba 2012a; Preunkert, Vobruba 2012) takes up impulses from both. The starting point is basically an action-theoretical approach; the challenge is that functionalism has some empirical plausibility in its own right. Hence, the approach focuses on this hypothesis: When a body of institutions of the European Union[5] is confronted with problems that are seen by relevant actors as threatening its existence and in urgent need of solution (Kiess 2015, Worschech 2018), they react by creating additional institutions, hence advancing integration.

In which key areas of integration has the pandemic policy had an impact? I focus on three key areas: health, mobility, and finance. In each area, I will first briefly describe the institutional situation before the pandemic. Then I will examine how the pandemic policy problems change institutional arrangements in the three areas. Finally, I will consider whether and why the changes will remain.

European Mobility Policy

Mobility policy played a central role in COVID pandemic policy.[6] The most important instrument of mobility policy was the regulation of border permeability. What has actually changed regarding borders and

---

[4] For a discussion of the possibilities and limitations of functionalist theory in general, cf. Merton 1968, Luhmann 1962, Wagner 2012.

[5] With this specification, my approach naturally also acknowledges its historical conditionality (see Fn. 3).

[6] See also Vobruba 2021a.

border-related action in the Schengen area during the corona pandemic, and what changes will be sustainable? In politics and social science, the freedoms of the Schengen regime are seen as a core element of European integration, which is endangered by individual Member States' unilateral mobility policy:

> "The COVID-19 pandemic presents an unprecedented challenge and has placed a major strain on the Schengen area, leading many more Member States to reintroduce internal border controls, at times jeopardising the proper functioning of the Single Market. The impact of these controls has been particularly felt by the lack of coordination, especially in cross-border areas. As internal border controls were re-established, trucks faced long hours waiting in queues to cross from one Member State to another, seriously disrupting supply chains within the EU. As such, the COVID-19 pandemic brought to the forefront the economic implications of Schengen and its intrinsic relationship with the Single Market. More than this, border closures represent a real concern for citizens especially in border regions, having had a real impact on their daily lives (European Commission 2021, 1).

In some social science–inspired contemporary observations, the policy of mobility restrictions has been elevated to a symptom of increasing national egoism and is seen as a threat to European integration as a whole (Krastev 2020; Hruschka 2020; differentiating: Wang 2021). What is realistic beyond the *Angstlust* of a disintegration of the European Union?

Key Points of the Schengen Code

The political field of European mobility and border policy is regulated by the Schengen Agreement. Pandemic policy thus encountered institutionalized European regulations. Unlike in other policy fields, such as health policy, the pandemic did not manifest an institutionalization deficit at the EU level and did not create immediate pressure for complementary institution-building. On the contrary, the Schengen Agreement allows for reacting flexibly to problems. The flexibility is institutionalized in exemption rules that provide that border policy can be temporarily shifted back to the nation-state level in case of problems. What are the key points?

The European Union's border-related mobility policy operates between border dismantling and border fortification (Vobruba 2003; Eigmüller 2021). In this sense, the Schengen Agreement is effective both internally and externally. Within the Schengen area, it regulates the basically free movement of persons. Article 22 of the Schengen Borders Code reads, "Internal borders may be crossed at any point without checks on persons, irrespective of the nationality of the persons concerned." As a consequence, internally, Schengen acts as a large-scale liberalization program (Vobruba 2016). The freedom of mobility within yields a common interest in controls vis-à-vis the outside (Vobruba 2007; Bach 2010, 171). Thus, those borders that are at the same time state borders and the EU's external border become a "double-coded border" (Vobruba 2012a, 92; Hilpert 2020). Article 5 of the Schengen Code regulates the modalities at the EU's external border: "External borders may be crossed only at border crossing points and during the fixed hours of traffic." Passage of the external border by third-country nationals requires: a valid travel document, usually a visa; sufficient financial means; a recognized reason for entry; no entry in the Schengen Information System (SIS)—that is, persons not wanted or otherwise undesirable.

Institutionalized Flexibility

The Schengen Code provides for exceptions to a certain extent for the regulation of both the external border and the internal area. Both the relaxation of entry controls at the external border and the reintroduction of border controls in the internal area are possible under certain conditions. "Border checks at external borders may be relaxed as a result of exceptional and unforeseen circumstances. Such exceptional and unforeseen circumstances shall be deemed to be those where unforeseeable events lead to traffic of such intensity that the waiting time at the border crossing point becomes excessive, and all resources have been exhausted as regards staff, facilities and organization" (Article 9 (1)). The exceptional resumption of checks at the EU's internal borders is governed by Chapter II of the Schengen Code (Articles 25 to 35). The principle is: "Where, in the area without internal border control, there is a serious threat to public policy or internal security in a Member State, that Member State may exceptionally reintroduce border control at all or specific parts of its internal borders for a limited period of up to 30 days or for the foreseeable duration of the serious threat if its duration exceeds

30 days. The scope and duration of the temporary reintroduction of border control at internal borders shall not exceed what is strictly necessary to respond to the serious threat" (Article 25(1)).[7]

The exceptional nature of these rules is emphasized by the fact that their use is described as a "last means" (para. 2). Under restrictively defined exceptional circumstances, an extension of up to two years is possible (Art 25(4)). Reasons, scope, and duration of the reintroduction of controls have to be reported to the Commission, and the European Parliament may request information from it. In principle, the proportionality between the danger to be averted and the controls must be examined. It is common to regard the exceptions provided in the Schengen Code as inconsistencies and their use as undesirable setbacks in the integration process. But it seems questionable whether this view can be sustained. In particular, the "migration crisis" of 2015 and the corona pandemic have unleashed pressures that would probably have broken the Schengen institutional complex had it not been for the possibility of making use of the derogation rules. In this perspective, the derogation possibilities in the Schengen Code are a flexibility reserve. The flexibility institutionalized by the exceptions makes it possible to absorb problems that would otherwise overwhelm the institutional base. Of course, hypothetical threats cannot be turned into evidence of the performance of the exceptions in the Schengen Code. But at least one should try to balance the two readings: Exceptions to free movement as a potential threat, or as a flexibility reserve of European integration. Of course, the boundary between the flexible handling of the rules on freedom of movement and a threat to integration is crossed when mobility restrictions mutate from pandemic policy measures to a question of principle of state sovereignty.

Restricting Mobility within the Schengen Area

Since the Schengen Code entered into force, the Commission has received 320 "Member States' notifications of the temporary reintroduction of border control at internal borders" (as of November 11, 2021).[8] Overall, the frequency of notifications increases over time. From 2006 to May 16,

---

[7] On the problems of precisely determining the two-year maximum ("overlapping risks," etc.), see Cebulak and Morvillo (2021).

[8] https://ec.europa.eu/home-affairs/system/files/2021-11/Full%20list%20of%20notifications_en.pdf

2015, there were 36 notifications. On September 13, 2015, the first notification (from Germany) was made to the Commission in connection with refugee flows. From then until the start of the corona pandemic, there were 81 notifications—and mostly, but not exclusively, related to refugee flows. The first reintroduction of border controls related to corona was reported (by France) on October 31, 2019. By November 1, 2021, there were then 196 more notifications of temporary reintroductions of border controls, almost exclusively with pandemic containment as the justification. Only since then have "terrorist threats" and "secondary movements"[9] dominated over corona reasons as causes for temporary reintroductions of border control.

While the Commission and the EU Parliament see themselves as guardians of free mobility, they have only weak means of intervention. On September 4, 2020, the Commission issued a set of rather feeble recommendations "to improve the clarity and predictability of measures restricting free movement in the European Union." The pandemic policy of the EU Member States was based on restrictive internal border policies, but there are strong opposing interests in mobility.

After border closures as first shock reaction, the borders were soon made permeable again for specific groups of people such as truck drivers, harvest workers, care workers, and commuters. However, this did not affect the much wider circles of the populations whose mobility was restricted in the interest of pandemic control. But their interests were also highly effective. The main mobility drivers are tourists and the tourism industry. The former are very many, the latter is very influential in some Member States. In 2016, about 400 million trips took place in Europe. About 40% of the trips of Europeans are abroad, most of which (about 80%) are trips within Europe. Delhey et al. (2020, 129ff.) conclude that Europe is the most densely integrated mobility network in the world. "One is by no means going too far out on a limb in stating that Europe is now almost fully integrated in terms of tourism (and EU Europe anyway)" (Delhey et al. 2020, 154; my translation). The expectations and practices of people generated by Schengen buttress the Schengen institution. It can be assumed that transnational mobility is now seen as a kind of customary right, and that restrictions on mobility are hardly accepted in the longer run. European integration is not irreversibly, but strongly secured by the "power of contact" (Deutschmann et al. 2018). Cross-border mobility in the Schengen area by no means came to a standstill during the pandemic. A few figures to illustrate. Statistics Austria reports a 52.7% decline in foreign arrivals in Austria in 2020.[10] That's a sharp drop, but it's still 15.09 million cases, or 30.18 million crossings of Austrian borders. The number of foreign arrivals in Germany decreased from 39.56 million to 12.45 million from 2019 to 2020. That's a reduction of about two-thirds—a lot for hotels, but still 24.9 million border crossings.[11]

Restrictions at the External Border

Nevertheless, the pandemic policy has an impact on the institution of "Schengen." Efforts to restore free mobility in the Schengen area have consequences above all for the external border. At the heart of the Commission's statement on strengthening Schengen in the context of the corona pandemic are proposals for controls at the EU's external border: "Since anyone crossing the external borders—by air, land or sea—can travel freely to and within the other Member States, Schengen's existence presupposes a high degree of trust in a robust management of the external borders" (European Commission 2021, 4). This is in the perspective of future health problems, of combating so-called irregular migration, and in particular of coping with "challenges related to the instrumentalization of migrants" (European Commission 20021d, 3–4). Reform proposals for the Schengen system entail information technology upgrades (Eurodac system). Similarly, the importance of cooperation with the outer periphery of the EU—in the sense of the European Neighborhood Policy as a pre-displaced migration defense—is emphasized. Measures in the interior are aligned in the same way. The European Commission (2021d, 8–9) proposes an intra-Schengen mechanism of "transferring irregular migrants" and the extension of the Advance Passenger Information system (API) to intra-Schengen flights: "This change would extend the toolbox of compensatory measures available to the Member States allowing law enforcement authorities to enable a risk-based data-driven approach within the Schengen area" (European

---

[10] https://www.statista.com/statistics/1262610/tourist-arrivals-austria/
[11] https://de.statista.com/statistik/daten/studie/946241/umfrage/ankuenfte-von-in-und-auslaendischen-gaesten-in-deutschland/

Commission 2021, 13). This includes selectivity of boundary permeability according to individual infection status.

All in all, pandemic policy as mobility policy together with the threat of the instrumentalization of migrants (as experienced in autumn 2021 at the border between Belarus and Poland) might result in a modest shift toward more coordination tasks at the EU level,[12] but it does not require complementary institution-building. The extensive use of derogations in the Schengen Code appeared undesirable to the Commission and Parliament, but they were not perceived as threats to the institutional set-up. On the contrary, with respect to internal borders, the Schengen Code's derogation rules allowed sufficient flexibility to conduct pandemic policy within the institutional framework already in place. With regard to external borders, the pandemic led to a continuation and acceleration of the long-term trend toward selective borders and ongoing technical but not institutional innovations in border policy.

Toward a European Health Union?

So far, EU health policy has been dominated by the subsidiarity principle. Significant parts of EU health policy developed indirectly, namely, deriving from areas of EU competence that have health policy effects. These include health protection at the workplace as an effect of regulatory social policy (Majone 1993), patients' rights abroad as an effect of freedom of movement (Eigmüller 2013), and consumer protection as an effect of standardization in order to build Europe-wide homogeneous markets. During the last decades, the Commission, the Parliament, and in particular the ECJ (Hatzopoulos 2002; Eigmüller 2013) were strongly engaged in accumulating competencies against the persistent but not necessarily successful resistance of the member countries (for an excellent summary see Eigmüller 2021, 115ff.; Vollard et al. 2016). As a result a "European Health Area" emerged, both as a set of institutionalized rights and as a feature of people's consciousness. Regulating pharmaceutical supply requires elaborated expert knowledge, and in 1993 the Commission founded the European Medicines Agency (EMA), which compiles recommendations for drug approval by the Commission. And in 2004 the European Center for Disease Prevention and

---

[12] At least this is something the European Commission (2021d, 13) is proposing.

Control (ECDC), an agency with information and coordination duties, was founded. All in all, the EUs competencies in health affairs basically consist of regulating demand and supply of medical treatments and medicine in a broad sense. It has created the conditions for cross-border demand for medical services to develop, as well as the institutional conditions for a Europe-wide market for pharmaceuticals by introducing and controlling uniform quality standards.

During the pandemic European health policy partly followed this path, but it also had to develop totally new instruments. What health policy tasks for the EU have developed in the pandemic?

EU Health Policy in the Pandemic, Path-Dependent

Accelerated vaccine licensing, vaccine purchasing, development of an EU vaccination passport—all these policy measures are executed by already existing EU institutions. As far as the EU had any competence in health policy, it was concentrated at the EMA.[13] The agency is responsible for making recommendations for the approvals of medicines by the Commission legally binding all members, which is important for liability issues. The centralized approval is compulsory for all relevant severe diseases.[14] Here, the pandemic policy could build on the existing institutional base. For the confirmation of vaccine development, the EMA established a task force to ensure permanent contact with the vaccine developers. What was new, however, was the public visibility of the EMA, hence exposing it to pressure.

The main objective was to enable vaccine to be made available quickly and safely, and to avoid competition among the Member States (European Commission 2020). This last point suggests a growth in EU competence within the health policy domain triggered by the pandemic.

---

[13] It is remarkable that for most of its finances the EMA has its own source: "For 2021, the total budget of the European Medicines Agency (EMA) amounts to €385.9 million. Around 86% of the Agency's budget derives from fees and charges and 14% from the European Union (EU) contribution for public-health issues and less than 1% from other sources." https://www.ema.europa.eu/en/about-us/how-we-work/governance-documents/funding

[14] https://www.ema.europa.eu/en/about-us/what-we-do/authorisation-medicines   Despite EU competence for approval of pharmaceutics, pricing and reimbursement remains with the Member States. Such interleaved competencies between EMA and national agencies sound irrational, but they enable expansion of EMA's administrative competencies as step-by-step facilitators.

EU Health Policy in the Pandemic, New

Worldwide pandemic policy started with national scuffles around masks. It resulted in fierce competition, put public procurement on the defensive against private providers, and offered opportunities for corruption. These negative experiences certainly paved the way for the Commission to assume responsibility for the procurement of vaccines. The Commission reacted relatively quickly. "As the pandemic moves across borders, so its socio-economic impact on each of the Member States spreads to the others. Against that background, it is essential that all 27 EU Member States have access to a vaccine as early as possible" (European Commission 2020, 2).

Then there was an egoistic alliance of some research-strong member countries, which the Commission captured by redefining it as a prefiguration of a Community strategy: "An important step toward joint action between Member States has already been taken in the formation of an inclusive vaccine Alliance by France, Germany, Italy, and the Netherlands. This alliance was formed to pool the national resources of those countries and secure fair access to vaccine supplies for the European population. The current proposal builds on the important groundwork undertaken by that Alliance" (ibid., 3). A distribution battle was emerging for a commodity that did not yet exist. The Commission emphasized the advantages of central procurement, echoing the bad experiences with mask procurement: "All EU Member States will be able to benefit from an option to purchase vaccines via a single procurement action. This process also offers vaccine producers a significantly simplified negotiation process with a single point of contact, thus reducing costs for all. Centralizing vaccine procurement at EU level has the merit of speed and efficiency by comparison with 27 separate processes. A truly European approach would avoid competition between Member States. It creates solidarity between all Member States, irrespective of the size of their population and their purchasing power. A pan-EU approach will increase the EU's leverage when negotiating with industry. It will also enable us to combine the scientific and regulatory expertise of the Commission and the Member States" (ibid.). In doing so, the Commission always emphasizes the caveat: "A common EU approach will always respect the principle of subsidiarity and Member States' competences in health policy: vaccination policies remain in the hands of Member States" (ibid.). These are some factors that caused only a reluctant shift of responsibilities for health affairs from the Member States to the Commission.

A Lack of Institutionalization and Experience

The main problem was that with the transfer of the purchase negotiations for vaccines, new health policy tasks at the EU level arose. The need for communitarization was obvious, but no corresponding institutions existed. The task for the Commission was to support the development of vaccines and to provide vaccine for 450 million people. The Commission acted not in its own right but on behalf of the member countries. Such pooled purchasing was a totally new community task for the European Commission and even more complicated because orders had to be placed long before vaccines were developed: "The Commission liked the extra responsibility. But whereas Paris, Berlin and Rome all have officials well accustomed to buying anything from a new type of frigate to a railway line, Brussels has little experience managing largescale procurement, certainly not at speed in a shifting land-scape" (*The Economist* April 3–9, 2021, 16).[15] The new task, which had to be mastered under time pressure and high uncertainty, encountered a European policy field that lacked any institutionalization in this sub-area. As a result, there was no routine in the Commission and no generalized public trust in its actions. "It was only in January (2021) that the extent of Europe's vaccine misfire started coming to light" (ibid.).

It soon became clear that the Commission was faced with risks that were difficult to calculate. According to Director General Sandra Gallina, of the Directorate-General Health and Food Safety (SANTE) of the European Commission speaking before the European Parliament on January 12, 2021, buyers had to choose between 65 vaccine developers at the start of purchase negotiations. Too little was ordered, and too much emphasis was placed on negotiating low prices. This became apparent when it became clear that the EU was being supplied by pharmaceutical firms on a time-lagged basis, and that savings were disproportionate to the looming economic costs of prolonged lockdowns. In addition, there were setbacks and delays in the development and production of vaccines—risks that were to be ex-pected, but for whose consequences the Commission was blamed across the board. Weak institutionalization and the lack of generalized trust in the Commission's health policy was used by the Member States to deflect atten-tion from the fact that they were involved in the negotiations themselves: "All

---

[15] And the *Economist* continues: "And because health is not usually the purview of the EU, the brightest Eurocrats typically prefer other briefs. The health commissioner in recent years has hailed from relative minnows such as Cyprus, Lithunia or Malta" (ibid.).

THE IMPACT OF THE COVID-19 PANDEMIC 319

participating Member States will be represented in a steering board, which will assist the Commission on all aspects of the APA (Advance Purchase Agreement) contract before signature. A joint negotiation team composed of the Commission and a small number of Member State experts will negotiate the APAs. The APAs will be concluded on behalf of all participating Member States" (European Commission 2020, 4). The Commission warned in advance that "the failure rate of vaccine development is high" and "there is no guarantee that a safe and effective vaccine will be available soon" (ibid., 9). In mid-2021 (see Tagesschau, May 8, 2021), the Commission made the largest vaccine purchase to date, with a total volume of 1.8 billion doses. In the process, the focus was shifted from favorable price to security of supply.

The Impact of the Pandemic

In order to assess the enduring impact of the corona pandemic in the field of health, I refer to the two strands of policies I introduced above.

EU health policy, path-dependent: EMA experienced an increase of public awareness—thus, also of political relevance—concerning the admission of new drugs and recommendations for their use. All in all, during the pandemic the EMA became an important institutional actor for building trust in health policy at the EU level. This development takes place without the formation of new institutions, but stabilizes the level of institutionalization that has been achieved. This is important not least because the EMA is an EU institution that has its own sources of funding beyond the EU budget, namely fees to be paid in the admission procedures.

EU health policy, new: The key pandemic policy task of vaccine purchasing created a complicated nesting of competencies between Member States and the Commission. The Commission acts on behalf of the Member States, while start-up funding comes from the European Structural and Investment Fund. Thus financing, purchasing, and distribution resulted in a confusing mix of competencies. The Commission acts as the purchaser externally and as the responsible party internally. In parallel, however, there is a "steering committee" of the Member States, which must agree to everything. In addition, the Member States (and at least in Germany, even the federal states) can purchase vaccine independently. What effects can be expected from this constellation? The dysfunctionalities can lead either to complete renationalization or to a gradual expansion of the Commission's competences as a reaction to obvious mutual dependencies within pandemics. The consciousness of mutual dependency led to the foundation of a new institution, namely the Health Emergency Response Authority (HERA).[16] This is a legal framework to strengthen the capacity of ECDC and EMA to act and to improve cooperation between the Commission and the Member States. It is primarily to perform information and coordination tasks.

The experience of the pandemic has led to numerous demands and proposals to strengthen EU health policy and to develop a "European Health Union." For instance, there is an initiative of the European Federation of Neurological Associations to strengthen EU health policy competencies. It starts with a useful outline of the development of competencies in recent years and then moves on to recommendations concerning increased competencies in health policy for the Commission. Similar proposals come from the European Public Health Alliance (EPHA), a network of NGOs, with reference to a study commissioned by the European Parliament. Basically "the EU must do more to improve how it uses its existing powers" (EPHA 2020).[17] The proposal of the European Commission is—significantly—partly a continuation and partly complementary institution-building. "It is proposing to upgrade the core agencies, the European Medicines Agency (EMA) and the European Centre for Disease Prevention and Control (ECDC), and to create a new one: the European Health Emergency Preparedness and Response Authority (HERA)" (Sipiczki and Lannoo 2021).

The Europeanization of Public Finances

The changes taking place in the field of public finances are publicly less conspicuous than those concerning mobility and health, but they far exceed those in the other two fields in terms of relevance for the EU integration process. The EU fiscal policy reacted to the corona crisis basically in a twofold way. In a first step, the Euro members fiscal room was widened. The Commission suspended the fiscal restrictions fixed in the Maastricht treaty. This widened the fiscal room of maneuver of the members of the Eurozone, in particular for temporary tax reduction in order to strengthen private consumption. But allowing all members to borrow more does not create equal

---

[16] European Commission 2020a.
[17] For an overview of the EU's existing competencies in health policies see Purnhagen et al. 2020.

chances to overcome the crisis as long as the conditions for debt are highly different for each country. And besides, it only supported the Euro members, when the pandemic was causing difficulties for all EU members. Thus, in a second step, more fiscal means were created. The Commission offered additional financial means, in particular by the SURE program (Support to mitigate Unemployment Risks in an Emergency, with a volume of up to €100 billion), "supporting short-time work schemes and similar measures"[18] in all EU Member States. This program, important as it was in itself in reducing unemployment, is seen as a precursor[19] of a much bigger and truly pathbreaking institutional innovation at the EU level.

The "NextGenerationEU"

The European Council decided on July 21, 2020, to start the "recovery and resilience facility" (also "NextGenerationEU," or NGEU), a financial instrument of €750 billion to deal with the economic fallout of the pandemic, focusing on health policy, ecological modernization, and digitalization. This is remarkable because during the euro crisis, the deficit countries that were most affected failed in their desire to take on joint debt due to the resistance of the others, largely orchestrated by Germany (De la Porte and Jensen 2021). The split between South and North is a nasty legacy of the euro crisis. The Council's decision for temporary borrowing by the Commission with proportional guarantees from the member countries was taken after relatively short discussion in July 2020, showing that most countries have learned from the financial and euro crises (exception: the "frugal four" including Austria, Denmark, the Netherlands, and Sweden). What will be the results?

Issuing bonds is not entirely new for the Commission.[20] "The EU has been operating three loan programmes to provide financial assistance to Member States and third countries experiencing financial difficulties: EFSM, BoP and MFA,"[21] In particular one might access this question by looking at

---

[18] https://ec.europa.eu/info/business-economy-euro/economic-and-fiscal-policy-coordination/financial-assistance-eu/funding

[19] In its Investor Call, the Commission (2021a: 7) itself names the SURE program "a useful preparation for NextGenerationEU."

[20] Though some authors try to insinuate this (see for instance Leino-Sandberg 2021).

[21] European Financial Stabilisation Mechanism (EFSM): Under Council Regulation (EU) 407/2010 of May 11, 2010 (as amended), EU financial assistance may be granted (in the form of a loan or a credit line) to a Member State in difficulties or seriously threatened with severe difficulties caused by

the smaller SURE program (100 billion, versus NGEU 750 billion). At the same time, the Commission sees the SURE program as a step toward a redistributive EU social policy, hence breaking with a long record of almost exclusively concentrating on regulatory social policy. Nevertheless, the program still does not install a direct relationship between the Commission and the population. SURE supports Member States not people. "The SURE instrument can be seen as an emergency operationalisation of the European Unemployment Reinsurance Scheme announced by the President of the European Commission in her Political Guidelines."[22] The program supports short-time work and similar measures. The first placement of (17 billion) "Social Bonds,"[23] as the Commission calls it, for financing the SURE program[24] was a great success. Lenders would have been willing to lend €233 billion. The Commission's demand for credit was thus more than 13 times oversubscribed. Accordingly, the interest rate for the EU members to whom the borrowed funds are passed on is extremely favorable: minus 0.102%.

Additional Institutions Required

Besides the much larger volume, the key difference between the two debt programs arises from the different issuance techniques, namely the shift from "back-to-back funding" to a "diversified funding strategy." Without going into too much technical detail (Preunkert 2020): This change has the

exceptional occurrences beyond its control.https://eur-lex.europa.eu/legal-content/EN/TXT/?uri=CELEX%3A32010R04075

Balance of Payments program (BoP): Under Council regulation (EU) 332/2002 of February 18, 2002 (as amended), the EU may assist Member States outside the euro area which are in difficulties or are seriously threatened with difficulties as regards their balance of payments.https://eur-lex.europa.eu/legal-content/EN/ALL/?uri=CELEX%3A32002R03326

Macro-Financial Assistance (MFA): The EU may assist third countries experiencing a balance-of-payment crisis with grants and/or loans on the basis of individual decisions of the European Parliament and of the Council. The instrument is designed to address exceptional external financing needs of countries that are geographically, economically, and politically close to the EU. https://ec.europa.eu/info/business-economy-euro/economic-and-fiscal-policy-coordination/international-economic-relations/macro-financial-assistance-mfa-non-eu-partner-countries_en

https://ec.europa.eu/info/sites/info/files/about_the_european_commission/eu_budget/eu_sure_social_bond_framework.pdf

[22] https://ec.europa.eu/info/sites/info/files/about_the_european_commission/eu_budget/eu_sure_social_bond_framework.pdf
[23] Concerning "Social Bond Principles" see the guidelines published by the International Capital Market Association (June 2020). https://www.icmagroup.org/assets/documents/Regulatory/Green-Bonds/June-2020/Social-Bond-PrinciplesJune-2020-090620.pdf
[24] SURE = Support to mitigate Unemployment Risks in an Emergency

effect of creating a dedicated issuance network. In essence, it connects the Commission with potential creditors via selected banks ("primary dealer network"). This requires the development of additional institutions within the Commission. In other words, the debt management triggers complementary institution-building at the EU level. Their tasks are already described in the decision of the Commission "on the establishment of the primary dealer network,"[25] specifying the duties of all participants, the inclusion of financial institutions in the primary dealer network, the control of the qualifications of the primary dealers, and the rules for exclusion and so forth. All in all, "the borrowing operations will be encoded in a robust governance framework, which will ensure coherent and consistent execution."[26]

The EU bonds will be placed in tranches between 2021 and 2026, using different techniques. The bonds have maturities of between three and 30 years. For liquidity reasons, it is necessary for the Commission to manage a cash reserve. With respect to institution-building, the effect of all these technical innovations is also crucial: NextGenerationEU institutionalizes public finance management as an EU competence and increases the Commission's autonomy vis-à-vis the Member States. "Given the volume, frequency and complexity of the borrowing, the Commission will have to undertake the debt management policy similar to those of large sovereigns" (European Commission 2021a, 10). A critical reading of the coverage rules (provision for repayment of the grants and for defaults on the loans) amounts to the Commission providing overcollateralization of up to 10 times the potential payment obligations. Attached to this is the suspicion that the Commission is securing financial leeway on a permanent basis. "The political signal is unmistakable: a margin is already being created here today, which will then be available in future crises and can be quickly activated" (Heinemann 2020, 17; my translation). This is meant polemically, but it fits the thesis of complementary institution-building.

Beyond such polemical "signal" interpretations, it can be summed up that the financing of the NextGenerationEU fund required the development of its own, new institutions. The lawsuit against NextGenerationEU before the German Federal Constitutional Court will presumably further

---

[25] COMMISSION DECISION (EU, Euratom) 2021/625 of April 14, 2021; Art 6. https://eur-lex.europa.eu/legal-content/EN/TXT/?uri=CELEX%3A32021D0625
[26] European Commission, "The EU's unified funding approach in a nutshell" https://commission.europa.eu/strategy-and-policy/eu-budget/eu-borrower-investor-relations/how-eu-issuance-works_en

the formation of institutions against their own intention. This is because the court did not grant the lawsuit any suspensive effect. The implementation of NextGenerationEU therefore creates a fait accompli. On May 31, 2021 the "Own Resources Decision" was ratified by all 27 Member States. On December 6, 2022, however, the German Constitutional Court finally rejected the complaints against the "Eigenmittelbeschluss-Ratifizierungsgesetz" (Own Resources Ratification Act) which translates NextGenerationEU into German law. Nevertheless, the court in its reasoning insists that community borrowing remains a rare exception. In order to put the EU Commission's debt competence on a solid footing, the best option would be to provide better constitutional safeguards for the Commission's future debt programs; in other words, to make complementary institution-building irreversible.

Immediate Success and the Manifestation of Additional Effects

On June 15, 2021, a first tranche of 20bn Euro was issued. It was seven times oversubscribed, indicating the big interest in investing in these kind of bonds. Reuters, a news agency, reports: "The new EU bond, due July 4 2021, was priced to yield 0.086%, according to the lead managers. It rallied in the 'grey' market pre-issuance, market participants said—further evidence of strong demand." (Bahceli 2021a) In addition, "the bond rallied sharply in the secondary market in further evidence of strong demand", Reuters added the next day (Bahceli 2021b). On July 2, 2021 it dropped for the first time beyond zero (Ranasinghe 2021).

As is well known, the interest rate situation has changed markedly since 2021. Of course, NGEU bonds are now also in positive interest rate territory. However, their relative position compared with government bonds with similar conditions has not changed. "EU bonds have traded at tight yield spreads relative to German Bunds, and below the GDP-weighted average of euro area sovereign yields, suggesting that the high credit quality of EU bonds is well understood by market participants" (Bletzinger, Greif, and Schwaab 2023). The finding of continued attractiveness is supported by two other indicators of creditor confidence. First: The yield curve of NGEU bonds by maturity shows the standard pattern, namely modestly higher yields at the long end. This indicates long-term creditor confidence in NGEU bonds. Secondly: At the same time, the difference between the selling and buying price (bid-ask spread), a measure of the liquidity risk perceived by market participants, has decreased. It is therefore possible to convert EU bonds into liquidity at relatively low transaction costs. However, they are still significantly higher than the bid-ask spreads of the 10-year bonds of important EU-members. "EU bonds' prospects for becoming a genuine euro-denominated safe asset could potentially be hampered by the fact that both SURE and the NGEU programme are foreseen to be one-off, time-limited pandemic emergency responses." (ibid.)

Obviously, the common funding of the NGEU represents advantages for less creditworthy debtors among EU Member States. But are there also effects that benefit actors beyond the immediate beneficiaries? In the short run, it is likely that EU bonds will put a brake on excessive negative interest rates (in particular for Germany). Because it can be taken as granted that EU bonds will pay slightly higher interest than German bonds. But there are some much more important, structural effects.

The great willingness to lend money to the EU will strengthen the euro as a safe investment currency and potentially as an alternative to the US dollar (Horwood 2021; Ranasinghe and Carvallo 2020), notwithstanding the fact that at present (June 2021) outstanding debts of the EU and of the United States relate 1: 20. (*The Economist* June 26–July 2, 2021, 60) The Commission concludes:

> Looking beyond the immediate economic and social crisis, a successful NGEU issuance programme will also strengthen the fabric of the Economic and Monetary Union, enhance the role of the euro in international capital markets and confirm EU leadership in sustainable finance. (European Commission 2021b, 9–10)

Positive effects of an internationally trusted euro reach beyond the obvious advantages for the Eurozone, its economy, and people. "About two dozen countries link their own currencies to it in some way" (*The Economist* June 26, July 2, 2021, 59). Corradin, Grimm, and Schwaab (2021), all from the European Central Bank (ECB), evaluated the impact of announcements of the ECB monetary policy and the Commisssion on fiscal policy:"Both ECB monetary and E.U. fiscal announcements had a pronounced impact on yields, mainly by affecting default, redenomination, and liquidity risk premia. The ECB's unconventional monetary policy announcements benefited some countries more than others, owing to unprecedented flexibility when implementing bond purchases. The E.U.'s fiscal policy announcements, by contrast, lowered yields more uniformly, possibly by moving fiscal risks onto shared budgets, lowering political (redenomination) risks through decisive action at the European level, and complementing the ECB's monetary policy aimed at improving the economic outlook" (Corradin, Grimm, and Schwaab 2021, 34–35).

Reporting in a similar manner on additional benefits of EU bonds by news media like *The Economist* is performative: From a sociological perspective, making advantageous effects beyond the immediate purpose of EU bonds explicit means mobilizing additional interests in favor of community debt. Notwithstanding a future test in practice, EU bonds are likely to be supported by a broad coalition of the interests composed by the Commission, by borrowing EU Member States and international investors on the one hand, and a kind of permissive consensus on the part of the populations on the other. This suggests that it will not be relinquished anytime soon.

Complementary Institution-Building in the Field of Public Finances

As a result of the non-deterministic theoretical approach, it is not possible to make certain assumptions about the future development of institutions at the EU level. However, the approach of complementary institution-building allows us to formulate probabilities of these developments.

Will there follow steps of complementary institution-building? Yes, this is very likely.

A) On the side of raising funds: In the course of the conversion of public debt to the EURO system, agencies were created with the "task of placing public debt on the financial markets" (Preunkert 2020a, 56; my translation), agencies that act on behalf but independent of the governments (finance ministries) of their countries. Is there an analogous agency as a spin-off of the EU Commission? In any case, the tasks of the Commission as issuer are formulated roughly analogous to the tasks of the German Finanzagentur (COMMISSION DECISION (EU, Euratom) 2021/625 of April 14, 2021; Art 6).[27]

---

[27] On outsourcing debt management to a separate agency, cf. Trampusch 2015.

B) On the side of the allocation of financial resources: As the volume of transfers from the Commission to individual member countries increases, so does the risk of misuse and the interest in controlling the use of the funds. Two institutional innovations point in the direction of meeting these requirements. One is the rule of law mechanism adopted by the European Council on December 10–11, 2020, which explicitly aims to protect the EU budget. It allows the Commission to withhold funding from NextGenerationEU if rule of law deficiencies in a member country jeopardize the proper use of funds (Nguyen 2020). Thus, a complementary institution is emerging to deal with problems that another may bring. The other institutional innovation is the European Public Prosecutors' Office, EPPO[28] (based in Luxembourg). It has existed since June 1, 2021. In contrast to the European Anti-Fraud Office, (OLAF), founded in 1999, the EPPO has the right of legal action: "The EPPO can bring criminal charges for misuse of EU funds and for a number of other offences, such as VAT and customs fraud" (*The Economist* August 21–27, 2021, 17). However in doing so it must rely on national courts, although it is an EU institution. These are almost textbook examples of the connections between institution-building, anticipated follow-up problems, and complementary institution-building.

Will these institutions be sustainable? Almost certainly: yes. I concentrate on the main new institution, the common debt.

With the Commission as a new (good!) debtor on the international financial markets, there is a potential competitor to Member States as debtors. On a global scale, this will lead to a weakening of the role of the US dollar as the world's reserve currency and thus to a shift in the balance of economic power between the US and the EU. Within the EU, this can lead to a paradoxical effect: The single currency and the ECJ's decision in 2000 that sovereigns must treat domestic and foreign creditors equally have strengthened competition among providers of bonds, hence already weakened the position of lower-rated sovereigns on the capital market (Preunkert 2020a, 34). Community borrowing will reinforce this effect. Though it is intended to facilitate the public financing of EU members with poorer credit ratings, it leads to (direct) access to the capital market becoming more difficult for precisely these countries, because potential creditors prefer EU bonds to the national bonds

---

[28] https://eur-lex.europa.eu/legal-content/EN/TXT/?uri=CELEX%3A32021D0856

of these countries. In the long term, this will mean that EU countries with poorer credit ratings will increasingly only be able—and willing—to borrow via the Commission. The huge institutional upgrading of the Commission as debtor creates a new player in the public debt market as a "configuration of power" (Preunkert 2020a, 13ff.). The position of governments as providers of bonds vis-à-vis potential lenders has already been weakened by the transition to a common currency area (Pagano and von Thadden 2004; Preunkert 2020a, 47ff.). Community debt now adds an additional factor: a new bond provider (debtor) which—as the development of the first NGEU bond tranches on the secondary market shows—is highly attractive to investors. As a result, this constellation in the relationship between Community bonds and national bonds could emerge. The countries with the highest ratings can borrow on terms more favorable than the Community debt, while member countries whose creditworthiness is below that of the Commission are fully dependent on it—just another argument for the irreversibility of joint borrowing.

A Theory-Oriented Conclusion

My analyses of the effects of the pandemic on European integration in the three policy areas of mobility, health, and public finances have yielded information that—I hope—speaks for itself. Instead of repeating this *in extenso*, I will therefore offer a theoretical conclusion as a kind of common denominator.

The starting point of my argument was that individual actors are overwhelmed with the management of the pandemic because of the collective-good problem and the prevention paradox. The problem that arises from this is essentially that solutions via self-organization by the people are very unlikely. So, state regulation is needed to produce the collective good of pandemic containment. This makes institutional politics central, and thus the classic sequence: "Institution building precedes awareness raising" (Lepsius 2013, 189; my translation).

In addition, the covid pandemic manifests global interdependencies. This applies to the routes of infection, to pandemic policy, and to the side effects of pandemic policy. Contagion cannot be kept away from individual states, and border closures do not work or are not practical with the rigidity that is medically required. Isolated pandemic policies of individual states are therefore illusory; transnational cooperation within the EU and beyond is required (Beck, Grande 2007). What are the effects for the EU's complementary institution-building? I have outlined this for the policy fields of mobility, health, and public finance.

In all three policy fields examined, actors' constellations are at work, in which the problems are taken up by relevant actors in an institutional context and dealt with under time pressure. In terms of implementation and results, the effects in the three fields differ considerably. The changes brought about by the pandemic in the policy field of mobility are striking but temporary. The Schengen Code represents a complex of institutions that could be adjusted to pandemic policies without directly changing the institutions themselves. The effects of the pandemic are more likely to be manifested in the fact that mobility policy development trends that exist anyway are reinforced by it.

In the policy field of health, two types of developments are triggered by the pandemic. On the one hand, the pressure of the problem leads to the path-dependent development of institutions that already existed. However, this institutional base was and is relatively weakly developed. On the other hand, there is a great deal of pressure to deal with problems, for which hardly any EU institutions are available. This is evident from the confusion of competencies between the EU level and the Member State level. The unraveling of this confusion in favor of the formation of new institutions at the EU level is not yet apparent, because the Member States are the relevant actors here and because there are hardly any points of contact at the EU level. There are, so to speak, no institutions to add yet. In addition, unclear competencies offer members the opportunity for blame avoidance—an effect that has become visible with the procurement processes of vaccines and hinders institution-building.

In the policy field of public finance, on the other hand, we find an example of exceedingly dynamic complementary institution-building. Connecting factors are already in place, plus the test by SURE. Strong interests on the part of the Commission, the divided interests of the Member States, and the change in expert opinions as a result of the bad experiences in the aftermath of the euro crisis have a reinforcing effect in the direction of complementary institution-building. The consolidation of complementary institutionalization is to be expected, as interests in retention are added to interests in the introduction of EU debt. With the issuance of community bonds, a whole bundle of additional benefits of community debt becomes manifest—and thus additional interests and supporters of community debt emerge.

What can be learned from this analysis for the sociological theory of European integration? A problem is never the cause of its solution, but only of the attempt of its solution. In order to explain the solution of a problem causally, a chain of problem perception, motivations (interests, values, attitudes), action strategies, power relations, and actions has to be thought between the problem and its solution. This presupposes that sociological theory focuses on actors in institutionally shaped actor constellations. In the course of European integration, institutions give rise to historically different actor constellations, which in turn have an effect on institutions. The actor constellations specific to political fields change over time and are therefore capable of resonating with different problems. Problem solutions lead to further institution-building and thus to follow-up problems. This is the dynamic of institutional European integration.

References

Alesina, Alberto, and Francesco Giavazzi. 2020. "Will coronavirus kill the European Union?" March 27, 2020. https://www.city-journal.org/covid-19-european-union.

Bach, Maurizio. 2010. "Die Konstitution von Räumen und Grenzbildung in Europa. Von verhandlungsresistenten zu verhandlungsabhängigen Grenzen." In *Gesellschaftstheorie und Europapolitik. Sozialwissenschaftliche Ansätze zur Europaforschung*, edited by Eigmüller, Monika, and Steffen Mau, 153–78. Wiesbaden: Springer VS.

Bahceli, Yoruk. 2021a. "EU launches landmark new program to near record demand-bankers". *Reuters*, June 15, 2021. https://www.reuters.com/article/us-eu-recovery-bonds-idUSKCN2DR0SB.

Bahceli, Yoruk. 2021a. "Debut EU recovery fund bond rallies sharply, investors await Fed." *Reuters*, June 16, 2021. https://www.reuters.com/article/us-eurozone-bonds-idUSKC N2DS0PZ

Beck, Urich, and Edgar Grande. 2007. *Cosmopolitan Europe*. Cambridge: Polity Press.

Bletzinger, Tilman, William Greif, and Bernd Schwaab. 2023. "The safe asset potential of EU-issued bonds." European Central Bank, Research Bulletin No. 103, January 16, 2023. https://www.ecb.europa.eu/pub/economic-research/resbull/2023/html/ecb. rb230116~e55fb14a74.de.html

Christie, Rebecca, Grégory Claeys, and Pauline Weil. 2021. "Next Generation EU borrowing: a first assessment. Policy Contribution 22/2021." Brussels: Bruegel. https:// www.bruegel.org/2021/11/next-generation-eu-borrowing-a-first-assessment/.

Constancio, Vítor. 2011. "Contagion and the European debt crisis." Keynote by the vice-president of the ECB at the Bocconi University/Intesa Sanpaolo conference on "Bank Competitiveness in the Post-crisis World" Milan. October 10, 2011. https://www.ecb. europa.eu/press/key/date/2011/html/sp111010.en.html.

Cebulak, Pola, and Marta Morvillo. 2021. "The Guardian is Absent. Legality of Border Controls within Schengen before the European Court of Justice." June 25, 2021. https:// verfassungsblog.de/the-guardian-is-absent/.

Corradin, Stefano, Niklas Grimm, and Bernd Schwaab. 2021. Euro area sovereign bond risk premia during the Covid-19 pandemic. https://www.berndschwaab.eu/papers/CGS_BondRiskPremia.pdf.

De la Porte, Caroline, and Mads Dagnis Jensen. 2021. "The Next Generation EU: An analysis of the dimensions of conflicts behind the deal." *Social Policy & Administration* 55 (2): 388–402.

Delhey, Jan, Emanuel Deutschmann, Monika Verbalyte, and Auke Aplowski. 2020. *Netzwerk Europa. Wie ein Kontinent durch Mobilität und Kommunikation zusammenwächst*. Wiesbaden: Springer VS.

Deutschmann, Emanuel, Jan Delhey, Monika Verbalyte, and Auke Aplowski. 2018. "The power of contact: Europe as a network of transnational attachment." *European Journal of Political Research* 57 (4): 963–88.

Doshi, Peter. 2011. "The elusive definition of pandemic influenza." *Bulletin of the World Health Organization* 89 (7): 532–38. https://doi.org/10.2471/BLT.11.086173.

Eigmüller, Monika. 2007. *Grenzsicherungspolitik. Funktion und Wirkung der europäischen Außengrenze*. Wiesbaden: Springer VS.

Eigmüller, Monika. 2013. "Europeanization from below: The influence of individual actors on the EU integration of social policies." *Journal of European Social Policy* 23 (4): 363–75.

Eigmüller, Monika. 2021. "Grenzen und Europa." In *Grenzforschung. Handbuch für Wissenschaft und Studium*, edited by Dominik Gerst, Maria Klessmann, Hannes Krämer, 257–66. Baden-Baden: Nomos.

EPHA, European Public Health Alliance. 2021. "How the EU can do more for our health." March 25, 2020. https://epha.org/how-the-eu-can-do-more-for-our-health/.

European Commission. 2020. "EU strategy for COVID 19 vaccines." Brussels, June 17, 2020. COM(2020) 245 final.

European Commission. 2020a. "Building a European Health Union: Reinforcing the EU's resilience for cross-border health threats." Brussels, November 11, 2020. COM(2020) 724 final.

European Commission. 2021. "A strategy towards a fully functioning and resilient Schengen area." Brussels, June 2, 2021. COM(2021) 277 final.

European Commission. 2021a. "Investor Call." June 8, 2021. Borrowing to finance the recovery: EU's upcoming issuance under NGEU. https://ec.europa.eu/info/sites/default/files/about_the_european_commission/eu_budget/gic_slides_08062021.pdf.

European Commission. 2021b. "On a funding strategy to finance NextGenerationEU." Brussels, April 14, 2021. COM(2021) 250 final.

European Commission. 2021c. "Drawing the early lessons from the COVID-19 pandemic." Brussels, June 15, 2021. COM(2021) 380 final.

European Commission. 2021d. "Proposal for a Regulation of the European Parliament and of the Council amending Regulation." (EU) 2016/399 on a Union Code on the rules governing the movement of persons across borders. Strasbourg, December 14, 2021. COM(2021) 891 final.

Goldmann, Matthias. 2020. "The Case for Corona Bonds. A Proposal by a Group of European Lawyers." *Verfassungsblog*, April 5, 2020. https://verfassungsblog.de/the-case-for-corona-bonds/

Heinemann, Friedrich. 2020. "Die Überdeckung der Next Generation EU-Schulden im Entwurf des neuen EU-Eigenmittelbeschlusses: Ausmaß und Haftungskonsequenzen." Erarbeitet anlässlich der Anhörung des Ausschusses für die Angelegenheiten der

Europäischen Union des Deutschen Bundestages am October 26, 2020. Deutscher Bundestag, Ausschussdrucksache 19(21)112.

Hatzopoulos, Vassilis. 2002. "Killing national health and insurance systems but healing patients: The European market for health care services after the judgements of the ECJ in Vanbraekel and Peerbooms." *Common Market Law Review* 39 (4): 683–729.

Hilpert, Isabel. 2020. *Die doppelt codierte Grenze und der Nationalstaat in Europa. Eine Untersuchung am Beispiel der Republik Italien.* Wiesbaden: Springer VS.

Hooghe, Liesbet, and Gary Marks. 2019. "Grand theories of European Integration in the twenty-first century." *Journal of European Public Policy*, Special Issue: Re-engaging Grand Theorie: European Integration in the Twenty-first Century 26 (8): 1113–133. https://www.tandfonline.com/doi/full/10.1080/13501763.2019.1569711.

Horn, Sebastian, Josefin Meyer, and Christoph Trebesch. 2020. "Europäische Gemeinschaftsanleihen seit der Ölkrise: Lehren für heute?" Kiel Policy Brief, No. 136/2020. Kiel: Institut für Weltwirtschaft. https://www.ifw-kiel.de/fileadmin/Dateiverwalt ung/IfW-Publications/-ifw/Kiel_Policy_Brief/2020/kiel_policy_brief_136_en.pdf

Horwood, Clive. 2021. "Next Generation EU issuance will boost euro's reserve status." OMFIF Official Monetary and Financial Institutions Forum, 16. June 2021. https://www.omfif.org/2021/06/next-generation-eu-issuance-will-boost-euro-reserve-status/.

Hruschka, Constantin. 2020. "In der Pandemie stirbt die europäische Solidarität." *VerfBlog,* March 18, 2020. https://verfassungsblog.de/in-der-pandemie-stirbt-die-europaeische-solidaritaet/; https://doi.org/10.17176/20200319-003230-0.

Hüther, Michael. 2020. "The European Union did not experience its 'Hamiltonian Moment'." *The International Economy Magazine,* p. 21. Summer 2020. Köln.

Kelly, Heath. 2011. "The classical definition of a pandemic is not elusive." *Bulletin of the World Health Organization* 89 (7): 540–41. https://doi.org/10.2471/BLT.11.086173.

Kiess, Johannes. 2015. "German Unions and Business: What the Crisis is About and How to Solve it." In *Aftermath. Political and Urban Consrequences of the Euro Crisis,* edited by Luís Baptista, Jenny Preunkert, and Georg Vobruba, 23–47. Lisboa: Edicoes Colibri.

Krastev, Ivan. 2020. *Ist heute schon morgen? Wie die Pandemie Europa verändert.* Berlin: Ullstein.

Last, John M. (ed.). 2001. *A Dictionary of Epidemiology,* 4th edition. New York: Oxford University Press.

Leino-Sandberg, Päivi. 2021. "How is ultra vires now? The EU's legal U-turn in interpreting." Article 310 TFEU. Verfassungsblog June 18, 2020. https://verfassungsb log.de/who-is-ultra-vires-now-the-eus-legal-u-turn-in-interpreting-article-310-tfeu/.

Lepsius, M. Rainer. (1999) 2013. "Die Europäische Union: Ökonomisch-politische Integration und kulturelle Pluralität." In *Institutionalisierung politischen Handelns. Analysen zur DDR, Wiedervereinigung und Europäischen Union,* edited by M. Rainer Lepsius, 185–203. Wiesbaden: Springer VS.

Luhmann, Niklas. 1962. "Funktion und Kausalität." *Kölner Zeitschrift für Soziologie und Sozialpsychologie* 14: 617–44.

Majone, Giandomenico. 1993. "The European Community between social policy and social regulation." *JCMS* 31 (2): 153–70.

Mau, Steffen, Heike Brabandt, Lena Laube, and Christof Roos. 2012. *Liberal States and the Freedom of Movement. Selective Borders, Unequal Mobility.* Hundmills, Basingstoke: Palgrave.

Mayntz, Renate. 2007. "Kausale Rekonstruktion: Theoretische Aussagen im akteurtszentrierten Institutionalismus." In *Sozialwissenschaftliches Erklären. Probleme der Theoriebildung und Methodologie*, edited by Renate Mayntz, 83–95. Frankfurt a. M., New York: Campus.

Mayntz, Renate, and Fritz W. Scharpf. 1995. "Der Ansatz des akteurszentrierten Institutionalismus." In *Gesellschaftliche Selbstregelung und politische Steuerung* edited by Renate Mayntz, and Fritz W. Scharpf, 39–72. Frankfurt a. M., New York: Campus.

Merton, Robert. (1949) 1968. *Social Theory and Social Structure*. New York: The Free Press.

Missio, Sebastian, and Sebastian Watzka. 2011. "Financial Contagion and the European Debt Crisis" (August 31, 2011). CESifo Working Paper Series No. 3554, Available at SSRN: https://ssrn.com/abstract=1920642.

Müller, Andreas. 2014. *Governing Mobility Beyond the State. Centre, Periphery and the EU's External Borders*. Hundmills, Basingstoke: Palgrave.

Nguyen, Thu. 2020. "The EU's new rule of law mechanism. How it works and why the 'deal' did not weaken it." Herti School, Jacqes Delors Centre. Policy Brief, December 17, 2020. https://www.hertie-school.org/fileadmin/2_Research/1_About_our_research/2_Research_centres/6_Jacques_Delors_Centre/Publications/20201217_Rule_of_law_Nguyen.pdf.

Pagano, Marco, and Ernst-Ludwig von Thadden. 2004. "The European bond markets under EMU." *Oxford Review of Economic Policy* 20 (4): 531–54.

Patra, Soumyajit. 2021. "The COVID-19 pandemic and a new sociology of social distancing." *Economic & Political Weekly* 256 (23). https://www.epw.in/engage/article/covid-19-pandemic-and-new-sociology-social.

Preunkert, Jenny. 2020. "Primary Dealer Systems in the European Union." MaxPo Discussion Paper 20/1. Max Planck Science Po Center on Coping with Instability in Market Societies, Paris. http://www.maxpo.eu/pub/maxpo_dp/maxpodp20-1.pdf

Preunkert, Jenny. 2020a. *Eine Soziologie der Staatsverschuldung. Über die Finanzialisierung, Transnationalisierung und Politisierung von Staatsschulden in der Eurozone*. Weinheim, Basel: Beltz Juventa.

Preunkert, Jenny, and Georg Vobruba. 2012. "Die Eurokrise—Konsequenzen der defizitären Institutionalisierung der gemeinsamen Währung." In *Entfesselte Finanzmärkte. Soziologische Analysen des modernen Kapitalismus*, edited by Klaus Kraemer, and Sebastian Nessel, 201–23. Frankfurt a. M.: Campus.

Purnhagen, Kai P., Anniek de Ruijte, Mark L. Flear, Tamara K. Hervey, and Alexia Herwig. 2020. "More competences than you knew? The web of health competence for European Union action in response to the COVID-19 outbreak." *European Journal of Risk Regulation* 11 (2): 297–306.

Ranasinghe, Dhara, and Ritvik Carvalho. 2020. "Game changer? How the recovery fund will shake up EU bond markets." *Reuters*, July 21, 2020. https://www.reuters.com/article/us-eu-summit-bonds-graphic-idUSKCN24M1ME.

Sandholtz, Wayne, and Alec Stone Sweet. 2012. "Neo-functionalism and Supranational Governance." In *The Oxford Handbook of the European Union*, edited by Eric Jones, Anand Menon, and Stephen Weatherill, 18–33. Oxford: Oxford University Press.

Scharpf, Fritz W. 1997. *Games Real Actors Play. Actor-Centered Institutionalism in Policy Research*. London: Routledge.

Sipiczki, Agnes, and Karel Lannoo. 2021. "Upgrading the EMA and ECDC, and creating a new agency. The EU Health Union in search of a definition and an open discussion."

May 12, 2021. https://www.ceps.eu/the-eu-health-union-in-search-of-a-definition-and-an-open-discussion/.

Trampusch, Christine. 2015. "The financialization of sovereign debt. An institutional analysis of the reforms in German public debt management." *German Politics* 24 (2): 119–36.

Verdun, Amy. 2020. "Intergovernmentalism: Old, Liberal, and New." *Oxford Research Encyclopedias. Politics.* August 27, 2020. https://doi.org/10.1093/acrefore/9780190228 637.013.1489.

Vobruba, Georg. 2003. "The enlargement crisis of the European Union. Limits of the dialectics of integration and expansion." *Journal of European Social Policy* 134 (1): 35–49.

Vobruba, Georg. 2007. *Die Dynamik Europas.* Wiesbaden: Springer VS.

Vobruba, Georg. 2012. *Kein Gleichgewicht. Die Ökonomie in der Krise.* Weinheim, Basel: Beltz Juventa.

Vobruba, Georg. 2012a. *Der postnationale Raum. Transformation von Souveränität und Grenzen in Europa.* Weinheim, Basel: Beltz Juventa.

Vobruba, Georg. 2016. "Borders Within the Dynamism of Europe. European Migration Regimes Between Exclusion and Inclusion." In *Migration in an Era of Restriction and Recession,* edited by David L. Leal and Nestor P. Rodríguez, 165–74. Switzerland: Springer International Publishing.

Vobruba, Georg. 2019. "Soziologische Gesellschaftstheorie. Einleitung 2019." In *Die Gesellschaft der Leute,* edited by Georg Vobruba, 2nd edition, V–XXI. Wiesbaden: Springer VS.

Vobruba, Georg. 2020. "Corona-Bonds gegen die Gefahr der doppelten Ansteckung." *Der Standard* (Vienna), April 8, 2020.

Vobruba, Georg. 2021. "Corona lässt bangen und hoffen." *Neue Zürcher Zeitung,* April 12, 2021.

Vobruba, Georg 2021a. "Mobilitätspolitik als Pandemie-Politik. Folgen der Corona-Krise für das Schengen-Regime." *ÖGFE Policy Briefs* (Vienna), November 19, 2021. https://www.oegfe.at/policy-briefs/mobilitaetspolitik-als-pandemie-politik-folgen-der-cor ona-krise-fuer-das-schengen-regime/.

Vollaard, Hans, Hester van de Bovenkamp, and Dorte Sindbjerg Martinsen. 2016. "The making of a European health care union. A federalist perspective." *Journal of European Public Policy* 23 (2): 157–76.

Wagner, Gerhard. 2012. "Function and Causality." *Revue internationale de philosophie* 66 (259): 35–53.

Wang, Zhongyuan. 2021. "From crisis to nationalism? The conditioned effects of the COVID-19 crisis on neo-nationalism in Europe" *Chinese Political Science Review* 6: 20–39. https://doi.org/10.1007/s41111-020-00169-8.

Worschech, Susann. 2018. "The 'making' of Europe in the peripheries: Europeanization through conflicts and ambivalences." *Culture, Practice & Europeanization* 3 (3): 56–76.

Epilogue

Stefanie Börner and Martin Seeleib-Kaiser

The COVID-19 pandemic and the subsequent policy responses in affluent European democracies have demonstrated the resilience of the welfare state during a severe public health, social, and economic crisis. After decades of criticism by conservative and market-liberal political actors and observers on the one hand, and the critique of permanent austerity and welfare state retrenchment by progressive actors and social scientists on the other hand, the modern welfare state has mastered the most severe stress test in its history. Moreover, public social policies, in the form of public health measures, income transfers, or labor market policies, have once again underlined the various functions of social policy. For most people in affluent democracies of Europe, the welfare state has delivered during the pandemic, providing publicly procured vaccines, health care services, income maintenance, and wage-subsidies. We can only fully understand the huge social benefits of the welfare state when we consider the counterfactual, that is, a world without public social policies. Imagine vaccines would have had to be privately procured; or people would have had to pay out of pocket for their very costly coronavirus treatment in the intensive care unit of hospitals instead of the treatment being provided by public health systems for free or covered by social insurance. What would have happened if states had not provided relatively unbureaucratic transfer payments to those on short-time work or those furloughed? *Grosso modo*: The state has fulfilled its social function! Obviously, this does not mean that the welfare state compensated or supported *all* individuals equally. Moreover, the COVID-19 pandemic also made the limits of the existing welfare state arrangements vividly clear, be it the limited sick-pay arrangements or short-time work benefits for low-wage or low-skilled workers, or the fragile to inadequate care conditions in long-term adult care institutions in many countries.

Stefanie Börner and Martin Seeleib-Kaiser, *Epilogue* In: *European Social Policy and the COVID-19 Pandemic*. Edited by: Stefanie Börner and Martin Seeleib-Kaiser, Oxford University Press. © Oxford University Press 2023. DOI: 10.1093/oso/9780197676189.003.0013

Not only did public social policies protect people against social risks during the pandemic, but these policies also contributed to the economic and political stabilization during lockdowns and beyond. In most countries, governments demonstrated that they are willing to use social policies to stabilize the capitalist economic system. Thus, the economic benefits of social policy, highlighted already in the late 1920s, have once again been corroborated (cf. Briefs 1930; Vobruba 1989). While the benefits of social policies have been emphasized for specific political economies more recently by various political economists (see Swenson 2002; Estevez-Abe et al. 2001), governments' responses to the COVID-19 crisis have evidenced the benefits of rapid and strong social policy interventions for the stabilization of the economy in *all* affluent democracies, irrespective of the specific political economy or welfare regime type. Policies have contributed to stabilizing the aggregate demand as well as to coping with the economic challenges triggered by the interruption of the global supply chains on the supply side. It is worth to once again imagine the counterfactual, that is, imagine the economic development during the pandemic without the huge sums infused by governments into the economy via social transfers to citizens or directly as subsidies to companies. Clearly these policies can be characterized as politics for the market in the medium and long term, with the aim of rescuing market participants and preventing the entire system from potential collapse by instrumentalizing public social policies against the market, called for and supported by capitalists, in the short term. In other words, the crisis has demonstrated once again the contradictions of the welfare state so clearly identified by Claus Offe (1984 [1993: 153]), who maintained that "while capitalism cannot coexist *with*, neither can it exist *without*, the welfare state."

In many countries, a minority of the respective electorates was skeptical or opposed to various public health policies and protection measures promulgated via executive orders or enacted through regular legislation. The political debate in many places focused on these minorities and did not sufficiently and effectively communicate the benefits of the various health and social interventions. Moreover, through the various measures—for instance the social benefits for the self-employed in many European countries—governments have shown that they were willing to pay a *risk premium* (Briefs 1930) for maintaining political stability, and used social policy instruments to increase or maintain political legitimacy. The United Kingdom, a case where different crises reinforced each other, makes this particularly clear. COVID-19 presented the government with an opportunity to embark upon a new social policy strategy that also addresses the United Kingdom's sense of nation, as Matthew Donoghue impressively shows in his chapter. The way political rhetoric and emergency policies have been connected in the United Kingdom is an especially stark example of welfare states' legitimization strategies in general.

The social policy response to the pandemic in Europe has shown that after decades of welfare state consolidation, adaptation, and policies characterized by growth to limits, the capacity of the state to intervene was considerable. Not only did countries financially spend more on existing programs, they also expanded and created new programs. As hypothesized by Peter Flora (1986) in the 1980s, a *crisis* could potentially lead to a further significant expansion of social policy. Historically, wars have been key drivers for welfare state development (Obinger and Schmitt 2020) and high taxation (Scheve and Stasavage 2016) in the 20th century. The question that arises from a historical comparative perspective is whether the COVID-19 pandemic can potentially be identified as a *key* driver for overcoming the impasse toward more redistribution within national welfare states. The chapters of this volume indicate that the pandemic has not brought about any *immediate* grand structural changes. Changes have been bounded by existing political and institutional constraints, but also reflective of and building upon opportunities that arose. As so often, incremental change, characterized by path dependence, has been a common response mechanism. However, this does not mean that new political ideas and social movements will not lead to a novel welfare state paradigm. The pandemic has challenged liberal interpretations of the welfare state and might give way to (re)new(ed) interpretations of public responsibilities, learning processes, and policy innovations in the long run.

This volume's analyses have shown that the COVID-19 pandemic has contributed to further EU integration in the social policy domain and supported the stabilization of national welfare states as well as their expansion. From a theoretical perspective, the question of institutional change and continuity, a guiding question of this volume, is core to assessing the recent social policy developments. Critical juncture, window of opportunity, or turning point are just some of the concepts scholars have been using to describe the challenges *and* opportunities linked to COVID-19 and social policymaking in Europe. For welfare state theory this phenomenon is not new but describes two main conditions of the welfare state: the welfare state (itself) *in* crises and the welfare state *during* crises (Vobruba 1990, 12). The chapter by Emmanuele Pavolini et al. demonstrates how national health systems in Southern Europe have undergone processes of piecemeal recalibration in the wake of the pandemic, policies very different to the cutbacks during the hard times of the 2010s—but they also show that these health systems have not been radically reformed. Similar patterns apply to other policy domains such as social security (see Chapter 1 by Daniel Béland et al.) or social assistance (Chapter 3 by Tatiana Saruis, Eduardo Barberis, and Yuri Kazepov). Based on their analysis of the fiscal consolidation of 2010s, Klaus Armingeon and Stefano Sacchi in their chapter raise the specter that welfare states might once again face a period of cutbacks. However, their research also shows that periods of so-called austerity do not last forever, but that states face "austerity fatigue" after a while.

The pandemic not only shed light on the strength and weaknesses of specific welfare state institutions and previous reform paths, but also on the working and financial conditions of particular social groups. As women are overrepresented in many front-line services and disproportionally belong to the group of essential workers in various economic sectors (e.g., health care and retail), they have also been disproportionally exposed to health risks and had to carry a disproportional burden in many countries during pandemic. Working parents faced difficulties to reconcile work and family obligations, due increased care responsibilities because of closures of child care facilities and schools. Very often it was working mothers that took up the additional care responsibilities. Although evidence for some countries, among others for the United States of America, suggests that women have been particularly hard hit by the effects of the pandemic on the labor market, the analysis by Katja Möhring et al. demonstrates no particularly high exposure of women to pandemic-related labor market risks in Germany—very likely the outcome of labor market regulation and welfare arrangements. Cecilia Bruzelius and Martin Seeleib-Kaiser's chapter suggests that institutionalized exploitation of seasonal workers continued in various EU countries due to a lack of enforcement by Member States, even though actors across the political spectrum have symbolically voiced strong support for labor and social rights during the pandemic. The challenges young people in Europe have been facing during the COVID-19 pandemic, namely aggravated transitions, insufficient social protection, and unemployment, are different in nature, as the chapter by O'Reilly et al. shows. In other words: although labor market regulations and welfare state arrangements protected many people during the pandemic, the pandemic did not expose people equally to risks, and public social policies did not protect people equally well. Moreover, the pandemic has also highlighted the shortcomings of existing labor market regulations and welfare arrangements, and the cases studied in this volume do not suggest that the reforms triggered by COVID-19 will benefit the most vulnerable groups.

Although very often characterized as an entity *sui generis*, the EU was confronted with very similar challenges as other federations in dealing with the pandemic, as shown by Natalie Glynn. Whether the EU will learn from the positive or negative experiences in some of these jurisdictions is still an open question. Irrespective, the EU has made significant inroads toward integration: Very few observers would have predicted at the outset of the pandemic that there would be significant steps toward a so-called *Transfer Union* or territorial redistribution, and the developments toward a European Health Union. It is already very clear at this point that the COVID-19 crisis has functioned as an important engine for social policy innovation and European integration, as the chapters by Mary Guy, Zhen Im et al., and Georg Vobruba show. Only history can tell whether we can speak of a critical juncture with regard to the social policy domain at the EU level, or whether the recent developments at the European level are even comparable to those nascent social policy developments in the late 19th and early 20th century that were associated with nation-building in many European nation states.

References

Briefs, Götz. 1930. "Der wirtschaftliche Wert der Sozialpolitik." In *Die Reform des Schlichtungswesens—Der wirtschaftliche Wert der Sozialpolitik*, edited by Vorstand der Gesellschaft für Soziale Reform. Bericht über die Verhandlungen der XI. Generalversammlung der Gesellschaft für Soziale Reform in Mannheim am 24. und 25. Oktober 1929, 144–170. Jena: G. Fischer.

Estévez-Abe, Margarita, Torben Iversen, and David Soskice. 2001. "Social Protection and the Formation of Skills." In *Varieties of Capitalism*, edited by Peter A. Hall and David Soskice, 145–83. Oxford: Oxford University Press.

Flora, Peter (ed.). 1986. *Growth to Limits: The Western European Welfare States since World War II*. Vol. 1 Sweden, Norway, Finland, Denmark; Vol. 2 Germany, United Kingdom, Ireland, Italy. Berlin: Walter de Gruyter.

Offe, Claus. 1984 [1993]. *Contradictions of the Welfare State*, edited by John Keane. Cambridge: MIT Press.

Obinger, Herbert, and Carina Schmitt. 2020. "World war and welfare legislation in western countries." *Journal of European Social Policy* 30 (3): 261–74. https://doi:10.1177/0958928719892852.

Scheve, Kenneth, and David Stasavage. 2016. *Taxing the Rich: A History of Fiscal Fairness in the United States and Europe*. Princeton: Princeton University Press.

Swenson, Peter. 2002. *Capitalists Against Markets: The Making of Labor Markets and Welfare States in the United States and Sweden*. Oxford: Oxford University Press.

Vobruba, Georg. 1989. *Der wirtschaftliche Wert der Sozialpolitik*. Berlin: Duncker & Humblot.

Vobruba, Georg. 1990. *Strukturwandel der Sozialpolitik*. Frankfurt am Main: Suhrkamp.

Index

For the benefit of digital users, indexed terms that span two pages (e.g., 52–53) may, on occasion, appear on only one of those pages.
Tables and figures are indicated by *t* and *f* following the page number. Numbers followed by n indicate footnotes.